THE MYTH
OF TANTALUS

"The unground is an eternal nothing," says Jacob Boehme, "but makes an eternal beginning as a craving. For nothing is a craving after something. But as there is nothing that can give anything, accordingly the craving itself is the giving of it."

Jacob Boehme, *Six Theosophic Points and Other Writings*

"It is the height of stupidity," says the Zen master, "to ask what your self is, when it is this self that makes you ask the question."

Daisetz T. Suzuki, *What Is Zen?*

At that subtle moment when man glances backward over his life, Sisyphus returning toward his rock, in that slight pivoting he contemplates that series of unrelated actions which becomes his fate, created by him, combined under his memory's eye and soon sealed by his death. Thus, convinced of the wholly human origin of all that is human, a blind man eager to see who knows that the night has no end, he is still on the go. The rock is still rolling . . . The struggle itself toward the heights is enough to fill a man's heart. One must imagine Sisyphus happy.

Albert Camus, *The Myth of Sisyphus*

Your cleverest poets . . . deny food and drink to Tantalus, merely because he was a good man and inclined to share with his friends the immortality bestowed on him by the gods. And some of them hang stones over him, and rain insults of a terrible kind upon this divine and good man; and I would much rather that they had represented him as swimming in a lake of nectar, for he regaled men with that drink humanely and ungrudgingly. But we must not suppose that he was really the victim of the gods' dislike

Flavius Philostratus, *Life of Apollonius of Tyana*

Philosophy will clip an angel's wings, Conquer all mysteries by rule and line, Empty the haunted air, and gnomed mine – Unweave a rainbow.

John Keats

One must imagine Tantalus, not Sisyphus, happy . . .

THE MYTH OF TANTALUS

A SCAFFOLDING FOR AN ONTOLOGICAL PERSONALITY THEORY

S. GIORA SHOHAM

sussex
ACADEMIC
PRESS

BRIGHTON • PORTLAND

2 4 6 8 10 9 7 5 3 1

First published 2005 in Great Britain by
SUSSEX ACADEMIC PRESS
Box 2950
Brighton BN2 5SP

and in the United States of America by
SUSSEX ACADEMIC PRESS
920 NE 58th Ave   Suite 300
Portland, Oregon 97213-3786

British Library Cataloguing in Publication Data
A CIP catalogue record for this book is available from the British Library.

Library of Congress Cataloging-in-Publication Data
Shoham, S. Giora, 1929–
    [Halikhe òTanòtalus. English]
    The myth of Tantalus : a scaffolding for an existential and ontological theory of personality / Shlomo Giora Shoham.— 2nd rev. ed.
    p. cm.
Includes bibliographical references and index.
ISBN 1-903900-43- 3 (alk. paper pbk.)
1. Ontology. 2. Personality. I. Title.
BD331.S45413 2004
126—dc22

                                        2004007297
                                        CIP

Typeset & Designed by G&G Editorial, Brighton
Printed by MPG Books Ltd, Bodmin, Cornwall
This book is printed on acid-free paper.

Contents

Contents

Contents

Preface & Acknowledgements

The Myth of Tantalus introduces a personality theory that is unlike other theories in the literature of psychology, social, psychology and personology. Freud, the initiator of theories of the human person, was interested in the psychological sublimation of sex. Hence, his psychosexual stages of development are all related to the sprouting forth of passions, conflicts, triumphs and disasters on the way to a personal grappling with objects and others. Only later in life did he realize the importance of death in Man's *Weltanschauung*, but he did not incorporate it into his theory. *The Myth of Tantalus* readdresses this imbalance by presenting a theory where in sprouting out towards development and relationship with the outside world, man alternates between conflict and a striving to revert back to earlier developmental phases. The transcendental longings and quests of Man are explored here not in their theological sense, but in their actual structuring of the human personality.

Self and Transcendence

This is the work of a cerebral rationalist who has had some mystical insights rather late in life. These experiences, which involved an intense longing for transcendence, were contrary to the author's logical *Weltanschauung*, his scientific training, his customary reliance on cognitive control and his natural revolt against the orthodoxy of a religious father. These circumstances provided an initial, personal introspective vindication of the potency of the longing for participation in unity, subsequently identified as one of the personality core vectors of our theory.

Experiences of elation, relief and the dissolution of the partitions of the self, so that it melts pantheistically into its surroundings, usually happens in times of severe crises when the outside environment inflicts blows with indiscriminate viciousness on oneself, one's kin and one's life-long professional interests. For the Author, experiences of blissful temporary dissolution of the self's cognitive partitions took place watching the sun set behind some ruins on the shores of the Mediterranean, while the waves, the darkening sky and the self fused into an opaque unison. On another occasion, by concentrating on the yellow petals of a wild chrysanthemum while the petals extended and widened, my whole self was engulfed into a vision of a single omnipresence. These experiences gave one the feeling that all external calamities were of secondary importance when taken within the timeless and spaceless context of transcendence as experienced through the inner Unity of self and object. At the time, however, I had severe doubts. The sporadic experiences of a blissful partaking in one's surroundings were interpreted by my cerebral cognition as a momentary spell of weakness, as a *ressentiment* rejection of the all-important achievement motive and the competitive goals of society.

Some time later, a thorough exposure to Lurianic Kabbalah, the writings of Al-Gazali and other Muslim Sufis, Taoism, Hinayana Buddhism and the accounts of the early Christian mystics, made it clear to me that their mystical experiences were authentic. After this realization, I could bring about a mystical experience without too much preparation. These experiences became more frequent. They conveyed the inner pre-existential Unity of all being which dwarfed the vicissitudes of daily chores and external disasters. It became clear that the attraction of most mystical religious systems stemmed from their ability to provide techniques for partaking in Unity, even if rudimentary and momentary, for those who had an intense longing for a mystical experience, but could not lift themselves up to a mystical experience by their own bootstraps. The Kabbalist *Tikkun*, the Quietist Hassidic *Devekut*, St. John of the Cross's "Ascent", the Yogi *Bukhti*, the Buddhist *Nirvana* and the Zen *Satori* are all different techniques, yet they are all similar in their aim of achieving a mystical partaking in Unity. The present volume gives proper attention to Man's longing for this mystical merger of self and object, within the context of our theory of the personality core.

Another major innovation presented in *The Myth of Tantalus* is related to what I have denoted as the Isaac Syndrome — the aggression of parents against their children to supplement the Freudian Oedipal pressures, which in turn are the aggressions of children against their parents. A full chapter is devoted to the Isaac Syndrome – a syndrome that covertly legitimizes the mass destruction, slaughter and pain inherent in war and political strife. The implications of the nationalization of sacrifice are immense and impact the religio-metaphysics of all cultures and peoples.

We shall show how myths and human behavior motivate both individuals and groups. Since myths are projected models of human behavior on all levels, they record past experiences as well as provide a structure for future goals. Myths are also an experience of overt behavior, as well as of covert dynamics, of the here and now, and of transcendence. Their dimensions may vary greatly, ranging from micro-myths, such as the names of persons and places (which express experiences or quests), to meta-myths such as the myths of Sisyphus and Tantalus (which represent the polar types of human behavior, on both individual and group levels). Myths vary with time and place. Every society and every culture has its own indigenous mythology, There is a continuity from the sacred myths of pre-history, in *ille tempore*,[1] to modern myths such as in those of the detectives Sherlock Holmes and Hercule Poirot, or the master spy, John Le Carre's Smiley, or Superman, who implements the dreams of omnipotence of the downtrodden, henpecked inhabitants of the megalopolis.

Myths can also relate to individuals. The offerings of Isaac or Iphigenia, signifying the sacrificial enmeshing of the young within the normative system of society, are prime examples. Then there are group myths such as the adventures of the Olympian gods and the tribal exploits of the German *Aesir*; indeed the Nazi movement itself may be studied as a collective myth.[2]

The mythological projections of manifest reality are mostly experiential and developmental myths, whereas the mytho-empirical anchors of the dialectics of yearning are, on the one hand, the separant myths of quests and, on the other, participant myths of longing. The myths of Tantalus and Sisyphus are meta-myths because they describe the predicament of Man, who cannot realize either his separant quests or his participant longings. These myths also constitute a combination of experiential projections and myths of yearning, and thus cover the whole range of mytho-empiricism. However, most myths can be identified either as experiential projections or as myths of longing. Experiential myths perceived as mytho-emperical anchors can provide the common denominators of experience. They may thus form a basis for inter-personal communication and could eventually become, if properly studied, meta-language. The myth of Tantalus, which describes how he was punished by being made to crouch beneath a stone, not knowing if and when it would crush him, is meta-experimental: it represents the basic existential condition of Man, thrown unto death. It is also the mytho-emperical anchor of the Heideggerian *Angst*, Kierkegaard's "fear-and-trembling" and our "desperation", as characteristic of human existence. Myths, as experiential projections, disclose things primordially,[3] register happenings before recorded history,[4] and, of course, project Man's development phases.

Myths of yearning are so abundant that they engulf all of our lives. Thrillers, science fiction, and detective books — all depict the myth of an ever-prevailing justice. These are typical myths of yearning, because we know that in real life justice, alas, does not always win and crime often does pay. Television commercials showing the flawless skin of cosmetic models are again myths of yearning, as are the Walter Mittyesque exploits of the "tough outside yet soft inside" cowboy who rides off into the sunset on his white horse, as the movie credits start to roll. Names are often myths of yearning; we call our children after prophets, kings and angels. Our family names are often synonyms for hope, happiness, joy, or wisdom; place names frequently denote success, progress, or glory.

The empirical value of a myth is directly related to the frequency with which it occurs in different cultures, and to its prominence within the mythology of a given culture. An apparent inconsistency in a myth does not necessarily lessen its mytho-empirical value; in many cases it may even enhance it. An illustration is the Kabbalist myth of the breaking of the vessels which depicts the actual sequence of human birth, and presents a less-than-perfect God, who cannot prevent catastrophic events in cosmogony. Yet the need to project the process of birth onto transcendence in mythical form resulted in the growth of this and its equivalent in other cultures, despite the attendant theological problems.

Mythogene and Mythology

The mythogenic structure is the connecting agent between consciousness and energy-matter that is structured into a model of a phenomenon to be realized subsequently as an act of creation. The durability and longevity of mythogenic structures are subject to natural selection and functional adaptability. In this domain, as in so many other Sisyphean dynamics of creation and entropy, Darwinian evolution reigns supreme.[5]

Once the mythogenic structure has been generated by projected experiences and yearnings, and formed into a self-regulating configuration, it has a life of its own. Hence, a mythogene is ahistoric. Consider the following: There is no independent evidence for the outright accuracy of the biblical account of Moses or the Exodus. A recent study by an American archaeologist concludes that the events recounted in the first ten books of the Old Testament can have no historical veracity.[6] Hence, not only Moses, but also Saul, David, and Solomon are all fictional characters. But such a view is not relevant to our present context. The mythogenic structure obeys W. I. Thomas's basic theorem of social processes, that if Man defines a situation as real, it becomes real in its consequences. Hence, if the mythogene has been projected, structured and legitimized by a given group, it motivates Man to generate cultural patterns by a process of revelation and creativity. Lévi-Strauss defines how the mythic structure links nature and culture, and how the mythogenic structures generate, grow and decline. Indeed, mythogenes are generated, developed and destroyed in a manner different from the growth and decline of historical entities. Leon Festinger has demonstrated how belief in prophets has increased just when their historical prophecies have failed.[7] Likewise, the serious proselytizing by the followers of Christ started after his crucifixion; likewise for the believers of Shabbatai Tzvi, the self-proclaimed seventeenth-century Jewish messiah, after he converted to Islam. The mythogenic structure moves itself, and us, its creators, in a feedback cycle of virtual reality; if we impute historical veracity to it and insist on incorporating it into our daily lives, we court disaster. The numerous Christs, Napoleons, and Elvis Presleys in insane asylums are all individual instances of the deranging effects of historicizing myths, whereas the Nazis' reviving and reliving of the *Elder Eddas* and the *Niebelungen Ring* was a catastrophic example on a group level.

A Note on Gender

Ideas are put forward using the masculine form. Arguments presented in this way are equally valid for the feminine. Any differences in the action/reaction due to gender are specifically mentioned in the text.

My Debt

It gives me great pleasure to acknowledge my debt to Albert Camus, one of my cultural heroes. I hope that he would have agreed with the thesis presented in this volume, had he lived, for the inherent ideas and philosophy are indeed Camusean, and reflect those in his epoch-making *The Myth of Sisyphus* and *The Rebel*.

With Gratitude

I wish to acknowledge with warm thanks the help given to me by my assistant, Yitzhak Stein, in collecting the sources and references for this book, and by my secretaries, Anne Weiler and Sheila Bahat, who worked their way devotedly and courageously through the intricacies of this work at the time of the first edition. I would also like to express my gratitude to my assistant, Mor Getz, for her devoted and expert editorial work in making this second revised edition possible. Special thanks go to my publisher, Anthony Grahame, since it was his insight that prompted me to revise the work and to present it in the form and structure herein.

Introduction:
The Away and Beyond is Right Here and Now

We burn with the desire to find solid ground and an ultimate sure foundation whereon to build a tower reaching to the infinite, but our whole groundwork cracks and the earth opens to abysses.

Blaise Pascal, *Pensees*

Personality theories have much to lose by pretending to greater coverage or rigour than they in fact possess. In following this time-honored primrose path to damnation, they easily leave the field of science altogether.

H. J. Eysenck, *The Biological Basis of Personality*

In this life everyone is a failure.

Anonymous

The Deprivations of Interaction

Upon Man's expulsion from the womb and his fall from the pantheistic omnipresence of early orality, he is left with a lifelong longing to annul the consequences of these catastrophes and revert back to the sheltered self-sufficiency of non-being. This longing, which can never be realized, creates much sublimatory dynamism that can never be fulfilled and quenched. This dynamism remains a lifelong passion that interacts dialectically with the force of growth. The chapters that follow will elaborate the difference between our conception of these core vectors of the self and the exposition of other personologists; we shall try to structure these vectors into concise models.

The conflict between the vectors of growth and regression makes the self an arena of constant battle. Moreover, the relationship between the individual and his surroundings is also marked by conflict, pain and deprivation, which alternate with sporadic spells of contentment from the very beginning of life. Out of the womb, the neonate needs shelter and food, which are not always forthcoming, and a bump on the head from a hard surface proves to the infant that his days of omnipresence are over. He has a limited *Lebensraum* in this world, which is going to be delimited further by his socialization into the normative system of his group. This deprivational interaction is not only painful, but also incomprehensible. Why has he been thrown out into this world? His *Geworfenheit*, to borrow Heidegger's apt term, is confounded by his sense of negative choice. Why has he been burdened by cognition? Why must he of all people serve as a channel to cosmic awareness? These are questions without answers. The individual is confronted with the outrageous silence of God and the catastrophic indifference of the Universe. All he has left is his intense longing for the blissful and perfect state of pre-awareness and non-being. This longing in itself may serve as a base for religious belief and mystical experiences. A previous work of the author – *Salvation Through the Gutters* – revealed how these pressures for the annihilation of cognition and separate awareness may express themselves as predispositions for a wide range of deviant modes of behavior.[1]

The present volume traces the formation in early orality of the boundaries around the self that are coagulated as a form of a scar-tissue following the conflictual traumas of the neonate with the breast, mother, their surrogates and surrounding objects. The longing of the self to disentangle and free itself from its delimiting boundaries is another lifelong passion, which we shall define and deal with. We shall be concerned with its inevitable frustrations: the barriers of meaningful communication between Ego and Alter; the reaching out of Ego towards Alter, only to be rejected because of misunderstanding, competition or sheer lack of interest; and above all, the tendency of Ego to project on Alter his subjective motives, assuming that Alter understands them, which he does not. Inter-subjective communication is a cherished myth, ever longed for but never achieved. The emotional subjugation of Ego by Alter, or vice versa, depending on the circumstances, which have been expounded philosophically by the Existentialists, becomes in our context a function of different levels of affect, sensitivity and hence vulnerability. If Ego is more deeply attached to Alter because of greater sensitivity or his ability or willingness to "open up" to him more thoroughly, he becomes so vulnerable that he is virtually dominated by him. As there can be no free flow of inter-subjective emotions between Ego and Alter, an emotional dialogue on an equal basis is an ontological impossibility. Consequently, the longing for dyadic emotional rapport is truly Tantalic, in the sense that the more Man longs for it, the less he is likely to achieve it.

This Tantalic dilemma of the inverse relationship between the intensity of Ego's desire to communicate with others and his ability to fulfil it, will be a main foci of our interest and explanation of human interaction. Novelists and playwrights with keen psychological insight, very often lacking in correlation-seeking behavioral and social scientists, have succeeded in portraying the devastating painful failure of Man to convey his miseries and sympathies to his fellow-men: Chekhov's bereaved fathers and estranged wives; Dostoevsky's "underground people", fuming inwardly with spite and *ressentiment* yet hardly noticed by others. The Theatre of the Absurd no longer bothers to deal with non-existent human communication: it lets its characters interact with the void. Jean Genet went even further: some of his *dramatis personae* perform a solipsistic passion in which they are both executioner and victim.

Even worse than lack of communication is Alter's tendency, both naïve and malicious, to take some parts of Ego's communications out of their original context and fit them into his own Gestalt, which is bound to be different both because of personality determinants and cultural imprints. The epitome of betrayal, however, lies in what has been denoted as the "Least-interest Principle", according to which Ego has less chances of being emotionally palatable to Alter if his needs and desire for communication are greater. In courting behavior, in business relationships, in the circles of social climbers, those who are radiating a desire to communicate, those who are emotionally involved from the outset, are less likely to fulfil their aim. The indifferent, the blasé, those who take others with a uniform, easy smile of shallow emotions are more likely to be on the receiving end of affective communication, for which they might have no desire or use. In interpersonal relationships, one seems to approach people by walking away from them.

While structuring our personality core model, we shall be greatly concerned with the inter-relationship between the polar components of our self-continuum: our interactive self, which reaches out towards the object, and the quietist self-defacing component of our self, which longs for the contentedness of pre-awareness and the bliss of nonbeing. We shall define and describe our continuum of the self and its structure within the personality core. An important dynamic that characterizes the interaction of the polar components of the self is following: We tend to admire and sometimes envy the non-involvement and peace of mind of the self-effacing, relatively self-sufficient modest man, even if we burn with ambition and are driven by achievement motivation, because the quietist component of our self, however subdued, projects its identification on to the person whose serenely detached behavior is diametrically opposed to ours.

Also, such real yet theoretically confused mechanisms, as Fairbairn's "Internal Saboteur", get a structural vindication by our continuum of the self. An activist, successful businessman, entrepreneur or academic "operator" may suddenly make a gross mistake or launch a self-defeating venture. This is the subterranean doings of the suppressed quietist vector of the self. On the other hand, a quietist mystic may find himself pushed by the subdued activist component of his self into an outburst of frantic activities, which may interfere for a while with his contemplative resignation. These dynamics may lead an individual to feel that whatever he is engaged with at the moment is not really important; if only he could be somewhere else, start his life in a new direction in line with his subdued polar personality core vector, he would find "real" happiness and fulfilment. But this is an illusion, a *fata morgana*, which if pursued would end in even more painful frustrations. The covert pressures of a dormant personality core vector to change entirely one's course of life as dominated by the other polar personality vector, have been discussed in the author's previous works – *Crime and Social Deviation*, *The Mark of Cain*, and *Society and the Absurd* – as potent pressures towards alienation and deviance.[2] As the present work is not directly concerned with deviant human behavior, so we shall touch upon problems of alienation and deviance only insofar as they relate to the structuring of our continua of the self and personality core models.

On the social level, we shall be concerned with the havoc that the lack of inter-subjective communication plays on the relationship between the individual and the normative system of his membership and reference groups. In the course of his socialization, the individual is enmeshed in a web of delimiting values and confining norms, which preach chivalry, loyalty, pity and honour. It takes a lifetime, to realize that they did not really mean what they preached, that they did not want him to take them so seriously, or that he should have taken their preaching in the double or multiple sense in which it was delivered. He finds out to his chagrin, horror or nausea, depending on his mental constitution, that brute force in social relationships is as all-important as it was at the time of the Borgias or among cave dwellers. He realizes that the Church, the Chief Rabbinate and the Ulema are mostly run by professional religionists, who do not believe in religion; and that lawmakers and law-enforcers are likely not to believe in the law when it has to be applied to themselves. He learns that friends are mostly defined as those who have common enemies; that good guys not only finish last but also that bad guys have to strike below the belt in order to survive, and the social élites in every régime, irrespective of ideology, subjugate the lower echelons, classes, castes or party members in order to perpetuate their power or augment their gain. If dyadic emotional relationships end up by the subjugation of Ego to Alter, or vice versa, the relationship of the individual to the normative system of society is initiated by subjugation, which is glorified into responsibility. This is precisely the burden of Sisyphus, which he tries to shirk off in vain. The Camusian Sisyphus is our model for the opposing vectors that determine the dialectics of relationship between the individual and social norms.

The Two Realities

Our point of vantage is the individual and his perception of objects, flora and fauna and other people around him, as well as his interaction with them. We have no intention of dealing with the world "out there", outside or beyond the individual's perception of himself and his environment. Philosophy has worn out some of the best human minds within the dead-end labyrinth of epistemology. The unchartered realms of transcendental belief are also outside our interest. We hold that the force field that divides the individual's perceptual world and the objects "out there", as well as the riddles of universal origins and ultimate aims, is sealed tight. No transit is possible or has ever been proved to exist. The present work is non-philosophical in the epistemological sense also because the individual self has no criteria for measuring the things "out there". To use an extreme mataphor: A spirochete within the brain of its syphilitic host cannot have any criteria for perceiving and evaluating the dimensions and nature of Man beyond the initial fact that it is embedded in a mass that is infinitely larger than its own dimensions and the form and contents of which it can know nothing beyond its tactile experiences. Our present work is also non-theological because we are not dealing with the unchartered areas of human belief. We are in the realm of personality theory, even if we deal with the interaction of the self with its surroundings as perceived by the self, or with the self's longing for partaking in Unity as determined by some pre-natal and early oral bio-psychological correlates.

Our continuum of the self presupposes two diametrically opposite cognitive systems: one that utilizes spatio-temporal precepts and has, therefore, logical, discrete and sequential perceptions; the other is holistic, timeless, infinite and synchronistic, and can be reached only by intuition or through mystical experience. Because human interaction with its surroundings, especially with other human beings and social institutions, is marked mostly by pain, deprivation and failure, as measured by the gap between expectations and achievement, Man has perennially sought solace in the other cognitive system. The mystics of all denominations promised recourse to the Unity behind the chaotic appearances of spatio-temporal reality to the aloneness (all-oneness) of omnipresent nothingness before existence. This "other" cognitive system has its origins in the memories embedded in the synaptic junctions of the brain of the blissful pre-awareness *in utero*, where needs were automatically supplied, or in early orality, where the neonate deemed himself pantheistically as the sole entity in existence. All this is not new. Our innovation, however, is in providing *a bio-psychological background to the development of the cognitive systems of the self and the relationship between them within the personality core.*

Bakan, in his exposition of the duality of human existence, says that: "this impulse (of Man to appreciate the nature of his existence) presupposes that the manifest is but the barest hint of reality, that beyond the manifest there exists the major portions of reality and that the function of the impulse is to reach out toward the unmanifest."[3] Our imagery is different: we envisage the forces of life and growth catapulting the organism out of the womb and into separate existence. This, coupled with

5

the rites of passage of socialization, create the pigeonholed loneliness of Man's normative existence. The opposite vector is Man's longing for the grace of irresponsibility of early childhood, for the pantheistic omnipresence of early orality and for the pre-natal bliss *in utero* of nonbeing. We also ask the "whys" of Man's longing for the "other reality". We claim that because his actual regression to previous developmental phases is impossible, he is motivated by surrogate regression mechanisms to long for the freedom of irresponsibility on the socio-normative level; to search for the melting-down of his separate self and seek fusion with the object on the ontological level; and to strive for the Unity of pre-awareness through *Unio Mystica* on the religious level.

The Core of the Self

Our concern in the present work is with some core mechanisms of the self and not with its peripheral traits or attributes. We assume that the bio-physiological structure of Man is a potential, albeit a formidable one, but still only a potential that interacts with an individual's surroundings to effect behavior and personality structure. We find it futile to indulge in arguments as to the relative importance to behavior and personality development of *soma* or interaction and learning processes. The bio-physiology of the organism is the raw material, which is moulded into shape by interaction. It would be equally superfluous to argue the relative importance for an edifice of the mortar or the efforts of the mason.

We envisage two basic vectors within the personality core, which embody both the biological potential and the interactive processes of the self. The first is the vector of growth, which is linked to birth and further developmental phases of the personality that are registered by the organism as catastrophes; the second is the individual's desire to revert back to his previous developmental phases and ultimately to nonbeing. These vectors, which we shall show later to be different in form and contents from the core characteristics of other personality theories, are the scaffolding on which our proposed models will be elaborated and construed.

Most personality dichotomies, which are explicit or implicit in all personality theories, stem from the basic division between the self and the object, not unlike Man's ten fingers being at the basis of the decimal system. Our two vectors are more ontological, in the sense that their dialectic ranges from awareness to non-awareness and from being to nonbeing. We shall demonstrate that the dialectical interaction between our two opposing vectors actually shapes the core of the self and moulds the Ego boundary out of pantheistic non-awareness.

A Note on Method

Our interdisciplinary synthetic exposition of the core self is not only different in form but also in content from the analyses of rather narrow segments of human behavior. One may try to analyze music as the scratching of catgut on horsetail hair; it may also be analyzed as mathematical functions of harmonies or it may be interpreted as a total cognitive and affective experience. The latter is analogous to our synthetic exposition of the core self. Our macro-synthesis perceives with due perspective the whole Gestalt of the core self, not unlike the impressionist's perception of an orange or a tree. On the other hand, the microanalysis of such an academic painter as Ingres tries to depict the ridges among the globules on the peel of the orange as well as the veins on the leaves of the tree. Our purpose in this volume is to provide a scaffolding for a personality theory rather than to present a fully-fledged theoretical structure. We shall not be concerned so much with peripheral personality traits, so that our theoretical scaffolding will hopefully determine the shape of our self models, yet we will not introduce all the walls, partitions and woodwork into our edifice. This will be done later in succeeding volumes, or by other masons.

The image of a scaffolding should not envisage a stratified structure. The dynamic nature of our models should be stressed and even our scaffolding of the core self should be regarded as systems in conflictual motion, held in balance by dialectical tensions. By utilizing dialectics, we do not assume a movement towards a given goal or a teleological objective inherent in the dialectical progress.

A theoretical system that tries to synthesize mystical experiences and achievement motivation, psychoanalytical premises and "hard data" findings, the writings of the Hasidim and cultural relativism, must inevitably be heuristic and flexible. If we did not have direct support, we would have to be content with circumstantial evidence. Sometimes we even experienced a "theory shock": we have construed some theoretical constructs without any shred of initial evidence to support it, only to be overwhelmed later by an avalanche of evidence for or against it. Naturally, we have incorporated the support for the vindicated premises and extracted from our exposition the discredited ones. It is my earnest wish that *The Myth of Tantalus* proves to be more than an intellectual exercise, because I believe, with Kurt Lewin, that there is nothing more practical than a good theory.

1

The Fist and the Open Hand

Man is born with his fists clenched, as if to say, "The whole world is mine", and he dies with open hands, as if saying, "I have inherited nothing from this world."
Ecclesiastes Raba 5:14

Everybody is born a king, but most people die in exile. Oscar Wilde

All that is absolutely worthwhile has something of the unattainable about it.
Morris Raphael Cohen, *Reason and Nature*

The *raison d'être* for another personality theory seems to be dubious considering the multitudes of existing theories, which very often differ from one another more semantically than intrinsically. Indeed, there is an amazing constancy in the description of the core characteristics of the personality in different ages and by different disciplines, the main variant being differences in language. This is even more apparent in the definition of personality itself. Gordon Alport's statement that "personality *is* something and *does* something . . . it is what lies *behind* specific acts and *within* the individual"[1] is much like Jean-Paul Sartre's conception of the "transcendental self". By a wider stretch of analogy, we may detect in Gilbert Murray's statement that "personality is always in process; the history of the personality *is* the personality"[2] a Heraclitean *panta rhei* – a dialectical conception of process as development, "Everything changes", "Everything moves". The Personality Theory proposed here may be vindicated on three grounds. First, it structures established theoretical statements into an entirely new frame of reference. Second, it introduces a range of ontological vectors and variables never before used in a similar context by personologists. Third, it presents new stages of personality development and resultant cycles of intro-psychic and inter-personal interaction.

The Vectors

The two opposing vectors that are the core of the Personality Theory, which we have presented elsewhere,[3] are "participation" and "separation". By participation, we mean the identification of Ego with a person (persons), an object or a symbolic construct outside himself, and his striving to lose his separate identity by fusion with this other object or symbol. Separation, of course, is the opposite vector. However, as the vectors are multidimensional, the pressures are much more likely to take place on the different planes of a space that represent the human personality than along a unidimensional continuum.

Of special interest is the fact that the subjective feeling of separation – Ego as an ontological entity, distinct from his environment – is a specific human quality. Other animals do not possess this ontological feeling of individuality. This *sui generis* quality of *Homo sapiens*, the ability to sense separateness, has been subject to diametrically opposite value judgments. Ernest Schachtel regards the "activity affect" leading to the elaborate interaction of Ego with the objects around him as an ever-recurring pleasure.[4] This interaction is not feasible if Ego is not ontologically separate. We, on the other hand, thread in the elegiac path formed by Sigmund Freud, Martin Heidegger and Mircea Eliade, where the coagulating of Ego's distinct identity is through painful encounters with obstacles, impediments and conflicts. Unifications are temporary and the desire for a blissful remerger of the individual and his entourage is a perennial longing expressed in religion, art and philosophy, but never fully attained in reality. Use of these opposing vectors of unification/fusion and separation/isolation as the main axis of the theory take place in conjunction with three major developmental phases. First of all, the process of birth: this abrupt propulsion from cushioned self-sufficiency into the strife and struggles of life outside the womb is a major crisis that is recorded undoubtedly by the newborn's psyche. This is in addition to any physical pressures that the process of birth itself might have on the cranium and the resultant impressionistic effects on the various layers of the brain. Indeed, we do not follow the "birth trauma" theorists, who stress the variability of birth-related physical violence as a clue to personality pathologies.[5] We build our premises on the separating effects of birth that are universal. These initiate the opposite vector of participation, which is a directional driving-force harnessing a diverse assortment of psychic energy towards union with given objects or symbolics. The fetus at birth is physiologically and psychologically capable of recording these colossal crises incidental to its birth, and it is traumatized by them into a life-long quest for congruity and unification.

The second process of separation is the crystallization of an individual ego by moulding of the "ego boundary". The infant shrieks and kicks his way into the world, but he still feels himself part and parcel of his entourage. However, this pantheistic bliss is gradually destroyed by the bumps and grinds he suffers from the harsh realities of hunger, thirst, discomfort, physical violence from hard objects in his surroundings, and a mother who is mostly loving but sometimes nagging, apathetic, hysterical or over-protective. All this cajoles and pushes the infant into coagulating a separate identity: to leave the common fold of unity with his environment and crystallize an "I". This individual self knows then that he is not part of and with everything, but *vis-à-vis* his surroundings and opposite everybody. This realization of oneself by being forced to leave once more the security of engulfing togetherness is registered by the sprouting psyche as a fall from grace. Why we are being pushed out is the great imponderable, the existence of which we are taking as given. The underlying theme of the present work is the fact of this *Geworfenheit* and the opposing life-long vector to overcome it.

The process of separation continues in full force as a corollary of socialization until one reaches, in Edwin Erickson's jargon, one's "ego identity", which is the post-adolescent's adjustment to the mandates of the normative system of society.[6] The making of the "responsible person", the "stable human being", is achieved by constant indoctrination by various socialization agencies – family, school, church, etc. These convey to him the harsh realities of life and urge him to "grow up", with the help of some rigorous initiation rites. What it amounts to is that the child spreads out his arms to embrace with naïve eagerness every person, object and beast. He exposes thereby his soft body and tender psyche to physical injuries and mental blows. These make him shrink with fright and pain. In due course, the scar tissue of experience and learning covers the sores and wounds. The child becomes less vulnerable, but also less sensitive; and he is more reluctant to expose himself with a loving embrace to his environment. This is the lore of the rape of innocence by life. The end product is separation of the alienated Man, who is basically lonely. The sneer of the "tough guy", who walks and needs nobody, is the folklore counterpart to the Protestant Ethic and the spirit of capitalism, who knows that "in this rat-race everyone is to himself". The strain to overcome the separating and dividing pressures never leaves the human individual. The striving to partake in a pantheistic whole is ever present and takes many forms; if one avenue towards its realization becomes blocked, it surges out from another channel.

Sometimes this quest for congruity will be directed against the limiting and dividing presence of the body itself. This would necessitate the coming to grips with various homeostatic and defence mechanisms of the organism. The Indian and Buddhist mystics achieved varying measures of freedom from the body through mental control and contemplation, whereas the early Christian Origen found it more expedient to castrate himself.

Socialization, however, goes on with varying degrees of intensity throughout life. The "balanced" and "responsible" citizen, and for that matter the "good party member", are pigeonholed products, which are geared towards mechanical solidarity with one another, but are emotionally and ontologically lonely. The inner vector of participation is still there. It makes the subjective *das sein* feel as the channel through which all creation flows. It also tries to reach in every direction and melt some of the partitions around it, so that it may experience a fusion of being with persons and things. This, no doubt, is rare and evasive, even for a short time, but a prolonged meaningful participation borders on the miraculous.

Indeed, our vectors would seemingly be diametrically opposed to the corresponding sociologistic solidarity and existentialistic individuality. However, the contrast here is largely semantic and not intrinsic. The Durkheimean conception of solidarity, being the end-product of successful socialization within the group, would be the epitome of separation. The levelling forces of indoctrination, the bumper effects of pushing back into place, of towing into line, are allocations of separate wishes for human beings to dwell in physical proximity but ontological distance. On the other hand, the subjective awareness of existence, which is by definition a property of the individual, can break its loneliness only by aligning itself to a similar entity, the embrace of a *pour soi* with a *pour soi*, a *das sein* with a *das sein*. Most Existentialists claim that this communication is ontologically impossible; but the fact is that Ego strives to find a meaningful link with others. This urge was in him from the beginning; from the time he was one with everything; from the time he was partaking in a pantheistic whole; from the time he was God.

Thus the three developmental stages that guide our analysis are: first, birth, which in its enormity, as far as the individual is concerned, would have its parallel in metaphysics in the cosmogony; second, the crystallization of the separate ego, which is the ontological coagulation of the "ego boundary"; third, the interaction of Ego with fellow human beings, which culminates in the ethical and affective "ego identity". Our developmental trinity is naturally different from that of the Freudians and the symbolic inter-actionists; our model proposes greater reliance on ontological parameters.

The various pressures towards separation occur in each development phase; each stimulus for the embryo is registered as a disturbance that has to be overcome. The various demands of the mother and the relevant others, before the crystallization of the ego boundary and after it, are also perceived as disquieting events, which one has to cope and compromise with. Later on, the various demands of the socialization agencies, to fit into the boundaries of the normative system and to gain one's "ego identity", are the semi-final or the final, as the case may be, separating pressures. After these, the individual is on his own, ontologically lonely and trying desperately to regain the togetherness of his lost fold. In this uphill climb, the individual may choose both legitimate and illegitimate paths, both strictly acceptable and deviant avenues.

An attempt to grade the intensity of the participation vectors may be presented in the following decreasing order: first, the reversal of birth, which is the most radical and would be linked, therefore, to the various techniques of *Unio Mystica* by the annihilation of the separate self; second, the dissolution of the ego boundary, which might result, in extreme cases, in insanity and autistic schizophrenia; third, the neutral-

11

ization of the socio-normative separation, which might display itself in crime and social deviance. Although our first examples of participation happen to be deviant, most attempts at participation are legitimate and institutionalized.

The quest for the expression of creativity, for instance, in any field is an institutionalised outlet for participation in the ontological sphere. Theodor Herzl aptly illustrated this when describing his feelings while writing *Altneuland*. He felt that he was soaring with an eagle, which lifted him above the cantankerous trivialities of routine existence. The deviant counterparts to these institutionalized attempts on ontological participation are retreatism, autism, suicide and other modes of self-destruction. In some forms of schizophrenia the patient "lets go", for he no longer wishes to hold on to his ego boundary, which was crystallized for him by his relevant alters. The pliable and one-way mirror soap bubbles that separate Ego from his environment melt down into a murky liquid; I and Thou and It sway together in a topsy-turvy camaraderie. The exhausted mountain climber is pleasantly lured down into an eternal sleep in the snow. Jack London's Martin Eden dives down and down into the ocean – the ultimate womb – realizing, with fulfilment, that there is no way back.

Our fascination with failure does not always stem from a sense of well-being – that by comparison we are a success – but from an identification with the anti-heroes of Saul Bellow and Bernard Malamud, who are not dominated by the "rat race" of achievement. We project on them our own desire to "opt out", to cast off the separating burdens of the social norms. In like manner, when in the midst of a struggle for power, position or money, one often feels a depressive urge to break down and faint away from the struggle and both its losses and victories; one also manifests a desire to lose oneself in the participatory cosiness of irresponsibility. Moreover, we might even look for losing battles, not because our "Internal Saboteur"[7] betrays us, but because our failure might allow us to regress to a lower common denominator of social participation.

The institutionalized religious avenue of participation is mysticism. For the Kabbalist, Man's task in the world is *Tikkun*, i.e. to mend, to glue, to make whole the original *Shevira*, the disastrous "breaking of the Divine vessels", which is the source of all evil and profanity. After this *Tikkun*, "there shall be perfection above and below and all the world shall be united in one bond".[8] This salvation shall be effected through *"Iyun"*, which is the negation of the self and its fusion with the divine whole.

The institutionalized avenues for religious participation in modern Western culture are sadly scarce. Consequently, many contemporary modes of participation are basically alternatives to mysticism. The deviant modes of religious participation did not begin with Jean Genet performing a black mass in a desecrated cathedral. The non-institutionalised avenues to salvation were just a further logical step from conventional mysticism. If purity and holiness were scattered in all directions by some cosmic catastrophe (e.g. the Kabbalistic "breaking of the vessels"), some of these fragments of sacred goodness have been stranded in dirt, impurities and squalor. One has to descend and dive in the mud to collect these shining gems. One has to wallow in profanity and sin in order to retrieve the holy particles that have been lost therein. Only then, when these stranded particles are re-embraced by the primeval source of holiness, will the Messiah come. This is the Gnostic and the heretic Judaic doctrine of Salvation through the Gutters.

Love is the institutionalized melting down of partitions between individuals. Sartre considered this participation through affect an ontological impossibility. Martin Buber, however, considered this fusion of souls as possible for some time, through a meaningful dialogue between Ego and Alter. The deviant attempts at affective participation put the blame on the stultifying regimentation and the impersonal levelling down of social institutions. If you are "turned on" by the right company (or the right amount of drugs), love is not only possible but almost a natural sequel. The "love-ins", as well as the inverted promiscuity of a Genet, are intense attempts at affective participation. Whether they succeed or fail is beside the point.

Ideology raises one's self by the bootstraps of Utopia, over the insignificant interest of the individual, to serve the Cause, the Party, or any other ecclesiastical abstraction. Here the end justifies the means. What are a few million dead, if their slaughter serves Utopia? What is some hardship for a few, if the Cause eventually shines forever? In order to build an edifice, one has to dirty one's hands. This is the ideological analogy to salvation through the gutters. Anarchy is the non-institutionalized avenue to ideological participation. This is the equality of chaos, the engulfing unity of *Tohu* and *Bohu* (chaos).

| | Participation | |
	Institutionalized	*Deviant*
Transcendental	Mysticism	Beatitude through sin
Ontological	Creativity	Self-destruction
Ethical	Solidarity	Anarchy and deviance
Social		
Affective	Love	Inversion

Figure 1.1   Avenues and Modes of Participation

The vector of separation operates on Ego from without, whereas the pressures towards participation are subjective and internal. A schematic summary of this premise is presented in **figure 1.1**.

Conceptual Analogies

The vectors of participation and separation have been studied in materially and semantically different contexts. Freud, Otto Rank, Harry Sullivan, Lucien Lévy-Bruhl, Eliade, Schachtel and many others have dealt with these vectors, but in a rather different way than proposed by us. However, it would be proper to point out the specific conceptual meaning of participation and separation in contra-distinction to similar concepts and theoretical frames of reference in the literature. Freud, in one of his later works, contrasted Thanatos (the death instinct) with Eros (the life force), which he regarded as the principle of unification.[9] But Freud did not develop fully this latecomer in his instinctual trinity of life, libido and death. Also, the biological processes of cell ageing and tissue decay probably seemed to him as rather flimsy bases for a major personality vector, as compared with the formidable energy of the libido. But for the Theory of Personality presented here, participation is firmly embedded in the major biological and ontological phases of human development. It is the striving to attain unity with groups, people, entities and symbolics that Ego has been separated from. One longs to discard the burden of responsibilities that the norms of society cast on the adult. Ego longs to waive his ego identity and be embraced by the relative freedom from responsibility within the family. He wishes to attain the pantheistic fusion with his environment before his ego boundary is forced on him through his interaction with his mother and other members of the family; but primarily he wishes to regain his blissful non-existence in the womb.

Our developmental phases, which are actually the three main signposts of separation – birth, the formation of the ego boundary and the formation of the ego identity – are also different in nature and process from the developmental phases postulated by Freud. He relied exclusively on sex for the exposition of these phases, which he actually denoted as psychosexual. This might or might not be a reaction formation (a psychoanalytical defence mechanism itself) to his persecution by the Viennese bourgeoisie for "wallowing in filth", i.e. sex. We, however, regard the libido as just one part in an assortment of separating pressures, which include birth and the ontological forces of being. One crucial corollary of our conception of separation as embedded in the bio-psychological phases of human development is that the separating vector becomes less potent with the achievement of each consecutive phase of development. This premise will have further significance later.

Rank[10] also bases his birth trauma theories on the separation processes, starting from birth and proceeding to subsequent separations from the sphere of influence of the mother, the family, the community, etc. The opposite vector is union with the back-to-the-womb urge. For the male, this urge is literally expressed in sex, whereas for the female it is achieved through identification. The Rankian hypothesis of the *regressus ad uterum* urge finds its pragmatical application in the modern cushioned houses, the deep wall-to-wall carpeting and the softening of sharp corners and angles. However, his basic value judgments are rather different from ours, and the direction of his vectors is diametrically opposed to ours. For Rank, the separation from the fold of the mother and the cushioning shelter of the family and the emergence out of it to gain independence and face reality are "good", whereas the urge for union, for *regressus ad uterum*, is an urge for nonbeing, for death, which for Rank is "bad". We, of course, do not necessarily share this value judgment. Moreover, for Rank, the fear of death catapults the individual away from his urge for union, whereas according to our conceptualization, the individual longs for participation but is obstructed in his efforts for union by all the separating pressures that operate on him: his separation-bound interaction with his mother, which culminates in the ego boundary, and the separating normative mandates within the family and other socializing agencies, which end with ego identity. Unlike the Rankian conceptualization, we hold that the striving of the individual for union presses him to overcome the separating factors of reality and individuality. On the other hand, society and the relevant others mould for the individual a separate existence, which he continuously resents. He, however, longs for the dissolution of his separate identity, for union with his entourage, for the bliss of nonbeing. For Rank, the quest of nonbeing is signified by fear. For us, participation is the dominant longing of a person throughout his life.

Andras Angyal, like Rank, sings the praises of the growing autonomy of a person, which "expresses itself in spontaneity, self-assertiveness, striving for freedom and mastery",[11] yet his opposite vector, homonymy, which is rather like our participatory urges of resignation and surrender, is conceived by him as complimentary to autonomy in a "balanced" personality.[12] This does not only differ in value judgment from our conceptualization – as Angyal sees in autonomy a self-fulfilling goal of the personality – but it also foregoes our conflictual model of two opposing vectors that can never rest in a complementary harmony. There is probably also a deep difference in mood here: whereas Rank and Angyal are more optimistic than Freud, we are less.

Sullivan has the two absolutes, which he denotes as absolute euphoria and absolute tension:

> The term euphoria refers to a polar construct, an abstract ideal, in which there is no tension, therefore no action – tantamount in fact perhaps to something like an empty state of bliss. The level of euphoria and the level of tension are inversely related. There is no zero or utter degree of either. Terror is perhaps the most extreme degree of tension ordinarily observable; the deepest levels of sleep, perhaps the nearest approach to euphoria.[13]

Sullivan's conceptualization may indeed be complementary to ours. Euphoria is one attribute of the process of participation and tension is an

15

attribute of the process of separation. Our vectors describe movements of the individual as related to some biological, psychological and sociological developmental stages, whereas Sullivan ascribes two opposing affects, which would accompany those movements. The emotions described by Sullivan occupy only a segment of the state of mind of the individual who moves along the vector of separation, or strives to regain participation.

Lévy-Bruhl speaks of the *participation mystique* of the primitive with his environment, which is the pantheistic feeling of togetherness, which a man imputes to the flora, fauna and inanimate objects around him.[14] This is indeed close to our conceptualization, but the usage by Lévy-Bruhl is different. We envisage participation as the constant driving-force that operates on the individual from the very moment of his birth, whereas the *participation mystique* is just one institutionalized result of our underlying vector towards unification.

Eliade speaks about the longing for the beginning as the primeval urge of the human race, which he has gleaned from his comparative studies of myths. Eliade relies also on Freud in his description of the blissful state of the infant before he was weaned.[15] Eliade's stress of the human longing for primordial bliss is rather similar to our vector of participation, insofar as we related Eliade's quest for the perfect origin to our urge for nonbeing through union.[16] However, we differ from Eliade's conceptualization insofar as we do not regard the vector of participation as a *regressus ad uterum* in order to be reborn subsequently,[17] because for us the negation of the separate entity of the individual is by itself the blissful end of nonbeing. Rebirth, therefore, would be the same catastrophe as the original event of separation. One has the recorded memory of one's original *Geworfenheit*, so that one does not wish to experience it again. We do not share Eliade's contention that Ego's motivation to revisit his formative years is to retrieve his past and to gain mastery over his origin. We maintain that the vector of participation aims towards annihilating the atomistic and artificial existence of the individual ego. The quest for the natal village or quarter, the longing for the lost familial fold, the striving for the pantheistic togetherness of the pre-weaning period, are just some of the later manifestations of the lust for suspended animation in the womb and the quest of the finality of nonbeing.

Schachtel speaks about embeddedness, which is the contented and cuddled absorption by the womb, the mother and the family, and activity effect, which is accompanied by the anxiety of emerging from embeddedness.[18] There are some similarities in Schachtel's conceptualization and ours, but the divergences are more profound. The main component of his embeddedness is Ego's homeostatic passivity, the sloppy slumber of not-doing. Our participation, on the other hand, is a tumultuous struggle up stream to reach the promised land of nonbeing, by overcoming the gushing waves of separation. With him, openness towards the world is the result of emerging from embeddedness; with us, to embrace the world means to embrace and be embraced by it through the melting of partitions, i.e. by participation. For Schachtel, embeddedness is synonymous with stagnation and conformity; with us, the separating effects of the social norms produce stagnating conformity. It is obvious, therefore, that although semantically our conceptualization is rather similar to Schachtel's, he assigns different values to his concepts. His vectors and our vectors move in diametrically opposite directions.

The Dual Orbits

Unlike all other conflict-based personality theories, we envisage not one but two concentric conflict systems, one within the other. The inner cycle consists of the separating pressures on the person that stem both from his biology and from his object relationships. These separating pressures are opposed by the participatory vectors, which stem exclusively from within the personality and operate from within Ego's psyche. The arena of this inner-conflictual cycle is Ego himself, whereas the outer cycle is the conflictual interaction of Ego with his surrounding alters, flora, fauna and other objects and symbols in his entourage. This double conflictual cycle differs from Freud's model, which is a single-conflict system between Ego's instincts and the normative mandates of society. Also, Freud confines his conceptualization of the Pleasure Principle to the strain process that leads to catharsis and release of energy, while focusing on Ego alone. Freud takes Ego as his unit of analysis; whereas for us, participation is a strenuous dialogue in which the loss of separate identity is Ego's coveted participation. The Greeks saw sleep and death as twin brothers, so that sleep brings recurring rejuvenation in the mornings. But the real prize is Thanatos – complete loss of separate identity. For Freud, Eros is in constant conflict with Thanatos; for us, Eros (unification) *is* Thanatos.

Sullivan, on the other hand, virtually ignored the inner conflictual cycle and focused almost entirely on the outer cycle of inter-personal conflicts. This stems from Sullivan's conception of the "self-dynamism" as being mainly based on the seeking of approval and avoidance of disapproval by others.[19] Freud's and Sullivan's personality theories are single-cycle, conflictual, monistic foci. Freud's instincts and Sullivan's social-interaction exclude the equivalents of our mainly psychogenic participation vector, which is mainly responsible for the duality of our personality core. Ego longs to dissolve his ego boundary and revert back to his pre-natal bliss. This is countered by the biological forces of growth, libidinal energy and the interaction with his surrounding objects. However, the second conflictual cycle is generated by Ego's longing for social participation with the surrounding alters. This is not just Sullivan's "approval", but also a quest for ontological union and social togetherness. This is countered by Ego's inevitable deprivational interaction with society and the separating pressures of social norms. Moreover, these norms, when internalized by

Ego, become the ever-present separating agent within the personality itself. The schema of our dual conflictual cycle is presented in **figure 1.2**.

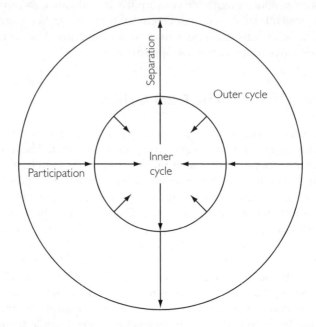

Figure 1.2   Schema of Dual Conflictual Cycle

The participation vectors try to assault the separating boundaries of the Ego and reach out to the surrounding others and objects, whereas the separation vectors stemming from the others interact with Ego and are partially internalized by him through socialization and normative indoctrination. The separating vectors within the inner cycle represent libidinal energy and biological growth processes.

After the primary biological separation of birth has taken place, the subsequent processes of separation and the ensuing developmental stages are affected by the deprivational interaction of Ego with his surrounding objects. We have traced elsewhere in detail these processes of deprivational interaction.[20] In the present context, however, we shall point out the relationship of our personality core vectors to this deprivational interaction. After the primary separation of birth, the instincts of self-preservation guard against the extinction of life in this new *separatum* by inducing it to cry for food and comfort. Yet, as we have pointed out,[21] the crystallization of the separate "I" and the coagulation of the ego boundary is affected though the dialectical interaction with the nipple that does *not* spurt food and with the mother who does *not* ease the pain and tension of discomfort. In other words, if the neonate would have all his needs immediately gratified, he would not have emerged from his pantheistic participation of early orality. This means that it is not the release of tension through the satisfaction of the biological needs that is the separating agent, but the conflictual interaction with a depriving object which constitutes the separating process. Consequently, ontological separation is not a corollary of instinctual need satisfaction but an interactional phenomenon. This premise that interaction begets separation will have further implications in our subsequent analysis. In like manner, we claim that social separation is not effected as Freud and Erickson postulated, by psychosexual developmental phases, but by the conflictual normative indoctrination and by the deprivational socialization within the family. These are exemplified by the numerous *rites de passage* studied by anthropologists[22] and the lonely burdens of responsibility cast on the post-adolescents in every human society so that they may be able to cope with the vicissitudes of adult life. This again shows that our vectors of separation after birth are psychosocial. The ontological and social separation, which constitute respectively the ego boundary and ego identity phases of development, may be concomitant but not dependent or necessarily related to the biological and libidinal releases of tensions.

The deprivational interaction as conceived by us between Ego and his entourage constitutes the outer conflictual cycle in our personality core model and fills some lacunae in Sullivan's "inter-personal dynamics" theory. Salvatore Maddi, for instance, complains that "it is not entirely clear why Sullivan should see conflict as inevitable" and that "Sullivan must be able to answer such questions as why he assumes inter-personal relations to be so fraught with disapproval".[23] We provide the reason for the inevitability of conflict and the disapproval by alters: without them, there would be no separate ego and the young of the species would forever remain in the care of their nuclear families until they are old and senile. Without deprivational interaction, "fraught with conflict and disapproval", no separate conscious "I's" would emerge from pantheistic early orality and no family would be able to extrude its young adults into the competitive loneliness outside it. In other words, no human society, as we know it, would be able to exist (to the chagrin of some and the rejoicing of many) without the deprivational interaction that sustains both ontological and social separation. Consequently, the stronger and the more intense the deprivational interaction (we shall elaborate later our claim that *all* human interaction is deprivational) of Ego with his entourage, the wider and the deeper is the separation. This means that our conceptualization rejects the Hegelian and Marxist creed of involvement through action. Our claim is that action and interaction, on both the individual and group levels, beget separation. Arthur Koestler's well-known continuum from the commissar to the yogi represents for us the whole range: from the active *Homo faber*, who manipulates his entourage and generates thereby maximum social separation, to the inactive and quietist Yogi, whose aim is to achieve the ultimate in participation by the annihilation of his separate being. In like manner, we have the range presented to us by anthropologists: between the "tool-oriented cultures", the societies of doers that are spurred by action and fuelled by achievement and consequently maximize social separation; on the other extreme are the "symbol-oriented cultures", whose fatalistic quietism is more amenable to the participatory goals of mystical union.

Having traced some of the mechanisms of ontological and social separation, we now proceed to analyze the interrelationship between the vectors of separation and participation as the basic dynamism of our personality core model.

The Tantalus Ratio

We have conceived our participation vector as the quest of the individual at every particular moment of his life to revert to an earlier developmental phase: to the irresponsibility of pre-puberty; to the grace of mother and the protection of the family fold; to the pantheistic omnipresence of early orality and the pre-natal bliss of nonbeing. These are countered by the instinctual and deprivational interaction vectors of separation, which except in the case of death, always have the upper hand. Yet the quest for participatory nonbeing is ever present and we tend to agree with the hypothesis that if Man had a special master-switch in his body by means of which he could end his life at will by pushing a button or lowering a lever, he would be bound to do it at one time or another. This also justifies Albert Camus' stance that the only valid philosophical question is whether or not to commit suicide.[24] We have pointed out elsewhere that the quest for participation manifests itself in numerous sublimatory substitutes, both institutionalized and deviant,[25] but actual participation is unattainable by definition. Marcel Proust can revive with super-sensitivity a lost childhood and a graceful mother through the hazy memories triggered by the taste of a *madeleine* cake, but even he cannot recapture the actual sensations of things past. We are forever looking for our lost childhood, for our narcissistic paradise, but no one can actually revert to pre-puberty, reconstruct the eccentric omnipresence of early orality or revive the sensations of blissful suspended animation in the amniotic fluid of the uterus. Participation is, therefore, a *fata morgana* shining hazily before one's craving eyes, but ever receding and never achieved. The countering separating vectors, both instinctual and interactive, augment this objective impossibility of participation. At any given moment of our lives there would be a disjuncture, a gap between our desires for participation and our subjectively defined distance from our participatory aims. We have denoted this gap the *Tantalus Ratio*, after the Olympian demigod who whenever he reached for fruit, a gust of wind would whirl it out of his reach, and when he bent down to drink from a seemingly fresh and sparkling stream of water, it turned out to be black mud. Even if he succeeded in scooping up some water in his palm, it sifted through his fingers before he could cool his parched lips.[26] This Tantalus Ratio, which is the relationship between the longed-for participatory goal and the distance from it as perceived by Ego, is dependent, *inter alia*, on the following factors:

1   The strength of the participatory vectors, as determined by the age distances from the developmental stages of birth, ego boundary and ego identity.
2   The fixations, in the Freudian sense, that Ego might have on the various developmental stages. These fixations would also be linked to the nature and intensity of Ego's deprivational interaction with his entourage and relevant others. These fixations would underlie a personality typology continuum, which we have denoted as *object-oriented* on one extreme and *idea-centred* on the other. This continuum would, no doubt, be linked to the vast number of the existing dichotomous personality continua that have been construed and measured by personologists.
3   The given culture in which the individual is reared, whether it tends to be a "tool-oriented" society of doers or a "symbol-oriented" culture that encourages mysticism, meditation and quietism.
4   A residuary unknown quality and quantity of variables, both on the personality and cultural levels, which affect the participatory and separating vectors and consequently the Tantalus Ratio, which cannot be determined at this theory-building stage.

Later, we shall elucidate further on these groups of variables, but the first step is to describe in more detail the Tantalus Ratio itself, and relate it to some other relevant expositions in the literature.

The Tantalus Ratio creates a strain, a tension between the longing for participation and the distance from it as perceived by Ego. This strain, the intensity of which is determined by the factors comprising the Tantalus Ratio, is the motivating force underlying Ego's action. On a rather low level of abstraction we may envisage this tantalizing strain as the rabbit lure moving ahead of racing dogs or the proverbial carrot tied up in front of a donkey's nose. This tantalizing strain is entirely different in nature from the opposing vectors that comprise the Tantalus Ratio. It is generated within the synaptic junctions of these opposing vectors and the tension is released by Ego's motivational movement towards some participatory goals or their sublimated alternative. In other words, the participatory and separating vectors comprise the crude psychic energy, whereas the Tantalus Ratio and the strain generated by it provide the motivational directions for Ego's actual behavior. This tantalizing strain may be both conscious and unconscious, and its operation is checked and regulated by the social norms from without and by some internal home-ostatic mechanisms. These are personality homeostatic mechanisms, which are not necessarily linked to biological mechanisms. Our hypothesis is that the psychic bases that underlie these homeostatic mechanisms were generated by the anxieties registered by each consecutive stage of separation. As each developmental stage from birth onwards was experienced by Ego as painful separation, accompanied by deprivational interaction, the personality clings to its present stability because each developmental change was a change for the worse and for more radical separateness. The psychic homeostatic mechanisms are, therefore, "The devil I know" defences, which make the personality adhere to stable states as lesser evils.

We have already mentioned that the actual reversal to previous developmental stages is, of course, a practical impossibility, but all the techniques of participation, both institutionalized and deviant, are a far cry from the intense longing for participation fuelled by Ego's memories of his earlier participatory developmental stages. This makes the Tantalus Ratio and the tension generated by it formidable energies, which are ever augmented and kindled by the impossibility of quenching Ego's thirst for participation. This, more than anything else, might account for Sartre's, the master phrase-maker, concluding elegy that "Man is a useless passion."

The groups of variables that we have hypothesized to be linked with the dynamics of the Tantalus Ratio are examined below.

Growth and Decline

Had Freud been more interested than he was in Judaic traditional sources he would have discovered a picturesque juxtaposition of Eros and Thanatos. "Man is born," says Ecclesiastes Raba, "with his fists clenched, as if to say, 'The whole world is mine'; and he dies with open hands, as if saying, 'I have inherited nothing from this world.'"[27] This illustrates the belligerent and aggressive life forces at the outset of life and the resigned submission towards its end. It also marks, in gross relief, the parabolic shift in potency of the Tantalus Ratio.

Freud's conception of the life cycle is an upsurge of bio-psychological growth that wanes and returns to non-life, to inanimate matter. Consequently, life's goal is the constancy and quiescence of death. There really is not much innovation in Freud's conception of the human life-cycle. It is as ancient as "dust thou art, and unto dust shalt thou return", or as contemporary as Heidegger's *Geworfenheit* towards death, or Søren Kierkegaard's fear and trembling unto death. Freud's mediator between the excitation of Eros and the quiescence of Thanatos is the *Pleasure Principle*. His earlier conceptualization of the Pleasure Principle is rather similar to our conception of the participation vector. For him, human pleasure consists in the release of energy, which leads to a return to a contented homeostasis; the overcoming of an irritation, which leads to inactivity, quietism, to the suspended animation of *regressus ad uterum*. Indeed, the Pleasure Principle may be regarded as a mechanism of participation insofar as its homeostatic sequel is the desired goal of relative contentedness. However, in a later work, Freud conceived the Pleasure Principle and the Reality Principle, Eros and Thanatos, as two embattled entities, rather like the two opposing deities in dualistic creeds, who fight each other the moment the infant is born.[28]

To us, the separation of birth is a catastrophe, which Ego strives to overcome all his life. One is thrown into a gushing stream, and one spends the rest of one's life swimming against the torrent: Sisyphus pushing his stone to the peak, which is nowhere in sight and which he never reaches.

Carl Jung's conception of the life-curve is not intrinsically different from Freud's Eros being siphoned into Thanatos through the cathartic release of energy by the Pleasure Principle. Yet Jung makes the parabolic progress from growth to inaction, to fit our conceptualization of the Tantalus Ratio. Youth, says Jung, is a seething cauldron of ambitions for shaping the future of both one's own and one's environment, but at the peak of this teleological parabola, at the middle of life, "death is born".[29] The subsequent descent towards death becomes then an ever-approaching goal, with corresponding changes in the ageing man's biology, *Weltanschauung* and personality. At the years of growth when the young man is pushed by his drives and social interaction to achieve any goal towards which his social group may direct him, the separating vectors are all-powerful, but from the second half of life onwards the participation vectors gain the upper hand, with an increasing interest in spirituality, transcendence and the approaching ultimates.[30] Indeed, the resignation of an old Ecclesiastes is the voice of participation: The futility of action, the vanity of hedonistic pleasure and the pointlessness of temporal existence. It praises the dead; it exalts inaction and glorifies nonbeing. The participatory longing for death in Jewish sources expresses itself in the conception of the ever-after as a spiritual unity where time, growth and achievement are superfluous. "In the world to come," says the Talmud, "there is no eating or drinking, no begetting children, no commerce, envy, hatred or competition, but only this: that the righteous sit with crowns on their heads and delight in the splendour of God's presence."[31] The renounced temporal items in this passage read like a list of separating drives of growth, sex and deprivational interaction, replete with the achievement motive. In the same vein, the temporal world is viewed as "a corridor before the world to come[32] which is wholly good".[33] Consequently, death is not only conceived as the strongest power in the world[34] but also as the ultimate good. This is apparent from Rabbi Meir's interpretation of God's statement on His completion of the work of creation, that "it was very good".[35] The very good here, says Rabbi Meir, "is death".[36] This seemingly anachronistic exaltation of death in Jewish sources fits into the wider context of the quest for participation, because death is the vehicle in which the righteous are brought to partake in the *Shechina*, the Divine Presence.[37] Death is also the ultimate refuge of the righteous from their incessant daily struggles with the *yetzer hara*, the evil

23

inclination that places temporal stumbling-blocks in the form of desires and profanities of the body in front of the spirit's craving for perfection. After death, the libidinal energies of this *yetzer hara* have no power on the spirit's craving for participatory union with the Divine Presence.[38] This brings to mind the various tormentors and mutilators of the body of all denominations who aim at numbing the separating pressures of libido and Eros.

We do not wish here to indulge in the intricate maze of depth psychology explanations of the flagellations of the ascetic and the projections, displacements and interchange of profanity and purity. Whatever reaction formation Jung might impute to Origen's self-castration,[39] for us his act of self-mutilation is a frontal attack on his separating libidinal instincts so that his spiritual ascent might be enhanced and facilitated. Origen's brutal attack on the separating vector of his Tantalus Ratio was in line with the Gnostic soul. Origen's is but one technique, a radical one to be sure, by means of which the aspirant participators aim to free the spirit from its temporal boundaries. Other ways, milder and less direct, have been employed to tip the conflict within the Tantalus Ratio in favour of the participatory vectors of spiritual union. One of the most common processes taking place in the second half of life is the strengthening belief in the eschatological partaking of the soul in Divinity. This, no doubt, shifts the Tantalus Ratio towards participatory components. In the *olam haba*, in the world to come, promises the Talmud, the righteous would bask in the glory of the Divine Presence and enjoy eternal spiritual bliss.[40] The souls of the righteous would be illuminated by the *Shechina* (the Divine Presence), "hidden under the throne of glory".[41] In the ever-after all the souls of Man would be fused into immortal unity. Man's soul, in contradiction to his body, is pure as God is pure, because He is the one who introduced it in the human embryo[42] and implanted thereby in Man part of Himself. The soul is thus part of eternal life, which reverts back to its perfect origins after temporal death. This, in essence, is also the Gnostic doctrine of "awakening", which has been adopted by the Kabbalah – which is the ascent of the soul out of its temporal exile, to be reunited with Divinity. Plotinus and the neo-Platonists conceived the release of the soul from the body after death as a spiritual communion with the Godhead. In like manner, Philo conceived death of the righteous (not the wicked, whose death is also spiritual) as the release of the soul from its temporal prison and its return to its home in God. Consequently, temporal death is longed for by the righteous and the blissful after-life is achieved by passing through the seemingly insignificant threshold of the confines of the body.

Paul Tillich lowers even further the stature of this threshold by regarding death as the passage from space-time existence to the eternal timelessness of the now, which is synonymous with God. This passage to the timelessness is a communion with Divinity, so that "He gives us rest in His eternal presence".[43] Death becomes thereby an optical illusion and the existence out of space-time confines becomes attractively feasible. Indeed, Jung urges us to reconsider the viability of spaceless-timeless existence which "partakes of what is inadequately and symbolically described as eternity".[44] Consequently, death is a transfer to a "higher" reality and to participation with eternity, which unifies the Ultimate with authentic Being. This brings eschatology to "just around the corner" and vindicates telepathy, clairvoyance, spiritualism and the whole Pandora's box of extrasensory perception.

The shifting of the intensity of the Tantalus Ratio, with the growth and ageing of the individual, stems from our conception of it as a strain between two opposing groups of vectors. This strain is the reservoir of the motivational energy of the individual, which may find institutionalized or deviant outlets, depending on personality factors and cultural mandates or restraints.[45] This is radically different from the generation and release of psychic energies. For Freud, a cauldron of somatic irritations and instinctual pressures generates psychic unrest, which is released by the Pleasure Principle and a relative homeostasis is regained, only to be aroused again by needs and drives. When the gratification of these needs is not readily available because of the lack of proper objects or cultural proscriptions, a vast maze of "defences" generates Ego's mental processes, as well as the whole of human culture. The similarity here between the Freudian obstacle course undertaken by the Pleasure Principle and the culture-generating delay of instinctual gratification and our Tantalus Ratio is more apparent than real. For Freud, direct need satisfaction is possible when the appropriate object is available, whereas for us, actual participation, i.e. a return to an earlier developmental phase, is not feasible, so that affective tension of non-fulfilment is ever present. Freud detected this ever-present restlessness in the human psyche and accounted for it by the discharge of the delayed drive tension into the soma.[46] However, we do not share Freud's insistence on every psychic process having a direct biological base. Our participation vectors are sustained by memories, mental records and fixations on earlier developmental phases. The effective and motivational energies are accumulated and directed by the Tantalus Ratio and subsequently released into an avenue that is a substitute for and a sublimation of the original participatory goals. These are unattainable by definition. There is some affinity in this point between our theorizing and that of Jung and Sullivan. The core personality structure as per Jung is a certain balance between the principles of equivalence and entropy.[47] This, no doubt, is contrary to our conception of the Tantalus Ratio as the personality core dynamism, which is never in balance. If the ratio achieves equilibrium it means that the personality has no affective and motivational energies, and the person is dead. Yet Jung says that complete selfhood is unattainable. Perfect entropy is never achieved. The person strives and longs for the perfect inner unity, for the mandala-shaped balance, but can never reach it.[48] This, at least, in dynamics and processes, resembles our conception of the Tantalus Ratio.

25

Sullivan also speaks of the inevitability of loneliness, although his inter-personal theory postulates that the individual strives for security through social acceptance, group togetherness and even physical proximity with others.[49] This, in essence, is very much like our Tantalus Ratio, where the longing for participation is an ideal never to be achieved. Consequently, the ever-present tension and the fluctuating excitation of affect, which may be reduced but never fulfilled, may be related to the Existentialist *Angst*. Heidegger's ever-present anxiety, which marks Man's existence, is the essence of his being. Or in Heidegger's own graceless Teutonic heaviness: "The of what of which anxiety feels anxiety in Being in the world itself."[50] This is also the unfulfilled, ever-present tension of the Tantalus Ratio, as expressed in unmatched clarity by Ecclesiastes. God puts eternity, longing and striving into Man's heart, "but without Man ever guessing from first to last, all the things that God brings to pass".[51]

The gist of our present premise is that the Tantalus Ratio is most powerful at the outset of life, and that it decreases in potency with each developmental phase, until it wanes to a low ebb in old age. We do not envisage the Tantalus Ratio as a mathematical quotient of precise dimensions. The methodological procedures for measuring the relationship between the participation and separating vectors are perforce rather vague at this stage of theorizing. The strength of the Tantalus Ratio is related first of all to the enormity of the separating forces in early childhood, which makes the participation vectors muster contrary pressures of corresponding potency. Second, the recency of the separating developmental events makes for vivid memories and sharply focused images of the lost participatory bliss. The child's frantic efforts to regain it would therefore be marked by a desperate surge of power to reverse the raw grief of the recent developmental calamity. These efforts are not yet mellowed and weakened by the sad knowledge of experience that direct participatory reversals are impossible. The separation of birth, which is registered by the neonate as a catastrophe,[52] as a cosmic "breaking of the vessels", is marked by frantic efforts to survive. The "mouth–ego" of the infant searches for the nipple, or for anything that will spurt nourishment. This, as well as the enormous pressures of growth at this hectic pace of development, constitutes the biological vectors of separation, which are at the height of their potency. And yet this is also the stage when the neonate has the strongest craving to revert back to his mother's womb, from which he was just a while ago so brutally expelled into an existence where mere survival involves effort and pain. This would be in keeping with what Schachtel denoted as his "law of embeddedness": "The more complete the state of embeddedness of the organism to any change in the significant environment, the less does the organism want to stir from a state of quiescent equilibrium in relation to the environment."[53] This means in our terms that the more violent the separating disturbance, the more powerful the corresponding striving for participation. And what is more violent than the separating expulsion of birth? Indeed, we claim that what John

Bowlby and other ethologists have denoted as the "instinct of clinging" of the primate to its mother,[54] as well as the less corporeal attachment of the human infant to his mother or mother surrogate, could be linked to the neonate's desire to regain the physical union with mother *in utero*. This could be the underlying motive for the clinging and attachment behavior of both primate and human infant, apart from the "functional" desire of the young to be close to the source of their nourishment and protection.[55]

The second major phase of separation, which is the coagulation of the distinct "I", the separate "ego boundary", is marked by the introduction into the battling forces of the Tantalus Ratio of the vectors of deprivational interaction with the object, which at the oral stage is the mother, the breast and the nipple. The ego boundary that separates the self from the pantheistic omnipresence of early orality is nothing but the scar-tissue that surrounds the *separatum* as a result of its deprivational interaction with its surrounding objects. We shall deal later with the varying contents of the ego boundary and the fixations that could result from excessive and traumatizing deprivations at the earlier and later oral stages. At this point, however, we hypothesize that the emerging self harnesses the participation vectors, to counter the separating effects of the deprivational interaction, which join forces with the processes of growth.

We have relied elsewhere on the "oralist" offshoot of psychoanalysis as describing the "mouth–ego" of early orality aiming to empty the object (breast), whereas at the later "biting" oral stage, the mouth–ego wishes to destroy in its fits of rage the non-obliging object (mother).[56] Apart from the need fulfilment and other developmental connotations that these urges to empty and destroy the object have, we may attribute to them participatory functions. According to the "oralists", the mouth–ego, at early orality, aims to swallow the object, so that pantheistic omnipresence is regained. At the later oral stage, when the infant's deprivational interaction with the object pushes it into developing a separating self, the destruction of the object by biting, which is the sole weapon that the mouth–ego possesses, is aimed to counter this deprivational interaction by elimination of the object. Also, when the depriving object is destroyed, the narcissistic mouth–ego reigns supreme and its omnipotence is regained. Consequently, the Tantalus Ratio at the stage of the crystallization of the self is very potent indeed. We shall later sharpen our distinction between the two oral phases with regard to the action of the mouth–ego. One of the "participation surrogates" that uses up the pent-up tension of the Tantalus Ratio is the extreme egocentricity of the child, which is a prolongation of the narcissistic omnipresence of early orality. This egocentrism lasts, according to Jean Piaget, up to the age of seven.[57] But here again the participatory vectors are fighting a losing battle, because egocentricity musters the counter-pressure of the socializers, who make it their duty to drive home to the child that "he is not alone in the world", that "one has to be considerate of the others", that "one has to

27

take the point of view of others and behave accordingly". This deprivational (from Ego's point of vantage) socialization eventually gains the upper hand until the young adult is extruded from the protection of the family fold and expelled by an endless variety of *rites de passage* to the final separation of adulthood. The participation vectors counter this separation to the burdens of responsibility by an intense longing for the graceful forgiveness of mother and the irresponsibility within the family fold. Most childhood memories become pleasantly idyllic and harsh, painful experiences are mostly repressed.

We do not rely on the Oedipal process as an explanation of normative indoctrination through the introjection of the father as a source of authority. We tend to agree with Melanie Klein, W. Ronald Fairbairn[58] and the other "oralists" who claim that guilt and a conscience may be acquired at a very early stage of development and forego the need of the resolution of the Oedipal complex as a source of normative indoctrination altogether. Social separation for us is achieved by the enmeshing of the individual by the parents and all the socializing agencies within a normative cocoon. Within this personal space allotted to him by the normative system, the individual *separatum* is supposed to mate, reproduce and assume his "proper place as a responsible citizen/subject/comrade in society". This is the "social involvement" decreed by every human society to its individuals. Each group either ascribes or expects from its members to fulfil certain positions within its structure: a witchdoctor, a priest, a sacred whore, a judge, a court-jester, a secretary-general of a party. These social positions are deemed, as a rule, to be taken or achieved after puberty, when the developmental stages of childhood have taken place and the young adult has been hardened by normative *rites de passage* and sent out from the protecting haven of the family fold to grapple with the burdens of "social involvement" without the chaperoning of elders and the grace of mother. The grown-up *separatum*, enclosed within his personal mesh of social norms, has to fight it out on his own without familiar extenuating circumstances.

This "social involvement", sanctioned by the normative system of the group and ingrained into the individual by the deprivational interaction of socialization, is, no doubt, an advanced stage of separation. Yet the Tantalus Ratio has enough tension stored up to send the individual off to some arduous "participation surrogates". These are rather like Freud's "defences", i.e. modes of release of libidinal energies, the direct satisfaction of which is blocked. If, for Freud, most but not all human behavior is "defensive", because some instinctual needs are directly fulfilled for us, there cannot be any actual or direct participation, so that the ever-present, although in varying degrees of potency, quest for participation is always expressed by participation surrogates. We have mentioned previously one such participation surrogate, i.e. the egocentricity of the child as an alternative to the pantheistic omnipotence of early orality. Another powerful and multi-directional participation surrogate operating at the "social involvement" phase of social separation is the achievement motive. It is submitted that pressures to achieve vary from culture to culture and from person to person, yet we may utilize the achievement motive as a proper illustration for the operation of the Tantalus Ratio within the context of its change in potency from childhood to old age.

The achievement motive may also illustrate how the cultural variable of the Tantalus Ratio is related to its other factors within the scaffolding of the personality core. We have evidence, for instance, that the achievement motive is stronger with persons who had unhappy childhoods and experienced unsatisfactory inter-personal relationships in their families. Those whose early family relationships were satisfactory tend to look for personal happiness and inner satisfaction rather than ambition and achievement.[59] In our conceptual framework this finding means that when the deprivational interaction in the family is harsher, it could traumatize the child into a fixation that would predispose the Tantalus Ratio to express itself into a higher achievement motive. Other fixations at earlier developmental phases could also predispose the individual to different attitudes towards achievement. Our age variable of the Tantalus Ratio is hereby linked to the variable of the personality type within the framework of the achievement motive. The cultural variable of the Tantalus Ratio has also been found to influence the achievement motive. Sebastian DeGrazia, for instance, contrasted the Weberian hypothesis as to the drive to excel (activist directive) inherent in the Protestant ethic of self-denial, thrift and hard work with the "quietist-directive" of Catholic other-worldliness and salvation through humility.[60] Other findings, however, indicate that the positive value that American culture places upon upward mobility striving is stronger than either the Catholic other-worldly salvation or the Protestant salvation through work.[61] The achievement motive would consequently vary in "tool-oriented" societies and in "symbol-oriented" societies. The achievement motive thus illustrates the multivariate nature of the Tantalus Ratio. The variables are only examined separately for our present purpose of theory building. The multivariate and interdisciplinary study of the Tantalus Ratio could subsequently be carried out by the empirically inclined taking the independent variables as well as the residuary unchartered variables as planes within a space. Louis Guttman's "Scalogram Analysis" might be an appropriate research tool for this purpose.[62]

The dynamics of the Tantalus Ratio are illustrated by the achievement motive as follows: the separating social norms decree the placement of each individual within the various positions of the social structure. These separating vectors are countered by participatory longing to cast off the normative burdens that regulate the "social involvement" of the individual within the social structure. However, the resulting tension within the Tantalus Ratio is directed through the achievement motive to "surrogate participatory" goals: by power and money, Ego dreams to regain the unconditional acceptance and graceful affection that he lost when he was

29

forced out of the protective family fold. With power, he aims to enforce on others his own particular vision of togetherness, and with money, to buy friendship and love, which are the prime modes of surrogate participation. By subjugating his membership or reference groups and manipulating at will the others and things in his entourage, Ego aims at re-incorporating his environment into himself, thereby regaining the narcissistic omnipresence of early orality. By having total control at their fingertips, with everyone around rushing to carry out at once the minutest of their whims, an Alexander, a Caligula and a Hitler sense the omnipotence of God. And yet, as we all know, these dreams of omnipotence have been as delusive with these tyrants as with the myriads of little Caesars in their executive suites, the *Napoleonchicks* serving as deans of faculties and the Christs in lunatic asylums. The fires of achievement with these, as with the other "pyramid-climbers", have been kindled by the Tantalus Ratio and directed towards defensive sublimatory "surrogate participation", because the way back to actual participation is inevitably blocked.

This rather simplistic view of the achievement motive may cause the serious students of upper vertical social mobility alternate fits of rage and scorn, but our purpose here is didactic and illustrative. We are well aware that the nature and manifestation of the achievement motive of a Genet, born to an unknown prostitute and raised by the *Assistance publique*, would be quite different from the ambitions of a Jack Kennedy; yet the nature of the propelling energies, not their magnitude and form, could be similar. Personality and cultural factors would also affect the potency of the achievement motive. We also have many findings classifying the levels of aspirations of youth, ranging from the non-aspiring to those who strive to change both their class memberships and economic positions.[63] We claim that these differences may be linked to the shifting relationships of separation and participation vectors within the Tantalus Ratio. It is quite irrelevant for our present purpose whether the achievement motive presses an individual to climb up the echelons of a legitimate structure or strive to become a head of a family in the Cosa Nostra: both are "surrogate participation" goals, fuelled by the Tantalus Ratio. It is, however, our task to trace the breakdowns of the involvement of Ego with his social positions and groups, because this marks a development phase that takes place later in life. It is marked by a decline in the separating vectors of social interaction and leads Ego down Jung's parabola of life towards resignation, inaction and a greater concern with the participatory ultimates of nonbeing. The relevant processes, however, are hopelessly complex. We have not undertaken in the present work to build a personality theory, *but only to construct a scaffolding for a theory* and describe some core personality vectors. Consequently, the processes by which the energy stored up by the Tantalus Ratio is cathected into the organism as affects – the day-dreaming, subconscious process and pathological manifestations resulting from the blocking of the cathected energies from expressing themselves into "surrogate participation" – are outside the scope of the present work. The achievement motive is the cathexis of energy into action, and as such we may trace its outward manifestation as Ego's social involvement within the framework of the maturation and developmental variable of the Tantalus Ratio.

The Tantalus Ratio, from maturity onwards, during most of the individual's adult life, is the relationship between his social involvement ordained by the separating social norms and the countering participatory pressures, which manifest themselves mostly by the surrogate participation of the achievement motive. At a rather high level of abstraction, we may trace the cathexis of the Tantalus Ratio into achievement to the two extreme poles of a continuum. Both of these mark, alas, the breakdown of social involvement, because achievement, being a surrogate participatory dynamism, does not satisfy the basic participation vector at the personality core. Consequently, the achievement motive is a self-defeating passion.

The path to one pole of the social involvement continuum leads through what sociologists and social psychologists have described and studied in a vast number of publications as anomie and alienation. Emile Durkheim, Robert Merton, Martin Seeman, Leo Srole, Joachim Israel, Richard Schacht and others[64] have traced the painful progress of the individual on the achievement pyramid, on which he is pushed to climb by the cultural mandates. He very often topples down on his climb from one achievement level to the other because the upper levels are bound to have less legroom than the lower ones. Also colour, creed and race barriers will keep him down, although he equipped himself with the formal climbing tools of education and proficiency required by the cultural mandates. Those who fell or were catapulted down from the tricky achievement pyramid might try to climb another one, an illegitimate one this time, only to discover that the climb upwards is as slippery on the deviant structure as it is on the institutionalised one. The rejects that lie broken in the gutters might develop an intense hatred towards the structure and hurl at it verbal venom, in impotent rage. They might also find themselves a protected niche within the structure and go through the motions and routines of existence, foregoing any attempt to climb further. They might also retreat and wait for better weather, in order to try again and assault the peak. All these have not really forsaken their quest for surrogate participation by achievement and their rejection of the coveted cultural goals is a "sour grapes" *ressentiment* negation of the fox in the fable. However, their real plight lies in the fact, almost never realized by the *ressentiment* anomiacs, that the goals they are after would never satiate their underlying craving for participation, which is unquenchable by definition. Utopians like Karl Marx, Herbert Marcuse and Franz Fanon, who assault the existing structures of society that render Man powerless, are oblivious of the fact that the difference between their visions of new structures and the existing one is that the former are still dreams, *fatae morganae*, kindled by their own quest for social participation.

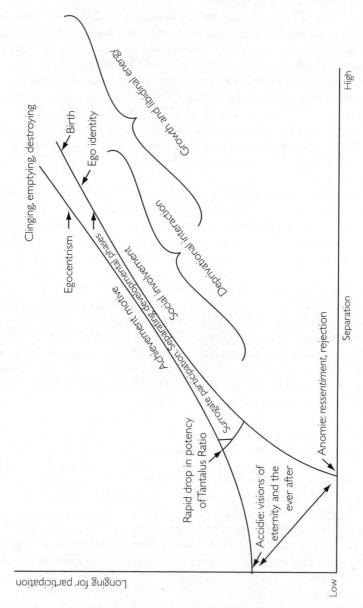

Figure 1.3 Maturation and Developmental Process

The other pole, the opposite extreme from *ressentiment* rejection, is reached by the accidiac,[65] whose breakdown of social involvement is outwardly similar but intrinsically different. When a social achiever on the climb looks down from one of his positions on the slope of the pyramid, or even from "the room at the top", his ennui, or the "so what" emptiness, might lend him the insight that another peak, another goal or another conquest would not ease his longing to achieve. This sudden insight might trigger in him a realization that what he is longing for transcends the social achievement slope. He would realize that the achievement motive is a sublimated substitute for the grace of togetherness in pre-natal Unity. This could be registered by him as a religious experience, a mystical communion, or a revelation of his own transcendental self behind the *Mayan* veil of temporality. He might join a Zen monastery, "do his own thing" among a group of "flower people" or junkies, leave his brokerage firm to pursue, *á la* Paul Gauguin, his inner vision of beauty, oblivious of his syphilis and the persecutions of the Tahitian priests, or gladly renounce his social position *á la* Camus' Judge Penitent, and pursue his own private vision of transcendence in lonely freedom. This task is "quite solitary and very exhausting. No champagne, no friends raising their glasses as they look at you affectionately. Alone in a forbidding room, alone in the prisoner's box before the judges and alone to decide in the face of oneself or in the face of others' judgment." [66] The accidiac is an outsider who has renounced the value system of his group and projects his craving for ultimate participation into his inner self, or more appropriately into transcendence. He hovers above the achievement pyramid and beyond the routines of social involvement; he becomes a quietist, nearer to the real goal of the participation vector and not its surrogates. The accidiac's non-involvement, his sloth, his claim to be outside the exigencies of the separating norms of the group make him one of the Seven Capital Sinners and gain him the spiritual death sentence of the Church. Yet he proves to possess the trump cards because the inaction, the quietism of the accidiac, brings him nearer to the goal of nonbeing of the participation vector.

The *ressentiment* rejects and the accidiacs are two ideal type extremes, between which a whole range of types may be placed. However, after the decline or breakdown of social involvement, the Tantalus Ratio has a poor store of cathectic energy left. The separating deprivational interaction is at its lowest ebb and the libidinal and growth energies decline.

Figure 1.3 illustrates the maturation and developmental processes as related to the separation and participation vectors of the personality core. It also relates to the maturation variable of the Tantalus Ratio and not to the personality and cultural variables, which shall be dealt with in subsequent chapters. We can see that the developmental stages of separation generate counter pressures and provide, thereby, the cathectic energy within the Tantalus Ratio. We have specified some of the surrogate participation modes here, again for illustrative purposes only, because in reality

33

they are far more numerous and their interrelationships far more complex. We have represented the primary separation forces of growth and libidinal energies as the social separating vector of deprivational interaction. Yet we cannot specify the actual extent of overlapping. All we can say is that the growth and libidinal energies operate on the fetus and neonate before the deprivational interaction of the infant with the object, and the interaction goes on after the growth processes have stopped and the sexual drive is on the decline. The regression is carried on throughout the social involvement phase. We have explained previously the progressive decline in the separating forces with each consecutive phase. The participation surrogates decline in potency because Ego is on his way to less activity, more resignation and inaction, which signifies the advent of nonbeing – the ultimate participatory goal. After the phase of social involvement is bifurcated, either towards *ressentiment* rejection or *accidie*, there is a sharp drop in the Tantalus Ratio. The individual has used up most of his cathectic energy. If he moves towards the anomic pole of the continuum, he broods with self-pity on the peaks he has lost, and if he heads towards *accidie*, he will have the quietist visions of eternity and the ever-after.

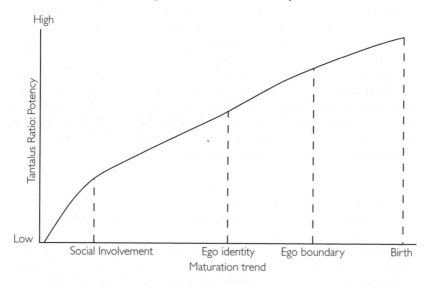

Figure 1.4 Decline of Potency of the Tantalus Ratio

The anomic *ressentiment* type of decline after the social involvement phase ends or deteriorates and moves, as seen in **figure 1.4**, towards the separation axis. The retired executive who realizes that the structure that sustained his job and the routines and the statuses of his work were not extraneous to himself, but *were* himself. The achievement motive structured his personality in the roles of his social involvement. When this involvement ended, he lost his crutches and sank into disintegration because his self-image was moulded by the pigeonhole of his social placement. The *ressentiment* dropouts who were rejected by the social structures before their retirement age becry with tears of gin-cum-grudges the rape of their innocence by "the system". Theirs is a fake innocence, because they still cling to the system, their only misgiving being that they ended up on the wrong end of its favours. These are the ludicrous tearful pleas for justice of a John Dean after his own manipulations of the Watergate mess ousted him from the power-game. The *ressentiment* anomics are still in the grips of the separating normative structure from which they have been rejected because the vicissitudes of the achievement motive will not let them make do with less than complete mastery. Western culture, as a rule, does not train its young how to become failures, or how to accept failure when it comes. The inner freedom of Camus' Judge Penitent when he is no more bound by the pomposity and play-acting of social roles and the burden of social positions is as conceivable to them as orgasm to a eunuch. The *ressentiment* anomics become lonely geriatric cases whose failing bodies afford them their main interest in an otherwise empty routine. The accidiac, on the other hand, anchors on transcendence, not as a mechanical means to prolong his temporal life in the ever-after, but as a participatory projection on the ultimate of nonbeing, which is right around the corner. He heads towards the axis of longing for participation in **figure 1.3**, because transcendence seems to him as the most feasible alternative to a waning temporal existence. This alternative is not deducted by logical inference, but by a mystical certainty ingrained by the quest for the omnipresence and non-awareness of the early and pre-natal phases of development. The *ressentiment* anomic is a Sisyphus burdened by repetitious routines and the futility of action, and yet he resumes his climb up the achievement pyramid. On the other hand, the accidiac is a Tantalus whose goals of participation are ever eluding him, but he always has before his eyes the dreams of mirages, however hazy, of participation in unity. Camus concludes his essay on the *Myth of Sisyphus* by saying that

> Sisyphus, returning toward his rock . . . contemplates that series of unrelated actions which becomes his fate, created by him, combined under his memory's eye and soon sealed by his death. Thus, convinced of the wholly human origin of all that is human, a blind man eager to see who knows that the night has no end, he is still on the go. The rock is still rolling . . . The struggle itself toward the heights is enough to fill a man's heart. One must imagine Sisyphus happy.[67]

This to us is happiness misplaced. Sisyphus is looking back and he knows that his climbing is futile and yet, like the *ressentiment* anomic, he longs to climb the slopes that have shaken him down. He knows every bolt in the assembly line, like the donkey that turns blindfolded a water-well precipitates the stone he stumbles on in every round he makes. However, the Tantalic blindfolded donkey imagines itself going ahead and not running around in circles. It has visions of making headway against all the available evidence to the contrary. It feels it in its bones.

35

The visions of the ever-after and the bliss of nonbeing are seen by the Tantalic accidiac as far away and receding; yet he has a vision, although blurred, to long for. Unlike Sisyphus, he has something ahead of him to strive for. Nobody knows what the hazy mirage ahead stands for, but it sustains the longing and the quest, which are the essence of the participation vector. This longing "is enough to fill a man's heart". One must imagine Tantalus, not Sisyphus, happy.

The
Sisyphean and the
Tantalic

2

An Ontological Personality Typology

To find a passage from the external world to the mental world is more important than to find a way to East India, no matter what statesmen may say.
                              Solomon Maimon, *Studies in Transcendental Philosophy*

For the greatest crime of Man is that he was born.
                              Pedro de la Barca Calderon

The second group of variables in the scaffolding of our personality theory
relates to the personality characteristics, traits and types as fixated in the
developmental phases. These variables will be linked to the developmental, maturation and ageing curve of the Tantalus Ratio. Finally, these two
groups of variables will be considered within the cultural context of the
symbol-oriented quietist and the tool-oriented activist cultures. These
three groups of independent variables, when related to the Tantalus Ratio,
are within the wider matrix of the participation and separation vectors of
the personality core. As we are constructing a scaffolding only of a personality theory, and not a fully developed and integrated theoretical
structure, we have left out from our theorizing an undetermined and
unchartered number of variables that are not clearly related to the personality core vectors.

Where are the Fixations Fixated?

Personality traits and types are centred on the key concepts of fixation,
which is, undoubtedly, Freudian in origin. Unfortunately, neither
Sigmund Freud himself nor his disciples have sufficiently clarified for the
uninitiated outsiders the mechanisms of fixation, although it seems to be
a central concept in psychoanalytic theory and practice. The original

Freudian formulation is that the libidinal energy is cathected towards the erogenous zones of the body, which also represent the major psycho-sexual developmental phases.[1] However, when parents or their surrogates over-indulge the infant or severely deprive him at any given developmental phase, he will muster a relatively large amount of libidinal energy to over-come the frustrations created by these over-indulgences or deprivations. He also will harness his libidinal energies to create alternative defensive outlets for the developmental growth processes, the "normal" manifesta-tions of which have been blocked. Consequently, the growth processes will be arrested or injured at a given developmental phase, because the libidinal energies have been expended to erect defences against the conflictual interaction with the parents, instead of to build the infant's personality. This butter versus cannons competition within the person-ality economy raises many questions that are not readily answered in the psychoanalytic literature. We do not propose to delve into extensive polemics, but one issue is highly relevant for our present purposes: what are the differential mechanics of a fixation caused by parental over-indul-gence and that linked to deprivational conflicts? There seems to be a degree of confusion in this matter. Salvatore Maddi is of the opinion that the fixation-causing mechanisms of over-indulgence and deprivation are quite similar. He says:

> The best that can happen is that the parents provide a modicum of instinctual satis-faction for their child. If they fall short of this modicum, by severely punishing the child for his need to receive and take, or by simply not having enough nurturance within them to make any difference, the inevitable conflict will be greatly intensi-fied. This intensification will require especially strong and ubiquitous defences, the employment of which are tantamount to a fixation, or arresting of growth. Once such defences are instituted, change and development are impaired. The parents can also exceed the modicum of oral gratification by trying to be more nurturant than is consistent with their own needs and duties. This deviation from the ideal also leads to an intensification of the inevitable conflict because the nurturance will be only superficially satisfying but will actually carry with it such resentment, and have so many strings attached, as to be counterfeit. Again, the child will be frus-trated and in pain, and have to institute defences of such intensity and ubiquity as to constitute fixation.[2]

On the other hand, such an authoritative interpreter of Freudian doctrine as Father John Nuttin describes the mechanism of fixation as follows:

> Fixation is produced by experiences in infancy, either of frustration or of intense gratification in the corresponding zones of the body. An intense satisfaction, espe-cially coming at a time when the child is otherwise in a difficult and tense situation, endows the seat of the pleasure with a special significance. The child subsequently will not be able to give up the type of infantile activity that afforded him this satis-faction. In like manner, frustration and excessive punishment relating to certain infantile activities compel the child to persist in his attachment to the forbidden area.

He may become "obsessed" by a certain type of activity either because it is a pleasure that was refused him, or because it was the occasion of a deep emotional
trauma.[3]

There seems to be a consensus here as to the fixating effect of parental
deprivation, but a wide divergence of opinion as to the nature of the
fixating effects of over-indulgence. Maddi's interpretation contains an
inner fallacy: he describes over-indulgence as a kind of force-feeding and
irritating nagging attention by the parents. If this is against the needs and
the wishes of the infant, it will be registered by him as pain and discomfort and will be similar to the effects of deprivation. However, if the
over-indulgence reduces tension and brings contentedness to the infant,
no libidinal energy has to be mustered to erect defences. Moreover, the
indulgence of needs, even to excess but gratifying to the infant, leads to
the coveted tensionless homeostasis of Freud's Pleasure Principle. The
cathartic release of tension incidental to the fulfilment of needs cannot
affect a pent-up cathexis of libidinal energy, leading to fixation. Nuttin's
interpretation of the fixating effects of over-indulgence is unacceptable to
us on different grounds. Our conception of the participatory vector in the
personality core of the individual pre-supposes an urge to revert back to
an earlier developmental phase: the carefree irresponsibility of pre-
puberty, the pantheistic omnipresence of early orality and the blissful
suspended animation in the womb. The wish to revert back to the earlier
developmental phases does not have to be reinforced by a pleasant interaction with parents. It is one of the two basic driving forces of Man's
personality. If our premise here, which is partially based on Freud's
Pleasure Principle, is correct, we are content because the satisfaction of
our needs removes the sensory irritations and tensions and brings us
nearer to the blissful automatic need satisfaction within the womb. There
the fetus takes exactly the amount of nourishment it needs, no more and
no less; also, the cosiness of suspension in the amniotic fluid, as well as
the constancy of temperature in the womb, makes the well-being of the
fetus so close to perfection that no human indulgence could match it. The
same holds true for the sense of exclusiveness and omnipotence of the
neonate at early orality. Consequently, the infant does not have to be
cuddled to wish to remain at early orality, because it registers the emerging
of the separate self from the pantheistic togetherness as an expulsion from
paradise. This brings us to our interim conclusion: that a fixation cannot
be effected by a contentedness incidental to a pleasure-giving parent –
child interaction. Deprivation and fulfilment, pain and contentedness
cannot have, to our mind, the same or similar fixating effects. Only deprivation, an acute non-satisfaction of needs and a traumatic injury may
cause fixation.

We may well ask ourselves now what are the dynamics of fixation;
otherwise, our theoretical exposition of the Tantalus Ratio as a personality core mechanism will have some vague spots. Here, too,

unfortunately, psychoanalytic sources are rather hazy, and Freud himself is not clear and takes too many things for granted. He says:

> The unconscious knows no time limit. The most important, as well as the most peculiar character of psychic fixation consists in the fact that all impressions are, on the one hand, retained in the same form as they were received, and also in the forms that they have assumed in their further development. This state of affairs cannot be elucidated by any comparison from any other sphere. By virtue of this theory, every former state of the memory content may thus be restored, even though all original relations have long been replaced by newer ones.[4]

The Freudian unconscious psyche seems to be the perfect databank, which stores all impressions as well as all possible interactions of these impressions with past and future ones, in a timeless progression. A fixation is, then, some sort of anchor on a given matrix of these impressions, but how this anchoring comes about Freud does not say. We propose an explanation that is based on our exposition of the developmental phases of the personality core.[5]

The coagulation of the separate self from the non-differentiated pantheism of early orality is effected by the deprivational interaction of the infant with its objects (breast, mother, its surrogates and the elements). In like manner, the separation of the child from the cushioning and irresponsibility of the family is brought about by the burdens of socialization and the normative *rites de passage* into puberty. If these processes, which are deprivational in essence, are more painful at a given developmental phase than the modal harshness (as measured by ego's own experience), a rupture, a developmental wound, is formed, which the psychic energies rush to mend. To be more precise: we envisage the developmental processes as an interplay between the separating forces of growth and interaction and the participating urge to revert back to an earlier developmental phase. The cathected energy resulting from the dynamic interplay between these vectors is the Tantalus Ratio. However, if the separating effects of the deprivational interaction were at a given space–time too intense or violent, the developmental process is temporarily disconnected. The separating injury has blown a fuse and short-circuited the developmental process. The participation vector and the cathected energies of the Tantalus Ratio repair the injury by surrounding and covering it with developmental scar-tissue, not unlike the scar on a wound. Yet the wound itself and the tender coats of scar-tissue are still exposed to conflict and more pressure, because the deprivational interaction of the nascent ego with its entourage is a continuous process. Consequently, the ever-thickening layers of the scar-tissue, which result from the trauma of the fixation, are more like a corn on a toe. The cathected energy whirls around the traumatized developmental area, covering it with excessive mental imprints, very much like the whirls and loops of the skin texture of the corn, which form a lump protruding from the texture of the skin. The corn is painful not only because of the pressure but because the excessive scar-tissue makes it more vulnerable. Because of the trauma, the whole area is over-sensitive. This, on a rather low level of abstraction, illustrates the nature of fixation. It is a combined outcome of the traumatizing injury and the excessive and frantic patching of layers of developmental scar-tissue by the cathected energies of the Tantalus Ratio. The harsher the trauma, the thicker would be the layers of the defensive scar-tissue. This should be related to our analysis else-where of the formation of the ego boundary.[6] The separate ego emerges out of the non-differentiated early orality through its deprivational inter-action with its breast mother and surrounding objects. The resulting boundary around the self is also a developmental scar tissue, but a fixa-tion is an over-traumatized developmental experience, which is more conspicuous, more sensitive and consequently more vulnerable than the rest of the developmental texture of the personality.

Our conceptualization of fixation, in contradistinction to the Freudian usage, is not related to pathological regressions but to the crystallization of character traits and personality types. We hold, also, that regression is not conditioned by fixation, but is a defensive flight to an earlier devel-opmental phase, the longing for which is ever present in the participation vector of our personality core. When the dynamic balance of the Tantalus Ratio is disturbed, by the separating pressures of growth or ego's inter-personal relationships suffering a disrupting blow, the released counter-pressures of participation catapult ego to visions of pre-puberty havens and to blissful dreams of early orality. Fixation is therefore a devel-opmental dam that traps both the disrupting blows of traumatizing interaction and the countering defences of the Tantalus Ratio. The anchoring of the personality traits on the fixation is the result of this massive concentration of painful experiences and the heaping of defences in frantic disarray. One is aware of a hand or a tooth only when they are painful, and one always gets hit on a sore because the same touch on normal tissue is hardly noticeable. Consequently, the severity of fixation is related to the magnitude of the developmental trauma and the corre-sponding intensity of defences mustered by the Tantalus Ratio. We have seen earlier[7] that the potency of the Tantalus Ratio is related to the matu-ration and ageing of the individual. Now we elaborate the premise that the intensity of the Tantalus Ratio is linked to the severity of fixation, which is linked in turn to character traits or types. In **chapter 3**, we shall try to link the Tantalus Ratio to the cultural continuum of tool versus symbol orientations and provide, thereby, the social dimension to our model.

Object and Self: The Crucial Dichotomy

Birth is, no doubt, an explosive event, the archetype of which in mythol-ogy is the act of creation itself; yet this colossal event is not registered by a separate awareness. Not until later orality does a separate self emerge out of a pantheistic mass and the "I" is confronted by the surrounding objects. This is the ontological base-line from which the inchoate being, i.e. the self, emerges out of the total being of early orality and the circumference of the *separatum*; the self is defined by the non-self, i.e. the object. This ontological revolution, which is registered by the individual as a separating catastrophe, is the basis of all Existentialist philosophy. Martin Heidegger's *das sein* and Jean-Paul Sartre's subjective *pour soi*, as contrasted with the object, the *en soi*, and the "they", the *das Man*. The *Eigenwelt*, the universe of the self, *vis-à-vis* the *Mitwelt*, the world of others, and the *Umwelt*, the inanimate world of things.[8] It is also the basis for the most numerous typologies in the study of Man's personality. This is only natural because the ontological division between subject and object is as readily employed in psychological dichotomies as the fact that Man has ten fingers is the sole basis for the decimal system. The coagulation of the self marks, therefore, the cutting-off point for the most basic developmental dichotomy: from birth and early orality to the phase where the ego boundary is formed around the emerging individual *separatum* and from later orality through the formation of the "ego identity" onwards. In the first phase, any fixation that might happen, and may imprint, thereby, some character traits on the developing personality, is not registered by a separate self capable of discerning between the objects that are the source of the fixation-causing trauma and himself as its recipient. The experiencing entity is a non-differentiated pantheistic totality.

On the other hand, if the traumatizing fixation happens at the later oral phase after the objects have expelled the self from their togetherness by a depriving interaction with it, the self may well be in a position to attribute the cause of pain and deprivation to its proper source, i.e. the objects. We propose a personality typology that is anchored on this developmental dichotomy of pre- and post-differentiation of the self. The moulding process is the nature and severity of fixation that determines, in turn, the placement of a given individual on the personality type continuum. However, the types themselves are fixated by developmental chronology: i.e. whether the trauma happened before or after the separation of the self from the non-differentiation type (the one who was fixated before the formation of the self – the *participant* or the *Tantalic* type). If the traumas fixate the personality after the coagulation of the self, the *separant* or the *Sisyphean* type is bound to emerge. We shall compare later our proposed typology with some of the leading personality taxonomies in the literature. However, its main asset, in the present context, is that it relates to the Tantalus Ratio and our personality core vectors. The Tantalic type is participation bound – ever visualizing and longing for the autarchic all-inclusive early orality, and the Sisyphean type is ever entangled by the vicissitudes of the object. **Figure 2.1** clarifies the bases of the typology.

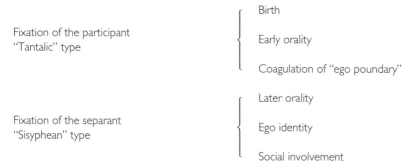

Fixation of the participant
"Tantalic" type

   Birth

   Early orality

   Coagulation of "ego poundary"

Fixation of the separant
"Sisyphean" type

   Later orality

   Ego identity

   Social involvement

Figure 2.1   Fixation and Personality Development

Although Henry Murray speaks of fixations within the womb,[9] we hold that the fetus is a non-differentiated entity possessing no self-awareness. Hence, the effects of fixations would be more conspicuous and decisive after birth and during the relatively short yet developmentally crucial period of early orality. After the differentiation of the self, the Sisyphean type may be fixated anywhere between later orality and post-adolescent puberty when the social norms finally enmesh the individual within the social identity of separation.

The main characteristics of the Tantalic–participant type in contradistinction to the Sisyphean–separant type will emerge in the course of our analysis, to be conducted along the following axis. We shall first distinguish and compare our typology with existing typologies. Our claim for innovation would have to be proved, in view of some rather close, yet superficial similarities between our typology and other personality dichotomies. Carl Jung's celebrated Introversion/Extroversion typology, for instance, which, Hans Eysenck claims, has been known and used in Europe hundreds of years before Jung,[10] seems to be very similar to our typology, but on closer scrutiny we may see that its bases are entirely different. Introversion/Extroversion and its semantic equivalents anchor on the dichotomy of self-orientation and object-orientation. This can happen only after the self is already separate from the object. It is entirely different from the basis of our typology, which contrasts the total non-differentiation of early orality and the plurality of self, others and things from later orality onwards. Also, Jung does not explain the developmental genesis of his types, so that his exposition is somewhat disconnected in this respect. We try to link our typology to the developmental phases of the personality by means of the dynamics of fixation. In our second line of analysis, we shall study some research findings that relate to various typologies and demonstrate that their findings are just intervening variables to the more basic dichotomy of participation and separation. Finally, we shall illustrate the two extremes of our typology by the character traits of the two founders of the Jewish Hassidic movement, Israel Ben Eliezer, the Ba'al Shem-Tov (1698 -1760) – the legendary Besht – who is our prototype for the separant–Sisyphean, and his foremost disciple – Dov-Ber (the Maggid) of Mezherich (d. 1772) – as the extreme Tantalic–participant type. The value of these illustrative types to our present purposes lies in the fact that these diametrically opposed personalities, whose character polarities expressed themselves in differences of religious doctrine, were the founders of an outwardly monolithic religious movement, which swept like wildfire the large centres of Jewry in eighteenth-century Russia and Poland.

For the past twenty-five years, since the publication of the first edition of this volume, we have devoted ourselves to developing the concept of mytho-empiricism. We believe that myths are the projected models of human behavior on all levels: they record the experience of the past and provide the basis of longing for the future. Not only do they express overt dynamics, they also serve as the most valuable key to understanding covert dynamics, such as those of the infant in the early oral phase.

All three crucial phases, or traumas, of the structuring of the self have their empirical counterparts (see Preface, page xi–xii). We may equate birth with the Kabbalistic "breaking of the divine vessels"; the coagulation of a separate self and formation of an ego boundary are projected as the myth of the Original Sin; and the offering of Isaac (discussed in **chapter 8**) serves as the empirical anchor for rites of passage from childhood to adulthood. These mytho-empirical anchors are discussed at length using Kabbalistic, Gnostic, Christian and Greek sources in *The Bridge to Nothingness: Gnosis, Kabbalah and Existentialism* (1993).

The underlying *leitmotiv* of our present analysis is that most existing character traits, both in the professional and folkloristic literature, may be linked to the more basic dichotomy of the separant and participant types. Also, the same outward manifestation of behavior may be related to diametrically opposite character traits. Asceticism, for instance, might be the reaction-formation involvement with food of the object-devouring separant, not unlike the food-obsessed abstention of the weight-watcher. On the other hand, the asceticism of the participant is motivated by his wish to renounce the hold that the object has on him through his needs, the satisfaction of which is an impediment to his desire for quietist inaction. This method of analysis has its pitfalls, rather like the dynamisms of psychoanalysis, which takes any outward behavior to represent diverse subconscious processes.

The fixation of our polar types is related to the crucial phase of the crystallization of the self, which we have described elsewhere.[11] We have relied on the object-relations theorists, especially Melanie Klein, W. Ronald Fairbairn, Donald Woods Winnicott and Harry Guntrip. These British "oralists" anchor their theorizing on the early and later oral phases, with a relative disregard for the later Freudian developmental stages. Their theories, together with our own reliance on the separating transition from the pantheistic non-awareness of early orality to the emergence of the self, serve as the theoretical foundation for the further elaboration of our present premise. We shall first present the "oralist" view and then explain how our conception is different.

We have stated in our previous exposition that the mother–child deprivational interaction at the oral stage is relevant not only for the process of the separation of the self but also to the contents of its encompassing ego boundary.[12] A tense, anxious, "empty", absent mother or a destroying "emptying" self are introjected into the nascent ego boundary and become "bad me". At the early oral phase, when the differentiation between the infant and his surroundings has barely been initiated, the empty breast, the neglecting mother, the hard objects and the recurring discomfort are still all "me". A fixation at this stage would result in an ego boundary dominated by a self-image of badness and surrounded by a hazy, amorphous and non-descript goodness, which hovers out in the un-chartered "there" and deals out in a rather erratic manner food and comfort. On the other hand, if the traumatic maternal deprivation and neglect is fixated in the later oral stage, after the division between self and mother (object) has been affected, the ego boundary would have a "good" self-image, fighting a rejecting bad mother (object). The polar types on our continuum would, therefore, be the "bad" ego boundary surrounded by the good objects, which ego aimed at "emptying" and "destroying", for which the evil self is to blame. At the other extreme, the "good" ego boundary is surrounded by aggressive and depriving objects. In order to structure further these rudimentary "bad" and "good" ego boundaries into our separant and participant character types, we shall avail ourselves of Saul Rosenzweig's typology of reactions to frustrations.[13] The extrapunitive reaction is characterized by aggression directed outwardly to the object. The defence mechanism accompanying this type of reaction is projection, the intropunitive reaction characterized by inner-directed aggression. The defence mechanisms accompanying this type of reaction are displacement and isolation. (The impunitive neutralizing and repressing attitude is irrelevant for our present context, since we are dealing with the polar extreme types of the continuum.) Our hypothesis is that Rosenzweig's types of reactions, which are measurable personality traits, have been fixated at the oral stage. These reactions, which are acquired presumably by a learning process, would be bound to the infant's complete reliance on the object (the mother or its surrogate). Consequently, the reinforcements, or the lack of them, would have such a marked imprint at the plastic oral stage that this polarity of reactions would be crystallized into lasting personality traits. But precisely these disturbances of infant–mother interaction constitute our fixations of early and later orality. Consequently, the synchronization of Rosenzweig's typology and our fixated types would result in the following more comprehensive description of our polar types. The intropunitive "bad me", fixated by the fear of destroying the good object (devouring the object, as described by the oralists), is the participant type. His vector of participation would be linked to his early oral fixation. Consequently, his

45

quest for participation would manifest itself by a tendency towards the annihilation of the self as the means to regain pantheistic omnipresence. The Tantalic participant would be guided by the visions of bliss of early orality (by definition, unattainable) as determined by the inner aggression towards the self, the crystallization of which ended the omnipotence of non-awareness, and the fixation at the early oral phase of development, which is the time-span within which this pantheistic non-awareness takes place. Our hypothesis is that the Tantalus Ratio of the participant polar type is less potent because he starts from the outset with the quietist character traits anchoring on inaction and the cathected energy is directed towards the annihilation of the self. The participant–Tantalic type aims at achieving participation by excluding himself from his ontological interaction with his surroundings, so that when he is transformed from a being to a nonbeing, the coveted state of omnipresent non-awareness would be regained. This is participation through self-annihilation, through the exclusion of the self from the ontological dramatis personae. The separant type, on the other hand, is extra-punitive. He has been fixated at the later oral phase, during or after the process of separation. The deprivational interaction with the mother/object provides a clear "bad" target for the "good suffering me". The devouring "mouth–ego" aims at swallowing, overpowering, manipulating the object and thereby gaining "participation by inclusion", i.e. incorporating the object figuratively or symbolically within the self. This, in turn, augments ego's involvement with his surrounding objects, with a resultant increase in his deprivational interaction with these objects. As we have stated elsewhere,[14] ego's deprivational interaction with his surrounding others, as well as social interaction in general, are the prime movers of separation. This is how the separant object manipulator is caught in a participation-motivated yet separation-generating Sisyphean cycle. The initial Tantalus Ratio of the separant type is relatively potent because the dialectics of participation motivated assault on the object, with a resultant separating counterattack, breed the highly charged conflicts between the participation and separation vectors of the personality core that constitute the Tantalus Ratio.

Klein, Fairbairn, and to some extent Karl Abraham, have rightly imputed an overwhelming importance to oral eroticism in the structuring of character and personality. Yet their theories relating to early and later orality, sucking, and biting, "emptying" the breast–mother or being deprived by it lack clarity since they do not provide clear-cut criteria for distinguishing between early and later orality. In contrast, we posit the coagulation of the separate self as the dividing line between early and later orality. Before the separation everything occurs within the pantheistic, omnipresent mouth–ego. However, after the separate mouth–ego gains its ego boundary the depriving breast–mother and surrounding objects are identified as such by the nascent ego and treated accordingly. The fixations at early orality may then be clearly related to a pantheistic unity of self, others, and objects, whereas the fixations at later orality are anchored on a distinct self, others, and objects.

The dynamics of congruity can operate by separant inclusion, through which the mouth–ego aims to swallow and incorporate the breast–mother and object, or by participant exclusion by which the mouth–ego aims to deface and annihilate itself so that it melts back into the object and fuses with the breast–mother. These dynamics result in the formation of a personality core continuum determined by the deprivational interaction between mouth–ego and breast–mother along the following lines. The mother axis has at one extreme the absence of the mother, the Jean Genet-type foundlings who grow up in institutions with very little care, where the nipple of a bottle, provided erratically and sometimes carelessly, is a surrogate breast, and the fleeting image of the passing nurse takes the place of the absent mother. The rejecting mother represents the other extreme. This includes a wide range of maternal attitudes, from the mother who openly rejects the child to the frustrating mother who does not fulfil the infant's needs for nourishment and comfort and is consequently perceived by the child as hating and rejecting it. The indifferent mother is the physically or mentally incapacitated mother or the mother who is overburdened with children and work; she is physically present but emotionally tired and detached.

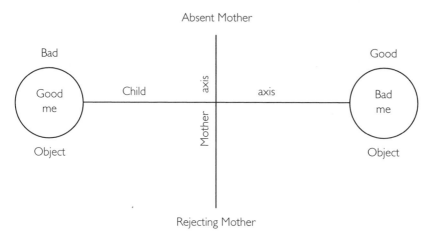

Figure 2.2 Dialectics of Mother and Child Relationship

The mother axis represents a skewed and anomalous continuum of maternal attitudes, since more or less normal maternal care does not predispose the infant to morbidity. One extreme of the child axis is represented by the negative (bad me) ego boundary surrounded by the good object (mother). At the very early oral stage, described by Freud as primary narcissism, by Fairbairn as "mouth–ego with a breast," and here as omnipresent pantheism, the mouth feeds on (empties) the breast and is temporarily content. However, disturbances in feeding and other related irritations generate the agony of want and pains of anxiety. Consequently, says Fairbairn, the infant infers that its feeding destroyed the nourishing, comforting breast. This to us is not tenable. At the very early oral stage the "mouth entity" is not capable of problem solving. Moreover, the me/object dichotomy does not yet exist. Therefore any pain, anxiety, and want that occur are in me and only in me because I am omnipresent, and there is nothing except the mouth-anchored me. Consequently, a fixation at the early oral phase results in the registration of a painful wanting (bad) me and a nourishing (good) something somewhere in the vague unchartered outside of me, which is, at this stage of awareness, outside of everything.

At the other extreme of the child axis is the good self, surrounded by the bad object (mother). The latter oral stage of development is characterized by a partial differentiation of the infant from the mother and the development of ambivalence towards her, manifested, *inter alia*, by the child's biting of the breast in moments of aggression. The emerging separation of self due to the deprivational interaction with mother creates an easily accessible source and a sequential explanation of the frustrations, deprivations and anxieties of the infant. The non-caring, non-feeding mother who is already separate from the suffering (good) me is all-apparent and very often in front of the child's mouth. This location of responsibility is accentuated by the vengeful bite.[15]

Unlike Abraham,[16] Klein,[17] and Fairbairn,[18] we hold that the mouth–ego's aggression towards and wish to swallow the breast–mother and object occurs only at later orality when both the breast–mother and surrounding objects have been existentially separated from the mouth–ego. *Per contra*, the early oral fixated participant mouth–ego is not aggressively oriented towards the breast–mother but wishes to deface itself and rejoin her in an early oral communion.

The main perception of the early oral self, once he feels the enticement and proscriptions of the breast–mother, is of a shameful, guilt laden "bad me." He is not as yet differentiated from his breast–mother and whatever happens occurs within his omnipresent self, thus there is no need for the oralist dynamics of incorporation and introjection of the breast–mother and objects. At later orality the breast–mother and objects are cognitively separate from the self, yet the longing to reunite with them still exists. If ego is early orally fixated he would long to deface himself in a participant manner and be incorporated in the object. A later orally fixated ego would aim to swallow and incorporate the object by separant inclusion. Since both melting back into the object and its physical incorporation are impossible, the personality core dynamics take the form of a dialectical interplay between the surrogate separant mechanism of inclusion and sublimatory participant processes of exclusion. Early oral traumas are perceived by the nascent self as happening within its omnipresence; the ontological deprivational interaction with the breast–mother is therefore registered by it as inherent badness and evidence of a "bad me". The sexual enticement transmitted to the mouth–ego by the breast–mother together with its concomitant proscription are felt by the mouth–ego as emanating from its omnipresent self, and hence as a source of shame and guilt. On the other hand, the later orally fixated separate self can and does impute its frustrations and forbidden sexual enticement to a distinctly identifiable "bad" and prurient breast–mother. These dialectics between an early orally fixated "bad me" surrounded by a good breast–mother and a later orally fixated "good me" – oppressed, tormented and bullied by a "bad" and obscene mother – provide a scaffolding for a personality-type continuum, a basis for ethical judgment, as well as for the range posited between the polarities of "pure love" and profane, "dirty" sex.

Our model rejects the oralists' basic notion of the internalization or the incorporation of the mother especially as formulated by Klein:

> Along with the child's relation, first to his mother and soon to his father and other people, go those processes of internalisation on which I have laid so much stress in my work. The baby, having incorporated his parents, feels them to be live people inside his body in the concrete way in which deep unconscious fantasies are experienced – they are, in his mind, "internal" or "inner" objects, as I have termed them. Thus an inner world is being built up in the child's unconscious mind, corresponding to his actual experiences and the impressions he gains from people and the external world, and yet altered by his own fantasies and impulses. If it is a world of people predominantly at peace with each other and with the ego, inner harmony, security and integration ensue.[19]

First, the idyllic and harmonious image of the child's unconscious painted by Klein is unwarranted by any shred of evidence or theoretical schemes outside or inside of psychoanalysis. Second, Klein and the other oralists do not explain how and why the child should internalize a parent psychically. At most, their expositions may account for the identification between parent and child but not for the "introjection" of the parent by the child. Our model utilizes the bio-psychodevelopmental fact of the infant's feelings of non-differentiated omnipresence at early orality to postulate an initial internalization of the breast–mother at that stage, and their later ejection by the ego-boundaried later oral self. A fixation at early orality on the inherent badness of a depriving mother or a sexually enticing and erotically stifling one introduces images of a host of petrifying Medusas and snake-coiffured Gorgons into the child's troubled psyche, since everything happens within the child's undifferentiated self. Third, the alternation between good/bad me, and good/bad breast–mother, cannot be readily explained by the fluctuations in the internalization of parents or the emptying of the breast–mother by the mouth–ego and vice versa. The disappointing, non-nourishing breast is a continuous affair, alternating with the bountiful milk-spouting breast at feeding.[20] More than these fleeting alternations are needed to crystallize the image of a "good/ pure" or a "bad/promiscuous" mother for life. We

49

aim to provide a durable developmental basis for the continua of positive and negative images of self and breast–mother and others anchored in the transition from a fixation at early to later orality, with a lifelong imprint on the self-image and the image of parents, other people, and objects.

At early orality the sexual imagery is exchanged exclusively within the mother–child dyad. The gender of the sexual imagery is focused from the very beginning and not blurred multisexually and uroborically as expounded by Erich Neumann.[21] For the mother, the phallic imagery aroused by the sucking of her breast is masculine, related experientially to her sexual intercourse; whereas for the child the phallic snake is feminine because it stems from the mother. Even if the phallic imagery transmitted to the child originated from the father, it is perceived as being feminine by the child because for him it comes from the mother.

Sex is conceived as vile and shameful by the child because it effected the ejection from the innocent, omnipresence of early orality. Before the Fall, primal man and woman were not ashamed,[22] but exposure to the fruit–breast and snake–phallus introduced shame into their relationship.[23] This is the shame of leaving the blissful togetherness of the mother–child dyad and of being with each other for the separant alienation of being *vis-à-vis* or against each other. Shame is the corollary of the existential loneliness of the crystallization of the separate self. The need to repress our sexual desire stems, therefore, from the shame of the mother at early orality aroused by her feelings of incestuous sex towards her child and transmitted to him. Guilt is also transmitted by the mother to the child at early orality, but by a different mechanism and with more profound implications. We agree with Klein that the Oedipal processes take place at the oral phase of development;[24] but as we shall try to demonstrate in **chapter 8**, their guilt anchored dynamics are different and their effects more spectacular than Klein envisaged.

The Other Dichotomies

The next step is to relate and compare our polar types to some of the most quoted personality continua in the professional literature. The innovation of our continuum of personality types stems from the premise, hitherto neglected by behavioral scientists, that the dividing border-line between the non-awareness of early orality and the coagulation of a separate self in later orality may fixate diametrically opposite ego–object relationships. Also, the early orality phase is actually a reflexive self–self relationship, because at that stage there is no perceivable object for ego to interact with. This, together with the personality core vectors of separation and participation which form the dynamics of the Tantalus Ratio, make our personality continuum *sui generis*.

Consequently, we shall be more concerned with differences than with similarities. Arthur Koestler, a political novelist and a popularizer of science, has presented a personality continuum that is closest to ours in its basic conception. This proves again our contention that intelligent and sensitive writers of belles-lettres are quite often better scientists than scientists. Koestler contrasts the archetypal yogi with the archetype of the commissar. The object-manipulating commissar believes in "change from without". He sanctifies action in its most violent form, i.e. revolution, through which he aims to achieve Utopia. The yogi, on the other hand, crouches in the colourless, warmth-less, "melting away" pole of the continuum. For him, only ultimates count. The yogi "believes that each individual is alone, but attached to the all-one by an invisible umbilical cord . . . and his only task during his earthly life is to avoid any action, emotion or thought which might lead to a breaking of the cord".[25] These are political types and as such are more related to the social variable of the Tantalus Ratio, which contrasts tool-action with symbol-quietist oriented cultures; whereas at this stage we are concerned with fixated personality types within a given, preferably constant, cultural setting. We shall later contrast the separant Besht and the participant Maggid, the two founders of the culturally homogeneous Hassidic movement, in order to demonstrate the two polar personality types.

The natural starting-point is Jung's introversion–extraversion continuum. There is a deceptive outward similarity between his polar types and ours. But as hinted above, there are basic dissimilarities both in form and in content between Jung's types and ours. First of all, Jung's types are not developmental personality characteristics. He does not offer an explanation how his types are moulded, nor does he give any explanation for the genesis of his four "functional modes" of thinking, feeling, sensing and intuiting, which are then cross-tabulated with the main dichotomy to form eight subtypes. Consequently, Jung's types are static taxonomies, which are not anchored on the developmental dynamics of the personality. Second, Jung postulates a turning inward of the introvert's libido so that "a negative relation of subject to object is expressed. Interest does not move towards the object but recedes towards the subject".[26] In contrast, our participant type wishes to annihilate the self, altogether. This self-effacement is the prime mover of his character structure. Jung's extrovert turns his libido outwards so that his subjective interest focuses on the object. Our separant type aims at devouring, overpowering and manipulating the object so as to incorporate it within him by gaining dominion over it. In other words, the aim of the separant type is still union with the object, but by including it within the self. Third, with Jung, the dichotomy is based on energy cathected towards the self in introversion and the cathexis of energy towards the object in extraversion. For us, the relationship is on a different contextual plane: the participant strives to annihilate his being into nonbeing and the separant aims to incorporate the object into himself.

There is probably no better way to illustrate the divergences between Jung's stance and ours than his reliance on Friedrich Nietzsche's celebrated dichotomy of the Apollonian and the Dionysian types. The Apollonian is the orderly shaper, whereas the Dionysian effects the ecstatic merger of Man, Nature and fellow-men by a welding surge of frenzy.[27] Nietzsche describes two different modes of action, whereas we contrast action with inaction. We therefore operate on two different levels of analysis. Our participant type aims at extricating himself from plurality and re-merging into archaic unity. The philosophical exponents of the participant *Weltanschauung* are Parmenides, Plato, Plotinus and their mystical disciples, who together with some leading Far Eastern creeds regard the spatio-temporal world as a chimeric plurality, which hovers over the reality of Unity. One's aim in life is to disperse this *Mayan* veil of plurality, which is painful yet trivial, stifling yet insignificant. The illusion of plurality creates relationships among the *separata* that breed evil. As evil stems from relationships that are intrinsically unreal, evil itself is unreal. However, if people define it as real, to use William I. Thomas' much-used aphorism, it becomes real in its consequences. This is the philosophical counterpart to our bio-psychological exposition of the participant type. It is the rational construct of ego's quest, fixated at early orality, to regain the non-differentiated Unity of his early developmental phase. Nietzsche's Apollonian introvert, on the other hand, aims at perpetuating the individual's separation. He is the measurer, the one who confines himself and others into categories and numbers; he is "the splendid divine image of the *principii individuationis*".[28] The Apollonian introvert extols the inwardly directed authenticity, in contradistinction to the "other directed" vulgarization of the extrovert. He compares himself with others and concludes that his preference of himself over others is justified. This is not unlike the existentialist's bias in favor of the subject: Sartre's exaltation of the *pour soi* and his dread of the petrifying "they"; Heidegger's subjective *das sein*, as compared to the shallow insignificance of *das Man*, the generalized other; and Søren Kierkegaard's siding with the subjectivist who is immersed in "eternal beatitude" against the barren "objectivist" who has much in common with Jung's extrovert. It must be clear now that the Apollonian-introvert is a *separatum* who cherishes and extols his separation and contrasts himself with the levelling down of conspicuousness and uniqueness, and hence inauthenticity, of the extrovert. In contrast, our participant's prime mover is the annihilation of his separate condition. Consequently, his orientation is ontological insofar as he contrasts his own quest for nonbeing with the separant's manipulation of being, whereas Jung's Apollonian introvert anchors on his self as a fortified unit of authenticity, as compared with the object-oriented extrovert. With Jung, the axis of the continuum is inner versus outer orientation; with us, it is being versus nonbeing.

The philosophical counterpart of our separant is expounded by the dialectics of Heraclitus, Hegel, Karl Marx and the myriads of their followers, who see in action the unifying agent between subject and object. Our separant sees in action, in contradistinction to the inaction of the participant, a means of achieving Unity with the object. In essence, therefore, the participant is process, i.e. action-oriented, whereas the extrovert focuses on objects. "Not only persons, but things seize and rivet (the extrovert's) interest." [29] In fact, both the separant and the participant types are action- and process-oriented. The former pursues ritualistically the manipulation of the object. A Sisyphus who looks upon work as his destiny, who "builds airplanes, no matter what they carry; roads, no matter where they lead; weapons, no matter what 'values' they defend or attack".[30] The Tantalic participant seeks the ontological defacement of the self, which is also unattainable. Both, therefore, are forever striving, manipulating objects or manipulating themselves in an endless variety of techniques. The strenuous pushing of the object uphill is the essence of the Sisyphean separant. Whether the stone is granite, gold ore or a chunk of the Holy Kaaba is irrelevant. In like manner, the Tantalic participant does not focus on himself, but pursues an illusive *Unio Mystica* by the obliteration of his separate state. Here again, it is not essential whether he does or does not achieve his aim. The striving, the agonizing thirst that cannot be quenched although fulfilment hovers (deceptively) within reach, is the essence of a Tantalus.

Another major difference between Jung's types and ours is that Jung envisages his extroverted-feeling type as dissolving himself in the object: "An assimilation of subject to object . . . occurs as almost completely to engulf the subject of feeling . . . it almost seems as though the personality were wholly dissolved in the feeling of the moment."[31] Our separant does not strive to dissolve his self into the object. This characterizes our participant. The separant, who is equivalent to Jung's extrovert, aims to overpower, to devour the object and incorporate it into his self. Finally, Jung's conception of his introvert is of one who safeguards his mental energies and hoards them into himself. The introvert, says Jung, "is always facing the problem of how libido can be withdrawn from the object, as though an attempted ascendancy on the part of the object had to be continually frustrated".[32] On the other hand, our participant aims to expend his mental energies to their utter limits, in the hope of achieving the quietist inaction of nonbeing or being engulfed by the object and embedded into it in an early oral unison.

The personality types and character traits of personologists other than Jung are so far apart from our continuum in form, contents and dynamics that detailed comparisons are superfluous. Freud's four character types, for instance, based on his four major developmental phases, have almost no tangential links with our typology. Also, as we have followed the British "oralists" in our theoretical orientation, we do not see any special self–object significance in the Freudian "anal phase" of development. We hold with Fairbairn that "whilst the breast and the genital organs are natural and biological objects of libido, feces certainly are not. On the contrary, it is only a symbolic object. It is only, so to speak, the clay of which a model of the object is moulded."[33] As for the Freudian Oedipal phase, most of its socio-normative aspects are incorporated in our last development phase of social separation[34] where we have postulated the enmeshing of the child within a pigeonhole in the normative system of society. A fixation at this phase would still contribute to the making of a separant type. Another example is Murray's theory. He adds two more types to Freud's four and has linked an elaborate system of needs to these types. Murray's conceptual matrix is totally different from ours and yet we may accept his hypothesis that a fixation may occur even *in utero*, and this "claustral type" may display a tendency to be amorphic in his attitude towards the object and extreme passivity in general.[35] These are also some of the characteristics of our participant type; the fixation also occurs much before the early oral phase, where the non-awareness of the fetus is even more complete. The above presentation of these dichotomies illustrates the relationships of our theoretical expositions to others. Even though the levels of analyses and conceptual matrices may be completely different, there are bound to be some tangential links and partial overlaps between one theory and another because, after all, the unit of analysis is the same human animal.

Some Empirical Anchors

There is a marked conceptual divergence, as well as a complete difference of method, between Jung's and Eysenck's analysis of the Extroversion/Introversion continuum. Needless to say, Eysenck's personality core theorizing and ours are widely apart, and yet we have located some empirical support for our premises in the vast wealth of research findings he has amassed in support of his theories.

For Eysenck, the extrovert is defined by his character traits, which are: sociability, impulsiveness, activity, liveliness and excitability; the introvert is marked by diametrically opposite traits.[36]

These are totally different dimensions than those that characterize our separant and participant types, yet some single outward traits in Eysenck's dimensions may be correlated with ours. The activity–inactivity traits, for instance, may be related to the quietist passivity of our participant, which decreases his deprivational interaction with the object and hence his separation. This is contrasted with the "object-devouring" activity of the separant. Consequently, we may avail ourselves of Eysenck's findings as to the "excitation" and "inhibition" of his polar types. We have to perform some conceptual *jonglerie*, because for Eysenck "excitation" and "inhibition" relate to the cerebral cortex. An "excited" cortex, therefore, would exert a restraining and inhibiting hold on behavior, whereas an inhibited cortex would loosen the reins over the individual, with a resultant increase in behavioral excitation.[37] Once we get used to this topsy-turvy terminology, we may be able to find empirical support for the dynamics of the Tantalus Ratio. Eysenck claims empirical soundness for his hypotheses relating to "reactive inhibition", which we prefer to cite in its original Hullian formulation. "Whenever any reaction is evoked in an organism," says Clark Hull, "there is left a condition or state which acts as a primary, negative motivation in that it has an innate capacity to produce a cessation of the activity which produced the state. We shall call this state or condition reactive inhibition."[38] This may include the dynamics of our opposing vectors of the personality core. We have hypothesized that the active separant vectors of growth and libidinal forces generate opposing pressures towards separant inaction. Although Hull and Eysenck had rather different aims in mind, the findings that support the mechanisms of the inhibiting reaction against the activation of the organism may serve as an empirical anchor for the dynamics of the Tantalus Ratio.

Of special importance is the findings surveyed by Eysenck that show a "stimulus hunger", i.e. sensation-seeking in the extrovert and a "stimulus aversion" in the introvert.[39] These are precisely our object-seeking separant and our quietist participant who strives for inaction, i.e. a state of non-stimulation. This is linked to Eysenck's findings that the introvert reacts favorably to sensory deprivation,[40] which is indeed close to the non-awareness of early orality and simulates a closeness to nonbeing, but is highly sensitive to pain. In contrast, the extrovert is relatively insensitive to pain, but suffers acutely when in a state of sensory deprivation. Here again we see the separant's need for activity and the stimulation of the object, whereas the participant suffers from stimuli that catapult him away from the coveted state of inaction. Consequently, he seems to develop a protective screen against stimuli and activation so that even a small amount would ring the danger signal. The participant, therefore, would have a low sensory threshold.[41] Of great value is Reed and Sedman's finding "that under conditions of sensory deprivation, feelings of depersonalization will be reported more readily by introverts than by extroverts".[42] This is the prime mover of our participant, whose desire for inaction is but a baseline for his quest for the dissolution of his ego boundary and for partaking in the omnipresence of early orality or even pre-natal nonbeing.

The "stimulus seeking" of the separant and the "stimulus aversion" of the participant may be related to the ingenious experiments of Petrie et al., who found that introverts tended to increase subjectively the size of the stimuli (augmenters), whereas the extroverts decreased it (reducers). This is related to the "stimulus hunger" of the extrovert–reducers and the "stimulus aversion" of the introvert–augmenters. Petrie also re-established that augmenters (our participants) were more tolerant of sensory deprivation and naturally less tolerant of pain.[43] We are aware that we are substituting Eysenck's introvert and extrovert with our participant and separant, but we are concerned here with only two character traits, i.e. activity and excitability, of the five that comprise his types. These two traits apply to our typology, whereas the others may not. It is therefore more appropriate to use our terminology instead of Eysenck's, which may cover more conceptual ground than we need.

The research findings surveyed provide an empirical anchor to the activist–quietist or the "interactive" dimension of our typology. We shall proceed now to link some pertinent findings to our ontological dimension: the "object-inclusion" of the separant and the "self-exclusion" of the participant. We may recall that the separant aims at "devouring" the object and incorporating it into himself, whereas the participant wishes to exclude, isolate himself and melt back into the object or the non-objective pre-awareness. Colquhoun and Corcoran have demonstrated that introverts are better task performers in isolation, whereas extroverts perform better in groups.[44] Furneaux states, "It is entirely consistent with the known characteristics of the extrovert to assert that he has a strong and continuing set to attend to stimuli associated with the activities of other people, and that the situations which lead him to enter states of high drive are predominantly inter-personal in character."[45] This better performance of the extrovert in group situations has been related to his stimulus hunger.[46] We hold that the higher motivation and drive in an inter-personal situation reported by Furneaux shows the dependence of the extrovert-separant on the togetherness of the group. He functions better not *vis-à-vis* the others, but *amidst* the others, within them and through them. The others thus serve the necessary medium for the better performance of the separant, because those others are vital catalysts and as such necessary components of his personality structure. Of even greater significance to our present premise are the findings that may allow us to link the separant (extrovert) to a higher "field dependence" than the participant (introvert), who would tend to be "field independent." These two concepts, as well as Witkin and his associates' later studies on "psychological differentiation", relate to the object, setting and environmental perception while performing a task. The "field dependent" displays a low psychological differentiation because he is dependent in his performance on cues stemming from the overall Gestalt and the background set of the situation. In other words, performance here is dependent on the configuration of the surrounding objects. On the other hand, the "field independent" and the one who displays higher psychological differentiation, relies on his own cognitive cues and not on the outward Gestalt of the objects.[47] Cohen and Silverman found that the field dependent, which like our separant is object dependent, was more vulnerable to sensory deprivation,[48] which again is a major characteristic of the separant (extrovert). As might have been expected, the separant's "hunger" for stimuli made him less vulnerable to pain and more field, i.e. object dependent.

We shall add here another trait, the empirical evidence for which has been extensively presented elsewhere.[49] We hypothesize that the separant is intolerant of objective ambiguity. He would grasp things, others and situations that are clearly defined by boundaries. On the other hand, the participant would be tolerant of ambiguities relating to objects, but he requires clear-cut abstractions. The objective haziness serves his quietist and mystical inclinations, but he is intolerant of any ideational ambiguities that may blur his concern with Unity and the ultimate reality beyond objective appearances.

The third normative dimension of our typology deals with self–object relationships. The participant type, which has been fixated at non-differentiated early orality, tends to be a depressive "bad me" surrounded by a good object, whereas the separant "good me" is the outwardly aggressive "good me" surrounded by a depriving object. Consequently, the participant would be "intro-punitive", the guilt-ridden self-blamer, whereas the separant would tend to be an "extra-punitive" blamer of others. We shall enumerate some traits that we hypothesize as related to our present dimension, although no empirical evidence has been found as yet in support of this hypothesis. We hold that the participant tending to blame himself, and consequently more ready to legitimize norms, would be "morally oriented", i.e. he is internally controlled by the deeply internalized norms so that external repressive sanctions are unnecessary to secure compliance. Our hypothesis is based on Ragnar Rommetveit's theory of the internalization of social norms;[50] it differs from expositions such as Julian Rotter's internal versus external loci of normative control. Rotter imputes to his "internal controller" a belief in his ability to manipulate the external world, as well as to change the political system by involvement in social affairs.[51] This characterizes not our participant but the diametrically opposite separant type. The latter would tend to be "sanction-oriented",[52] being outwardly aggressive he would not tend to legitimize norms but would comply with them for fear of sanction only. Consequently, the separant would be a higher risk-taker than the participant, since the separant tends to manipulate objects and operate through others. He tends to be "other-directed", as described by David Riesman.[53] The "other-directed" has his normative antennae ever attuned to others and their approval. Consequently, he tends to be a conformist, in the sense of Douglas Crowne and David Marlowe's approval motivation and need for affiliation.[54] All the character traits mentioned above, both hypothetical and those that have been empirically verified, are by no means an exhaustive list but are a mere illustration of measurable parameters to tie our theoretical dimensions and typologies to empirical anchors. Also, they may be useful indicators for the adequacy of our personality core vectors as the underlying sources for the various behavioral patterns and traits. The typology dimensions and their corresponding traits are summarized in **figure 2.3**.

There is a link between our present typology and the developmental maturation dimension of the Tantalus Ratio (analyzed in **chapter 1**), namely that the separant starts with an initial, more potent Tantalus Ratio than the participant. This is in line with our contention that any heightened separant activity musters a corresponding quietist reaction. Consequently, the cathected energy generated by the Tantalus Ratio is

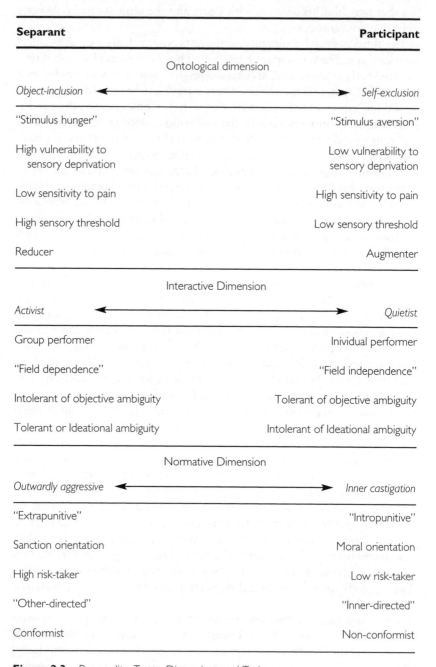

Separant   **Participant**

Ontological dimension

Object-inclusion ⟵————————————⟶ Self-exclusion

"Stimulus hunger"   "Stimulus aversion"

High vulnerability to   Low vulnerability to
    sensory deprivation   sensory deprivation

Low sensitivity to pain   High sensitivity to pain

High sensory threshold   Low sensory threshold

Reducer   Augmenter

Interactive Dimension

Activist ⟵————————————⟶ Quietist

Group performer   Inividual performer

"Field dependence"   "Field independence"

Intolerant of objective ambiguity   Tolerant of objective ambiguity

Tolerant or Ideational ambiguity   Intolerant of Ideational ambiguity

Normative Dimension

Outwardly aggressive ⟵————————————⟶ Inner castigation

"Extrapunitive"   "Intropunitive"

Sanction orientation   Moral orientation

High risk-taker   Low risk-taker

"Other-directed"   "Inner-directed"

Conformist   Non-conformist

Figure 2.3   Personality: Types, Dimensions and Traits

higher. As might be expected, the separant type has higher chances of ending his days as a disenchanted "sour grapes" *ressentiment*-laden object manipulator *sans* object, whereas the participant would age into a Tantalus, ever-chasing elusive ultimates and hazy transcendence.

Square Bolts in Round Holes

It is in the nature of a continuum that as one moves along it, one dimension increases while the other decreases. Therefore, any participant, except the ideal polar type, which does not really exist, would have some covert separant traits lurking inside him. Also, the vector of the Tantalus Ratio, which operates in opposition to the fixated personality type, exerts hidden pressures that manifest themselves in the desire of one type to be involved in the activities of the diametrically opposite type.

The enormity of this dialectic and its vast effect on human behavior has been the subject of wild conjectures, but has not been chartered or deeply investigated: the attraction of opposite types in sex, marriage and friendship; the participant–depressive Nietzsche, dreaming up the separant power-manipulating Superman; the self-destructive melancholic Lord Byron, ever courting the active involvement of politics and war; and Don Quixote, the hazy, contemplating, archetypal participant carried away by the glory of action and picking a fight with a windmill. The opposite examples are also legion: Charles de Gaulle, a genius power-manipulator retiring for carefully calculated periods to his country retreat; Howard Hughes, the ruthless business and industry carnivore secluding himself in the most widely publicized solitude; and David Ben-Gurion, a most adept political wheeler-dealer, ardently admiring the neo-Platonist mystics and self-exiling himself for official meditation in the Negev, yet not relinquishing for a moment his political interests and activities. The sad truth is that one type is incapable, because of his psychic constitution, to play the roles of the other type in an optimal manner. One type has constant covert wishes to play the roles of the opposite type, but once given the opportunity, he is likely to fail. The same is bound to happen if one type is forced or manoeuvred into performing the tasks that are more suited to the other type. Jung even goes as far as saying that the reversal of type roles may cause physical harm to the organism because physiological factors may well be the underlying basis for the personality type's differentiation.[55] The far-reaching conclusion here is that the vast array of social roles and statuses, as well as social placements and personal affiliations, throughout man's life are very much influenced by his fixated personality type, which was formed in the remote oral phase of development. Consequently, the possibility of learning and unlearning the basic personality traits are sadly limited. This echoes Martin Luther's sincere confession in front of his tormentors that he could not behave differently even if he wanted to.

59

We are well aware that the burden and formidable responsibility of the mother in shaping the destiny of her child through behavior that might have been quite insignificant at the moment is too heavy for any mortal, yet determining her child's fate is precisely what the mother does through her interaction with her infant at the oral stage.

Any meaningful communication between the two polar types is exceedingly difficult. One type cannot comprehend the significance of the other type's action, neither to himself nor to others. The participant who is ever absorbed by ultimates and the great and deep truths away and beyond has difficulties in understanding that the easy success of the separant in his social interactions has nothing to do with his abstract principles, ideological system or depth of thinking, but is more often than not a result of the separant's skin-deep easy smile and his adeptness at flattery at the right moment and place. For this very same reason, a separant who has been ousted or has retired from his social position, or a social-climber whose name and ageing face no longer appear in the gossip columns, collapses completely because he does not possess the participant's interest in inner transcendence. He is the soap bubble supported by a shallow and fragile net of object relationships.

The Hassidim

We shall illustrate our two polar types with the personalities of the two main figures among the founders of the Hassidic movement, the Besht and the Maggid. This religious, messianic, mystical and social upheaval virtually revolutionized the social and cultural structure of eighteenth- and nineteenth-century East European Jewry. Hassidism is considered not only a major religious and social movement in Judaism but also a unique phenomenon in the history of religions. "Hassidism," says Shimon Dubnow, "created the type of believer for whom religious ecstasy was more important than the learning of the Torah . . . It provided the oppressed Jews with a subjective feeling of spiritual supremacy and although it could not ease their actual subjugation it made them feel superior to their oppressors . . . In the real world of God, the Jew is the master and his tormenting '*paritz*', the feudal landlord, his slave."[56] This search for the inner reality behind temporal appearances elevated the Hassid and made him "walk with God".[57] Spiritual ascendance was open to every Jew through prayer and devotion, in contrast to the arduous elevation by learning prescribed by rabbinical orthodoxy. No wonder that the Hassidic movement scored quick victories over the formalist rabbinical "*mithnagdim*" and gained the adherence of the rank and file of East European Jewry as well as a great many of the mystical Kabbalists.[58]

According to Martin Buber, the essence of Hassidism is the continuous redemption of daily routines, the sanctification of everyday life. Salvation does not lie in awaiting the end of time but in the beatification of every minute speck of temporality. "The redemption of temporal profanity is the task of the Hassid, his meals are offerings and his table an altar."[59] Buber imputes to Hassidism the basic belief that temporality is a state of separation, and participation in unity is eternity. This doctrine, which Hassidim probably inherited from Gnosis and the Kabbalah, has a patent relationship to the personality core vectors and constitutes a *prima facie* justification for our choice of the Hassidic movement as an illustrative source for our personality types.

The main channel through which the Hassid seeks participation in unity is prayer. "People think," said the Rabbi of Koretz, "that one prays in front of God; this is not true because prayer itself is the power and glory of Divinity."[60] The ecstasy of prayer brings out the sparks of divinity that are embedded in the individual and catalyzes their return to their origin. "In prayer," said the Rabbi of Kotsk, "words surge out from the core of the soul, and the whole soul is engulfed and raised by the prayer to partake in Unity."[61] Were one to ask what the single main characteristic of Hassidism is, this unifying prayer would be the most likely answer. It is an outcry *de profundis*, ranging in intensity from a silent murmur to a shriek, to be redeemed from the squalor of temporality and to raise one's dire existence to the stature of divinity. Hassidism claims a most ambitious goal for prayer by any religious standard: to have divinity permeate every second and every speck of temporal existence.

Another characteristic of Hassidism is that redemption by partaking in unity is a continuous process. Every act, every moment in the Hassid's life, should be raised to heights of grace by aiming to weld the sparks of divinity in temporal existence to the *Shechina* – the divine presence. Salvation is, therefore, not conceived as the spectacular coming of the Messiah or the resurrection of Jesus Christ, but rather as a continuous and painstaking process. Redemption is ever present and yet never final. There is always another moment and another act to be redeemed. Consequently, the longing of the "divine sparks" in every individual to unify with the divine presence can never be fully quenched. Here again, one may note the analogy between this Hassidic conception of continuous redemption and the participation vector.[62] The individual *separatum* ever longs for participation in unity. This longing, like the Hassid's quest for redemption, is continuous precisely because it cannot be fully satisfied. Both the Hassid's quest for redemption and our longing for participation derive their strength from the impossibility of their fulfilment. The longing for redemption of the Hassid stops when he ceases to live, and the core personality vector comes to a standstill with the ultimate participation, which is nonbeing and death.

The Hassidic movement experienced a relatively short period of growing and flowering from the middle of the eighteenth to the middle of the nineteenth century, and then a century of decline through the advent of secular learning and an essentially secular Zionism. Hassidism was no match for these powerful temporal creeds and the *coup de grâce* came with the disintegration of the *Shtetl* and the Holocaust. This weird and powerful movement (with its historical and sociological constancies and outwardly homogeneous façade) was triggered by two diametrically opposite personalities who illustrate our polar character types. The fact that these two divergent types founded one religious, ideological and social movement only makes the personality differences stand out in relief from the common social background.

The differences between the Besht, the prophetic founder of the Hassidic movement, and the Maggid, its doctrinaire systematizer, are not related to mere forms and styles but rather to contents and essentials. We do not claim exclusiveness for this character typology, and it may well be that the great students of human types would attach different labels than these to the Besht and the Maggid as prescribed by their specific conceptual systems. Jung would have found character analogies between the Besht and Origen, whom he regarded as the archetypal extrovert. He would also find character similarities between the Maggid and the introverted Tertulian.[63] If Nietzsche had come across the teaching of Hassidism he might have detected Dionysian outbursts of divine frenzy in the Besht, whereas the Maggid would have appeared to him as an Apollonian manipulator of ideas, immersed in inner contemplation. A student of Far Eastern religions might regard the Besht as a Karma yogi who strives for redeeming union through action and the manipulation of his environment, and the Maggid as a Dhyana or Jnana yogi who seeks union by meditation and knowledge. This may be so, yet our contention is that the personalities of the Besht and the Maggid, in their totalities, cover the widest range of characteristics of the separant and participant types and not just a single or a few of them. Moreover, most of the traits displayed by these two Hassidic sages that are relevant to our typology are either irrelevant or inapplicable to the personality continua surveyed at the beginning of this chapter.

The main characteristic of the Besht was that, like the separant type, he sought union through the manipulation of others and the activation of objects in his environment; whereas the self-effacing Maggid strove, like the participant, to achieve union by quietist inaction and the annihilation of the self. The Besht preached a constant radiation of pathos and energy in order to reach the scattered particles of divinity that are in everything and everywhere.[64] "There is no place," said the Besht, "which is devoid of the divine particles. In trees and in stones, in every human act and even in his sins these particles are present."[65] Apart from the interesting partial absolving of sins, the Besht also decrees here the boundless arena of human action that has to aim towards every object. Divinity is strewn everywhere and the task of Man is to reach through to it by the proper techniques. The Maggid, on the other hand, did not aim to reach the divinity in objects. He aimed to annihilate his own awareness so that his immersion in divinity would follow as a matter of course.

The Besht forced himself on the object through action, trying to gain access thereby to the particles of divinity embedded in it. The Maggid tried to achieve a similar goal, i.e. union with the ultimate, by melting into it. The Besht overpowered the object, while the Maggid manipulated his inner psyche. These divergences are aptly illustrated by a Hassidic tale recounted by Shmuel Y. Agnon:

> When the Besht had a difficult task before him, he would go to a certain place in the woods, light a fire and meditate in prayer – and what he had set out to perform was done. When, a generation later, the Maggid of Meseritz was faced with the same task he would go to the same place in the woods and say: we can no longer light the fire, but we can still Speak the prayers – and what he wanted done became reality.[66]

This tale is taken out of context and the story it tells is basically allegorical, yet the message is pertinent: the Besht, the doer, kindles the fire and brings about the performance of the task. The Maggid, on the other hand, does not act but prays. He focuses on his thoughts and transforms them into reality. The Besht reaches to the object; the Maggid transforms himself.

This book is not a tract on the history or philosophy of religion, but the distinction between the polar personality types of the Besht and the Maggid might help clarify an argument between contemporary students of Jewish mysticism. Rivka Schatz Uffenheimer sides with Gershom Scholem against Buber's interpretation of Hassidism as a continuous beatification of the object and temporality. She calls Buber's description of the Hassid's dialogical sanctification of the object as "an untenable secular interpretation" of Hassidism.[67] In fact, Buber deals[68] in Hassidism as expounded mainly by the Besht, whereas Schatz-Uffenheimer deals with the quietist Maggid and his pupils. These are not different interpretations of the goals of Hassidism, but rather diametrically opposite ways to achieve these goals as determined by the polarities of the personality structure of the Besht and the Maggid. Indeed, the polarity of the character types of the Maggid and the Besht manifested itself also in prayer, which is the anchor of Hassidism and its path, means and tool of redemption. The Besht described union through prayer as the astronomer's quest for the stars. The words of prayer carry with them the spirit that looks through the object with an X-ray concentration to reveal the sparks of divinity within it.[69] The Maggid, on the other hand, saw in contemplative prayer a means of being immersed in the sacred names and words, in order to be stripped of the profane garments of existence, to rid the inner immanence of the confines of spatio-temporality, and to disperse into the nothingness of unity.[70]

The Besht seems to have adopted the prayer techniques (*Kavanot*) of the Lurianic Kabbalists. These techniques involved the manipulation of words and symbols in intricate combinations in order to reach the higher spheres of divinity. These *Kavanot* contained, no doubt, elements of magic and conjuring. The secret permutations of symbols were regarded as "special keys to open the gates of heaven".[71] These object-manipulating *Kavanot* are in line with our characterization of the separant Besht. His goal of union was actually a goal of dominion. By activating the object and gaining access to it through the magic-like praxis of the *Kavanot*, the Besht tied the divine sparks of temporality into his own pneumatic spirituality. This dialogical link with the object and the manipulation of spatio-temporality by the ecstatic praxis of magic was also expounded by Albertus Magnus who said: "When the soul of Man falls into a great excess of any passion, it can be proved by experiment that it (the excess) binds things (magically) and alters them in the way it wants, and for a long time I did not believe it, but after I had read the nigromantic books and others of the kind on signs and magic, I found that the emotionality (*affectio*) of the human soul is the chief cause of all these things."[72] The Maggid rejected the object-activating *Kavanot*. For him, prayer meant the annihilation of the self. "The ancients," he said, "had the *Kavanot* which were the keys to open the (divine) gates but we don't have the keys of the *Kavanot* any more. We have to break our own hearts in order to gain entry."[73] This is typical of the self-effacing style of the Maggid, who did not openly contradict his teacher and mentor, but the message is clear. The Maggid saw in the mechanistic *Kavanot* an inadequate technique of ascendance. The proper mode of prayer that achieves real union is the destruction of separate awareness, "to break one's heart into a great many fragments until it melts like water".[74] The Maggid expounded the doctrine of the self-annihilating *Devekut* as the essence of prayer, in diametrical contrast to the object-activating Kabbalist *Kavanot*. This doctrine of *Devekut* (devotion) was conceived by the Maggid as a pantheistic and acosmic perception which describes the essence of God as penetrating all existence and embodying everything: the whole earth is the Holy One, and it is the world which stands within the Creator.[75] One may note here that *Devekut*, as the main attribute of prayer, was deemed to achieve pantheism. This is precisely the predominant vector in the personality core of the participant who strives to regain the pantheism of early orality. Thus, the Maggid assigned the task of destroying the individual consciousness and negating his existence to *Devekut*: "The purpose of Man is to abolish. . . reality and to return to the mystical *Ayin* (nothingness) which preceded creation."[76] The *Devekut* through prayer was deemed to bring about the complete metamorphosis of the self from being to nothingness. "It is impossible for anything to pass from one existence to another without it becoming *Ayin* (nothingness) at the point of transition."[77] A further corollary of the Maggid's doctrine of *Devekut* was that prayer should aim at the total negation of consciousness. Any intellectualized *Kavanot* should be avoided, since they hampered the *annihilatio* of being. The uttering of the words of prayer should be automatic, lest their contents lead the Hassid away from the spiritual and direct contact with unity. "One should stand still and bring the words of prayer to the world of bliss."[78] According to Schatz-Uffenheimer, this is the annihilation of consciousness; yet the "divine world of bliss" may be linked, for the purpose of this personality typology, to the fixation of the participant type on the blissful non-awareness of the early oral phase.

The styles of prayer of the Maggid and the Besht were also widely divergent. The Maggid seems to have followed the quietist and restrained form of prayer, which was more suitable for the achievement of self-negation. This type of prayer was practiced by some Christian mystics and the Sephardic Kabbalists of Bethel in Jerusalem.[79] The worst offence was to ask anything for oneself, one's family, business, or any temporal entity, since needs are just the superficial attributes of plurality.[80] This again brings to fore the longing of the participant for the needlessness and omnipresence of early orality. The Besht, on the other hand, advocated the stormiest style of prayer. According to the Besht, prayer had to force its way through the partition that separates Man from God, just as in our conceptualization the separant aims to force his way to the object. One may use all kinds of body movements, song, and dance in order to reach this ecstatic ascendance. The Besht used a very interesting analogy with sexual intercourse: "Prayer is an intercourse with the Divine Presence. Like an intercourse, one should gain entry by moving and wriggling but later one can be still and be glued to the *Shechina* (the Divine Presence) with the utmost attachment."[81] This is the separant seeking union with the object, using sexual imagery to illustrate the coveted attachment, and decreeing an activist, ecstatic frenzy as the vehicle for gaining access to the object. The imagery of sexual intercourse is quite apt here, since the separant's aim is to achieve dominion over the object. The male is described as the active agent, whereas the divine presence is seen in the passive female role. The ecstasy of prayer should be so forceful that all the objects in one's surroundings should seem to be swirling with charged emotions. This may be linked to a story about the barrels that caught the frenzy of the dancing Besht and danced together with him,[82] a story that shows the Besht's activist hold on the objects in his environment. Unlike the Maggid, the Besht saw in prayer a way of influencing spatio-temporality, and in times of stress prayer for him was the prime solution. It opened the gates of prisons,[83] and the force of the ecstatic frenzy brought the needs, pains, and worries to the attention of the divine presence.

Another doctrine in which the character polarities of the Besht and the Maggid manifested themselves was the quest for the "divine sparks". The Kabbalistic doctrine of the *Shevira* – the cosmic catastrophe of the breaking of the divine vessels, which was interpreted as the mythological counterpart to the separation of birth[84] – which was adopted by Hassidism, saw the task of Man to effect a *Tikkun*, a redeeming of the broken vessels by helping the strewn sparks to reunite with their divine origins. The Besht preached involvement with every fauna, flora and inanimate object in order to make contact with the divine sparks that constitute their sacred essence. There are, therefore, no more important or less important people, more or less essential things in God's world.

Everyone and everything are equal before him. Consequently, the Besht urged his followers to reach rapport with every minute object, any commonplace chattel, and every man in the street in order to reach their sacred sparks and unite with them. Buber saw in the Besht's doctrine a realization of his dialogic philosophy.[85] This may be so, yet for our purposes the Besht's doctrine of *avoda begashmiut* – worship through the concrete or within spatio-temporality – is evidence of his object involvement, of the separant's activation of his entourage in order to link whatever essence it might have to himself. The Maggid, on the other hand, saw the process of union with the sparks of divinity as emanating within and from the psyche. Divinity rests in the contemplative thought of Man, and this thought, which is part of the divine presence, may partake of the holy sparks embedded in spatio-temporality on the condition that Man annihilates his self. "The wisdom is within reach of the worthy yet in order to reach it they have to think they are dust . . . "[86]

"Wisdom is nothingness."[87] In order to reach unity with the divine sparks beyond the temporal appearances of plurality, one has to annihilate the self. This was the Maggid's participant mode of achieving unity with the strewn sparks of divinity. The ultimate religious goal of redeeming the sacred sparks exiled in spatio-temporality was the same for both the Besht and the Maggid, yet they approached it from diametrically opposite poles in line with their polarities of character.

Another major premise that is approached in similarly divergent ways is the Kabbalist *Tzimtzum* (contraction), which was incorporated into Hassidism. The Besht seems to have adopted the original Lurianic version of cosmogony, according to which God contracted himself from a part of infinity in order to make place for the world.[88] This rather weird doctrine, which poses many theological dilemmas, fitted the Besht's activist and object-manipulating separant character: God and temporality are in a constant pulsating interaction. Divinity contracts to make space for temporality and then sends out rays to activate it. God not only regresses within himself to make adequate *lebensraum* for the world, but also accommodates spatio-temporality and Man in another way: this contraction of divinity within itself, this *Tzimtzum*, dimmed God's immense radiance so that it might be bearable and perceived by Man.[89] The conception of the contraction of divinity and its interaction with temporality fits not only the Besht's separant character type but also some of our hypotheses as to its genesis. Invoking our methodological premise (see Preface, pages xi–xii), namely, that myths – and Kabbalist cosmogony is a "real" myth – many times may be interpreted as a projection of personal developmental history, the contraction of divinity, to make place for temporality, is conceived by the Besht as a process of pain and evil.[90] In other words the genesis of being is affected through a painful interaction. This fits the description of the coagulation of the separate self out of pantheistic infinity through the deprivational interaction with the object.[91] It also supports our contention as to the fixation of the separant type after the later oral phase, when the separate self has already crystallized.

The Maggid, in contrast, related the doctrine of *Tzimtzum* not to cosmogony or to objective processes but to the cognitive dynamics of the psyche. The human cognition, as it were, traps divinity by means of its thought processes. Yet God is an obliging prisoner because he contracts himself so that he may be contained within the human consciousness. "It is like a child," said the Maggid, "who induces his father's mind to get involved in his puerile play, in like manner the worthy induce, in a sense, God to partake of their thought . . . when they think of love they bring God to the world in love, as stated in the *Tikkunei Zohar*: a king is imprisoned in the tresses of the mind."[92] This contraction of divinity is reversed and God is released from his human bondage by the annihilation of the self.[93] God and Man are then united in infinity. The participant Maggid thus made the bold assertion that divinity, in the semi-exiled state of contraction, generated the human cognitive processes. The redemption, i.e. the release of divinity, is affected by the obliteration of the boundaries holding it captive within the human consciousness. This, in effect, is the goal of ontological participation that aims to revert to the pantheistic non-awareness of early orality. The fixation at early orality is also apparent here, in that the encompassing of part of pantheistic infinity within the boundaries of the nascent self – when the perception of extra and intra-psychic processes are as yet interchangeable – takes place at this developmental stage.

The Besht's attitude towards evil was on the Lurianic Kabbalist doctrine of the divine particles embedded in all creation, fauna, flora, objects – and even evil acts; sins, thereby, contain vestiges of divine goodness. One has to grapple with evil and extract its divine core of goodness; this is the essence of repentance.[94] This again shows the activist Besht's separant desire to overpower evil, to manipulate it, and transform it into good.[95] For the Besht, the *yetzer-hara*, the evil passion, was the proverbial whore sent to tempt Man. One had to fight, conquer and rule her.[96] Indeed, the Besht appears to have taken his eagerness to unearth the goodness from within the evil acts to quite unorthodox extremes. Also, the ability to cope with evil makes it less ominous. Thus he did not share, for instance, the Kabbalists' and some of his contemporaries' abhorrence of ejaculation during sleep.[97] He also held that the greater ecstatic piety of the penitent had more vigour in it and was therefore more acceptable to God than that of those who had not sinned at all.[98] The Besht did not share the antinomian extolling evil, but saw in it a choice object for manipulation and conquest. When the bad, annoying object (breast) withholds its nourishment, it is bitterly attacked and forced to spurt its inner goodness.

The Maggid seemed almost to disregard sin and evil. For his quietist, participant personality, evil was trivial, an attribute of the illusion of plurality. When one delves through the superficiality of appearance into the unified core of reality, evil disappears.[99] The Maggid advised his disciples not to heed distress and misfortune because this led Man away from the concentration needed to cast off temporality and seek union with divinity.[100]

The Men

The Besht was orphaned in infancy and was raised by the community in a school for the children of the poor.[101] This, no doubt, was a prime example according to the model of the separant post-oral fixation on the object. The young Besht proved to be a runaway and a truant, and his guardians despaired of making a *"mensch"* out of him.[102] For a while he roamed the streets and market places and mingled with the simple folk and labourers. The Besht did not give up this gregarious mixing with the man in the street, even after he was established as a religious leader. The Maggid, on the other hand, true to his participant quietism, rarely came out of his resigned detachment to brush elbows with the common men. The Besht occupied himself with an assortment of manual labours. He dug clay and operated a public house. He also learned the miracle healers' art of magic from the "Ba'alei-Shem". This transformation of one state of spatio-temporality to another is the ultimate in the separant's quest for the manipulation of the object. The ultimate state is one desired by the "Ba'al-Shem", the magician, who shows mastery over the object and incorporates it, thereby, into his extended self. This mastery over the object manifested itself in the Besht's dominion over nature.[103] He conversed with animals, made the rain fall, and revived the dead.[104] Scholem seems to be baffled by the fact that mysticism and magic, such as the miracles performed by the Besht, seem to be closely connected in the Hassidic movement.[105] How can a true mystic, he asks, also be a magician? Well, the answer seems to be that there are here two distinct trends represented by two different personality types. The participation longed for by the Besht was a hunger for God and his creation, and the manipulation of spatio-temporality was a means of gaining dominion over it. The separant aims to swallow God the way the post-orally fixated infant aims to swallow the object. The Maggid, on the other hand, was an *agape* mystic and, like the Taoist and Zen Buddhist, realized the givingness of grace and the omnipresence of the divine state by the effacement of self-awareness and the annihilation of the self.[106]

The separant Besht sought the object in order to devour it. He hungered for stimuli, for action, for the concrete in order to sap out the divine vitality within them.[107] He also had a high excitation barrier; it was very hard to make him fly into a rage.[108] The Besht opposed mortification of the flesh and asceticism. "One who harms his body," he said, "harms his soul and delight in mortification comes from the sinister powers."[109] This almost hedonic quest for stimuli was rejected by the quietist resignation of the Maggid. His asceticism would seem to be linked to his participant aversion of stimuli. The Maggid could not cope with too much excitation, and his inaction-seeking personality trait filtered the incoming stimuli, so to speak, so that a bare minimum passed through; yet this small volume was enough to saturate his psyche. The high excitation level of the Besht also made him cherish joy and seek ecstatic festivity. "The Divine Presence does not hover over gloom but over joy. . . . Worry and gloom are the roots of all the powers of evil."[110]

The activist Besht was described as a fiery mountain bursting with energy.[111] With this overpowering energy he aimed to engulf the object; this is the energy that flows from Man while clinging to concrete objects and carrying out even the minutest act of everyday life. This is not unlike our conception of the libidinal energy that is stored in the Tantalus Ratio and cathected onto the surrounding objects. We have already mentioned that the separant Besht used sexual imagery when describing the attainment of the trance-like, clinging (*Devekut*) to divinity. He actually described a process of making love to the object. The participant Maggid, on the other hand, also used sexual imagery, but with him it is the concentration of all being during prayer and its flow in union into the divine presence. All his might is concentrated in this flow, like in a spurt of semen in ejaculation.[112] This wish to shoot-back one's spark of divinity into the divine presence is the participant's craving to reunite with the perfection of nonbeing of early orality.

The key concept of the Besht's relationship with the object was *avoda begashmiut*, to work (serve God) through the concrete. Spatio-temporality is only the garment of God who is everywhere and in everything: "no place is devoid of Him."[113] Man has to work through the concrete appearance of things, nature and fellow men in order to reach divinity that permeates them. An illustrative instance is the dull witted shepherd who blew his whistle on the Day of Atonement in the house of prayer. All the worshippers became frightened and confused, but the Besht said that the shepherd's whistle made it easier for his prayer to reach divinity.[114] This "worship through the concrete" is linked to the beatification of daily routines. The activist Besht decreed the sanctity of all human activity: "the least among the servants of the king, he, whose task it is to sweep the forecourt free of dirt, sings a merry song as he works, for he does what he is doing to gladden the king (God)."[115] The essence of *avodah begashmiut*, as expounded by the Besht, is a constant struggle with the concrete: "If this is the service of men in the world, to the very hour of their death: to struggle time after time with the extraneous, and time after time to uplift and fit it into the nature of the Divine Name."[116] This is precisely the main personality trait of the separant, fixated at a post-oral phase, he sees himself in constant struggle with the object, with the ultimate aim of overpowering it. The separant's quest also involves an openness and exposure to the object. "Alas," exclaimed the Besht, "the world is full of enormous lights and mysteries and Man shuts them from himself with one small hand." [117]

The Besht's focus on the interaction with the object made action itself a central theme in his teaching. Indeed, any kind of work or occupation was a prime value for the Besht and a medium of worship. The story about Enoch is typical: he was making shoes and with every stitch of the needle he was unifying God with the Divine Presence.[118] "Just as the strength of the root is in the leaf, so the strength of Man is in every utensil he makes, and his character and behavior can be gauged from what he has made."[119] Buber used this object relationship as expounded by the Besht to construct his *diologica* premise of an I–thou relationship between Man and his surroundings.[120] Yet the Besht himself focused on the dynamic action, on the activity, *per se*, as the manifestation of divinity. He preached: "You should know (worship) God in all your ways."[121] This is the sanctification of the act, the equivalent to Hegel's bridge of action between subject and object and the Protestant ethic of salvation through work. It is also an apt illustration of the separant's focus not so much on the object as on the interaction with it. The professed aim of the Besht was to free divinity from its enclosure within spatio-temporality, but the outward manifestation of his doctrine, at least as perceived by his admiring disciples, was dominion over Man, nature and things. The Besht communicated directly with objects: he conversed with fowl and plants;[122] he controlled the stars, moon and clouds; he diverted the course of rivers,[123] flattened mountains and controlled the angel of death.[124] Buber tried to distinguish the Besht's mastery of spatio-temporality from mere magic. The magician tries to impose his subjective wish upon the object, whereas the Besht aimed at a unification of God in Man and God in nature.[125] The wishes of Man and divinity coincide, and the change in the perception of the object is a correlate of this dialogic union. This may well be so as far as religious philosophy is concerned, yet for the present purposes the Besht's anchor on the need to break through the "outward garments" of nature in order to partake of its covert divinity is equivalent to the separant's quest to "swallow", i.e. dominate, the object by the overpowering frenzy of action.

The Besht was a charismatic leader who recognized in himself a call for leadership.[126] His overflowing charisma manifested itself in an immense ability to influence other people, who were instantaneously captivated by his spell.[127] He also imposed his doctrines by displays of argumentative authority, winning contests with the followers of Rabbi Isaac Luria,[128] the sixteenth-century founder of the most influential Kabbalist system which bears his name. He was also the supreme arbitrator and judge of his followers. The Besht was, no doubt, a man of the people who despised the elitist aloofness of the learned rabbinical scholars. He admonished one of his followers who preached morals to his community while keeping apart from them and not mixing with the people around him.[129] This lends credence to Buber's interpretations of the Besht's doctrine of lowering oneself to the stature of a friend as the basis for a face to face dialogue between I and Thou.[130] However, for this study, the *dialogica* is an interim stage with the ultimate aim being to incorporate alter within the activist's ego sphere of awareness. It is not a merger on a basis of equality but rather, as Buber himself states, "an overpowering effort of Union".[131] The separant Besht did indeed strive for union with *alter*, but his personality structure was such that he envisaged this union on his ontological terms, with himself as senior partner. This is by no means a derogatory portrayal of the Besht's personality but an inevitable corollary of the separant's effort to reach the object with himself as the base. In contrast, the self-effacing participant seeks union on the object's terms, with the ultimate aim of losing all vestiges of separateness or uniqueness, by melting away into the object.

The separant's link with other people was a tie to the Besht's extended self, dependent on alter's complete trust and entailing, therefore, to a great extent, alter's subjugation. The Besht used to give his followers an amulet containing his name. The amulet was believed to help them because they trusted him: "The amulet is the permanent symbol of his direct influence at the given moment. It contains his name and thus represents him. And through this pledge of personal connection, the soul of the recipient is 'lifted'."[132] This is the modus operandi of the separant, who reaches alter by a symbolic extension of his self through his name. He ties him by a bond of trust and then "uplifts" him to the realm of his *pneuma*. Indeed the Besht was very much dependent on the loyalty and solidarity of his flock. Once when they left him to pray by himself he admonished them, "By going away and leaving me alone, you dealt me a painful separa-tion."[133] The expression "separation" here is important. The Besht felt the pains of separation as the snapping of the umbilical cords of the togeth-erness of which he is the centre. This centrism of "The Tzadik" anointed the Besht as the incarnation of the living Torah, which radiated from him unto the community.[134] Indeed the Besht saw himself as the "vessel for God",[135] the duct through which God emanated into the world. This portrays the separant's sense of uniqueness, of being an exclusive seat of ontological awareness. The "miraculous power of the Besht to cling to God"[136] made him, so to speak, responsible to God on behalf of his community, so that a direct partaking of the community in God was effected with the Besht as the divine channel. Indeed, the members of the community when sitting together with him felt that he was addressing directly each one of them.[137] Consequently, each one felt as though he were on the receiving end of a direct line to the divine presence, with the Besht as the central exchange.

The separant's post-oral fixation and his deprivational interaction with the object may be inferred from the Besht's statement that, "the service of men in the world to the very hour of their death is to struggle time after time with the extraneous".[138] This expresses the separant's aim of manip-ulating the object and struggling with it in order to "uplift and fit it into . . . the Divine Name".[139]

The doctrines of the Maggid and his main personality characteristics would seem to be diametrically or rather symmetrically opposite to those of the Besht. The participant Maggid's aim in life was self-annihilation, in order to become *Ayin*, i.e. nothingness. If the Besht aimed at devouring the object, the Maggid longed for the omnipresence of early orality when no differentiation between self and object had yet been effected. Naturally, pantheistic participation entails the nonbeing of self-awareness or a *separatum*, which interacts with an object. The participation in unity involves the abrogation of relationships that are the ontological manifestation of plurality. If the self melts into nothingness, the disappearance of the object is an automatic sequel, and pantheistic omnipresence is achieved. Only when Moses hid his face, i.e. annihilated his self, explains the quietist Hassid, in a causalistic manner, did he partake in divinity.[140] Indeed, the Hassidic view is that all the world is full with divinity. "There is no place devoid of him."[141] Consequently, the *separatum* only has to rid himself of the confines of his ego boundary, in order to merge into the boundlessness of pantheism. Hassidim describe this pantheistic state of nonbeing as "complete rest in God's lap".[142] This recalls the contentedness of the fetus' suspended animation *in utero* and the blissful omnipresence of early orality. The pantheistic doctrines of the quietist Hassidim bear a striking similarity to our conception of the personality core of the participant personality type. The Hassid believes that God cannot reveal himself if the separate individual is active. Only when all the interfering self-consciousness and self-awareness of ego is blotted out can divinity be perceived in all its boundlessness.[143] In like manner, the participant personality type longs for the obliteration of all vestiges of apartness and conspicuousness as a means of regaining the blissful participation of early orality. The participant Maggid preached, therefore, that Man should annihilate himself, and that with the disintegration of the ego all spatio-temporality would disappear, and pantheistic omnipresence would reign supreme. He interpreted scripture to fit this doctrine: "Wisdom is to be found in nothingness," and "Thou shall know what is above you," meant that "everything which is above you comes from within you" – or, by coming out of the confines of oneself one may reach divinity above.

The dominant aim of the Maggid was the quest for Ayin – nothingness. "When the self becomes nothingness," said one of the Maggid's disciples in his master's name, "the will of Man becomes identical with the will of God." [144] It was deemed to be of symbolic importance that the self, Ani in Hebrew, has the same letters as nothingness – Ayin – but in a different order. "The work of creation," said the Maggid, "was the making of essence out of nothing but the worthy turn essence into nothingness."[145] This annihilation of the self into nothingness "restores the unity which was disturbed by the work of creation".[146] It also aims at returning the participant to the non-differentiated state of unity in early orality prior to the ontological separation of the self.

Buber compared Eastern and Christian mysticism with Hassidic mysticism and found some disparities that were relevant for his context of analysis. However, he finds similarity in the teachings of Al-Hallag[147], the Muslim mystic, and of Meister Eckhart, who preached the quest to "return to the primary essence before what he was before creation".[148] In the context of the personality core dynamics, these doctrines of the Muslim and Christian mystics are identical to the participant Maggid's fixated quest to regain the unity of nothingness of early orality.

Unlike the activist Besht, who prescribed the reaching out to God by violent movements during prayer, the quietist Maggid's technique of achieving self-annihilation was total immobility in prayer.[149] The participant worships without moving a limb, "shouting his prayers in complete silence". By shutting off spatio-temporality he facilitates the merger with unity. Another technique for reaching nothingness advocated by the Maggid was "automatic prayer".[150] The mechanical reciting of the words of prayer without relating to their contents made for a monotonous ritual, numbing the senses, not unlike the monotonous incantations and repetitious liturgy in religious and magic rites that effect a similar dulling of consciousness and numbing of self-awareness. For the Maggid, this achievement of nothingness was the greatest of miracles,[151] since it turned Man into God. This is a logical sequel to the partaking in pantheistic unity. Heaven, earth, Man and the universe fuse into the omnipresence of divinity.[152] This unity through nothingness may be experienced just for the shortest of instances, but the enormity and intensity of bliss is supreme and cannot be described in any temporal scale of pleasures.[153] This coincidence of nonbeing and blissful non-awareness with pantheistic unity is clearly linked to the participant's fixation on the omnipresence and non-differentiated self-sufficiency in early orality or *in utero*. As a wild conjecture, one may also relate the participant Maggid's "true" monotheism, i.e. his anchor on the partaking in unity, to this fixation on objectless early orality. In contrast, the separant Besht often followed the doctrines of Lurianic Kabbalah, which is covertly and sometimes overtly dualistic.

It should be noted that the process of self-annihilation, as expounded by the Maggid, had the dialectical effect of turning nothingness not only into something but also into everything. By defacing one's separate individuality one merges into the pantheistic totality of God. In addition, the Maggid expounded the doctrine that God is, as it were, imprisoned in Man's conscious thoughts.[154] The annihilation of Man's thought and self-awareness releases God from his spatio-temporal confinement. Consequently, Man's metamorphosis into nothingness is both his own return to the grace of unity and the granting of divinity its freedom from human bondage. This amounts, in a sense, to the resurrection of God, since a limited or confined divinity is not God and is a contradiction in terms. The participant personality type is marked, therefore, by more than a touch of ontological megalomania, linked perhaps to his early oral fixation when the self, or to be more precise, his non-self, and everything were one. As a matter of fact, he was everything. Then comes the separation into individual consciousness, which encompasses only a fragment of the early oral omnipresence. This particle of the pantheistic everything is now imprisoned in the ego boundary of the individual self. The annihilation of the self is also the release of this particle of everything, so that God and Man reunite into the perfection of nothingness.

Unlike the activist Besht, the Maggid shunned action and advocated an attitude of indifference towards the results of an act.[155] He preached to his disciples that the divine presence rests with Man only when he is passive and not active.[156] He also opposed the active pursuit of good deeds, since this is motivated by the desire for rewards or by other object related passions, and not by the desire to immerse oneself in divinity.

The separant Besht sought the solidarity of the fold, the togetherness of the admiring others who regarded him as the "channel of God". The participant Maggid, on the other hand, was uninterested in social status and position and disregarded the separant achievement motive. The social sphere rested on the lowest plane of his mystical activity.[157]

The Maggid himself postulated the existence of two diametrically opposite social relationships incidental to the religious doctrine of the two polar personality types. He "differentiated between *Tzadikim* [the Hassidic saintly rabbis] who succeeded in maintaining the dialectic tension between social life and the mystic life and *Tzadikim* who were compelled to withdraw from the people because their contact with society was liable to result in their downfall".[158] Very rarely does a subject of investigation voice the demonstration of a hypothesis, the way the Maggid did in his differentiation between the gregariousness of the separant and the resigned isolation of the participant.

The Maggid, unlike the Besht, was an ascetic, who shunned all passions and rejected sex that was not for the purpose of procreation.[159] He also rejected his share in the ever-after, so that he could pray and worship God without the enticement of rewards.[160] In his aversion to stimuli he shut himself off from the harassment of too many events, since a very small amount of incoming energy is enough to activate the participant, and any excess of it would, so to speak, blow a fuse and cause complete disorientation.

Since the participant was fixated at early orality, when a boundless "bad me" was surrounded by a vague, non-descript "good object", which was continuously injured or "emptied" by the "bad me",[161] he tends to be depressive. Indeed the Maggid seems to have suffered episodes of deep depression for which he sought help from the Besht. Yet the quietist Maggid fought despair, because despair, like rewards, tie Man to the spatio-temporality of human existence.[162] To a large extent the Maggid preached social isolation and solitude as a prerequisite for *unio mystica*.[163] Unlike the Besht, the Maggid taught that even in a crowd of worshippers one should pray as if one stands alone before God.[164] The underlying intuitive conviction of the participant is that spatio-temporality is a chimeric nuisance recorded by the senses, which cannot possibly be real. With the attainment of self-annihilation all relationship disappears and with it evil, sin and pain. Why should one be affected by the worries of the here and now when spatio-temporality itself can be cast off at will like a garment?

The separant Sisyphus anchors on the interrelationship with the object, whereas the participant Tantalus seeks the blissful fruits of *unio mystica*. These are the passions kindling the vectors of our polar personality types. However, Sisyphus' object-stone keeps rolling and the mystical fruits of Tantalus are forever receding. This is the essence of the Tantalus Ratio: its strength is measured by unachieved aims because its fulfilment is not only impossible but is tantamount to impotence.

We have studied here in detail two great Hassidic figures, representing our two opposed personality types. In *The Bridge to Nothingness* we elaborated on the figure of another great Hassidic sage, Rabbi Nachman of Bratzlav, in comparison with a Christian mystic, Kierkegaard, both of whom represent participant existentialist rebellion, as presented in the final chapter of this volume.

Entropy

With the passage of time, and especially with old age, the conception of temporality and space changes drastically. This was demonstrated by Haim Hazan in his study of a day care centre for the elderly.[165] In old age entropy sets in and the separant structures of time and space that link the old to the here and now become more fluid and ultimately disintegrate. The inmates of old age homes have a grand future in their past. In old age we become more brittle and vulnerable. The young are more adaptable and flexible, whereas the old are more rigid, ossified, and hence more susceptible and weak. Toughening through experience is a fairy tale for the young. Experience makes us less immune to the blows dealt us by our surroundings. The old are weak, their libido exhausted and their prime mover – the core dialectics of their separant quests and participant longings – has entropied and drained out of their system. Jacques Brel portrays this process with the touch of a master in *Les Vieux*.[166]

In the first part of life, the Sisyphean separation forces push for activism, creativity, and passions; later in life participant Tantalism takes over. As Jung said, in the second half of life, death is born and Man anchors more on transcendence. Early in life, death is remote and time is spent indiscriminately, but when old age sets in the fact of *Geworfenheit zum Tod* becomes glaring, the order of priorities is reshuffled. If authenticity is reached the waning energies are mustered for the bare essentials. Earlier in life, separant proficiencies are more apparent. Most mathematicians, physicists, and natural scientists make their greatest achievements in their twenties – very rarely in their thirties. Humanists, philosophers and theologians mature in old age. When Solomon was a youth he sang the passionate Sisyphean Song of Songs; in his maturity he preached his proverbs; and in old age he wrote the participant Tantalic laments of Ecclesiastes.

The young feel the need of the group. The attitudes of their peers are infinitesimally more important to them than those of their elders and socializers. In old age the need for peers decreases and the reliance on transcendence increases. Youth possesses the courage and bravado of the inexperienced, while the mature and the old realize that the *angst und sorge* of life are in earnest. The hormones of youth push them to wine, sex and song, but when slavery to the glands subsides, a Reish Lakish [Rabbi Shimon ben Lakish], an Augustine, and a Leo Tolstoy become saints. Our programming seems to invest everything in youth; and once the tasks of fertility, creativity or whatever transcendence destined us to carry out has been accomplished or is no longer possible, it loses interest and permits the old to entropy, atrophy, disintegrate and rot. As time is not a factor for our programmer (who exists in the timelessness of eternity) he lets the aged linger in their own limbo and putrefy at their individual pace. Youth is a bait for life, for growth, for love and for procreation in the here and now, whereas old age is an advertisement for the futility, deceit and pain of being in the world and serving time in the prison of history. Hence, old age looks and smells bad like the precursor of death that it is. Here though, the participant Tantalic vector intervenes to teach maieutically the separantly disintegrating old the wisdom of revelation. Those of the old, who do not realize that passion, growth, power and Sisyphean activity must decline or subside, suffer from anomia, despair and depression; however, those who realize that revelation is more imminent in old age might experience a renewed sense of meaning and purpose in their metamorphosed existence. Thus, the *Midrash* teaches us that the ignorant old, or, in this context, the inauthentic old who do not experience the enlightenment of revelation, become demented; whereas the enlightened old, i.e. those who gain a novel insight and meaning in their life through revelation (as discussed in **chapter 10**), the more they age, the more they become serene.[167] They do not rage, but go gently towards the approaching night.

Separant
and Participant
Cultures

3

The Social Component of the
Tantalus Ratio

Produce! Produce!
Were it but the pitifulest infinitesimal fraction, produce it in God's name! 'Tis
the utmost thou has in thee: Out with it, then up, up. Whatsoever thy hand
findeth to do, do it with thy whole might. Work while it is called today; for the
night cometh . . . wherein . . . no man can work.

Thomas Carlyle, *Sartor Resartus*

In Sicily, it doesn't matter about doing things well or badly; the sin which we
Sicilians never forgive is simply that of doing at all.

Guiseppe Di Lampedusa, *The Leopard*

The first dimension of our exposition of the Tantalus Ratio related our
core personality vectors to the growth, maturation and decline cycle of
the individual. While the Buddhists plot the cycle on the circumference of
the *Samsara* wheel, on which birth and death are mere signposts of endless
reincarnations, we see the cycle of spatio-temporal existence as one swing
of a pendulum that originates in nowhere and moves towards an
unknown end. Our second dimension consisted of the polar fixations of
the personality. The Tantalic participant type has been fixated at the pre-
differentiation stage of pantheistic omnipresence, whereas the Sisyphean
separant has been traumatized by his object relationships after the coagulation of his ego boundary at the later oral stage. The present third
dimension is provided by the various socializing agencies that ingrain into
the individual the norms of cultures, which may also be classified and
placed on the participant–separant continuum. These three dimensions
comprise, in fact, the whole ontological realm of Man's existence. The
first developmental dimension plots the movement of Man in time and
thus relates the Tantalus Ratio to temporality. The second dimension
relates the personality core vectors to the differentiation of the self from

the non-self and provides the spatial boundaries between ego and his surroundings. In other words, it concretizes for ego his object relationships within a given space. The third social dimension relates the vectors of the Tantalus Ratio to ego's relationship with his group and its norms. These three ontological dimensions may be connoted, therefore, as the temporal, spatial and ethical components of the Tantalus Ratio.

Although the ethical and spatial components of the Tantalus Ratio may have some overlapping zones, the exposure to normative indoctrination begins after the spatial differentiation of the ego boundary from its surrounding objects has already been completed. Consequently, whatever the attributes of our present analysis, it has the additional effect of linking the psychogenic or intra-psychic and sociogenic factors of the personality within a unified theoretical matrix.

Patterns of Culture and Social Character

The taxonomy of cultures along a continuum and its relationship to a given personality structure necessitates, at a minimum, two basic assumptions. First, that cultures possess some generalized traits that may be measured and ranked on a pre-determined typology or scale. Second, that these traits could be related to the character of the individual person. By adopting both these assumptions, we find ourselves in good or bad company, depending on taste or value judgment. Oswald Spengler and Arnold Toynbee have adhered to both these assumptions in their epoch-making works on the growth and decline of cultures. Indeed, Spengler compares the ages of cultures to the ages of Man: "Every culture," he says, "passes through the age phases of the individual man. Each has its childhood, youth, manhood and old age."[1] Spengler and Toynbee introduced the dynamic temporal dimension to the study of culture. We, fortunately, do not have to follow their giant strides. Whatever the similarities and disparities between the growth, maturation and decline of cultures and individuals, they remain outside the scope of the present work, which focuses exclusively on the individual. The temporal dimension of the individual's growth and decline and his spatial object relationships are related to his upbringing within a given culture. However, we have to confine ourselves to the effects of socialization and cultural transmission on the personality of the individual as the sole matrix of our analysis. The task ahead is therefore to provide the culture context for the temporal dimension of growth and the spatial object relationships of the individual's personality core.

Indeed, the current anthropological conception of culture as the "super-organic"[2] patterns of symbolics and instrumentation generated by the interaction of groups and individuals, and transmitted by learning does lend itself to abstract classifications. The crucial question is: Are these patterns Platonic ideals projected by the mind of the anthropologist into the rarified ether of abstraction, or are they generalized descriptions of processes actually taking place in societies? If culture "is what binds men together",[3] and it does so by "symbolating" human interaction[4] through relating forms and appearances to qualities and attributes, it involves, by definition, the abstraction and ordering of "Gestalts".[5] In other words, the processes of cultures by themselves are manifested by configurational patterns. This may also be gleaned from some of the key concepts in the definition of culture. A symbol is a value- or meaning-laden sign;[6] and meanings and value judgments are readily expressed in generalized patterns. The "super-organic" is manipulated by tools and the instruments (means) to achieve cultural goals are regulated by norms. Yet rules and norms are constructs that are the choice objects for paradigms and classifications; *prima facie*, therefore, we may accept the feasibility, contrary to the vehement objections of some ethnographers, of ordering cultures into generalized configurations and patterns. Or to use Spengler's flowery language, "to paint the portrait of a culture".[7] Indeed, Ruth Benedict and her cultural-relativist colleagues and disciples have demonstrated how patterns may be identified by the direct observation of cultures. Claude Lévi-Strauss and his structuralist school have also shown that cultural processes in "savage" societies are incidental to the classificatory passage from things to symbols, notably the totemic generalizations from the concrete to the abstract.[8] The structuralists thus identify in societies not only patterns but whole systems of functions underlying the overt cultural processes. For Benedict, cultural patterns stem from "unconscious canons of choice that develop within the culture . . .'[9] so that it selects some segment of the arc of possible human behavior, and insofar as it achieves integration, its institutions tend to further the expression of its selected segment and to inhibit opposite expressions".[10]

These habit formations, symbols, meanings, values, cultural goals and the means to achieve them crystallize into "total culture patterns"[11] by which cultures may be identified and tagged. It should be stressed that the ordering of cultural patterns into schemas, paradigms, continua and matrices may vary according to the purpose, frame of reference and the theoretical orientation of the observer. There can be no universal criterion to measure the validity of the classification of culture patterns. The value of a classification should be determined by the specific aims and needs of a given theoretical concern. Lévi-Strauss aptly states this as follows:

> The real question is not whether the touch of a woodpecker's beak does in fact cure toothache. It is rather whether there is a point of view from which a woodpecker's beak and a man's tooth can be seen as "going together" (the use of this congruity for therapeutic purposes being only one of its possible uses) and whether some initial order can be introduced into the universe by means of these groupings.

We may thus observe in the literature a vast array of taxonomies of cultures that serve an *ad hoc* aim of the researcher. On the micro level, we may find Francis L. K. Hsu's classification of cultures by their dominant dyads: Japan, according to his criteria, is a father–son dominated society, whereas American culture is dominated by the husband–wife dyad.[13] On the macro level, David Riesman and his associates identified the traditional, inner-directed societies within the matrix of transitional growth and economic development.[14] The typology that is closest in its general objectives to our own is the one presented by Benedict, who followed Spengler's tradition of cultural relativism. We have pointed out in the conceptual clarifications in **chapter 2** that Friedrich Nietzsche's Dionysian–Appolonian typology, which has been adopted by Benedict, differs both in form and contents from our Sisyphean and Tantalic types. We shall also distinguish later between our typology and Spengler's Faustian and Appolonian types. However, the cultural-relativist method of identifying dominant social characters within a culture, which may be arranged between two poles of a continuum, suits our present methodological purposes. By this method, we may characterize a culture according to its position on the continuum. This position is never static because it shifts with time and social change.

Our second assumption relates to the nature and viability of a "social character". To Erich Fromm, a social character does not consist of the peculiarities by which persons differ from each other, but of "that part of their character structure that is common to most members of the group".[15] The social character is, therefore, an attribute of individuals that displays the characteristics of a culture as ingrained in them by the socializing agencies. As our focus is on the individual and not on the group, we are concerned with this social character as the manifestation of internalized culture within the personality structure. Riesman, who uses, *mutatis mutandis*, Fromm's definition of social character, relies for the sources and genesis of this social character on Erik Erikson, who says: "Systems of child training . . . represent unconscious attempts at creating out of human raw material that configuration of attitudes which is the optimum under the tribes' particular natural conditions and economic-historic necessities."[16] Erikson's social Darwinism cum Marxist material dialectics is too concrete and harsh for us to serve as an explanation for the rather volatile concept of social character. We prefer to see the social character as a "collective representation", in the sense used by Lucien Lévy-Bruhl,[17] of acts, symbolics and transitional processes from the concrete to the abstract displayed by groups in their interaction with the individuals comprising them, or with other groups. This involves the transmission of the "social character" from the group to its young and from generation to generation by a process of learning and socialization, and not by biological heredity as postulated by Carl Jung.[18] The social character is the psychological type of a character as displayed by a collectivity and not by the individuals comprising it. Yet when the group implants this social character on the individual, it provides the necessary link between the phylogenetic and autogenetic bases of the personality structure.

Activist and Quietist Cultures

As we have pointed out, each taxonomy fulfils the specific aims of a given theoretical structure; ours is to determine the interrelationship of the Sisyphean–Tantalic personality type continuum with the separant–participant continuum of cultures. Consequently, we have to define our cultural continuum and describe the polarities of our social characters, and this, to be sure, is no mean task. Once, the author was sitting in one of the *tavernas* in the Plaka, on the slope leading to the Acropolis and overlooking the whole of Athens. He was sipping Ouzo and reading Lev Shestov's *Athens and Jerusalem*. He was swept by his eloquent contrast between Socrates, "the man who is led by reason alone", and the biblical Psalmist who "cries to the Lord out of the depths of his human nothingness"[19]. The reason-, fact- and thing-oriented Socratic Greeks versus the intuition-, faith- and revelation-bound biblical Jew. Yet when he looked beyond the ruins of the Agora towards the horizon, there was a striking similarity between the hills around Athens and the Hills of Judea around Jerusalem. The same scalding heat, the same bare rocks, the same cruelty of Nature served as a physical setting for the activist, object-manipulating post-Socratic Greeks and the quietist, contemplative and self-effacing Judea of Ecclesiastes. The "portrait of a culture", however, depicts only the predominant cultural traits and patterns, but every culture is perforce pluralistic and displays, to varying degrees, the patterns of the opposite polar type. This is the main reason for the continuum being the most suitable methodological artifact to describe the polarity and range of social characters. Also, some basic ideas and innovating modes of thought and observation displaying either participant or separant attitudes might or might not have been representative modal values and attitudes of a given society. In all likelihood, many great names studied today with reverence and admiration were eccentric recluses shunned and ridiculed by their contemporaries. We shall therefore use the ideas and insights of savants to help us formulate, define and illustrate our concepts; but for the description of cultures as separant or participant, we shall rely mainly on original documents.

The polarized characteristics of the Sisyphean–separant and Tantalic–participant social characters permeated the *Weltanschauung* of keen observers from times immemorial. Parmenides founded the Eleatic school of philosophy on the premise that reality is static. We have here the basic tenet of inaction common to the participant ideals of Taoism, Hinayana Buddhism, the Muslim Sufis and the quietist Hassidim. Heraclitus the Ephesean, on the other hand, postulated the universality of flux, the strife between opposites that sweeps everything into a dynamic flow of change, a constant torrent of action – the basis of Hegelian dialectics as well as the Marxian creed of historical materialism, which postulates salvation through action. The first polarity characteristic of a separant culture is, therefore, an orientation on action. The second polarity relates to the contrast between Unity and plurality. The participant culture decrees that one has to rid one's thought from the illusory perception of the senses in order to reach the monistic wholeness behind the deceptions of plurality. Consequently, the Parmenidean sphere, which is the omnipresent monistic wholeness, is also a three-dimensional mandala – the prevailing symbol of the Far Eastern participant cultures. The separant conception of reality follows the pre-Socratic Pythagoras and, of course, Heraclitus, who saw the Universe as ordered into measured pluralities that follow the logos: the universal formula of sequence and dynamic harmonies within inter-related boundaries. This brings us to the third polarity, which contrasts the invariance or constancy ideal of the participant cultures with those of the relationship-oriented separant. If plurality is illusion, the veil of *maya*, and the sole reality is Unity, then relationship is also illusory because Unity cannot interact with itself. Moreover, for participant cultures, relationship is not only a deceptive mirage but also the source of evil, sorrow and pain. For the separant cultures, on the other hand, relationship with spatio-temporality and other human beings is the frame of reference of human concern, which has to be coped with by integration, adjustment and solidarity. The fourth polarity is the separant cultures' focus on reason, on the inherent schemas, formulae and models that "explain" Man and his Universe, whereas the participant cultures tend to distrust and reject logic while relying more on intuition and revelation. Indeed, Spengler colours his following statement by a participant value judgment when he says: "Reason, system and comprehension kill as they 'cognise'. That which is cognised becomes a rigid object, capable of measurement and subdivision. Intuitive vision, on the other hand, vivifies and incorporates the details in a living inwardly-felt unity."[20]

The fifth polarity that we found useful is the separant tool orientation, i.e. a culture geared towards manipulation of objects and the participant symbol-oriented culture in which ideas and belief systems are anchored on inwardly contemplating individuals who are immersed in "doing their own thing".

Our five polar characteristics of the social character are presented in summarized form in **figure 3.1**. These patterns are by no means exhaustive but rather illustrative: they point out the highlights of a given social character, but do not constitute a precise definition. We shall construct later a matrix of these pairs of polar patterns and analyze variables that result from the interrelationships of these patterns, but first we have to discuss the extreme types that we shall place at the poles of our continuum of social characters.

Our usage of the continuum as a tool describing social character means that no culture may be tagged by one monistic label. Consequently, in every participant social character there are separant patterns, and vice versa. In Judaism, for instance, *Yom Kipurim*, the Day of Atonement, is a participant, self-effacing ritual in which the individual strives to partake of Divinity through self-humiliation and defacement. On the other hand, *Yom Hapurim*, the feast celebrating the deliverance of the Jews from Haman, Ahasverus' evil *wazir,* is written in Hebrew like the Day of Atonement, less one syllable: *ki*. This led the Lurianic Kabbalists to link the two festivities: the Day of Atonement being *Yom ke Purim*. Consequently, the "lots" cast by children and adults in play on the festival of Purim are compared with the "lots" of life and death cast by God on *Yom Hakipurim*, the Day of Atonement. And yet Purim is a separant ritual of frenzy in which individuals strive to reach each other through the ecstatic togetherness of wine, song and dance.[21] The ideal-type separant or participant culture does not exist in reality, but the patterns that indicate the presence of one polar type of social character or its opposite may be arranged on several continua representing the various cultural areas. These multidimensional measures may subsequently be placed within a three-dimensional space in which the two extreme planes represent the participant and separant social characters. We may try and search, for illustrative purposes, for two cultures that may be rather close to the ideal-type constructs at the extreme poles of our theoretical space continuum. At the separant extreme, we may well place the northwest European societies that have been kindled by the Protestant Ethic and burst forth with the full-blown flames of the "American Dream". On the participant pole, we may place the cultures dominated by the Hinayana Buddhist doctrines of quietist self-annihilation.

Separant	Participant
Object manipulation	Self-manipulation
Reason	Intuition
Relation	Constancy
Plurality	Unity
Action	Resignation

Figure 3.1 Polar Patterns of Social Character

It might well be that the separant–activist trends of northwestern European cultures have their origins in the ethos of the Germanic tribes hammering their way all over Europe, carrying Thor's hammer as a symbol of power and conquest. They even dispensed with the fear of the ever-after by having Odin, the God of Battle, send his Valkyrie maidens clad in armour to carry the slain warriors to eternal bliss in Valhalla. There is no doubt that the achievement-motivated, power-backed manipulation of less-powerful societies and the scientific conquest of nature, which marked the advent of northwestern European societies in the last centuries, has been boosted by the Protestant Ethic. There seems to be a separant trend running through Martin Luther's sanctification of work as a sacred calling, John Calvin's stress of achievement as a proof of predestined worth, Hegel's action as the necessary bridge between subject and object, and Karl Marx's decree to harness all means of production in order to mould Man's (dialectical) future. The separant culture is Sisyphean because its aim of incorporating spatio-temporality within itself by its total control is unattainable. Hyperactivity channels itself very often into routine and aimless ritualism, social engineering is more likely to lead to the social death of totalitarianism or the robotic zombies of *1984*, and the scientific manipulation of matter seems to achieve the suffocation of air, the death of water and the perfect sophistication of artifacts for mass-murder. And yet separant striving to reach the perfection of Utopia through the dialectics of action is never-ending, like Sisyphus' continuous struggle to roll his rock uphill.

At this stage we anticipate some critical reactions to our focus on religion as an anchor for the identification of cultures along our space continuum. This is warranted both by theoretical considerations and empirical findings. First, religious affiliation has been found to correlate with a great many attitudes and modes of behavior, as well as with the structure and contents of social institutions.[22] Religion may serve, therefore, as a significant identification tag. Although many other social institutions, norms and cultural goals in a given culture are relevant for our classification, we may observe that most, if not all, of our pairs of polar patterns of social characteristics are reflected in the religious doctrine of a given culture. Second, most of human history, to risk a sweeping generalization, has been related, influenced and many times totally dominated by religion. The "unchartered region of human experience", to use Gilbert Murray's fortunate phrase,[23] is the domain of religion. Although the areas of our "positive knowledge" are expanding, most of the rather swift human journey from an involuntary beginning to an unknown end is governed by unchartered areas of incertitude, confusion and chaos. Consequently, religion reigned supreme in human societies throughout history, the most notable exception of which was evident in the twentieth century. Even Marxism has been denoted as a "secular religion", and Bertrand Russell has made the following ingenious analogies:

Yahweh = Dialectical Materialism
The Messiah = Marx
The Elect = The Proletariat
The Church = The Communist Party

The Second Coming = The Revolution
Hell = Punishment of the Capitalists
The Millennium = The Communist Commonwealth.[24]

Yet, if we try to place Communist China, the most ardent adherent to the Marxist secular religion, on our continuum, we may decide that its position is not on the very far separant pole, because it still has some vestiges of the Taoist and Buddhist participant social characteristics.

As for empirical evidence, we have ample proof that the Catholics' other-worldly orientation, their conception of labour as a curse, a corollary of Original Sin, which are incidentally participant quietist traits, make them less achievement-motivated than the Protestants,[25] and this would determine, *inter alia*, their placement considerably far from the separant extreme of our space continuum.

On the participant extreme of our continuum we have placed Hinayana Buddhism of the Southern Theravada School. The Hinayana is the "small vehicle", as condescendingly labelled by the Mahayana Buddhists, who called themselves the "great vehicle". We shall deal later with some of the Hinayana doctrines as expounded by the Pali Canon; at this stage, we shall only try to justify its placement on the participant extreme of our space continuum. First, the Hinayana rejects temporal existence as a burden because all action and interaction is irritation, friction and suffering (*dukkha*).[26] Second, the *Samsara*, the cycle of growth, maturation and decay – the essence of the individual's separate condition – produces disharmony and desire, which are the harbingers of evil. Third, plurality is an illusion generated by the perception of the separate self. Nirvana, therefore, is achieved by the annihilation of the individual self and "awakening", thereby, into the blissful reality of Unity.[27] We may actually identify in the Hinayana doctrine at least four out of our five main patterns of the participant social character, namely: quietist inaction, rejection of temporality, self-defacement and the belief in the omnipresence of Unity behind the veil of plurality. Although the Hindu yoga is very near to the participant pole, it is somewhat removed from the extreme position of the Hinayana. For yogis, for instance, the temporal world is vile and full of suffering and pain, but it is, nevertheless, real and not illusory.[28] Also the aim of yoga, although quietist in essence, is not to annihilate the separate self, but to separate spirit (*Purusha*) and matter (*Prakrti*).[29] Mahayana, the northern school of Buddhism, has even more separant traits in it and is therefore is further removed from the participant pole occupied by Hinayana Buddhism. Suzuki, when expounding the Mahayana doctrine, states: "In Mahayana Buddhism, each soul is not only related as such to the highest reality, but also to one another in the most perfect network of infinite mutual relationship."[30] The element of relationship here assumes the reality of alters and consequently of object relationships, which generates, in turn, separant action and interaction. Mahayana lowered, also, the Hinayana emphasis on *dukkha*, the pain of

85

interaction, and preached with a zeal becoming of a Calvin: "Work out your salvation with diligence."[31] Zen Buddhism, which evolved from Mahayana doctrine, is even more separant. It seems that Zen influenced the rise of the business class in nineteenth-century Japan. "Zen discipline," says Suzuki, "is simple, direct, self-reliant;" *Satori* (individual enlightenment) is attained not by ritual but by "one's inner life".[32] This, to be sure, is rather similar to the Protestant Ethic. Indeed, Zen flourished in its full bloom in Japan, the most separant culture of the Far East, which cherishes self-reliance, responsibility, cleanliness, order and energetic performance.[33]

The above description of the extreme poles of our space continuum, and some of the criteria for placing social characters on it, will help us later in our subsequent wider analysis of cultural character patterns. The next step is to discuss the relationship of our present social character continuum to the Tantalus Ratio and its personality core vectors.

The Tantalus Ratio and Social Character

The Tantalus Ratio of cultures, i.e. the dynamic relationship between its participant and separant patterns, may well resemble the developmental curve of the Tantalus Ratio of individuals. We shall not deal with the development of cultures, because this work is concerned with the personality structure and development of individuals and not of societies. In other words, we shall not attempt the formidable task of relating the age of a culture, its growth and decline, to its Tantalus Ratio. Our task is to trace the interrelationship of separant and participant patterns within a specific culture at a given time, in order to relate them to the personality core vectors of the individual personality. The rest of the chapter will therefore deal with the concordance or conflict of the types of personality and the types of culture within which they were socialized. Consequently, the various tags given to cultures by the cultural relativists may be relevant for our present context, but not their developmental analysis of these cultures within the matrix of social change. We may avail ourselves, for instance, of Spengler's description of the Faustian culture as focusing on becoming, which in our context would mean that the Faustian culture displays separant patterns of activist striving; whereas his statement that the decline of a culture is its fulfilment,[34] being a developmental observation, is foreign to our present context. In like manner, Benedict's comparison of patterns of cultures, although based on the Nietzschean typology, which differs from ours, is relevant to our frame of analysis precisely because it compares cultures as they are and not within a developmental matrix. On the other hand, Riesman's analysis is mostly developmental and is based on criteria of economic growth, social cohesion and conformity to normative systems. This makes it foreign to our analysis, for conformity or non-conformity to cultural mandates is not necessarily correlated with separant or participant social characteristics.

Consequently, the crucial part of our present analysis relates to the factors that determine the patterns of a culture, at any given time, to display participant or separant characteristics. This, to be sure, is impossible if we aim at comprehensive causal explanations, which can rarely be accomplished in the behavioral and social sciences. We may, however, point out some basic processes, the foremost of which seems to us to be "collective fixations". We do not subscribe to Jung's postulate that social character and cultural patterns are transmitted genetically through the inherited gene structure. Socialization is a good enough explanation, for our purposes, for the transmission of cultural patterns associated, for instance, with the Protestant Ethic or with the brutal Japanese training for cleanliness. We do claim that fixations, i.e. traumatic developmental processes, are as crucial in determining the social character in a culture as they are for the crystallization of personality types, yet collective fixations are not just the sums of individual fixations in a culture. We may rely here on Lévy-Bruhl's conception of the collective as defined by him within the context of his central notion of "collective representation":

> The representations which are termed collective . . . may be recognized by the following signs: They are common to the members of a given social group; they are transmitted from one generation to another; they impress themselves upon its individual members (but) their existence does not depend upon the individual; not that they imply a collective unity distinct from the individuals composing the social group, but because they present themselves in aspects which cannot be accounted for by considering individuals merely as such . . . Collective representations have their own laws.[35]

In **chapter 2** we traced the formation of individual fixations and their relationship to the personality core vectors. Indeed, we had to trace the etiology of these fixations, because this is a treatise on the structure of the individual's personality. But we do not have the onus or the tools to study the etiology of collective fixations. All we have to do is to ascertain their prima facie existence. Consequently, we shall examine some basic tenets of a social institution (religion) in order to find some clues and at least circumstantial evidence for the existence of participant and separant collective fixations.

The religion of cultures approaching the participant pole of our space continuum would tend to be truly monistic insofar as they stress the exclusive reality of Unity and the illusion of plurality. If religions display, under the outward shell of a monotheistic Godhead, a division of dominion between a duality of conflicting powers and a triumvirate of trinities, they would tend to move their corresponding cultures towards the separant pole of our space continuum. Taoism, for instance, which is truly monistic in this sense, postulates: "The great Tao flows everywhere, to the left and to the right. All things depend upon it to exist and it does not abandon them."[36] We may recognize here the omnipresence of the pre-differenti-

87

ated or even pre-natal self, when everything and everywhere is full with the exclusive wholeness of Unity. The energy of being flows dynamically to all sides, but it is not cathected to a distinct object because there is no distinct object to focus on. Consequently, the great Tao has its energy of being fixated on the totality of non-differentiated Unity. It "flows everywhere". The second verse of Chapter 34 of the *Tao Te Ching* ends with the reassurance of care and non-separation, which brings to the fore the autarchic sufficiency of self *in utero* and in early orality. In the second part of Chapter 34 Lao Tzu spells out what seems to us another projected image of the blissful contentedness of early orality: "To its accomplishments it (Tao) lays no claim. It loves and nourishes all things, but does not lord it over them."[37] Food and shelter flow gracefully from a nameless whole, and there is no painful deprivational interaction with an object because no object has, as yet, been coagulated from the non-differentiated whole. The omnipresent Tao seems to be a projection of the collective fixation of Taoism on the non-differentiated phases of human development as expounded by us in **chapter 2**. An even clearer indication of this collective fixation may be discerned in Chapter 25 of the *Tao Te Ching*, which postulates:

> There is a thing confusedly formed,
> Born before heaven and earth.
> Silent and void
> It stands alone and does not change,
> Goes round and does not weary.
> It is capable of being the mother of the world.
> I know not its name
> So I style it "the way" (Tao).[38]

We have here most of the characteristics of early orality – the unlimited, formless and boundless mass before any contrasting or delimiting object emerges to confine the boundaries of being. The collective fixation of Tao anchors on the omnipresence of Unity. The dynamic energy of being whirls around vigorously, but it is not cathected to an object. It has the potential of motherhood, because in the undifferentiated stage of early orality, mother, world and self are fused into a pantheistic whole. The omnipresent being is nameless at this stage because the ego has as yet no boundaries; the "I" has not been formed. The collective fixation of Taoism on the ego-less early orality is especially apparent in Chapter 21 of the *Tao Te Ching*.

> The Tao is something blurred and indistinct.
> How indistinct! How blurred!
> Yet within it are things.
> How dim! How confused!
> Yet within it is mental power.
> Because this power is most true
> Within it there is confidence.[39]

The free-flowing energy is cathected within a formless mass, which has some indistinct images at the fringes, but the predominant entity is a boundless power within an engulfing nothingness. Taoism is immersed within an infinite whole on which its collective fixation is projected.

If the previous passages from the *Tao Te Ching* have left many sceptics still not convinced as to the collective fixation of Taoism on the early non-differentiated phase of human development, we have Chapter 20 of the *Tao Te Ching* using the following imagery:

> I alone am tranquil, and have made no signs,
> Like a baby who is yet unable to smile,
> Drifting, as if being attached to nothing.
> But I value seeking sustenance from the Mother (Tao).[40]

The imagery here is of suspended animation *in utero* and the non-awareness of early orality, yet the sustenance and nurture is sought from the mother, which is none other than the formless, pantheistic Tao. Another Taoist text by Chuang Tzu states the ideals of sanity by reference to "The baby (who looks) all day without winking: that is because his eyes are not focused on any particular object. . . He merges himself with the surroundings and moves along with it."[41] This is even more relevant because the Taoist collective fixation projects a *post facto* idealization on the merger between subject and object in the early phases of infantile development.

Hinayana Buddhism also displays a collective fixation on early non-differentiated omnipresence insofar as its conception of Nirvana is a negation of spatio-temporality through "the dying out, the waning out, the ceasing to be"[42] of the separate individual self. Nirvana is actually the manifestation of this collective fixation on early or even pre-natal phases of development. It sets the goal of reverting back to the pre-birth stage, which involves the annihilation of consciousness. Nirvana also aims to negate the process of becoming. Change is of the essence of the perception of time; the quietist static goal of Nirvana postulates the negation of temporality. Another goal of Nirvana is the dissolution of concrete form. This may be related to the formation of the ego boundary at the later oral stage, which Nirvana aims to disperse in order to revert to the non-differentiated state of early orality. Nirvana aims also to destroy composite plurality[43] because relationship, which is the basis for pain and suffering, disappears the moment composite plurality is abrogated. The single sentence that expresses in a concise manner the collective fixation on non-differentiated omnipresence of the Hinayana conception of Nirvana is: "Foregoing self, the Universe grows I."[44] Another monistic religion, although less participant than Taoism or Hinayana Buddhism, is Upanishadic Hinduism. The Hindu collective fixation is on the *Atman*, the omnipresent self who tilled the Universe all by himself. This is the typical description of the non-differentiated being before the separation

89

of the "I" from the amorphic mass of non-awareness. The omnipresent *Atman* is in a state of *ananda*, constant bliss,[45] that is rather like the self-sufficiency of the fetus *in utero*. The Yogic *Purusha*, the all-embracing person, which is similar to the Gnostic "Primeval Man" and the Kabbalist "Adam Kadmon", is without relation, inactive, indifferent without desires, and free of any temporal attributes.[46] The omnipresence of *Brahman* is expressed negatively: he is without duality, without any contrasting opposite or object.[47] This is in line with our claim that the collective fixation of the monistic, extremely participant religions is on the pantheistic, pre-awareness, objectless stage of human development. Consequently, any plurality that is the result of the illusory division of the primordial self, the *Atman, Purusha* or *Brahman,* is unreal – a chimeric veil of *maya*. Of more importance is that the participant collective fixation on early non-differentiation negates the primary duality between subject and object, which is the anchor of the separant fixation. "All is *Brahman,*" say the Upanishads, "all duality is falsely imagined."[48] Moreover, all classification and ordering, which in Sanskrit derive from the root *matr*, is also the etymological source of matter. Consequently, not only is plurality *maya*, but concrete matter and spatio-temporal objects are, perforce, also illusory. Of special importance is the Sanskrit root *dva*, which is the source both of "divide" and "two". This indicates that the primary act of division separates the Universe into an "I" and "not I". The moment the ego boundary is crystallized, the world is divided into two: the subject and the object. This division is a traumatic catastrophe for the omnipresent pantheistic self and is registered, as we have pointed out elsewhere, as mythical projections of a fall from grace.[49] This primary division may be the focus of a separant collective fixation, but for the monistic religions, which are collectively fixated on pre-differentiated Unity, all division is evil because it is the source of painful interaction, and salvation is essentially the annulment of the *mayan* dividing boundary between subject and object.

In the more separant Mahayana Buddhist doctrine there is already a division between pairs of opposites, whereas the Kegon School of Buddhism, with its doctrines of *Jijimuge* and *Rijimuge*, is evidently collectively fixated on a duality where *Ri* is the non-divided plenum and *Ji* the concrete object.[50] The traumatic fixation is centred on the division from the plenum of Unity, "When the One trembles at the birth of Two,"[51] but after the birth of the "two", and the subsequent division into pluralistic spatio-temporality, the separant collective fixation imputes reality to objects. Consequently, separant religions are preoccupied with subject–object relationships and the place of the plurality of separates in the scheme of Divinity. This they have accomplished by proclaiming that every man, fauna, flora and inanimate object is blessed with a core or particle of Divinity, which is enshrined in them. God thus enters the body of the devout *separatum* in the manner of the Greek *Enthousiasmus*, in contra-distinction to the more participant *Ekstasis*, which is the emerging of the soul from the body to partake in Divinity,[52] as well as in all items of creation. Separant rituals of absorbing the Divine parts of God are apparent in the eating of the God-beast or the drinking of its blood, the sacred priestesses or holy virgins who were impregnated by Divinity, the Hermes liturgists who beseeched God to "Enter into me as a babe into the womb of a Woman", and Markos the Gnostic, who preached that the devout should "Prepare thyself as a bride to receive her bridegroom".[53] This is the separant process of "inclusion" by which the *separatum* is tied to Divinity, which is also its perfect origin by the absorption of part of its Divine Presence. We have traced this process in **chapter 2** when we described the separant strain of Hassidism as practised by the Besht and his *Avoda-Begashmiut*, which is the sanctification of profane temporality by reaching the Divine Sparks that are embedded in all parts of creation. This "positive mysticism" is very much apparent in Protestantism, which emphasizes the direct communion of individuals with God so that "everyone could get renewed energy by direct contact with the Divine".[54] As a sweeping generalization, we may say that most sects in Christianity, except such esoteric mystical doctrines like Meister Eckhart's, are separant insofar as they postulate a deistic God *vis-à-vis* a distinct self, others and objects. The same holds true for Judaism, with the exception of the Kabbalists.

91

Ten Pairs of the Composite Polar Patterns

I Tool and Symbol Orientations

The classification of cultures along a continuum of either tool or symbol orientations is implicit in the work of many anthropologists and has been expressly mentioned by one of them.[55] Indeed, in societies where reason and logic guided the manipulation of nature, tools were the means of harnessing the energy of muscles and natural resources to further Man's dominion over his surroundings. The Neolithic potters and weavers, the Mesopotamian and Egyptian irrigation technicians, the Roman aqueduct engineers, the *Homo faber* of the Industrial Revolution, the commissars of the five-year plans, the builders of the Great Society, the sponsors of the Great Leap Forward – all were aiming to subjugate their surroundings to what seemed to them their immediate or future needs, but in terms of their collective fixations they were activating the objects in their surroundings according to their projected conception of order and function. Thus, tools and artefacts become the means of incorporating the object within the extended reign of the self. Tool orientation displays the instrumental nature of a social character that aims to harness and control the object so that it fits into a preconceived cultural goal. Consequently, the level of technological development as measured by the various students of economic growth[56] is a proper index for separant tool orientation. On the other hand, the intuitive self-centred symbol orientation foregoes any kind of instrumentalism in all areas of culture. It does not need the structured avenues provided by separant cultures to enjoy art, such as exquisite paintings hung in unfit conditions together with other "exotic" collector's items in the villas of the rich, or shallow explanations by celebrated art critics. Participant symbol orientation may reach aesthetic fulfilment by immersion into the mandala-like kaleidoscopes of rainbows reflected from a drop of dew hanging on a cherry blossom. Music in separant cultures is performed by highly specialized professionals who direct their orchestrated art to an audience straight-jacketed in formal evening-dress, whereas participant symbol orientation loses itself in the throaty undulations of torch-singers whose excellence is determined by their ability to bring some hours of self-oblivion to their listeners. The objects of Nature surrounding the participant are not targets for assault and conquest. His symbol orientation makes him adjust with his environment in a pantheistic-bound symbiosis because one should not be unduly violent to one's partners in Unity.

Separant tool orientation reaches outwards to things as well as to structured relationships between objects in a manner described by Ortega y Gasset as *alteracion*. This outward-reaching activity is contrasted by him with a contemplative journey into one-self (*ensimissmarre*).[57] Indeed, the symbol-orientated, quietist, intuitive manipulation of ideas has no common grounds with the activist goal-oriented manipulation of objects. A discourse between the two is bound to be very much like Maxim Gorky's fable on the dialogue between a hawk and a snake on the pleasures of flying.

The religions of tool-oriented cultures are either truly polytheistic in the sense that the plurality of spatio-temporality is taken to be real without an underlying wholeness and is believed to be controlled by a plurality of deities, or Divinity is believed to activate the plurality of objects by embedding parts of it in the individual *separatae*. Indeed, the truly polytheistic Olympian gods are the deities of an activist, tool-oriented society of doers. The ancient Greeks' collective separant fixation on the object is apparent from the fact that the Olympian gods never claimed to have created the spatio-temporal world; they conquered and subjugated it.[58] This is the separant's projected wish to incorporate and dominate an already existing object. The Greek gods are activist doers. Zeus controls the weather; Apollo is an archer; and Hephaestos is a craftsman, a toolmaker. The Olympian gods try both to imitate Nature in its constant cycles of change and to control it. They represent power and action with no unified *telos*[59] or ultimate goal. It seems as if they held that the manipulation and control of their surroundings are a proper reward in themselves. This indeed is the essence of tool orientation, that the activist manipulation of the object should not be a means to a further end. Hard work is its own reward says the Calvinist. Sisyphus, to paraphrase Camus, must find happiness in the endless struggle with his stone.

Deistic monotheism does not, in itself, make a religion participant. This holds true for the monotheistic interpretation of the Olympian religion by Zeno, who still conceded the reality of daemons,[60] as well as for the dualistic and Trinitarian strains in Judaism, Christianity and Islam. In these, the separant manipulation of the object manifests itself in the doctrine that parts of Divinity are impregnated in every individual and object, and one may reach Divinity through these particles. The Mahayana Buddhist doctrine is different in form but not in essence and has, therefore, a discernible measure of object manipulation, rationalism and tool orientation. It preached "openness" towards the outer world, i.e. the concrete temporal surroundings, and to other human beings. In like manner, the Kegon School of Japanese Buddhism, the harbingers of Zen, preached that the parts of objective reality retain their individuality within the universal whole.[61] This is a far cry from the original doctrines of Hinayana Buddhism, according to which all separate individualities and objective realities are *mayan* illusions. Consequently, Zen adheres to object manipulation as a means of bridging the gap between subject and object, and the tool orientation of the Japanese culture is a possible influence of this aspect of Zen Buddhism. The Sisyphean nature of this separant attempt to bridge between subject and object is pointed out by the more symbol-oriented and participant Hindu (*Samkhya*) Yoga, which calls this attempt *avidya* (ignorance) because to link the reality of the omnipresent true self (*Purusha*) with the illusory object (*prakrti*)[62] is non-sense by definition.

When we reach the separant extreme of our space continuum – the protestant northwest European and North American cultures – the "Man over Nature" tool orientation reigns supreme. If economic growth and wealth is the main index of tool orientation, we have the assertion by David McClelland that the average person in northern Europe or the United States has several times as much wealth at his disposal as the average person in most of Africa or Asia.[63]

The tool orientation of industrialized societies is a direct corollary of production requirements and the need for specialized skills. The extreme separant cultures are primarily rational manipulators of their surroundings, i.e. tool-oriented, because instrumental activities sustain their cultural goals of successfully coping with material needs and controlling their physical environment. Participant symbol orientation is related to cultural patterns that advocate the non-rational, contemplative, intuitive pre-occupation with the individual self in order to remove the confining boundaries between subject and object. Murray describes the last period of Hellenism in a manner that fits our conception of an intuitive self-probing symbol orientation:

> This sense of failure, this progressive loss of hope in the world, in sober calculation, and in organized human effort, threw the later Greek back upon emotions, mysteries and revelations, upon the comparative neglect of this transitory and imperfect world for the sake of some dream-world far off, which shall subsist without sin or corruption the same yesterday, today and forever.[64]

When sober calculation, i.e. reason and logic, and organized endeavours of controlling nature, amassing power and wealth, i.e. manipulation of the temporal environment, have failed or proved to be worthless, one is ready for the pursuit of participant absolutes and probing into oneself for intuitive revelation. However, the most expressive symbol, to risk a tautology, of symbol orientation, is the mandala. A Tibetan mandala described by Jung depicts the concentric circles of contemplation, the shutting off of the outer rims of temporal desires and concrete objects until one reaches the centre of "the One Existent, the Timeless in its perfect state".[65] "The goal of contemplating the processes depicted in the mandala," says Jung, "is that the Yogi shall become inwardly aware of the deity. Through contemplation, he recognizes himself as God again, and thus returns from the illusion of individual existence into the universal totality of the Divine state."[66] The mandala stands, thus, for the extreme form of self-manipulating symbol orientation, of shutting off by contemplation the illusions of objective spatio-temporality and the *Samsara* wheel of growth and pain, relation and evil, so that the self-god reverts to its original, undivided perfection of Unity.

In Hinayana Buddhism, the self-defacing aspect of symbol orientation is manifest in the goal of Nirvana, which is "the shattering of the house of self".[67] By contemplating away one's ego boundary, the separateness of the self is dissolved and the exiled individual "awakens" into the Universal Self. The growth and interaction of the *Samsara* wheel is all *dukkha* – irritation, friction and suffering – which also characterizes the Sisyphean ordeals of tool orientation, because the object mocks its manipulators. In the last analysis, it is never fully subjugated and "swallowed" by the "mouth–ego" of the voracious self, but by relinquishing their involvement with the object, which is illusory anyway. The Hinayana Buddhists comply with their collective fixation of the pre-differentiated total self with its visions of well-being, perfection, wholeness and bliss.[68] One of the stories chosen by McClelland to measure the achievement motive is an Indian tale that states the moral at the outset:

> The world is an illusion. Wife, children, horses and cows are all just ties of fate. They are ephemeral. . . We should not clamour after riches, which are not permanent. As long as we live it is wise not to have any attachments and just think of God.[69]

This might be the only *Weltanschauung* possible in a culture in which a large segment of the population is born, grows, copulates and dies on the pavements of cities, and here the corpses are picked up in the morning by garbage vans. But as a cultural pattern it signifies the rejection of tool-oriented activism and the adherence to the inwardly-bound extinction of the objective surroundings and relationships. The symbol-oriented social character is so immersed in an inner flow of symbolic meanings that the externalized symbols of separant European origins, e.g. flags, nationality and social ideologies, seem to him trivial or grotesque. What is a painted piece of cloth compared with eternity! The contemplative symbol-oriented social character can shut off external "reality" almost instantaneously. A Chinese Buddhist friend of the author used to shut off the world at will and lose himself instantaneously in deep meditation. He used to ridicule his Occidental friends who needed drugs to be "turned on". His participant symbol-oriented cultural setting enhanced his proficiency of intuitive self-oblivion, whereas the activist "sober" rational background of his Occidental friends was an impediment to their aim of achieving a temporary refuge from their ontological loneliness. "Do your own thing" was the creed of the "Woodstock Nation", but this was no mean task for a WASP, college-educated chronic "joiner".

2 Welfare State versus Social Traditionalism

The separant object relationship with human groups is based on the dual credo that all aspects of social life can be planned and that this planning should lead to "progress", to a sheltered and cushioned life from cradle to coffin in the bosom of the Welfare State. The conviction that human interaction may be predicted, controlled and planned is shared by the peoples' communes in China, and the industrial psychologists and community planners in the United States. Both believe in the amelioration of the lot of Man by "social engineering". It is rather significant that economic growth, which is the main manifestation of the separant tool-oriented societies, is also linked with anti-traditionalism and the ideal of progress through innovation.[70] This is a *prima facie* link between our two composite patterns of the separant social character. Innovation here is not necessarily non-conformist to the cultural system because planned innovation – or to be more exact, openness to economic and social innovations – may be deemed to be functional for the development of a tool-oriented industrialized society. Consequently, receptiveness to change and innovation may be a built-in and planned characteristic of a separant tool-oriented culture.

The planning of housing projects, slum clearance, health services, education and welfare schemes do seem to be the general trends in industrialized societies. Whether a controlled economy is better or worse than free enterprise for economic growth is irrelevant in our context. What is relevant is that tool-oriented economic growth does seem to be linked with social reconstruction plans, social welfare and "social engineering". The rational manipulation of material objects seems to go hand-in-hand with the planned manipulation of people.

The separant social character traits of tool orientation and social planning are closely linked with the idea of progress: the Hegelian and Marxist dialectical zigzags towards a "New World", the Spencerian liberal focus on a better and more bountiful future, and the Unitarian belief in the "progress of mankind, onward and upward forever". It is our contention that the idea of progress is a separant value judgment. Any attempt at objectively measuring the cultural progress of societies does not really hold water. Alfred Kroeber's attempt, for instance, to attribute to the "advanced" cultures more humaneness and psychological maturity than to the "retarded" cultures[71] seems to us a sad joke. Are napalm bombs more humane than poisoned arrows? In separant, more "advanced" industrialized societies, people do not kill each other with axes; rather, in cold blood, they give each other fatal heart attacks and peptic ulcers. We have analyzed elsewhere[72] the societal disintegration and value breakdowns that are inevitable corollaries of economic growth, achievement-motivated specialization and the pressures towards conformity in "socially engineered" cultures. Much else has been written about anomic trends and alienation of the individual in "progress"-bound societies. Yet the best illustration of the value judgment inherent in the idea of progress is apparent from the following South American anecdote, which has its equivalents in many other cultures: Pedro lies in the pampas, warming himself in the sun, and a Yankee tourist stops his big car on the passing road, comes over to Pedro and reproaches him for idling away his life, laying there in the sun. "Why don't you teach yourself to drive?" says the Yankee. "Buy an oil truck and transport oil to port." "And what then?" asks Pedro. "You buy another truck," answers the Yankee, "and another, and another, and then you buy an oil well." "And what then?" asks Pedro. "Money flows in and you don't have to work anymore." "Then," says the Yankee, "you buy yourself a nice villa, sit on the lawn and warm yourself in the sun." "But that is exactly what I'm doing now," retorts Pedro.

Another criterion of "social progress" mentioned by Kroeber is that more "progressive" cultures are less superstitious, whereas retarded cultures are dominated by magic.[73] Here again, the criterion for progress seems to us to be based on a value judgment and an illusion. Kroeber could not have been aware of the millions flocking to the movie-houses all over the United States to partake vicariously in the brutal sights of exorcism. The black masses, the Jesus freaks and occult circles in the United States and Europe have an ever-growing number of initiates. On the other hand, South American societies undergo a tremendous upheaval of social change marked by surges of economic growth, yet readers of the novels of Gabriel Garcia Marquez sense the animistic pantheism by which the Latin American Indian is engulfed, irrespective of the instrumental "progress" or "retardation" of his culture. Indeed, Claude Lévi-Strauss has demonstrated that the totemic classificatory systems are as logical as a quadratic equation; and because the "primitives" define them as real, to use William I. Thomas's theorem, they become real in their consequences.

If we examine the attitude of the truly monistic religions, e.g. Taoism and Hinayana Buddhism, progress is inevitably defined as an illusion in league with the *Samsara* wheel. The value judgment of progress is apparent in the Sufi parable on progress, which depicts the donkey that turns the wheel to draw water from the well. Its eyes are wrapped in a rag so that it may think that it is moving ahead and not going around in circles. Consequently, the idea of progress as related to a culture is so value-laden that it cannot serve as a social characteristic of a culture. Its seemingly defining attributes seem to dissipate when compared with the more basic polar patterns in our paradigm.

The participant social character tends to be traditional in his social attitudes because he does not accept the notion of the betterment or the amelioration of the human condition by "social engineering". First, for the participant, all human relationship is evil by definition. The participant ideal is to statify all relationship, including human interaction. Consequently, any social welfare scheme is a sham because it intends to substitute one evil hue with another vile shade. The participant therefore regards social progress as trivial pre-occupation with illusion. For him, the misery on the pavements of Calcutta is neither worse nor better than the inevitable misery in the palace of a Maharaja. The participant traditionalist does not believe in change and social welfare. He anchors himself on an embodied environment where objects and people are fixed within a rigid structure that serves as a setting for the ritualistic merry-go-round of temporal existence. The traditionalist feels that these cycles of misery should be kept on the lowest level of activity until the liberating nonbeing rejoins one with eternity. Di Lampedusa's Don Fabrizio, the archetypal Sicilian traditionalist, does not oppose "social engineering" and progress – they just have no place within his quietist frame of reference.

3 Scientistic or Mystic

The separant social character is concerned with the relationship of objects within the framework of reason and logic. The interrelationships among all items of spatio-temporality are believed by the separant to be measurable. Taxonomies, variations, correlations and matrices describe and "explain" all phenomena. One has only to find the proper indices, scales and significance tests to apply to the given research populations for the "inner or outer scheme of things" to come out. Micro- and macro-relationships are being designed into "models", clusters, multiple regression curves and other modes of surrogate causal relationships. Even the irrational, the mystical and the subconscious are subject to logical analysis and relational dynamism, although they themselves deprecate the explanatory value of reason. The mystical social character acknowledges the existence of logical interrelationships, but they seem trivial to him. The Upanishadic Indians knew mathematics quite well, but they were not motivated to apply it to a balance sheet or production curve. The participant mystic prefers intuition to logic and inactive constancy to the Samsara wheel of relationship.

The belief in science is a reliable symptom of separant trends, even in participant cultures. The leaders in "developing" countries profess adherence to science in the time-honoured ribaldry of Evelyn Waugh's Black Mischief and Anna's King of Siam. Cultures that have almost completed the metamorphosis from a participant to a separant social character have raised science from a means to an end in itself. In Japan, for instance, "scientific living" has become a cultural goal.[74] Indeed, the means-ends continuum is relevant in the present context. The moralistic choice of ends is an impediment to the goal orientation of scientism in separant cultures. Morals in both their internalized form of conscience and the external controls of social norms are a limitation on the range of actions and hence participant in essence. The proponents of scientism in separant cultures usually abhor moral checks on their activities as regressive, medieval and reactionary. Scientific goals are deemed, in separant cultures, to justify means, and "bleeding hearts" moralists impede the progress of mankind. Some conspicuous examples for the triumph of science over "redundant" protests of moralists are the Manhattan Project and the control group of syphilitics in a follow-up study who were untreated and left to rot because the killing of the spirochetes in their blood would introduce an intervening variable and bias the results of the study. It might well be that the scientism of a culture is the most conspicuous evidence for its separant social character. Weber, when describing the Occidental cultures imbued with the Protestant Ethic, says "a rational, systematic and specialized pursuit of science, with trained and specialized personnel, has only existed in the West in a sense at all approaching its present dominant place in our culture".[75] The scientistic anchor on the rationality of the interrelationship among the *separata* of spatio-temporality scorns irrationality and dismisses disconnected causal sequences as superstition and illogical premonitions based on intuition as dangerous nonsense. Precisely this rejection of rationality, the distrust of logic, the view of structured relationships as useless (apart from their aesthetic grace within the confines of a mandala or the mind of a meditating philosopher) and the intuitive grasp of immutable constancy behind the deceptive outward relationship among *separate*, are the essential tenets of mysticism. The change from separant rationality to participant mysticism in the late Hellenistic culture is forcefully depicted by Murray:

> There is a change in the whole relation . . . to the world . . . (there) is a rise of asceticism, of mysticism, in a sense of pessimism: a loss of self-confidence, of hope in this life and of faith in normal human effort; a despair of patient inquiry, a cry for infallible revelation; and indifference to the welfare of the state, a conversion of the soul to God.[76]

This passage illustrates the change from scientistic realism to the intuitive groping into the self for mystical revelation.

As scientism is the most prominent symptom of the separant social character, so is mysticism the most conspicuous polar trait of participant cultures. Indeed, one may safely use mysticism as the main criterion for ranking participant cultures and most of the other social character traits would correlate with it. The extent of a culture's pre-occupation with ultimates, its lack of interest in concrete objects, its collective representations being imbued with "an infinity of imperceptible entities," [77] is also the extent and measure of its mysticism. For the mystical social character, the dichotomy between subject and object is illusory. His collective fixation is anchored on the pantheistic wholeness before the "I", separated from the non-differentiated omnipresence of non-awareness. The mystical social character displays an overpowering "need and the ardent desire to be merged in one common essence".[78]

The mystic rejects measurement, reason, logic and orderly formulation. "The Tao that can be expressed," says Lao Tzu, "is not the eternal Tao."[79] Expression in concrete, discrete or ranked form is foreign to the mystic social character; it functions and perceives through the amorphic Gestalt of intuition. Henry Bergson, the ardent advocate of intuition, speaks of "mystic experience taken in its immediacy, apart from all interpretation". "True mystics," he says, "simply open their souls to the oncoming wave."[80]

Indeed, the aim of the mystic Hinayana Buddhist is to escape the fetters of form (*rupa*) so that the delusion of separate selfhood disappears and subject and object are fused into Unity. This *Unio Mystica* in insignificant variations is also the goal of the Gnostics, the disciples of Eckhart, the Lurianic Kabbalists and the Muslim Sufis. Lévy-Bruhl also invokes this mystical fusion between subject and object when he describes his "law of participation" of primitive societies. "In the collective representations of primitive mentality," he says, "objects, beings, phenomena can be . . . both themselves and something other than themselves . . . they give forth and they receive mystic powers, virtues, qualities, influences, which make themselves felt outside without ceasing to remain where they are."[81] When the partitions among self, others and things melt away, there can be no relationships any more, but a static everlasting wholeness. Indeed, the mystic social character is conditioned by his collective fixation on non-differentiated pantheism to grope beyond the confines of reason for the perfection of Unity behind the deluding confines of plurality.

4 The Carnivores and the Downtrodden

The cycles of growth and decline of cultures have been linked in the works of the cultural relativists with powerful aggression and meek submission respectively. As we are not concerned with social change, the cycles themselves are not within our present focus of interest. However, when a culture is politically aggressive it tends to fit within our separant matrix of manipulating and controlling human beings as objects of subjugation. Readers of the first-hand account by Alexander Solzhenitsyn in *The Gulag Archipelago* of the techniques of subjugation used by the Stalinist régime are overwhelmed by the reality of horror, which is lacking in the second-hand accounts by Arthur Koestler and in the nightmares dreamed vicariously by George Orwell. Solzhenitsyn's realistic terror seems to be emitted by the total objectification of human beings by the Stalinists. In most other instances of overpowering or subjugation of Man by Man, the victims were regarded as persons, albeit evil, dominated by the Devil, treacherous or mad, but still persons; but in the Gulag, the inmates were not people, they were objects, things. The regime's manipulation of its subjects – victims – is performed in a disinterested manner, destined to achieve total submission, so that a person becomes a resilient chunk of clay that yields to the minutest pressure of its master-moulder. The victim's wife is forced to divorce and denounce him, and his children are taken away to study in special institutions, the curricula of which includes, *inter alia*, the study of their father's crime, not because the régime aims to get even with a traitor, but because it holds that these methods are bound to achieve "better" results. The inmates in the Gulag have to become reified zombies in their abject obedience so that they may be proclaimed as "rehabilitated". Solzhenitsyn's captors who threatened him with a mock death sentence prior to his deportation to Germany were not staging an act in the tradition of the Theatre of Cruelty; they were just "going by the book". They were performing their duties according to their training to make human beings succumb thoroughly to the power of the State: to make things out of persons. However, the ultimate in the separant objectification of people was brought to perfection by the Nazis. I was present at Adolf Eichmann's trial in Jerusalem and was struck by the fact that there was a complete breakdown of communication between the defendant on the one hand and the judges, the prosecution and the other dramatis personae in the trial on the other hand. They were accusing him of slaughtering people, whereas he was presenting his operation as the organization of transports of *things* to be cremated in the ovens of Auschwitz as if they were so many sides of bacon to be smoked or ceramic pots to be glazed. The separant power manipulation of people in its extreme form tends to level the stature of all items in spatio-temporality to one inanimate category. People, flora, fauna and the elements reach a common denominator *vis-à-vis* the separant power structure: they become objects for an impersonal, rational and organized subjugation. The organization aspect here is quite crucial: if the annihilation of self-awareness, which aims to achieve participation in Unity, is always a solitary process, the separant objectification or annihilation of people is inevitably a planned project executed through bureaucratic structures by "organization men".

The participant social character is essentially powerless and he protects himself from the bullying brutality of political predators by building an inner shield of assertion based on longing for transcendental Unity. This sanctuary may be founded on the collective fixation of the participant on blissful pre-awareness, but for the politically oppressed and downtrodden participant, this anchor on an inner sense of worth is many times his only defence against becoming a thing, a reified object. In this way, the powerless participant holds his own and does not succumb to the ultimate aim of the separant predator, who is not content with the mere physical subjugation of others but expects people to extinguish their "inner sacred spark" and become lifeless inlays within organizational structures. The inner sanctuary of the participant social character is aptly described by Montaigne, who said: "I can bow only with my body, but not with my mind." Novelists have successfully depicted this inner-directed defence of the politically downtrodden. Nikos Kazantzakis makes his Greeks re-enact The Passion, which is the epitome of the participant ideal of martyrdom, the partaking in Divinity by the sacrifice of the self, as a defence against the cruel oppression by the Turks. Elie Kazan shows in his *America, America* how an American family centres its *raison d'être* on an inner sense of dignity, which cannot be shared by their tormentors, and Curzio Malaparte, who describes the Neapolitans perennially conquered by outsiders, their sons enslaved and daughters molested, but in the final round of contest, they have the trump-card – nobody can destroy their inner conviction of self-worth, which is shielded by a surrounding fence of utter contempt for their worthless oppressors.

The carnivore traits of the separant social character make him seek power, respect the capacity for leadership, and hold in high regard quick and effective decision-making. Indeed, McClelland provides us with an empirical anchor to our present premise when he relates that totalitarian and "police states" are high in "n" power, i.e. political authoritarianism marked by a "strong desire to dominate and control others unchecked by a friendly interest in those others"[82] (low in "n" affiliation). This is precisely the characteristic of the politically aggressive carnivore, which aims to manipulate people as if they were inanimate objects. The separant believes in the channelling of power through organized and specialized structures in which only results count and failure to achieve them for whatever reason, justifiable or not, is the ultimate sin. The separant power élites were perennially harnessing the existing ideologies and religious dogma to serve their aggressive ends. The politically carnivorous Jesuits used the maxim *perinde ac cadaver* (obey like a corpse), not so much as a directive for themselves, but for others, preferably their victims. It is typical that the simile demands people to obey like a cadaver, a lifeless object. The Samurai have applied Zen to develop Bushido (the Way of the Warrior), the art of war in which fighting is conducted in effortless efficiency.

The participant social character is usually a member of a society of political losers. Cultures that have been victimized and exploited for so long that meek political powerlessness became a *Weltanschauung*, a way of life and a second nature. The participant political herbivores readily yield in uncritical obedience at the slightest show of authority. Koestler describes India, which is a typically participant, politically passive culture, as follows:

> (Indian culture) sets a premium on uncritical obedience, penalized the expression of independent opinion and proclaimed, in lieu of the survival of the fittest, the non-survival of the meekest … Out of the sacred womb of the Indian family only political

yes-men could emerge. Their compliance to the will of the leader was not due to opportunism or cowardice, but to an implanted reflex.[83]

The participant cultures in the Middle East have been marked, for centuries, by powerlessness. Readers of the humane diary of a rural prosecutor in Egypt, Taufiq El-Haquim, may sense the total submission of the fellahin to the local "kingpin", the headman appointed by the central government. He may kill with impunity anyone he likes, rape women and confiscate property. If someone "up there" in Cairo becomes unduly inquisitive, his palm is easily greased with part of the loot. Lawrence Durrell's *Alexandria Quartet* depicts the Levantine urban élites as utterly passive, being swayed aimlessly by whiffs of decadence and jostled around by the more aggressive Occidental social pressures. Indeed, Anwar al-Sadat was literally right when he proclaimed that in October 1973, the Egyptians won their first partial victory in five hundred years. One of the most forceful portrayals of participant powerlessness is Di Lampedusa's Sicily. A culture that has been dominated, violated, exploited and bled white by carnivorous conquerors for twenty-five centuries has slumbered into self-centred drowsiness. "[Sicilian culture] is a centenarian being dragged in a bath-chair round the Great Exhibition in London, understanding nothing and caring about nothing, whether it's the steel factories of Sheffield or the cotton spinneries of Manchester, and thinking of nothing but drowsing off again on beslobbered pillows with a pot under the bed."[84] The participant is disinterested in the mechanical object manipulation of separant industries. The passive participant social character aims to obliterate its consciousness, to shut off the vicissitudes of relationships, to annul the temporal appearances of plurality by physical death, in order to "re-awake" into Unity. "Sleep," says Di Lampedusa's Don Fabrizio, "that is what Sicilians want, and they will always hate anyone who tries to wake them . . . All Sicilians' self-expression, even the most violent, is really wish-fulfilment; our sensuality is a hankering for oblivion, our shooting and knifing a hankering for death; our languor, our exotic vices, a hankering for voluptuous immobility, that is for death again; our meditative air is that of a void wanting to scrutinize the enigmas of Nirvana."[85] This almost perfect formulation of the participant quest for self-annihilation is coupled with a deep distaste and distrust of the separant's compulsion for management, administration and bureaucracy.[86] "The Sicilians," says Don Fabrizio, "never want to improve, for the simple reason that they think themselves perfect; their vanity is stronger than their misery; every invasion by outsiders upsets their illusion of achieved perfection, risks disturbing their satisfied waiting for nothing."[87] We have here the inner shield of the powerless participant against the assault of the carnivorous separant. Of more importance is the clear expression of the longing of the participant social character, which is motivated by his collective fixation on pre-differentiated non-awareness for the perfection of nonbeing.

102

5 Exaltation and Lethargy

The separant social character tries to force his way to the object by frenzy, ecstasy and exaltation. He is the Hassid who follows the doctrine of the Besht to make daily life Divine. The Hassidic *Avoda-Begashmiut* is the beatification of daily routines; the raising of every contact with objects and others to the stature of an exalted happening. This is also the Mahayana principle that real Nirvana rests in the *Samsara* wheel of routine life. Through the love and wisdom of the *bodhicitta*, the Mahayana Buddhist sanctifies all the objects in his spatio-temporal surroundings. The participant, on the other hand, seeks Unity by the quietist lethargy of the Maggid and the "dying out of the self" of the Hinayana Buddhist. The separant Mahayana Buddhist is an optimistic realist and a pragmatic positivist, whereas the Hinayana Buddhist is a self-effacing depressive who uses intuition to see through the delusions of reality.

In like manner, the earlier Raja Yoga as expounded by Patanjali's Yoga Sutras, displays the participant's collective fixation on the omnipotent (*sarvakarta*) soul[88] and the everlasting bliss to be attained by the release (*moksha*) from the *Samsara* wheel and the confining bonds of the object as represented by the body and spatio-temporality.[89] The later Hatha Yoga has the separant's fixation on the object. It aims to gain mastery over the object by rites of purification, cleansing and techniques of body control that extend to their "personal space" and perception of time.

Hatha Yoga is literally a violent effort to affect a union between the sun (*ha*) and the moon (*tha*).[90] This brings to the fore similar methods by the Hassidim to achieve union with the object through the ecstatic rites of prayer.

The striking similarity between the social characters of the separant Hassidim, the followers of the Besht, and the Mahayana Buddhists, stems from their frantic efforts to overpower the object, or at least to make contact with its Divine core. In Hatha Yoga we also find the technique of *bhakti* devotion, which like the Hassidic *devekut* aims to achieve contact with the core of Divinity in the object. Indeed, we may find in some of the expositions of Hatha Yoga the value of ecstasy in obtaining Nirvana.[91] This brings to mind the violent Hassidic "Upharazta", the "break-through" to the Divine Sparks within the object by means of prayer. Thus all three separant doctrines, which are quite divergent in their origins, postulate the active frenzied reaching out to the object. The Hatha Yoga is a potent, and often violent technique of controlling the object. Mahayana Buddhism reveals its collective fixation on the object by postu-lating that "every blade of grass shall enter into Buddhahood",[92] whereas the epitome of separantism is found in the Mahayana offspring – the Kegon School, which scatters the universal Buddha into every particular thing.[93]

Mahayana Buddhism is affirmative and "positive" in the liberal bour-

103

geois sense, insofar as it advocates the acceptance of temporal reality and not its rejection. One has to seek salvation within the *Samsara* wheel,[94] not unlike the duty of the Hassid to seek joy even in the worst trials that befall him. The Mahayana focus on the object is also apparent in its anchor on the person of the Buddha as the intermediate channel of enlightenment.[95] Again, this is similar to the Hassidic sanctification of the *Tzadik*, the righteous man, as the medium in which Divinity is personified. The separant doctrines of Zen go even further than the Mahayana in affirming the natural environment of the self: by the dialectic *jonglerie* of equating reality with the void of Nirvana, Zen not only affirms the existence of reality but also all its material manifestations. The Zen adherent must appreciate art, manual labour and the natural universe[96] because "The highest attainment was to enter into awakening without exterminating the defilements *(klesa)*"[97] of everyday life. Here the *Samsara* wheel has completed a full cycle with a leer of triumph. Its trump card is that Zen actually advocates active involvement with the object and joyful interest in the business of day-to-day existence. This more than anything else signifies the Sisyphean nature of the object involvement of the separant social character. He may call his daily burden *klesa*, i.e. defilement, refuse and other bad names, but once he realizes that the *Samsara* wheel, which is a Sisyphean rock in a Buddhist attire, is his only possible destiny, we should visualize Sisyphus, to borrow Camus' metaphor, as a happy man.

The Zen *chih chih* (direct pointing and direct awareness) aims at circumventing the ritualistic and symbolic barriers that surround the object. The Zen adept finds salvation within his seemingly vile surroundings because he is able to reach the core essence of people, flora, fauna and things in an immediate directness. The Zen shortcut to all the objects in one's environment, "in front, behind, in all ten directions",[98] is deemed to ensure enjoyment, love and compassion amidst the spikes of suffering, hatred and despair of the wretched cycle of life. The Zen master's involvement with the object amounts to an affirmation of spatio-temporality. "Don't be antagonistic to the world of the senses,"[99] is the sage's advice to the initiated.

The separant's means of object involvement is the forceful assault on his surroundings by a controlled and regulated frenzy. This is nothing else than the release of energy cathected within the Tantalus Ratio and aiming it towards the object. The separant medium of exaltation as a means to reach the object is manifest in the violent control and body manipulation techniques of Hatha Yoga: the *chih chih* direct access to things as postulated by Zen and the ecstatic *devekut* (present in each particle of Creation) by means of which the Hassid reaches Divinity. Exaltation also screams from the grandiose art of the European romantics who court agony vicariously as a lever for reaching a timeless glory, yet this is the separant's vision of lifting himself up by his own boot-straps towards an eternal infinity. In music the frenzied exaltation of a Hector Berlioz "tries to do away with the division (between himself and the infinity of aspirations) by extending and exalting his being towards the infinite he aspires to on earth".[100] The more grandiose the goal of the romantic the greater the agony – and what is more remote than infinity? The romantic, therefore, is a true separant, blasting away the ecstatic trumpets and reaching out in exalted glory towards the grandeur of an impossible union: ego seeking the object in vain, and in ever-recurring Sisyphean cycles.

The Taoist ideal of *wu wei* (non-action) epitomizes the lethargic non-involvement of the participant social character. Passive lethargy is also of the essence of Nirvana, as apparent from its etymology, which is *nire* cessation of *vritti*: movement.[101] In like manner, Patanjali's exposition of the Raja Yoga is the "process by which one could attain release (*moksha*) or isolation (*kaivalya*) of the soul from involvement with matter and its doings".[102]

The aim of the participant Raja Yoga is *citta vritti nirodha*: the cessation of the movements of the mind. This advocacy of inaction and immobile lethargy stems, *inter alia*, from the participant social character's collective fixation on omnipresent Unity. If plurality is an illusion, what use is there in manipulating a non-existing object? The separant's effort to control or be involved with people and things is a worthless passion. The only reality is the self minus its spatio-temporal consciousness, which is an objectified illusion. The pure person (*Purusha*) is what is left after the awareness of movement, action and plurality is dispersed. The "plenum void" is then felt as the inner expansion of Unity, which expands and dissolves the chimeral world of the senses into the totality of no-objects, no-things and no-consciousness. This is the Taoist principle that "the true mind is no mind (*wu hsin*)".

The separants' conception of the object as real makes for the basic dichotomy of self and object, which trails after it a horde of false dualities of good–bad, right–wrong, strong–weak, and an endless succession of others. These dualities call for choice and judgment, which entangle the self in the infinite swings of dialectical conflict. The participant's anchor on Unity grants him the freedom of infinity unbound by opposites or discrete boundaries of separate objects. Consequently, in the participant's universal Unity the possibilities are endless, so that:

> Something and Nothing produce each other;
> The difficult and the easy complement each other;
> The long and the short off-set each other;
> The high and the low incline towards each other;
> Before and after follow each other.[103]

For the participant, the lethargy of inaction and non-involvement is a source of freedom and power. Lao Tzu sings the praises of detached inaction and advises his disciples that "the sage keeps to the deed that consists in taking no action. . . Do that which consists in taking no action, and order will prevail."[104]

This relates to the blissful inaction of *Unio Mystica*, but even on a more mundane level we may observe that those who were immersed into their inner universe of ideas, while keeping a measure of detachment from their surroundings and non-involvement with their societies, gained some freedom and even power. A Diogenes has less to lose by asking Alexander to move out of his sunlight and a Baruch Spinoza may retain his freedom by refusing the inevitable involvement in the intrigue of a prince's court, which comes together with the job of a philosopher laureate.

The participant social character's passive lethargy towards the object is anchored in Unity. Consequently, the delimiting forms (*rupa*) are hindrances to the path of perfection[105] and have to be dispensed with because forms are of the essence of plurality and generate the trials of relationships. Also tagging, labelling and name-calling are obstacles to participation in Unity, because:

> The way that can be told is not the constant way.
> The name that can be named is not the constant name.
> The nameless was the beginning of heaven and earth.[106]

This is the collective fixation on preconscious Unity, since "The named was the mother of the myriad creatures"[107] and the harbinger of plurality, relationship, *Samsara* and suffering. Conceptual definition should also be avoided because one kills Nirvana by defining it. "For the Extinguished One there is no measure and nothing is there to define him by; when all appearances come to an end. The ways of language, too, have reached a stop."[108]

"The end justifies the means" is essentially a separant–activist maxim, for whom only results count and a worthy failure is a contradiction in terms. On the other hand, the participant is basically a moral social character because morality, i.e. rules of conduct, check, limit and curb behavior. Morality narrows the choice and range of action and, therefore, tows one closer to the participant ideal of inaction. The dynamics of the Tantalus Ratio as related to the social character are the counter-curbing effect of the participant norms on the power-based activism of the separant to reach the objective goal.

The separant Hatha Yoga in the form of Tantrism disregards moral convention and advocates the infringement of norms. The separant Zen awakening entails a release from all convention, including morals, whereas Hinayana Buddhism imposes morals and limiting norms on action in line with its participant ideal of static inaction and lethargy.

Finally, we may end our comparison between separant exaltation and participant lethargy by a musical note: there is a marked similarity among the musical scales of the quietist Hassidim, the self-effacing smoky music of the Middle East and the mystical Gregorian chants. Their music is well suited to the participant's search for the torpor of permanent sleep and the oblivion of temporal extinction. On the other hand, the separant music bursts at its seams with ecstatic pomp and romantic glory. Berlioz's *Requiem*, George Handel's *Messiah* and Ludwig van Beethoven's *Emperor* overpower their audience and engulf all the objects within the range of their sound vibration in a turbulent torrent, which aims to pierce a hole in the sky and carry away with them every particle of Creation.

6 Time and the Void

Relationship within plurality pre-supposes sequence and order, and therefore time. Temporal awareness is of the essence of the separant social character. The future-oriented Protestant Ethic regards the "fruitful", "positive" use of one's time as one of the dimensions of salvation, whereas the materialist dialecticians see temporal determinism, or in their jargon, Historical Necessity, as salvation incarnate. For the participant, time is the dimension of finitude that sustains the forms of matter and determines the sequential order of the spikes on the *Samsara* wheel. The participant seeks constancy in Unity, which is infinite and therefore timeless. The separant social character's collective fixation on the object relates time to space in a dynamic yet inseparable Gestalt, consequently our separant is intrinsically different from Spengler's Faustian cultural archetype, who gives priority to "time, direction and destiny over space and causality".[109] For our separant social character, time and space, and hence direction and causality, belong to the same objective configuration. Consequently, the participant social character's disengagement from the bonds of time entails freedom from the confines of space because the two together make up concrete reality, like two atoms comprising a molecule of matter. When one of the atoms is destroyed or separated, the molecule disintegrates. Our simplistic example is illustrated in a more sophisticated manner by the Hinyana Buddhist state of *Jhana*, which is both a unified one-pointed awareness, i.e. without substance, and focused in one moment (*ekak-sana*) of the present without a past or future, i.e. timeless.[110] In like manner, the participant Sufi achieves his aim when he frees himself from the slavery imposed upon him by the time cycle of objective reality and creates his own subjective time, which is the eternal present of "no time".[111]

The separant social character is "future-oriented" because one has to have a "life plan" to prove one's worth in the here and now as a proof of worth before God. Another reasoning is: "we fast today in order to feast tomorrow"; or because a succession of five-year plans will zigzag us dialectically towards Utopia. "Remember," says Benjamin Franklin, "that time is money,"[112] and money is a sign of Grace, Power and Wisdom in the successful manipulation of objects. Consequently, the separant holds punctuality and timetables in high esteem; he is ruled by schedules, dates and deadlines. He has to "fill the unforgiving minute with sixty seconds of long-distance running". He abhors waste of time or spending it uselessly. He is annoyed if his watch has stopped or does not run properly. He feels guilty if he sleeps late in the morning, even on holidays, and he is gripped by anxiety when he is not certain of the time.[113] The shape of the day as determined by orderly routines encased by fixed time sequences gives the separant a sense of security. It reassures him that by ordering his time he can control the space around him and determine his destiny.

The participant, on the other hand, has a constant sense of temporal failure; being an outsider, a non-participant observer of the daily routines, he is in a better position to see the pointlessness of clinging to the spikes of the *Samsara* wheel. The separant Sisyphean does not have the perspective for it. He is too involved in his ever-failing attempts to overpower the object. The participant longs for infinity. History for him is far from being the omnipotent propellant, the separant prime mover that runs the world. For him, history and time are just whirls and ripples of the *maya* curtain, the veil of illusions that the Upanishadic *Moksha*, the liberation, disperses. The *mayan* illusion is both time and form (*rupa*), which are inseparably bound together. Consequently, the participant's vision of the eternal now involves the dispersion of the obscuring fog of time, sequence and form, and revealing behind it the constancy of Unity.

7 Achievement and Resignation

One of the most conspicuous patterns of the separant social character is the achievement of cultural goals, which involves the active manipulation of one's environment. The desire to achieve a higher social status than one's parents, to gain more money, to acquire more power within the various structures and institutions of society are some of the indices of the separant social character's achievement motivation. Moreover, the normative system as a whole, as well as the cultural imagery in art, communication channels, folklore and education in a given society, reveal the inherent value-judgments favouring or derogating the achievement motive.

For McClelland, the foremost student of the achievement motive in separant societies, the mythological achieving archetype is Hermes: "the patron of the upwardly mobile Athenian merchant entrepreneurs, reflects their aspirations and characteristics, as seen both by themselves and others."[114] The active object manipulator, who is out to swallow the world, is portrayed in quite pejorative epitaphs:

> He is . . . litigious, skilful at making the worse appear the better reason. He lies brazenly to Apollo. He tries a mixture of trickery, bluffing, flattery and cajoling to persuade Apollo to let him keep the cattle, and it succeeds. These are the essential traits of the impudent and smooth-talking self-seeker that haunted the Athenian agora.[115]

The negative value judgment apparent from this portrayal of Hermes, the conniving *arriviste*, does not really support McClelland's contention that Greece of the Homeric "Hymn to Hermes" (circa 520 BC) was an achievement-motivated culture. We might even claim that the whole theme of *hübris*, of exceeding one's lot in life, of *meden agan* (nothing in excess) and having the Gods jealously smite those who leave the Golden Mean, which is so dominant in pre-Socratic Greek culture,[116] is anti-achievement. Hermes might well suit the archetypal imagery of the achiever, but the separant activist who is fixated on the object is more elaborate. Indeed, Max Weber's original conception of the salvation-bound Calvinist portrays in greater depth our object-manipulating upper-mobile activist. According to Weber's thesis, achievement in itself is not the aim, but success, the accumulation of wealth and "making good" in the here and now is proof of ontological and transcendental grace. Consequently, these divine signs of worth should not be exploited, but should be reinvested to augment the overt proof of salvation. This is the separant ideal of fulfilment, determined by his fixation on the object, in which the successful manipulation of one's environment gives one the (illusory, Sisyphean) feeling of incorporating the object into oneself. Therefore, the Protestant Ethic decrees thrift, saving and non-indulgence in worldly pleasures, but to invest and grow rich in power, money and goods so that more objects are amassed within the space of one's personal control. This is echoed in John Wesley's command to his flock: "We must exhort all Christians to gain all they can, and to save all they can; that is in effect to grow rich."[117]

The achievement motive as a trait of the separant social character, which is expounded by the Weberian thesis, should not be confused with the semi-instinctual impulse of acquisition displayed by most fauna and, especially, by ever-greedy Man. Weber aptly phrases this thus: "Pursuit of gain, of money, of the greatest possible amount of money, has in itself nothing to do with capitalism. This impulse exists and has existed among waiters, physicians, coachmen, artists, prostitutes and beggars."[118] For the separant, mere acquisition is not important: what is crucial is that another factory, another bank, another invention, another region, another peak is the successful subjugation of the object "out there", which thereby becomes part of the expanding self. Gothic architecture is the embodiment of the achievement motive, in which each arch and every spire reaches up for the splendour above.

The United States, Western Europe and other pluralistic societies seem to have an abundance of off-beam groups, the aims of which range from political violence to mysticism. Yet even today, for the overwhelming majority of people in countries with a competitive economy, money is the prime yardstick of success. "In some large measure," says Robert Merton, "money has been consecrated as a value in itself; over and above its expenditure for articles of consumption or its use for the enhancement of power."[119] In other words, money in itself as a symbol of worth, and not necessarily the things it can buy, is the separant's proof of grace. The separant is not a hedonist who indulges his pleasures with the material means at his disposal. He is a Sisyphus, always trying to climb higher in an ever-increasing need for reassurance that he can control his stone object. "In the American Dream," continues Merton, "there is no final stopping point. The measure of 'monetary success' is conveniently indefinite and relative. At each level . . . Americans want just about twenty-five percent more (but of course this 'just a bit more' continues to operate once it is obtained)".[120] This, indeed, is the apt portrayal of the Sisyphean – pushing uphill a burden increasingly becoming heavier with time and fatigue.

The achievement motive is, no doubt, ingrained in the young through socialization. There is ample evidence that, due to different accents in the modes of socialization,[121] the activist Protestant is more motivated to achieve than the participant Catholic controls. The Protestant parents and socialization agencies stress self-reliance, independence and self-help, whereas the Catholics stress the authoritarian curbing of activities and the stricter obedience to delimiting norms. One study points out that Catholic parents buy more equipment, e.g. playpens and walking harnesses designed to curb the free activities of children.[122] The ingenious studies of Winterbottom showed that high achievement scores were related to the socialization by parents, especially by mothers to competitiveness, energetic activity and independence.[123] Naturally, in participant societies in which religion has a strong hold on education, socialization will be geared towards implanting in children resigned inactivity and apathy towards worldly success goals.

For the separant social character, achievement is a duty, "a calling", which must be pursued with diligence, thrift, sobriety and prudence.[124] This externalized manipulation of the object is contrasted with the deadly sin of sloth, the passive slumber of lethargic non-doing, which is one of the signs of the participant quietist ideal.

On the social level, the indices for high achievement motivation are the various measures of economic growth, e.g. power and energy outputs, per capita consumption of electricity, number per annum of registered patents, etc.[125] However, the traits of the high-achiever as indicators of the separant social character are more elaborate and quite sophisticated. The separant achiever is "brisk, energetic, restless and dynamic",[126] which relates to the activity dimension of the separant achiever; this dynamism is not free-floating but directional, and is cathected towards a well-defined object. The separant achiever tends to be a traveller.[127] This could well be related to the achiever's efforts to realize his ambitions, but for our context we may visualize the achiever as literally covering more "turf" as a symbolic act of incorporating within his personal space the new places he sees and visits. The separant achiever is a social *arriviste*, a pyramid climber.[128] He aims to break through the traditional and ascribed statuses in order to secure some room at the social top. Social liaisons, including marriage, are planned largely by their upwardly mobile potential to lift one up to the "right people", "the jet set", "the beautiful people", or the social register. The patrician noblesse tend to belittle or even disregard their ascribed statuses; not so the nouveaux riches and the snobs, for whom their achieved status is a reinforcement of their belief in their ability to control their environment. The separant *arriviste* is obsessed with success and failure. For him, "losers" are the generic type "who didn't make it". In a separant culture, the "loser" takes the place of the witch and the bogeyman, to frighten recalcitrant, "bad" children who bring home poor grades. Success is relative. Consequently, the *arriviste* also tries to "achieve" by belittling others and explaining away their success. The Sisyphean climber forever strives upward; consequently, the efforts in themselves cease to be the means and instead become part of the goal. This is so because, deep down, Sisyphus knows that salvation through absolute achievement is a Utopian dream, yet still thinks that one should roll the stone uphill even if it rolls back from time to time. The separant social character sings: "We shall overcome" while bearing his burden. "Be a king in your dreams," preaches Andrew Carnegie. "Say to yourself, 'My place is at the top.'" "The cultural manifesto is clear," says Merton, "one must not quit, must not cease striving, must not lessen his goals, for not failure, but low aim is crime."[129]

The Sisyphean essence of achievement is apparent on all levels of analysis: the subjective–psychological, the relational–interactive and the social. Subjectively, the achievement motive can never be quenched. There is also some evidence that the appetite grows with each new possession, title or position of power. Past achievements are disregarded or taken for granted, whereas future achievements cannot have any sense or measure of fulfilment because in a separant culture, there are no upper limits for aspirations. The separant *arriviste* rows frantically upstream. He goes through all the strenuous motions of moving ahead, and all the gushing torrents with which he has to struggle provide him with an immediate sense of motion; yet in moments of truth, when he looks towards the shore, he realizes that he has not advanced at all. The achiever's maxim of *per aspra ad astra* makes the *arriviste* a frantic racer towards infinity whose subjective perception of distance has no beginning and no end, no departure and no arrival.

The Sisyphean element in the interactive process of achievement is twofold: First, when one strives frantically to achieve a job, a soul-mate, or a position of power, one generates so much antagonistic opposition that one's goal seems harder to achieve the more strenuous one's efforts to gain it. In contrast, when one is nonchalant or emotionally indifferent towards a certain object, one is in a better position to coldly calculate its successful acquisition. Willard Waller illustrates this element in courtship interaction by what he calls "the principle of least interest". Waller says: "That person is able to dictate the conditions of association whose interest in the continuation of the affair is least."[130] And Ross states, in similar vein: "The thing is common and its rule is simple. In any sentimental relation the one who cares less can exploit the one who cares more. In the man–woman relation and the mother–child relation we see this

III

plainly."[131] Our claim is that this least-interest principle holds true not only for courtship behavior but also occurs when striving to achieve any object, position or power.

The other mode of the Sisyphean dialectics of achievement is that after so much intensive and strenuous effort is spent to achieve an object, when it is finally secured, the taste of triumph is flat. The seemingly endless waiting and the exhausting efforts to gain the coveted goal use up ego's energies within the Tantalus Ratio that are cathected towards the specific object, so that no enthusiasm is left for the object itself when it is achieved. The gist of this premise is that ego's chances of gaining love, consideration and social esteem are lower if he strives for them frantically than if he displays towards them a condescending nonchalance.

The least-interest principle might also be a partial explanation for the separant Zen maxim that "By their very seeking for it they produce the contrary effect of losing it."[132] We may envisage the Zen sage Bodhidharma, in a manner that is sure to enrage the orthodox Zen scholars, winking at us in sly scorn and advising that if we wish to get something, we should not be too eager and the desired object will be ours. This is a practical advice for those who wish to manipulate successfully the *Samsara* wheel. Zen indeed concedes that spatio-temporality is a *mayan* illusion, yet one may achieve *Satori* (enlightenment) even in the chimeral context of *Samsara*. Consequently, one has to be involved in *Samsara* and manipulate spatio-temporality to the best of one's ability. The Zen doctrine that one has to try to manipulate objective reality without the impeding load of emotional affectation seems, therefore, a practical advice to the "go-getter", which is only slightly more sophisticated than the advice given in manuals, like "How to succeed in business without really trying". This is the inevitable result of separant Zen's desire to eat one's cake and have it, i.e. its claim that objective reality is an illusion, yet one's involvement in it lends it an operational concreteness, which one might as well turn to one's personal advantage. This should be carried out in a real or feigned nonchalance so that other people's competitive covetousness should not be aroused and impede the effortless acquisition of the desired object.

On the social level, the Sisyphean nature of achievement is linked to the rather complex phenomenon of alienation. Elsewhere we have dealt at length with the serpentine concepts of anomie, anomia, accidie and alienation, and their relationship to the breakdown of human involvement with their groups.[133] We shall discuss this concept in **chapter 5**. It seems that the common denominator of the various expositions of alienation on the social level is the Sisyphean gap between levels of aspiration and levels of actual achievement. The achievement motive breaks down with the failure to manipulate the object in complete fulfilment of ego's aspirations. One reaches a point when one realizes that the objective environment is not as pliable and yielding as one is led to aspire by social norms, and one's desires as determined by the collective fixation on the object. Hegel's exposition of alienation is anchored on the inevitable rift between the world spirit (*der Weltgeist*) as embodied in the self and in its counterpart in the concrete objectiveness of nature. The self's striving to reach absolute totality is countered by the existence of concrete reality. A dialectical relationship ensues in which the self interacts with the object in order to fuse into absolute totality. Yet this is impossible because concrete reality is necessary for the definition of the consciousness of the self. Consequently, this dialectical merry-go-round cycles around itself *ad infinitum*.[134] This, essentially, is the recurring Sisyphean failure to gain full control over the object.

The burden of striving to control the treacherous stone has been imposed on the demi-god by his Olympian elders. The achievement motive ingrained by separant socialization is the mortal counterpart to the Sisyphean stone, and alienation is the inevitable gap between aspirations and actual performance.

The young Marx carries on Hegel's separant ideal of reaching the Absolute Universal Spirit by the dialectical intercourse between subject and object. He follows Hegel in conceiving the realization of Man through his labour. By the creative manipulation of the object, the subject flows over to the object and fulfils itself. "It is just in his work upon the objective world that Man really proves himself as a species being," says Marx, in Teutonic heaviness.

113

This production is his active species-life. By means of it nature appears as his work and his reality. The function of labour is, therefore, the objectification of man's species-life; for he no longer reproduces himself merely intellectually, as in his consciousness, but actively and in a real sense, and he sees his own reflection in a world he has constructed.[135]

But Man's labour in capitalist societies becomes alienated because of *Entausserung*, or "exterioration" of labour.

First, that the work is external to the worker, that it is not part of his nature; and that, consequently, he does not fulfil himself in his work, but denies himself, has a feeling of misery rather than well-being, does not develop freely his mental and physical energies, but is physically exhausted and mentally debased. The worker, therefore, feels himself at home only during his leisure time, whereas at work he feels homeless. His work is not voluntary but imposed, forced labour.[136]

We claim that the assembly line chaplinesque estrangement of the product from the producer is not the exclusive domain of the capitalist system. Every separant culture stressing the pace of production as a function of the achievement of individuals and groups is bound to create the impersonal assembly lines or Kafkaesque halls of push-button clerks in which the object controls the worker, the way Sisyphus is virtually enslaved by his stone. In participant cultures, on the other hand, the created object is an extension of the self: the Persian carpets of Shiraz, the copper inlay of the Damask coffee-trays, the personalized carving of a

Ming Dynasty teapot have indeed absorbed the creative energies of the labourer-artist and become, thereby, the embodied reflections of his aesthetic inner dreams. The participant artisan does not aim to control and overpower his product *qua* object, but to express himself through his creation, which becomes, thereby, a work of art.

Durkheim's exposition of the anomie society is directly related to a Sisyphean breakdown of achievement aspirations. He postulates that when the normative barriers to aspirations in traditional, stable, socially immobile and inactive societies, which would fit in our matrix of the participant social character, are shattered because of rapid social change, the society plunges into a separant spree of achievement. Consequently, the boundless aspirations of the separant social character make fulfilment impossible.

> Nothing gives satisfaction . . . agitation is uninterruptedly maintained . . . Now that (the manufacturer) may assume to have almost the entire world as his customer, how could (his aspirations) accept their former confinement in the face of such limitless prospects? Such is the source of excitement predominating in this part of society (that) the state of crisis and anomie (are) constant and, so to speak, normal. From top to bottom of the ladder, greed is aroused without knowing where to find an ultimate foothold. Nothing can calm it, since its goal is far beyond all it can attain.[137]

This is the incarnation of the Sisyphean curse inherent in the self-defeating achievement motive of the separant social character.

We have mentioned the core expositions of alienation, both Marxist and Durkheimian, and related them to our basic social character typology. Each of the two seemingly divergent expositions of alienation generated mountainous amounts of literature both theoretical and empirical. Georg Lukacs's exposition, in the Marxist tradition of the "reification" of Man, i.e. his becoming an objectified neuter, has much in common with existentialist phenomenological thought,[138] whereas Merton and others, in the Durkheimian tradition, analyze the failure to achieve social goals through culturally sanctioned avenues.[139] Ritualism, for instance, as envisaged by Merton, which is the resigned relinquishing of the achievement motive because of repeated failures and the complete focus on the rigid routines of life, is the modal state of mind of the ageing assembly line employee.

The participant quietist sees wisdom in looking a step ahead beyond alienation, which is a common sequel to the separant achievement motive, and advocates resignation, non-aspiration and the negation of striving. This doctrine is embodied in the third Noble Truth of the Buddha, as expressed in the Hinayana tradition according to the Pali Canon: "And this, brethren, is the Aryan Truth about the ceasing of suffering. Verily it is the utter passionless cessation of, the giving up, the forsaking, the release from, the absence of longing for, this craving."[140] The craving, the desire to grasp (*trishna*), to gain, is *avidya* (ignorance), because one can never quench this craving for achievement. Consequently, by foregoing at the outset the craving for achievement, one escapes from the trials of the Sisyphean cycles of motivation (*Samsara*).[141]

The separant achievement motive may be included in the generic Pali concept of *tanha*, which is the "thirst or craving, causing the renewal of existence (the *Samsara* cycle), accompanied by sensual delight, seeking satisfaction now here, now there – the craving for the gratification of the passions, for continued existence in the worlds of sense".[142] Indeed, the Hinayana doctrine is radical in its approach; it postulates not only the annihilation of desire but also the cessation of object involvement, on which all motivation is based. The Hinayana Nirvana is supposed to be attained, *inter alia*, by the renunciation of greed (*lobha*), hatred (*dosa*) and illusion (*moha*). Note that the craving to possess the object generates the achievement motive; its competitive nature breeds hatred and its ever-augmenting positive feedback nature has a built-in self-defeating illusion. Consequently, the separant achievement motive is the most conspicuous antithesis to the participant ideal of Nirvana. Indeed, one cannot even strive to achieve Nirvana, because the moment one strives for something, an object relationship comes into being; whereas Nirvana is the dying out of relationship, which causes conflict and suffering and resigned dissolution of consciousness into boundless Unity.

Participant Taoism rejects the achievement motive because it involves the active cathexis of energy towards a concrete object. Achievement is "inferior *te* (because it) is active and has an aim",[143] whereas the resigned, quietist, self-defacing Tao is the "superior *te* (because it) is non-active and aimless".[144] It seems that Lao Tzu had a deeper insight into the origins of the achievement motive than contemporary behavioral scientists: they trace its genesis to economic systems and social institutions, whereas he rightly links it to the separant social character's active, purposeful onslaught on the object.

8 Homo Faber and Fatalism

Work, industry and activity, as aims in themselves, are traits of the separant social character quite distinct from the achievement motive. Achievement aims to overpower the object, control it and incorporate it into ego's "personal space"; work aims to link the subjective and objective into a "meaningful" system of relationship. Work became a calling, a vocation and a creed to such varied separant social characters as the Protestant northwestern Europeans, Soviet Russians, Zionist settlers and Maoist Chinese. But for the more participant Catholics, it remained a curse.

The separant "religion of work" brings to fore the Hassidic *Avoda-Begashmiut* – "work in the concrete" – which seeks to reach the Divine Sparks in the object so that a bridge can be built between Divinity in Man and Divinity in the object. Work also involves the rational systematization of the object in relation to ego, and places Ego within the temporal world, irrespective of his position in it. Man's sheer placement within the social system and the structure of things depends on his work. Indeed, work, the cathected activity of Man, has been the perennial basis for the separant expositions of human interaction: from the Hegelian identification of work, action as the catalyzer that unites subject and object within the Universal Spirit, to the Parsonian analysis of action within the infinite permutations of four squares, which make up his social system. Fromm aptly describes the separant *Homo faber*, the industrious social character, as follows:

> In discussing the productive character, I venture beyond critical analysis and inquire into the nature of the fully developed character that is the aim of human development... The "productive orientation" of personality refers to fundamental attitude, a mode of relatedness in all realms of human experience. It covers mental, emotional and sensory responses to others, to oneself, and to things. (Productiveness implies that Man) is guided by reason, since he can make use of his powers only if he knows what they are, how to use them, and what to use them for... Productiveness means that he experiences himself as the embodiment of his powers and as the "actor"... One can be productively related to the world by acting and by comprehending. Man produces things, and in the process of creation he exercises his powers over matter... His power of reason enables him to penetrate through the surface and to grasp the essence of his object by getting into active relation with it.[145]

Fromm presents the productive *Homo faber* as reaching out to the object in a meaningful relationship with it, a relationship that is effected by activity guided by reason. For Fromm, productivity is the panacea for Man's loneliness in the world and he follows, thus, Hegel and Marx in regarding action/work as the saving ontological bridge between ego and the object. And yet Fromm senses the separant's dilemma, for which he gives a pseudo-solution:

> Human existence is characterized by the fact that Man is alone and separated from the world; not being able to stand the separation, he is impelled to seek for relatedness and oneness . . . it is the paradox of human existence that Man must simultaneously seek for closeness and for independence; for oneness with others and at the same time for the preservation of his uniqueness and particularity... the answer to this paradox . . . is productivity.[146]

We can see Sisyphus burst into a painful grimacing leer and retort that Fromm confuses a blessing with a curse. One should ask him if the active link with the object is graceful, or even at all feasible. Granted, ego strives to break out of his ontological loneliness by reaching out to the object – but does he succeed? Sisyphus will point to himself and assure us that Man's ability to interact with the object is limited. One can be very much involved with the object, but as for an everlasting meaningful relationship based on reason, Sisyphus will nod his tortured head in sad despair. The active object manipulators sense many times that "the Universe is out of control". The physicists reach a point in the micro-level of subatomic particles or the macro-level of galaxies where reason and meaning break down into chaos. The frenzied productivity of Man, which is intended to attune him to the object, hastens the destruction of the atmosphere and water tables, and deepens slavery to oil. By supplying nuclear reactors to states like North Korea and Iran, it brings everything closer to the ultimate bang that will fuse ego and object into a macabre unity of *Götterdammerung*.

For the participant Catholic, action, work and any kind of labour are inflicted on man as a curse following the Original Sin. Consequently, the medieval church held the patent participant position that "inactivity and idle contemplation are ways of avoiding sin".[147] The Reformation radically changed the Catholic attitude towards labour, and in line with its separant *Weltanschauung*, regarded it as the prime vehicle to salvation. Luther preached that work is like prayer,[148] and prayer is the manner by which the separant strives to reach the object. We may recall that the Besht saw in *devekut*, devoted prayer, the means of reaching the Sparks of Divinity in the object. Therefore, work became a sacred ritual, a Divine process that links the subject and object together. Consequently: "A cobbler, a smith, a farmer, each has the work of his trade, and yet they are like consecrated priests and bishops."[149] If labour brought an instant of sanctity, work became a duty, a pleasure and a religion all by itself and for itself. Work had also a therapeutic function, because it protected Ego from his anxiety of being alienated from God.[150] In our context, this would mean that work makes Ego feel that the Divinity in himself and the core of Divinity embedded in the object could be linked within the rational and meaningful matrix of action. The temporal world, for the Calvinists, was corrupt and chaotic; only disciplined, strenuous and constant labour could transform it into the Holy Community.[151]

Consequently, Protestantism of the low churches bred a social character for whom "continuous and systematic work"[152] was a calling, a duty, a way of prayer, the core of his faith and *raison d'être*. If one observes Lutheran Germans, the Dutch, the Scots (not the High Church English, who never took their Protestantism seriously and defined a gentleman as one "whose hands are white as a lily") and the Bible Belters, one is struck by the fact that they cannot relax. Even when on vacation, they are intensely busy with their fishing, hunting and motoring equipment, so that outwardly their activity is not less strenuous than in their regular jobs. They look obviously uneasy when they are not occupied with something. Their collective fixation on the object makes them feel guilty if their efforts to reach it are relaxed or suspended even for a moment.

Specialization is the natural outcome of the separant's preoccupation with the object, because it makes for a deeper, more thorough contact with the object and fosters a more intimate acquaintance with it. Yet it is precisely this over-specialization that enhances the Sisyphean plight of the separant: the atomized immersion into a narrow segment of a project turns labour into a mechanical repetitive activity and the workers into "specialists without spirit", engrossed in "mechanized petrification, embellished with a sort of convulsive self-importance".[153] This is Weber's apocalyptic vision of the "lonely crowd" – Sisyphus turning knobs on assembly lines and punching calculator keys at the specialized super-structures of modern megalopolis.

Note the marked similarity between the Occidental *Homo faber* and the activist Zen follower. *Satori*, the Zen enlightenment, takes place within the *Samsara* wheel of spatio-temporal reality. It involves an aware-ness of a goal, a purpose, and the proper means to achieve it. Zen stresses fruitful productiveness, diligence and the industrious performance of one's task as much as the Calvinists and the Boston Bay Preachers. Zen is violently active in trying to reach over to the object. "Zen technique," says Christmas Humphreys "like the explosives used in logging, is designed to break the jam in the river."[154]

The participant social character is a fatalist. He is resigned to his fate because any activity that is goal-directed and designed to affect Man's relationship with the object is less than futile because there is no object and one cannot act and react in a void. Indeed, Mao learned the hard way that a participant social character cannot be changed by decrees. Consequently, the Communist régime, whose very essence is separant activism, had to drag the spirit of Confucius, which still seemed to influ-ence the Chinese social character, from its grave to combat Confucianism's participant maxims of inaction, tranquillity, obedience and fatalism.

For the participant Hinayana Buddhist, *Karma*, which is the temporal condition of Man within the misery of the *Samsara* wheel, is literally "action".[155] Since action, doing, pre-supposes an object relationship that is goal-oriented, the Taoist *Wu-wei*, i.e. non-action, as well as the Buddhist *akarma*, non-directed action, take out the object cathexis from ego's behavior and render it free, i.e. accepting things as they are without striving to disturb the given state of spatio-temporality. The non-action of *Wu-wei* signifies the fatalist acceptance of facts and events, not because one despairs of controlling the object, but because any essence outside the self is either part of the omnipresence of the Tao or flickering illusions too trivial for attention. The reality of the Taoist *Wu-wei* non-action is an inverse growth process that avoids breaking the continuity of Unity; consequently, object relationship is an ontological impossibility.[156] This non-interactive process does not strive or reach out; it yields acceptance. "To yield," says Lao Tzu, "is to be preserved whole." By fatalistically submitting himself to the vicissitudes of his environment, the participant cancels its effect, like training oneself to ignore through acceptance the monotonous drone of heavy traffic or the predictable nagging of a wife.

The fatalistic acceptance of his surroundings permits the participant to ignore them and build up his inner grandeur. "Sicily wanted to sleep," says Di Lampedusa's Don Fabrizio, in spite of (outside) invocations: for why should she listen to them if she herself is rich, if she's wise, if she's civilized, if she's honest, if she's admired and envied by all, if, in a word, she is perfect . . . this sense of superiority (which) dazzles every Sicilian eye, and which we ourselves call pride (is) in reality blindness.157

And yet Don Fabrizio aims to build an inner sanctuary to ward off the miseries of the outside world; but he does not succeed. Participation is a goal, an ideal that, by definition, cannot be attained. The same is true for the Tao, the Nirvana and the *Samadhi*. These are ideal perfect states, the quest of which is ingrained into the social character of the participant by his collective fixation on the bliss of pre-awareness and omnipresent non-differentiation; but their attainment is impossible. The participant, therefore, is a Tantalus seeking perfection in elusive, ethereal, ever-receding Unity – the way the separant Sisyphus chases his galloping object-stone.

9 Nobs and Snobs

The separant social character would tend to be more socially mobile, both vertically and horizontally, whereas the participant is likely to have economic, religious, legal and traditional barriers to his mobility. Many criteria have been devised to measure the social mobility within societies.[158] However, in the present study we are not concerned with measures, but with the most generalized traits that are linked with the social mobility of the participant and separant social characters. Outwardly there would seem to be much resemblance between Ferdinand Tonnies' traditional, integrated and socially stable *Gemeinschaft* and his industrialized, impersonal and diffuse Gesellschaft,[159] and our participant–separant continuum as related to social mobility. However, Tonnies' is more of a macro-sociological description, which naturally ignores motivation and object relationship, which is the backbone of our analysis. This holds true for Weber's description of the traditional and more participant in contradistinction to the instrumentally rational and more separant types of social action.[160]

When we discussed achievement, we studied motivations and aspirations, but here we consider actual mobility, irrespective of covert aspirations. Henri Pirenne, the master historian, describes the fluctuations in mobility in capitalist societies as follows:

It is as if the capitalists, who have up to that time been active, recognize that they are incapable of adapting themselves to conditions which are evoked by needs hitherto unknown and which call for methods hitherto unemployed. They withdraw from the struggle and become an aristocracy which if it again plays a part in the course of affairs, does so in a passive manner only, assuming the role of silent partners; in their place arise new men, courageous and enterprising, who boldly permit themselves to be driven by the wind actually blowing and who know how to trim their sails to take advantage of it.[161]

This is the process in which the separant social character turns into a passive élite, non-active participant who leaves the stage for another layer of social-climbers to try and make good. Di Lampedusa's patrician Don Fabrizio chooses to rest on his ascribed laurels and live the passive life of an onlooker. He lets Don Calogero, the nouveau riche wheeler-dealer, be elected to the senate, because having been at the upper social strata for a very long time, Don Fabrizio cannot be excited by high class; the empty rituals of high status bore him and he has lived long enough to see that Sicily ended up the worse with every new wave of social change. The participant Don Fabrizio chooses the constancy of quiet non-involvement, made possible by the comforts of his ascribed status.

The major characteristic of the separant social-climber is his insatiable hunger for the object. His quest to reach or possess the object is different in essence from the achiever's wish to prove his worth with his material possessions; the social-climber needs his acquisitions as a status symbol. He is not an ascetic or frugal hoarder of wealth, but rather a show-off, conspicuous consumer. The quest for the object would make the social-climber rush after it from place to place, but his ultimate objective is upper mobility. Consequently, he would be attuned to people, especially to those whom he defines as instrumental in securing him a "room at the top". His emphatic focus on other people is not made with the aim of achieving dialogic rapport with them, but relates to their social status *vis-à-vis*

himself. The attitude of the social-climber towards people would be as to objects in the Existentialist sense. The separant's hunger for people, which is linked to his collective fixation on the object, is not for friendship and emotional solace, but as an affirmation of the "right" status. He seeks to achieve this by being seen in the company of the "beautiful people," by being invited to the yacht of Onassis, by going with *tous Paris* to the charity ball organized by Madame Guy de Rothschild, or being thrown into the Kennedy swimming pool. He is not seeking approval in the Douglas Crowne–David Marlowe sense, in order to reinforce a vulnerable self-esteem.[162] Neither is he motivated by McClelland's affiliation, i.e. "establishing, maintaining or restoring a positive affective relationship with another person",[163] which in non-jargonized language simply means friendship; the social-climber's "other directedness"[164] is mainly related to the "status cues" of other people that indicate the "right" occupation and the "proper" behavior for "a person like me". Consequently, the upper-mobile separant is a "joiner". He joins the voluntary organizations that would ensure his exposure to members of his reference groups to whose status he aspires. The separant social-climber, being attuned to the "relevant others" who pass judgment on his eligibility for membership in their group, would do his utmost to convey to them his posture and the modes of behavior and attitudes that he thinks would meet with their approval. The vertically upper-mobile separant is essentially a poseur, an actor constantly wearing a mask moulded for him by the expectations of the élites in his reference groups.

Morality, i.e. the normative checks on the choice of means to gain a higher status, is relatively ignored by the social-climber. Morals are internalized controls that would hamper the free, ready and "natural" pose and demeanour of the "pyramid climber" as required by the current *arbiter elegantiarum* and the social pacesetters.

Social Darwinism reigns here in the sense of the survival of the fittest. Those who do not comply with the rather elaborate and shifting expectations of the significant others would topple down from the social pyramid replete with the corroding bile of *ressentiment*. The upper-mobile separant will climb the social ladder better if he does not get unduly attached to people on his way up. This might mar his clear judgment as to the best ways and means to reach up to another echelon on the social ladder. The social-climber must adhere to his view of other people as objects, as inanimate things. Finally, the mobile social character is more likely to be bred by an industrialized, urbanized, commercialized and secular social setting. Conversely, an agricultural, rural, traditional and non-technological social setting is less likely to breed the "rags to riches" Horatio Algers or the likes of Somerset Maugham's snob in *The Razor's Edge*.

The participant of contemporary cultures' collective fixation on the static constancy of inaction tends to confine and limit social mobility by ascribed statuses guarded by the grace and sanctioned by the damnation of God. Indeed, India, which is one of the most participant contemporary cultures, still bars social mobility by the rigidly ascribed statuses of the caste system. Tradition, which lends normative support to class, status and the whole social structure, is also a strong barrier to mobility. This is made apparent by the classical exposition by Weber, who said, *inter alia*:

> The derivation of the legitimacy of an order from a belief in the sanctity of tradition is the most universal and most primitive case. The fear of magical penalties confirms the general psychological inhibitions against any sort of change in customary modes of action. At the same time, the multifarious vested interests which tend to become attached to upholding conformity with an order, once it has become established, have worked in the same direction.[165]

Laws, customs, mores and economic obligations may virtually bind people to geographical locations: the feudal system in medieval Europe, the permanent binding of the Russian peasant to an aristocrat's plot of land during the reign of the tsars, and the lifetime tenancy of the Middle Eastern fellahin to the lands of the Effendis are some representative illustrations. Status is also a strong barrier to mobility. Finally, in savage societies in which each individual mystically partakes in the common totemic soul, social mobility is pointless.[166] These societies, which would probably be placed on the very extreme pole of participation, clearly show the inverse relationship between the participant social character and social mobility. In like manner, social mobility to the Hinayana Buddhist, for whom any kind of struggle within the *Samsara* wheel of becoming is both

121

futile and vile, is one of the manifestations of *dukkha*, the painful misery of relationship, including social interaction. The participant Taoist, Hinayana Buddhist and the Upanishadic yogi would abhor social mobility as the composite incarnation of the inevitable suffering of action and the lying illusions of object relationship.

10 Salvation and Utopia

Dealing with subjects that have been documented so well, such as Utopia, is both exasperating and frustrating. If one dares to ignore previous analyses, one risks the adventure of the poor devil from a remote mountain village in Tibet who recently invented the bicycle all by himself. On the other hand, if one chooses to delve into the previous expositions, one wages a losing battle with the colossal minds of the likes of a Karl Mannheim. Yet we have no choice but to relate conceptually at least to Mannheim's Utopian mind. Our separant social character seems to be quite apart from Mannheim's Utopians. The revolutionary who actually undertakes to topple an existing "*utopia*" (social order) according to some wish-image embodied in ideologies is a Utopian as per Mannheim's definition.[167] Our separant aims much higher. He wishes to achieve complete harmony between subject and object. This is a true Utopia, which is literally "no-place", because no one has ever succeeded to attune oneself completely to one's object, although the separant Sisypheans will forever try to reconcile themselves with their stones. Mannheim's Utopia is a state of existence that is unattainable relative to the point of view of a given social order,[168] whereas the separant's Utopia is absolutely unattainable from any point of view, although he never ceases striving towards it due to his fixation on the object. For Mannheim, Utopias are spatial wish-images, whereas temporal wish-images are chiliasms.[169] Our separant aims for perfect attunement with the object on both the temporal and spatial dimensions when these two are also in harmony between themselves. It seems that our conception of the separant Utopia is more in line with the conventional sense of the term as expressed by the socio-political structures dreamed up by a Plato or a Thomas More. These are the subjective visions of the separant projected on the object in an integrated and ordered schema that does not allow for any dishevelling or frustrating disjuncture between ego and his objective entourage. This Utopian vision is projected into space at a future point of time, but the process leading to it is dialectic. The present rather chaotic disarray is jostled to its antithesis by a conflictual quake. A stable state is momentarily formed, only to be pushed into another dialectical zigzag and so on, *ad infinitum*, which must contain, as per the separant vision, somehow, somewhere in its fluctuations the philosophers' stone, which will perform the alchemy of closing the rift between ego and the object. Utopia is as necessary for the object-manipulating separant as Sisyphus' determined optimism that eventually he will reach a *modus vivendi* with his stone. The separant

Utopian, irrespective of his political label, cathects his frenzied energies towards the object in order to mould it, with himself as visionary, into the Just Society, the Classless Society or the Great Society. The participant, on the other hand, abhors history. For him, it is not a necessity but bondage. He aims to rid himself from the object altogether by destroying his awareness, which binds him to the concrete. His fixation on pre-differentiated omnipresence makes him seek salvation in timeless spaceless Unity. "Nothing so much hinders the soul from knowing God," says Eckhart, "as time and space. . . if the soul is to perceive God, it must stand above time and space. . . if the soul is in the act of taking a leap beyond itself, and entering into a denial of itself and its own activities, it is through grace."[170] This is the Tantalic "leap of faith" into the unknown and the unattainable, because without time there are no measurements and without space no one knows the distance to salvation. Between inactive unity and salvation one has to pass through oblivion, but this in itself is a relationship and a sequence in time, so that we are once again back at an insoluble paradox. The participant seeking salvation is a Tantalus chasing a *fata Morgana*, whereas Sisyphus, on the other side of the continuum, makes his rock look like the philosophers' stone of Utopia.

There is essentially no intrinsic difference, for our purpose, among the various types of Utopia described by Mannheim. The Chiliasts, who are kindled by a messianic outburst of revolutionary energy, are not aiming towards the ever-after, but like the anarchists, their contemporary counterparts, they aim to disrupt the here and now into a lawless paradise. Yet this vision of the world to come is the projection of an ecstatic Thomas Münzer on an activist God who would surely lend a helping hand to mould the object according to the exact specifications of the Chiliast prophet. In like manner, the anarchist Utopia of a Michael Bakunin is as paradoxical, contradictory and chaotic as its author's mind. The liberal Utopia is anchored in the evolutionary process of progress: the optimism of "tomorrow is another day" and "things do turn up to be better if one has perseverance and patience to wait". The Kiplingesque Man projects his "ifs" onto the object and eventually, despite all the trials, people, things and beast are moulded into Utopia, with ego in the guise of Superman supplying the proper happy ending to nursery rhymes.

Surely, the Utopia of the Chiliast Hassidim is a far cry from the apocalyptic visions of a Herbert Marcuse or a Franz Fanon, yet both display separant object relationship. The Besht links himself to the object by *devekut* (devoted prayer), but the dialectics of violence fuse Man and things somewhere towards the end of time, within the harmony of the Hegelian "universal spirit". Words, jargon and images differ, but the separant brands of Utopia are very much alike, as well as the processes allegedly leading to them.

Utopia is an active process of becoming, whereas salvation is a reflexive extinction of the self. The participant does not fight objective reality; he disperses it into oblivion by blotting out its awareness. He hankers with

Di Lampedusa's Don Fabrizio for "voluptuous immobility" and the saving grace of his collective fixation on omnipresent Unity. The participant does not pray to God because his inner sense of perfection, when projected outwards, makes him synonymous with God. The quest for salvation through the quietist dissolution of the self into Unity was shared by Taoism, Hinayana Buddhism, the Gnostics, the Mithras cultists, the Muslim Sufis, the disciples of Eckhart and the Maggid of Mezherich. This quest is echoed in the prayer of Markos the Gnostic, who wished "that thou mayst be what I am and what thou art. . . I in thee, and thou in me!"[171] This is also the participant aim of terminating the ontological loneliness of the self by its reciprocal fusion with the object so that "the false and separative self is slain and the true self [the universal Buddha, *Atman*, *Purusha*, Tao or Nirvana] steadily developed".[172] The participant just about to reach Nirvana recognizes the futility of the Sisyphean's desperate efforts to control the object. "Thus Nirvana," says Alan Watts "is the equivalent of *Moksha*, release or liberation. Seen from one side, it appears to be despair – the recognition that life utterly defeats our efforts to control it, that all human striving is no more than a vanishing hand clutching at clouds."[173] Well, we were cautious and specified that the aspiring Buddhist is just about to reach Nirvana, because if he did, we shall never know it. Also, striving for Nirvana is a contradiction in terms so strongly elucidated by the separant Mahayana and Zen Buddhists. The clever, almost too clever solution of the Japanese Zen is not to search strenuously for *Nirvana* in the away and beyond of the void, but to find *Satori* (the Zen salvation awakening) in the readily available spatio-temporality, with the obvious result that Zen co-exists with a most activist, rabidly competitive object-manipulating culture. So when one seems just about to get hold of Nirvana, it vanishes into the fumes of the Yokohama chimney forests and the endless rows of almond-eyed girls assembling transistors at Mitsubishi. This is a re-enactment of the Tantalic myth in Kabuki attire, replete with receding mirages and dire metamorphoses.

We have now traced the traits of the separant social character, with its vigorous cathexis on the object and the self-defacing participant drifting effortlessly towards blissful oblivion and reawakening in Unity. This rather abstract, paradigmatic analysis has to be anchored on some initial empirical referent. In **chapter 4** we shall illustrate our polar social characters by the Jews and Arabs conflicting and contrasting with one another in Israel (and previously in Palestine). This chapter will conclude with a synthesis between the separant Sisyphean and Tantalic personality types (as expounded in **chapters 1 and 2**), and the separant and participant social characters as analyzed above.

Jews and Arabs

4

The Relationship between Personality Types and Social Characters

No worry, fear or weakness. We, our fathers and forefathers, dreamt from time immemorial of a State of Israel, and now this dream becomes a reality, and our eyes shall see the State of Israel from Dan to Beersheba, if not further on . . . and this sweet and strong link which ties us to the heroes of Israel fighting the Philistines, shattering the Greek altars and defending the stronghold of Massada . . . We are sure to win. How can it be otherwise?

Moshe Salomon, *Scrolls of Fire* (from the diaries of Israeli youths who fell in action during the War of Independence)

I have no political power and I cannot possibly have any political aspirations. I embody in my existence an absurd: I have to be neutral in a conflict of which I myself am the object. The two nations have an equal historical right to the same piece of land. Each one has his own truth and I am very pessimistic. It seems to be God's wish that the Arabs and Jews live side by side, but he forgot to tell them how to do it.

Haidar Akal, an Arab student at a Jewish University

Jews and Arabs: An Illustration

In **chapter 3** we analyzed the Sisyphean and Tantalic social characters on a rather high level of abstraction. For didactic and illustrative purposes we drew our examples from the extreme cases on our continuum: Taoism and Hinayana Buddhism on the far participant pole and the Protestant Ethic and the American Dream of the far separant extreme. We found it best to illustrate our empirical referents by middle-range cases that were not too extreme. Although extreme cases do highlight the contours of an abstract argument and tie our theoretical argument to an initial empirical outpost, it is more useful to use as illustrations some modal types of social characters, as far as their placement on the separant–participant continuum is concerned. Jews and the Palestinian Arabs have been exposed to each other's cultures, often violently, for the greater part of a century; the contrasts between them are readily comparable since they have co-existed side by side within the confines of a relatively small area. Hence, their relationship will illminate in bold relief the separant–participant continuum.

The predominant cultural profile of the Jewish *Yishuv* (the pre-independence Jewish community in Palestine) was strongly influenced by Ashkenazi Jews, who were mostly of East European origin and who brought with them to Palestine a hybridized *Weltanschauung* of European culture, as absorbed by and adapted to the East European Jewish mentality. This generalized statement is bound to enrage professional cultural anthropologists, yet no statement about any cultural attribute of the Jews, which is inevitably complex, may pass the carnivorous scrutiny of the critics, unless it has a serpentine chain of saving clauses or provisos or if it rests on such a high level of abstraction that it means almost anything, i.e. nothing. Thus we shall try to steer between the Scylla of over-complexity and the Charybdis of ethereal abstractions by relying heavily on original statements and sources, and leaving the final judgment to the reader. We shall, however, mention an observation on cultural osmosis that seems to apply to East European Jews, who were the political and cultural élite of the *Yishuv* and are still the dominate power in present-day Israel. Raphael Patai, an anthropologist who has researched contemporary Middle Eastern culture, noted:

> It has been observed that the Jews tend to assimilate to their environment in relation to the cultural enticement it offers them. German Jews, for instance, were a more assimilated group than the Polish, because German culture had more to offer them than Polish culture. Actually, this is but the specifically Jewish variant of a general tendency observable in culture contact situations: it is in the higher type of culture which is more readily absorbed by those originally partaking of a culture which they feel to be of a lower type.[1]

We may safely conclude, therefore, that the *mélange* of Western European culture, as filtered through the East European ghettos and *shtetls,* dominated the social structure and institutions of Palestinian Jewry. This holds true for the Israeli cultural scene, although Ashkenazi Jews are not a numerical majority in Israel; Oriental Jews (Jews who immigrated to Israel from areas formerly under the Ottoman Empire, together with a relatively small number of Ladino-speaking Sephardic Jews) constitute approximately 60 percent of the population. Consequently, except for religious ritual and some assorted folkloristic mores, Ashkenazi East European patterns of culture, overlaid by some West European lacquer and polish, dominated the Palestinian Jewish community's social institutions and cultural system. Naturally, these patterns served as the starting point for the development of what may be called the Jewish Israeli social character during more than fifty years since the establishment of the State of Israel. There seems to be little doubt that the ideological founding fathers and the cultural ancestors of the nation's élite were members of the Second Aliya: the wave of Jewish immigration from Eastern Europe, which started in the middle of the first decade of the twentieth century. The crucial part played by the Second Aliya in moulding the ideology, values and cultural traits of the Israeli labour movement, which constitutes the cultural and power élite of Israel, is attested by one of its leaders, who says:

> We, the vast majority of the labour movement, those who came here many years after the beginning of the Second Aliya and those who were born and grew up in this country, all of us feel around us the atmosphere of the Second Aliya which virtually reared us and which ingrained its imprint on everything which happened in the Jewish community. This is largely due to the fact that the core of the Second Aliya is also the core of all the communal settlements (Kibbutzim) as well as the labour organization. Moreover, every one of us wishes to partake of the spirit and values of the Second Aliya.[2]

The Second Aliya has been a reference group, an ideological anchor as well as a source of values for the vast majority of the Jewish population in Palestine.

The social character of these founding fathers may be gleaned from some original documents and letters written by the members of this Second Aliya. The late David Ben-Gurion uses in his Jubilee Address activist expressions that we have identified as characteristic of the separant social character. He talked about the industry and perseverance of the pioneers: their social interests in communal living, in education, in managerial organization, in the political power of the Jewish community and its labour force, in continuous fighting for Jewish labour against cheaper Arab labour in Jewish settlements. He constantly used the expression "to conquer" whenever he mentioned learning Hebrew, acquiring land and introducing Zionism to the youth of the Diaspora. Above all, he stressed, in separant fashion, the value of work and labour not as a means but as a goal in itself.[3] Another leader of the labour movement described the Second Aliya as the bridgehead for the forces of progress breaking out from the ghetto to build a new life.[4] Again, we have the image of a forceful liberation from the confines of the lethargic and fatalist resignation of the ghetto life and a surging out to control one's fate in a new environment. Of special importance is the cultivation of the land and the direct contact with Nature,[5] which stands in direct contrast to the peddlers, shopkeepers, the scholars and the detached *Luftmensch* of the Diaspora. This exists in the realm of the separant's quest of the object, in contradistinction to the manipulation of ideas and the intellectual self-sufficiency of the yeshiva scholar. The Second Aliya had many ideological upheavals and conflicts, mainly between radical leftist factions adhering to "pure" Marxism, which they imported from their native Russia, and nationalist Zionists.

127

Eventually, an ideological synthesis of socialist Zionism was reached and, with a few variations, it became the professed ideology of the Israeli labour movement to the present day. Finally, the Second Aliya members were largely puritan ascetics who pursued their activist goals of building new settlements and a new society very much like the founding fathers of the American Dream who were kindled by the Protestant Ethic of fulfilment through work.

Nevertheless, the *prima facie* separant traits of the Jewish Israeli social character do not indicate an extreme separantism. In like manner, but in the opposite direction, Muslim Palestinian Arabs display a participant social character, but less so than Taoists or Hinayana Buddhists, who negate time, space and worldly involvements and ambitions, which seem to be pointless, and hence are on the extreme participant pole of our continuum. This view is upheld by Patai:

> To regard this world as one of "suffering and change" as "a tiny shore which must be left" in an urge to reach "the infinite expanses of the Great Void" is not typical of the whole of the Orient but only of South Asian culture, as exemplified by Hinduism . . . Middle Eastern culture has avoided this extreme.[6]

Most Palestinian Arabs are Sunni Muslims, which is the dominant religious sect in Islam. Islam dominates the culture, the values and the way of life of the Arab, even if he is not religiously observant in the strict sense of the word.[7] The participant core of Islam is already apparent in its name, which literally means resignation and giving oneself up to God.[8] Islam anchors itself on Unity (*tawhid*) and on the participant doctrine of relating the multiplicity of appearances inwardly towards one centre.[9] "Islamic art," says Seyyed Hossein Nasr, "seeks always to relate the multiplicity of forms, shapes and colours to the One, to the Centre and Origin, thereby reflecting *tawhid* (Unity) in its own way in the world of forms with which it is concerned."[10] This is the mandala-like strain from the circumference inwards towards central Unity. Also Sufism, which is the mystical component of Islam, is ingrained in the main current of religious doctrine, unlike the mystical trends in Christianity, which were regarded by the Ecclesia as esoteric and sometimes treated as heresy, or in Judaism, where mysticism was shrouded in obscurantist secrecy and became the realm of the initiated few. The historical reasons for the prominence of mystical Sufism in Islam may be attributed to the fact that Al-Ghazali, who had in Islam a stature equivalent to St. Thomas in Christianity or to Maimonides in Judaism, effected in the eleventh century a synthesis between the doctrine of the orthodox Muslim Ulama and the mystical teaching of the Sufis. Since then, the participant *Weltanschauung* of the Sufis was institutionalised within mainstream Islam.[11] Consequently, the participant Sufi doctrine permeated the cultural system of the Middle East and had a major role in moulding the social character of the Palestinian Arab.

The foremost participant doctrine of Sufism is that the spatio-temporal self must die in order to become aware of one's eternal essence (*azal*).

Figuratively, this is analogous to a snake peeling off its skin.[12] The goal of Sufi participation is "the liquefaction of the outer crust of man's being, thus revealing to Man his own divine centre, which is the 'Throne of the Compassionate' (*arsh al-rahman*)".[13] Of special importance for our present theoretical structure is that this Sufi quest for the inner infinite being, through the dissolution of the outer shell of the finite being, is a continuous and constant driving force that determines Man's behaviour throughout his existence. This is very much like our basic participant vector of the personality core, which constantly presses for the dissolution of the ego boundary and for ontological extinction, yet is never attainable throughout Man's temporal existence.

The collective fixation of participant Sufism on the original bliss of pre-differentiated omnipresence is apparent from its mystical goal, which is the perfect stature of *ahsan taquim*,[14] the primordial bliss of Man before he was separated from the Divine Presence. The longed-for omnipresence of the individual *separatum* is achieved when Man and the cosmos become interchangeable, i.e. when the individual soul unites into the universal cosmic soul. "Everything which is in the cosmos," says the Sufi Master, "is to be found in the soul; equally, everything in the soul is in the cosmos. Because of this fact, he who masters his soul most certainly masters the cosmos, just as he who is dominated by his soul is certainly dominated by the whole cosmos."[15] However, the most conspicuous evidence for the Sufi collective fixation on the unlimited bliss of pre-awareness is its professed goal of a spiritual return to the Edenic state not in the ever-after but in the here-and-now by the effusion of the inner image of perfection through the burst seams of the boundaries of the self into the omnipresent Universal Man (*al-insan al-Kamil*).[16] This reminds one of the Gnostic and Kabbalist primordial man, but Gnosis and the Kabbalah never achieved the influential stature that Sufism gained through its official integration into the main stream of Islam. The Sufi participant quest for annihilation, for the defacement of the self and the release from plurality into Unity, thus stamps its indelible mark on the Arab social character and its participant traits.

The social characteristics of Middle Eastern Arabs have been described by anthropologists, travellers, politicians and novelists as Levantinism. We have already pointed out the complexity of this concept and the heterogeneity of the phenomena that it purports to describe; our sociological definition of Levantinism was the shallow absorption of the patterns of one culture by another.[17] This definition of one of the attributes of social change, which is not confined to the Middle East, is outside our present context. We are not concerned here with cultural change as such, but with the placement of a given social character on our separant–participant continuum based on some of its conspicuous traits. Indeed, our task is similar to the one undertaken by a cubist painter who uses the conspicuous, seemingly unrelated characteristics of an object to create his compositions.

The origins of Palestinian Arabs have never been fully unearthed from the turbulent and chaotic history of the Middle East. However, it can be stated that the overall Islamization of the majority of the inhabitants of Palestine was a gradual process that began in the seventh century when Muslim armies conquered Palestine from the Byzantine Empire. The indigenous population, which was a heterogeneous conglomeration of ethnicities and religions, soon learned the advantages of becoming Muslim, especially when all the disciples of the Prophet Muhammad were automatically exempt from taxes.[18] Gradually, the Palestinian Arabs' social character crystallized over the centuries and it is generally believed that both the Crusaders' and the Turkish rule were too external and superficial[19] to effect any crucial changes in its major traits. The social character of the Palestinian Arab is the result of a continuous process of "Arabization" by an endless flux of the nomadic Bedouin tribes who chose to exchange their harsh and precarious existence as herdsmen, smugglers and highway robbers for the softer and more prosperous life of the fellahin, the rural peasants who constituted the great majority of the Palestinian Arab population.

The conflicts between the two divergent social characters of Jews and Arabs may be interpreted by a political frame of reference that is imperative, but relates only to a small segment: the external, visible parts of the iceberg, of the cultural divergencies between the two cultures. A deeper analysis reveals the intrinsic polarities of the two social characters in every possible area of contact. Consequently, the relationship is almost never a cultural intercourse but a cultural clash. Thus, we observe that except for several numerically insignificant movements mostly sponsored by Jewish intellectuals for peaceful coexistence between Jews and Arabs, and the "Canaanites" who preached for the estrangement from traditional Judaism and integration within the indigenous Middle Eastern culture, the relationship between the two cultures has constantly been marked by misunderstanding, strife and hatred. It is quite typical that Jews sponsored these two movements for cultural *rapprochement*. From the outset, the Arabs were dismayed over and antagonistic towards the influx of Jewish foreigners, who it seemed had covetous designs on the land and who were importing a bizarre and vulgar culture.[20] If the antagonism of the urban Arab population towards the Jews had a predominantly political base, the rural fellahin were opposed to the Jews on a wider cultural basis: the fallah regarded the Jew as a barbarian who was ignorant of the elaborate participant mores and ritual so important in the Arab peasant's way of life. The Jews "cannot speak", i.e. the Jew is oblivious of the elaborate verbal preliminaries and courtesies that have to be exchanged among civilized people (namely Arabs) when they meet. He is a "heathen who does not know God" and lets his women walk like prostitutes half-naked and in shorts.[21] "The Jews," said an Arab coachman in abrupt finality, summarizing his views on the subject of cultural contact between Jews and Arabs, "have never known us and we never managed to acquaint ourselves with them."[22] This cultural distance, despite a geographical proximity, becomes understandable when we contrast in the following pages the social characters of Jews and Arabs in Palestine according to the ten pairs of variables representing the separant–participant polarities described and analyzed earlier.

East is East and West is West

"There is nothing which can stand against the Will. If there is a Will, the dream comes true." This was the separant credo of Theodor Herzl, the founder of Zionism. If one wishes strongly enough, one can successfully manipulate one's environment. The ability to reach out to the object and subjugate it to one's will has been the unwavering belief of the Zionist pioneers. Toil, hardship and suffering are the inevitable corollaries of fighting one's hostile environment, but the brave and persevering ones shall overcome. This is the message preached by Joseph Vitkin, another founding father, to his pioneer disciples. "Your goal shall be achieved only after immense toil and heavy casualties, and wars, constant wars with nature, men, disease and hunger, but your war has to be a war of deeds and not of words."[23] The activist object manipulator believes in action, not in words, symbols or intentions; but the action must be properly harnessed and applied to the object in a rational and organized manner; only then shall it yield to Ego's will. The Second Aliya pioneers were not self-oriented, but always related themselves to action, to others and to the land, while stressing that their mode of action *vis-à-vis* the object was struggle. They constantly spoke of the conquest of labour in the Jewish settlements over cheaper and more experienced Arab labour as a goal equivalent in importance to the conquest of land, i.e. the acquisition of increasing amounts of soil for agriculture and of land for new settlements.[24] The vigorous pent-up pioneering spirit of the founding fathers seemed to be cathected in a frenzied ecstasy towards their new surroundings. The following striking imagery used in a corporation charter by a group of settlers from the First Aliya is another illuminating illustration of our premise: "The toil of the hands and the sweat of the brow ties the created object to its creator by links of guts and nerves which will never be severed again."[25] This is the separant activist ideal of synchronizing the subject and object into everlasting harmony. The Second Aliya founding fathers were possessed by labour, constant activity and the need to complete one task and immediately look for another; idleness was the ultimate sin, because it made one resemble the lethargic Arab fellah. There can be no failure and if one attempt is not successful, one must start all over again,[26] with Kiplingesque determination to go through another Sisyphean cycle.

In contradistinction to the well-intentioned and functional activism of the Jewish settler, the fellah is enmeshed in magic threads woven around

131

himself. Oswald Spengler has described the social character of the fellahin quite perceptively, although he did not posses first-hand knowledge. He envisaged the fellah as being passively subject to "planeless happening": concrete reality and events do not fall into a meaningful relationship with his person. To him, they are devoid of significance; it is as if they occur on a different plane of spatio-temporality.[27] This vicarious impression of the fellah is upheld by the first-hand and moving account of the Egyptian village by Taufiq El-Haquim. He depicts the fellah as downtrodden by the feudal landowners, the government and corrupt law-enforcers. His blood is poisoned by the parasites of the Nile waters and his vision is dimmed by trachoma. The misery of the external world is too formidable for his senses so he finds refuge in his inner world of fantasies and make-believe.[28] He rejects the viability of outside reality and accepts the constant lies of the people around him as part of his absurd surroundings. He believes in his failing senses least of all. If the separant Jewish pioneer believes in deeds and not in words, the Arab fellah is entranced by symbols and words. He is carried away by verbosity. His inwardly directed imagination is so fierce that symbols and words make up his inner reality. He puts so much energy and force into the articulation of words and the sacred synonyms of God and the Prophet that deeds become superfluous. When an Arab talks about his prospective ventures, he does so with so much flowery imagery and intense elaboration that the words become imbued with a magic essence of their own and deeds seem to be *de trop*.

The Jewish pioneers were fiercely anti-religious, partly in reaction against the scholarly religiosity of the Diaspora Jew. In contrast, the participant Arab fellah is pantheistically immersed in a creation that is part of an omnipresent God. The constant evocation of the ever-present Divinity bears witness to the fellahin's collective fixation on early non-differentiated Unity. The Muslim creed, laced with generous doses of Sufi mysticism, makes the Arab snap quite often into participant stretches of self-seeking oblivion. It is not an uncommon sight in an Arab village to see some fellahin crouched with their legs tucked under their bellies, in the style of the Orient, and their gaze transfixed for hours on the flow of water in an irrigation channel or on the half-crescent on top of a mosque. Temporary self-oblivion and dimming of awareness is also sought after by the myriads of Middle Eastern coffee-house patrons who sit long hours in lethargic, almost catatonic postures, sipping Turkish coffee and smoking water-pipes, sometimes loaded with hashish.

The strong mystical Sufic undercurrent in Islam effected its essential negation of spatio-temporality. Together with the Hellenistic neo-Platonists, the Gnostics and the Kabbalists, it longs for the extinction of the multiplicity of self and its remerger into pantheistic Unity. The Sufi Master leads his disciple by the proper method (*tariqah*) to shed the outer peels of his cognition and make the divine core of his self-travel inwardly to the transcendental centre of spaceless Unity and the Divine Presence (*Hudur*).[29] The Sufi *tariqah* effects, so to speak, a transcendental voyage not within time or space, but outside and beyond spatio-temporal dimensions altogether. The participant goal of Sufism is to annul the ontological separation of Man from his Divine origin. One has therefore to annihilate one's self and die to the world of the senses, greed and temptation, although one may still be in the midst of it. Sufism is the "Muhammadan poverty" of the soul, which is not being seduced by the chimeral enticements of temporality.[30] The goal of the Sufi, as defined in a nutshell by Junayd, "is that God makes thee die to thyself and become resurrected in Him".[31] Without the religious terminology, this Sufi formula is precisely the direction taken by our participation vector and its aim of annulling separate awareness and reverting to nonbeing.

Like extremely participant creeds, the Muslim does not regard the objective world as a *mayan fata Morgana*. Instead, he holds the involvement with the object as a futile pastime, very much inferior to the contemplative involvement with the self. For the Sufi, action and tools to manipulate his environment are necessary for coping with the vicissitudes of existence, but he regards the Western obsession with gadgets and the separant's hyper-activism as an avenue for salvation, as the epitome of folly.

The Arab is virtually engulfed by rituals that cushion him into a cocoon of magic meanings that lead somewhere to the far away and blunt the painful friction of object relationship. We claim that the rituals, manners and politesse of the Arab in his intercourse with other people is a participant means to blunt the separant trials of deprivation and suffering inherent in human interaction. It is impolite, for instance, to contradict an Arab's statement, because this either makes him a liar or an ignoramus.[32] Consequently, Arab repartee is an endless chain of mutual consensus and each party tries to excel in praising the wisdom of the other. A Westerner who is enraged when a "promise" made by an Arab is not kept, misses the point. The Arab did not want to offend him by not promising to grant his request, although he knew quite well that he could not make his promise good. The fellah may have despised the direct and "functional" approach of the European and adjudged him as coarse and impolite, but how could he offend his guest by declining to grant his wish. To do business with a fellah, one should make the subtle evaluation beforehand – what he can and cannot do – and not force him to promise to supply goods he cannot possibly deliver. He must make promises, as ordained by the canons of the participant ritual, which, in turn, softens the sharp spikes of interaction. It was quite inevitable that the practical, goal-directed Jewish pioneers, who valued "deeds and not words", would be despised and ridiculed by the fellahin for their lack of manners. There were some attempts by the pioneers to learn and practice Arab rituals of interaction. However, this endeavour, like similar attempts by separant social characters to adopt participant patterns of behaviour, proved to be a failure because the underlying separant activism and goal-oriented behaviour of the Jewish settlers did not change, and the Arabs saw through their outward demeanour and mannerisms, which were not related to a deeper participant *Weltanschauung*.[33]

Except for the inevitable rituals that dominate Arab religious worship, there is an additional participant element in the monotonous recital of prayers and innumerable adorations and praises of Allah and his Prophet. These effect a certain blunting and dimming of awareness, which is deemed to bring the worshippers closer to Divinity. This may remind us of a similar participant technique used by the quietist Hassidim, which was to recite their prayers mechanically without relating to the meaning of the words of the prayer, so that the intellect may be neutralized and not interfere with the longed-for immediacy of contact with the Divine Presence.[34]

Rituals also permeate the routines of daily life. The vendors of goods in the colourful marketplaces and bazaars in the Arab villages announce their wares through recitation of verse, song and music. Even the peddler of *tamar-hindi*, a musky, oriental beverage, heralds the drink by the clacking of brass castanets. This lends an aesthetic aura to the drudgery of life, softens the sting and grimness of human interaction and extends Ego's personalized style on his immediate surroundings. In this manner, the object is not overpowered or subjugated by a goal-directed tool orientation, but rather the participant's entourage is softened, tenderized and made pliable, so that the deprivational interaction with the object becomes less strained.

Music plays a central role in the life of the fellah. His idea of blissful leisure is invariably centred on the hours-long muted spasms of torch-singers like Um Kalthoum or Firouz. The smoky voices assault the senses and the jerky rhythms of the music affect a simulated shaking-off of reality and welcome a somnambulistic slumber. Unlike separant pop music, which catalyzes a frenzied "turning-on", the Arab torch-singer courts a "turning-off", a participant extinction of awareness.

The participant's aesthetic non-functional approach is ever-present in the craftsmanship of the Arab: tools are ornamented, damascene tables and chairs, as well as Persian carpets, are triumphs of personalization of objects by their makers, who aim to imprint part of themselves into their creation so that their relationship with it is not marked by contrast and conflict but by a sense of belonging to a common pantheistic whole.

Finally, Arab rural architecture yields to the contours and structure of the terrain. An Arab village appears to sprout naturally from the hilltop. The village does not fight the slope of the mountain; it gives in to it by moulding itself with the concave or convex curve. Jewish architecture assaults the terrain. It scatters square, ugly but functional blocks of concrete houses in geometrical sequences. Newly-erected semi-skyscrapers dwarf the ethereal silhouette of the Old City of Jerusalem, nestling amidst the Judean hills, and the Hebrew University of Jerusalem erected its functional concrete cubicles on a ramp of limestone that was Mount Scopus before huge bulldozers scraped off its upper half.

Change and Stagnation

The Zionist pioneers believed in the total planning and restructuring of the Jewish *Yishuv*, so that it became a creative antithesis to the diffuse and non-productive intellectualism of the Diaspora Jew. The social engineering advocated by immigrants of the Second Aliya amounted to a virtual revolution in human relationship and resulted in the unique experiment in communal life in the form of the kibbutz. The motto of the Second Aliya leaders was the complete change of all the social institutions of the Jewish community, from the structure of the family through education to planning and control of the economy.

The most radical innovation in social engineering made by the Zionist pioneers was the kibbutzim (communal farms), which in their ideal form were meant to supply the needs of every member, while the members themselves would contribute to the best of their ability. One of the major tenets of the kibbutz movement was the common rearing and education of children, which affected the structure of the basic family structure and the interrelationships within it. Complete equality of women in both rights and duties was another basic doctrine of the kibbutz movement and the ideology of the pioneers. These virtual revolutions in the social institutions advocated by the Zionist social planners were diametrically opposed to the traditionalist, religious, kinship-bound fellahin. Social and economic egalitarianism was totally foreign to them. Communal life and equal rights for women borders on sacrilege and outright promiscuity.

The separant Zionists' adherence to their ideology and to their group, as well as their nationalism, was also incomprehensible to the fellah, whose relationships with his environment were permeated by mystic and pantheistic projections. These in themselves were the symbols and symbolics that dominated the fellah's cognitive structure, and there was no place in it for the highly abstract ideologies and constructs of nationalism, socialism, material dialectics and the other *isms* that characterized the political jargon of the Jewish pioneers. The following incident, recalled by one pioneer, Netta Harpaz, illustrates this premise:

> We had decided to organize the Arab labourers in the orange grove in which we, the Jewish pioneers, were also employed. We talked to them about the solidarity of the working classes, we proved to them the strength inherent in being organized for achieving a common cause, we explained to them their rights for fair wages and we urged them to demand together with us a raise in our daily wages. They said that they were convinced and they declared their agreement to our common plan. The next day all the Jewish labourers were fired. It seems that the Arabs notified the owner of the grove of the subversive plan. The Arabs stayed on the job and they openly laughed at us, "the stupid Jews". We were bitterly disappointed. We could not understand how fellow workers betray their colleagues and their class and how they double-crossed those who were ready to fight for the common cause of the working classes.[35]

This is not a tale about good and bad guys or the naïve do-gooder against the conniving double-crossing scoundrel, but a typical instance of a conflict between two diametrically opposed social characters.

The managerial aspect of social planning was also central to the pioneers' ideology and party discipline; it had the jargonized name of "ideological collectivity", and was expressly incorporated in the charters of kibbutzim and labour organizations.[36]

In the economic realm, the pioneers envisaged a controlled economy managed and directed by the labour organizations. Indeed, the major role played today by the powerful Israel labour organization, the *Histadrut*, which controls a large segment of the Israeli economy and has a large percentage of salaried employees registered as members, had been envisaged by its founders, who stated the *Histadrut's* goals more than eighty years ago, as follows: "The *Histadrut* unites all workers in the country who live off the fruits of their own labour without exploiting the labour of others, for the purpose of arranging all the communal, economic and cultural affairs of the working class in the country for the building of the labour society in the Land of Israel."[37] Other aspects of social engineering and planning are also prominent in the original writings and visions of the pioneers. Sports, body–building and physical prowess were very much advocated, in contrast to the sickly and physically weak image of the Diaspora Jew. Mental health, order and cleanliness were the other prerequisites of the pioneers and their offspring, the Sabras, destined to recover, resurrect and rebuild the Promised Land. In contrast, the socially conservative fellah believes in God and the Koran and not in the social changes conjured by Man. New ideas frighten him, because in his experience most changes turned out to be for the worse. The ideas of social progress are quite foreign to the fellah. Planned families, prophylactic medicine and communal hygiene are either vile or useless. The fellah in Palestine up until some decades ago, and many Mount Hebron villagers to this very day, regard disease as a misfortune they have to learn to live with. The fellah believes that most plagues of the Middle East are the germs of Westernization imported from time to time by the self-styled harbingers of progress, which to him brought regression, death and stagnation. Often, "experts" are sent to him from abroad. They are mostly starry-eyed graduates from Western universities. They bring new books, ideas, techniques and schemes for such praiseworthy aims as raising the standard of living, uprooting malaria, trachoma and syphilis, introducing more efficient and less corrupt bureaucracies and installing a postal service or a telephone system that really works. Reality is hardly cooperative; there are no roads for heavy trucks to transport equipment. There is no money or trained workers to construct the roads, and very few understand technical matters. The population is too entrenched in its traditional routine. The Western idea of hard work, the concept of accuracy – of time itself – is foreign, undesirable or meaningless. What is the big hurry? And the great dream deteriorates into rusty, unused or broken equipment; the clerks continue their perennial slumber, with timetables and efficiency charts decorating their desks or walls. The dust from the unused time-and-motion charts slowly covers the ideas of progress or innovation.

The whole idea of social welfare is also foreign to the fellah. Social workers and welfare officers are scorned because they "poke their noses in other people's business". Also, if the fellah gets something for nothing, he usually regards the giver as a feebleminded sucker. Some villagers had their taps connected to the Israeli water system after the Six Day War. They were ecstatic with the free water brought to their houses, but they were not thankful to the Israelis. They were beside themselves with glee for cheating the Jews out of water for which they would have had to pay the local water authority half a pound per gallon.

Reality and Illusion

The founding fathers preached realism, a Zionism of the present and not of the ever-after, as promised by the Orthodox Rabbis in the Diaspora and the old religious communities in Jerusalem and Safed. For the pioneers, "concrete realism" was a blessing, and "fantasy" a sin. One must plan the solution of problems with vigour and imagination, but the problems have to be "realistic", and the goals "concrete". "Progress" and "development" were other passwords used by the pioneers in their writings, addresses and conventions. Progress and development were related to the latest methods in agriculture, irrigation and construction. Progress was also equated with total adherence to the scientific method as a panacea for the reconstruction and revival of the Palestinian swamps and wastelands. "Socialist Zionism," said Nahman Sirkin, one of the prominent early leaders, "revives the healthy and progressive elements in Judaism and makes them the bridgehead for the future . . . Socialist Zionism fights the sick elements in Judaism which stem from religion and traditionalism . . . Its allies in this struggle are science and light."[38] In the separant vocabulary of the pioneers' progress, development and science were the forces of light, whereas religion and tradition, which were the major components of the social character of the fellahin, stood for stagnation and darkness. Although mainstream Zionism rejected Ahad-Ha'am's vision of a Jewish state that would become the Light of Nations in spiritual and scientific matters, it still regarded the rational and scientific rebuilding of Palestine as one of the major goals of Zionism. The separant regards the preoccupation in science, *per se*, as detached intellectualism, not vastly different from the scholasticism of the Talmudic scholars in the Diaspora. Science should be harnessed for the goal-oriented manipulation of the environment and used in the service of realism, development and progress.

Realism for the Palestinian fellah was the acceptance of constant occupation by foreigners and recurring political disasters. Reality also meant the cruelty of the Middle Eastern elements – i.e. frequent droughts, precarious rains, regular raids by nomads and swarms of crop-eating locusts from the surrounding deserts. No wonder reality was unpalatable to the fellah, whose mystically oriented religion assured him he could never find contentment in reality. Indeed, the so-called stations (*maqamat*) of Sufism are techniques of neutralizing reality in preparation for one's mystic partaking in God. The second station, for instance, is the attainment of spiritual solitude (*Khalwat*), so that "Changes in the concrete temporal world do not alter his inner secrets and calamities sent by Heaven do not cause the bird of love to fly away."[39] When one reaches this station, reality becomes blunt and its sting is less painful. Reality cannot be but painful because "For seventy years the carnal soul, i.e. Man's temporal self, which interacts with reality, cries in agony with the desire of receiving a single favour and does not receive anything but pain and hardship."[40] This is the Muslim mystics' sad summation of Man's temporal life. Consequently, the interim goal of the Sufi is to surround himself with a no-man's-land of detachment so that he becomes indifferent to reality, then "Disaster and well-being, favour and privation are the same for him."[41] The ultimate goal of the Sufi is to lose himself in God; through the mystic strains of Islam the fellah is also imbued with an underlying quest of renouncing reality and annihilating himself into pantheistic Unity.

The managerial orientation of the Jewish pioneer in achieving his goals of "progress" and "development" are foreign to the social character of the Arab, because there is almost no organization and institutionalized management in Islam, which is very much a solitary contemplative religion. A Muslim may pray by himself or in a group. There is also no priesthood, in the ecclesiastic sense, that could have built and sustained elaborate managerial structures.

The fellah tries to lose himself in his environment in many other ways. His dress conceals and mars the contours of his body. His mud huts merge with the landscape. The domes, round corners and fluid lines of his houses are haunted by ghosts, spirits and superstitions, which make for a hazy, ethereal complement between the fellah's inner and outer worlds.

Power and "The Children of Death"

When the physically weak, pale, sickly, tender-handed, intellectual Jewish pioneers came to Palestine to work the land in the searing heat, they were scornfully labelled by the Arab fellahin as "Awlaad El Mout", "The Children of Death". Yet the Arabs' observation was only skin-deep: They did not realize, to their later detriment, that behind their weak exteriors, the pioneers had ferocious willpower.

A poet, on whose otherwise mild-mannered prose and idyllic poetry generations of Palestinian Jews were reared, preached: "Nothing enhances malice, injustice and violence more than weakness – be strong, and you will have right on your side and justice."[42]

Many Zionist extremists cherished and sanctified the fiery verses of their leader: "Defy every hardship and obstacle, disown your blood and soul for a glory unknown, to die or the mountain to conquer – Jodefet, Massada, Beitar,"[43] which were strongholds of Jewish freedom fighters.

Yael Dayan, in a largely biographical novel, describes the upbringing of her father, Moshe Dayan, whose parents were Second Aliya pioneers:

> During the spring, the children of Beit-On would play "Who is strong?". The leader of the group would get up, hands in his pockets and would ask: "Who is strong?" Then one would get up: "I am strong"... the children's chorus... demanding, teasing, challenging: "Show us you're strong!" This was the point of the game, to show that you could do whatever you didn't believe you could do, and every spring the children of Beit-On jumped from the cliffs or climbed the trees or swam in the deepest part of the lake, and every spring, as the children grew up, the targets became harder to achieve.[44]

The slogan inscribed on the flag at one of the first Jewish settlements in Palestine was "Here you shall learn misery and faith". These first settlers, the "Biluyim" (formed from "Beit Israel Lechu Venelcha," The House of Israel – let's go!) were a special breed. The pioneers who settled the Wild West were hardy, rugged and tough, but the Biluyim were starry-eyed, soft-muscled intellectuals, getting bloody blisters with every raise of the shovel. Their only strength was their will, the will for self-fulfilment through hard manual labour, and their single-minded battle to implement the goals of Zionism.

This violent pioneering spirit took many forms, such as draining marshes and swamps in malaria-infected areas, single-handedly guarding herds and property against attack from Arab hordes, quickly establishing new settlements with limestone-fortified wooden perimeter fences in hostile areas. This was the phenomenon that Ben-Gurion called "the miracle of the pioneers", the unbelievable spectacle of urban youth, unfamiliar with manual labour, pampered by luxury, coming to the country not for spontaneous heroism, or to fight, but for a life of tedious and continuous courage and heroism, every day, every year, every decade.

The power-based nature of the pioneers' frantic activism is also apparent from the structure of their labour force. Some of the pioneers were organized into "labour legions", which were administered through a military-like system with severe displine.[45]

Joseph Trumpeldor, the one-handed hero of the pioneers, envisaged the rebuilding of a Jewish Palestine as a military operation. "We should not forget even for one moment," he wrote, "that this nation of peddlers and petty artisans has to be resurrected in his land and become a nation of land cultivators. We have, therefore, to plan everything beforehand and organize: 1. Construction groups. 2. Temporary labour conquest groups. 3. Groups of permanent settlers. 4. Military units. 5. An organization of reconnaissance groups."[46] The language of military operations permeates most of the activities of the pioneers. They preached for the conquest of labour, economic enterprises and political positions; for the occupation of the wastelands and the centralized ownership of property; they waged war against the "parasites", i.e. the bureaucracy of Baron de Rothschild's settlements, which received financial support even in the absence of work.

They saw themselves as soldiers constantly on their guard, fighting against a hostile physical environment, an antagonistic Arab populace and a lethargic, decadent old Jewish community subsisting on alms and handouts. The separant pioneers rejected the moralistic arguments against their ideology of force as weakness. They offered historical materialist defences of their strategy, such as their conviction that if their goals were just, then the means to achieve them were just too. They even welcomed hardship with a Nietzschean mood, that suffering might eventually become a source of strength.[47]

The Palestinian Arab had been politically subjugated for centuries, first by the Turks, then by the British and today by the Israelis. The Palestinian refugees who fled to Arab states in 1948 have never been fully accepted. Most are kept near the Israeli border in refugee camps so as to create reservoirs of cheap labour and new recruits for the various terrorist organizations, and so that international pressure can be exerted on Israel. Essentially, Palestinian Arabs have never ceased being politically powerless. Spengler's statement, made at the beginning of the 1900s, that the "Fellahin are rigid objects of a movement that comes from outside and impinges on them unmeaningly and fortuitously,"[48] still applies today.

An Arab proverb says that Palestine is the centre of the world because the turbulence of fighting never ceases there. Indeed, wars have been ravaging the people and the lands of the eastern shores of the Mediterranean from time immemorial. Apart from the physical destruction of towns and villages, this has pressed the inhabitants into servile docility. At first, the Turks mercilessly crushed every show of independence or political ambition. This political servility continued under the protectorates of many European powers, which won concessions and "capitulations" from the disintegrating Ottoman Empire for their semi-independent economic and political activities, under the guise of protecting the holy places and safeguarding the rights of religious minorities. The British mandatory regime discouraged Palestinian ambitions of political independence, and subsequent wars with Israel made the realization of these ambitions even more remote. The constant oppression of the Arab by politically aggressive cultures made him lower his head in obedience before authority and readily succumb to any show of force. The Arab developed techniques of self-defence characteristic of the powerless and downtrodden. This is illustrated in the following maxims, which for the Arab are time-honoured social norms:

"Kiss the hand you cannot bite."

"Whoever marries my mother shall be called father" [one should not oppose authority].

"The dog of the Emir should be treated like an Emir."

"If you need something from a dog, call him Haj Ahmed."[49, 50]

This abject oppression and powerlessness made the participant Arab fly into lies, deceit and denial whenever he came in contact with authoritarian figures, but he sought refuge through isolation from any symbol of power and resigned himself to his external fate, which he alleviated by day-dreaming and courting temporary oblivion.

The epitome of political and social powerlessness seems to be the lot of the Egyptian fellah as portrayed by El-Haquim, which still holds true today. The *umdeh*, the headman of the village, is appointed by the central government. He is virtually the absolute monarch of the village, and treats the fellah as his slave. He is the legislator, the judge and the policeman. He imposes on the fellah as many taxes as he wishes. The fellah only has duties. He has no rights, but the worst he can do is complain because then he is as good as dead. The headman can do with the fellah as he wishes; nobody will dare interfere in his area of jurisdiction. If a representative of the central government visits the village, it is only to demand his share of the spoil, which is where his inspection terminates. Even if he wanted, he could not investigate illegalities because in the village the *umdeh* is the law and offenders are declared ad hoc, based on the mood of the headman. Nobody is really acquainted with the laws of the central government, and in the rare cases when they are used, it is only to levy more taxes and put more restrictions on the fellah, who has thus no choice but to suffer in silence.[51]

The abject oppression of the fellah, his total dependence on a precarious nature, and his lack of personal and economic security make him seek solace and refuge in another plane of essence and meaning in which spatio-temporality is less threatening and in which he can develop a certain measure of indifference towards his hostile surroundings. He finds this in the participant Sufi doctrine that the finite may be blurred into insignificance and an inner essence then projected, temporarily at least, onto the higher stature of graceful infinity.

The Ecstasy and the Lethargy

The pioneers of the Second Aliya were constantly afire with their ideals of activism and conquest. Their visions of the future made them euphoric with ecstasy, and after a hard day of manual labour they would dance the *horra* until midnight,[52] very much like their activist Hassidic ancestors who tried hard to force their way to Divinity by frenzied dances of "Ufaratsta".[53] The pioneers' image of their collective life is that of a beehive: overflowing with activity, swarming with a life of constant labour, wishes, goals and desires all sprouting outwards in ever-accelerating frenzy; and when the parent beehive can no longer contain the teeming growth of new life, a young swarm separates itself from its origins and seeks new pastures and new grounds.[54] The separant's fixation on growth and the separation of the self from the object is portrayed here with vivid imagery. When one reads the accounts of the pioneers in the original Hebrew one is struck by the force of the expressions, which invariably convey a sense of urgency augmented by an almost uniform level of ecstasy-laden words following one another at staccato speed. Some illustrative Second Aliya expressions were: "Primeval longing for action" and "The blessed inner fermentation helping us in our struggle towards our goal". Not only are these the dynamics of a collective fixation on the object, they are also a conviction that a powerful assault will harness it into the grand design of subject–object harmony envisioned by the separant pioneer. Consequently, a "searing character", i.e. one bursting with nervous energy, is a laudatory trait for an agricultural engineer. The construction of an oil refinery is described as a divine task,[55] which calls to fore the separant Hassidic "*Avoda-Begashmiut*", i.e. sanctification of daily routines by reaching out to the Divine core of the object.[56]

The separant pioneer is optimistic because no problem cannot be solved. As Harpaz said: "We have to look for small solutions to small problems and big solutions to big problems."[57] The solutions exist; one only has to find them and make the corresponding problems and answers fit together. The pioneer believes in his ability to command and successfully manipulate his environment. Here in Palestine he must be master of his destiny, because in the Diaspora he was its slave. Hope, constant hope despite recurring failure, is his motto and anthem. The participant Arab, on the other hand, does not believe in his ability to command his environment. He knows better than to put his trust in treacherous Man and the cruel elements. He is not an optimist because his past experience did not reinforce this. The most he allows himself to expect from his environment is not to be hurt by it. The fellah puts his trust in God because whenever he tried to trust Man or Nature he received an unpleasant surprise. Consequently, he tended to retreat from spatio-temporality into an inwardly directed quietism, which to an outside observer appeared as indifference, stagnation and despair. These were precisely the states of mind that were considered anathema by the separant pioneers. Berl Katznelson, the charismatic leader of the Second Aliya, preached optimism "not so much because of the beauty of hope as because of the ugliness of weakness and lethargy, which amounts to the betrayal of the Cause".[58] It is also typical that the pioneers worshipped the optimism of youth and resented the resignation of old age, whereas the Arabs equated old age with wisdom, and village elders were always the bearers of traditional authority – though this has suffered enormously in recent decades

142

because of exposure to the secular and separant norms of Israeli society.

The fervent separant ideologies of the Jewish pioneers were utterly incomprehensible to the participant Arabs. They could not understand how the Jews could ever hope to combat the afflictions and vicissitudes of the elements as ordained by God and the essential inhumanity of Man to his fellow men. To them, resignation and lethargy seemed the safest way of life because one cannot possibly fight one's lot in the evil here and now. Solace may only be found in quiet self-effacing prayer, and hope only lies in longing for the *ahsan taquim*, the "perfect origin", a kernel of which is embedded within one's soul.

Haste is from the Devil

Socialist Zionism believes in historical necessity, yet time works for those who cherish and respect it. Time will bring the Zionist victory over the hostile environment if the battle is waged with punctuality and efficiency. Goods must be delivered on time; tomorrow will never come for those who delay today's tasks.

The separant Zionist is both past- and future-oriented; conversely, the participant fellah is present-oriented. The Arab is not just indifferent to temporal sequences, like the Latin American's *mañana* – he rejects it outright. *Alajale min a'shaitan*, i.e. "to hurry is to be under the devil's influence", is a religiously sanctioned Arab more, signifying contempt and disdain of action structured and paced by time. When asking an Arab the time of arrival at a destination while travelling by mule or modern car, the answer will likely be *"caman shewoy"*, "in a little while". This same answer will be given with relaxed constancy whether the distance is ten kilometres or a hundred, or whether the travel time is one hour or ten. A Bedouin measures distances by cigarettes, i.e. the time unit is the distance covered by a camel rider when smoking one whole cigarette. If asked the distance between Beersheba and Gaza, a Bedouin is likely to answer "ten cigarettes".

Time for the fellah is vile because it harasses him out of his convenient fatalism and participant lethargy. The fellah is not indifferent to time – he is hostile towards it. He resents the temporal boundaries of finitude, which curb his participant longing for infinity.

143

The Driven and the Lazy

David McClelland has found modern Israel to be high in achievement motivation.[59] This may be traced to the separant spirit of its founding fathers. "We worked to the verge of physical exhaustion," wrote one of the pioneers, "because of our ardent wish to succeed in everything."[60] The perennial belief that the Jews were the Chosen People translated itself into the infallibility of the Jews in the attainment of their Zionist goals. If the Protestants' temporal success was taken as proof of predetermined worth, the success of the Zionist dream was meant to reinforce belief in the uniqueness and choice of the Jewish people.[61] Every obstacle was readily met with enthusiasm as a worthy challenge, because the more serious the obstacle, the greater the achievement and resultant proof of worth.

Competition is the natural companion of the achievement motive, and employers in Palestine took due notice and advantage of the competitiveness of the Jewish pioneers. They would place two Jews among a group of Arab workers hoeing an orchard and challenge the Arabs' ethnic pride against the Jews' claims to superior performance, even in menial tasks. A competition would then ensue, to the delight of the orchard owner.[62]

Achievement, obstinacy and perseverance in pursuing high ambitions are foreign to the Arab's social character. He longs for a life of unharassed rest and uninterrupted leisure – the outward manifestations of the quietist ideal of peace of mind. Also, there was little reinforcement for ambition and achievement in the Arab village because, in its traditional closed social structure, the barriers to aspiration were strong and high and made any possibility for upper mobility sadly remote. The abject poverty and the disease-ridden existence of many of the fellahin make sheer survival a feat in itself, so that no further ambitions are entertained. Finally, the symbol orientation of the fellah and his participant collective fixation on non-awareness predisposes him to spend a great many of his waking hours in day-dreams and fantasies. Often with the help of hashish, his fertile imagination may allow him to perform the exploits of kings, poets and warriors without the cumbersome mediation of reality.

A Religion of Labour

The reaction-formation against the ghetto Jew, Sholem Aleichem's *Luftmenschen* resulted in the cult of manual labour among the Zionist pioneers. If there was anything approaching the sacredness of religion in the largely non-religious Jewish community of Palestine, it was the religion of labour. This was directly linked to the supreme goal – building the country and the state with one's own hands. If the British gentleman had to show his status by keeping his hands as white as lilies, the supreme status symbol among the pioneer aristocracy was coarse, horny hands:

> All of us go to help in the Kibbutzim – they have a severe labour shortage there. We work, our hands are calloused and bleeding, and we sweat: blood and sweat have soaked the rocks of Jezrael Valley and Galilee from times immemorial; this is the only way a man fructifies his land, his country and his life.[63]

This is the forceful portrayal of the separant activist fighting desperately for meaningful ties with the object.

Another negativistic antithesis to the scholarly and learned élite of the

Jewish Diaspora was the detached intellectualism by the pioneers. This stems directly from the cult of manual labour. If, previously, social status was gained by familiarity with the Talmudic labyrinth, or the attainment of a university degree, now the coarse, calloused hand was waved with scorn at the "unproductive" intellectuals and their futile, "parasitic" existence.

But this anti-intellectualism was never raised to the status of a positive value, as in some totalitarian movements. Among youth in the *Yishuv*, intellectualism was considered superfluous and a luxury because there were other urgent and seemingly more important things to do.

> It is very difficult for a person who grew up in the middle-class family to get used to a life of manual labour and agriculture, but this is absolutely necessary. Not that we shall force anyone to work with his hands, or that we are against intellectuals as such . . . we shall always have enough doctors, but we are in great need of good farmers.[64]

The separantism of the pioneers is evident in the independent, supreme stature that they assign to labour: the active manipulation of the object is not a means but an end in itself. For many pioneers, the ideal of menial labour was stronger than, and preceded the political goals, of Zionism.[65] For them, work was both the source and *raison d'être*. Direct, immediate contact had to exist between the pioneer and the object. One had to work the land, to hold the plough, to lay the bricks. Mediate, vicarious contact with the object was not good enough. Tending the wine bottles in the wine cellars, for instance, was deemed to be an inferior task.[66] Only actual contact with the soil was regarded as worthy labour.

The belief in personal fulfilment through labour was so fierce that many times the pioneers agreed to work without pay and only for their meagre meals. Work was considered a panacea for all problems and a balm for every illness, not unlike the learning of the Torah as a cure-all for the Diaspora Jew. Work, for the pioneer, was a creed and a blessing chosen willingly and joyfully, whereas for the fellah it was a dire necessity. He toiled his land for a livelihood like his fathers and forefathers before him. The fellah was a "natural" and skilled labourer, but he could not understand why the pioneers glorified a necessary evil and made it a cherished ideal.

The pioneers' collective fixation on the object is also apparent from the "halo effect" that the ideal of labour had on the normative system of the Jewish community. Industry and perseverance are the natural attributes of a good labourer. Labour was also the normative basis for the cultivation of a sense of duty and notions of responsibility. Finally, the pioneer had to love his work. He had to perform his task with devotional *devekut*,[67] i.e. with emotional attachment to the object; and here the separant cycle is complete. From a collective fixation on the object, one derives the motivation to manipulate one's environment, to harness it into one's vision of harmony as projected outwards, to build a system of duties and

145

responsibilities based on the manipulation of the object and derive emotional satisfaction from the relationship with it. "In the beginning, however, was the action,"[68] stated a pioneer leader, echoing unknowingly and unwittingly the cosmological primordial archetype of Genesis, thereby signifying that active object manipulation is both a prime mover and the way to personal fulfilment. Aharon David Gordon, the Tolstoyesque labour prophet of the pioneers, preached that one should be originally linked to labour as the essence of one's existence, and through work the Jewish nation would tie itself to the land and create its culture.[69] The Hegelian–Marxist notion that action is the necessary bridge between the subject and object, and the separant Hassidic premise that one has to work one's way towards the object in order to reach its divine core, is readily apparent.

The Arab fellah is a fatalist because he knows from experience and from observation that one cannot successfully manipulate one's environment however hard one may try, and that the only way to cope with the succession of calamities waged on him by Man and the elements is to accept them as they come. The fellah likes to posses material goods, but if he has to work hard for them, he can do without them. The material needs of the fellah are not great and he will not exert himself for no need. Work is not an aim in itself, far from it. Work and labour are the result of the fallen state of Man, and industriousness is not virtuous because one does not make a virtue out of necessity. Work has value if it is invested in handiwork or in the decoration of a tool, a utensil or the minaret of a mosque; then it is a work of art, the expression of the inner personality and the extension of the self.[70] The Arab is resigned to his fate because God has ordained it. It is blasphemous to fight against one's destiny, which is the expression of God's will. Also, the way of the outside world has been determined by God's will, which manifests itself pantheistically in all creation. The fellah has learned to his detriment that whenever he has tried to manipulate reality to improve his material lot he has usually been beat, abused and pushed back into his place by the village headmen, the greedy government officials, the calamities of nature or festering disease. He has interpreted this as visitations of Divine scourges, to avenge his hubris. He was quick to learn these lessons of humility taught to him by God, and he resigned himself to the acceptance of his assigned miseries as his inescapable lot in life. He only burrows deeper, searching for the spark of Divinity that is embedded in his soul, in order to project it outwards and surround himself with the truth of pre-being (*al-haqq*) as an antidote to the precariousness of the spatio-temporal world (*al-khalq*).[71]

Social Mobility

The structure of Israeli society is flexible and in constant change. This may be largely due to the vast ethnic heterogeneity and the cultural diversity

146

of the population. Although Jewish immigration to the country was not steady, it was continuous from the beginning of the nineteenth century. This state of social flux cannot support rigid barriers to upper social mobility. It is true that Ashkenazi Jews of European origin have higher social positions than the oriental Jews, but this stems from economic, historical and educational reasons. Oriental Jews who immigrated to Israel after the establishment of the state had less education and vocational training, so their placement within the existing social and economic institutions was precarious and problematic. There are no legal or formal barriers to the upper mobility of oriental Jews, and great efforts have been made to lower informal barriers by raising the educational and vocational standards of the younger generations of oriental Jewish immigrants. There is also no rigid class barrier in Israel to impede upper mobility. A rigid class structure based on traditional and economic criteria and sanctioned by use over hundreds of years is clearly nonexistent in Israel.

The pre-1948 Jewish community in Palestine was basically an egalitarian society whose élites were people who displayed a devotion and ability to implement the ideologies of the group. After the establishment of the state, the criteria for social stratification and upper vertical mobility became conventional, i.e. economic affluence and status in the power structures of government and business. Regarding the latter, no normative or structural barriers to the aspiration of their achievement existed. On the contrary, the objective necessity for professional and executive manpower constituted an immense impulse and impetus towards aspiration, achievement and mobility.

Mobility in the Arab village, when compared to the rather open-endedness of Jewish society, is quite limited. Boundaries against upper mobility are first and foremost the semi-feudal rental system, in which fellahin cultivate land that they do not own and pay the landowner up to half the annual crop yield. Although there are some vestiges of limited land reform, fellahin usually do not own land. Those that do may also be bonded to it, since either the entire plot or part of it may be owned collectively by the extended family (*hamula*), or even by the entire village. The fellah may be confined to his land and to a low level of production because of heavy debts to the village loan shark, to whom he may owe enormous sums of cumulative interest that he can never hope to repay. This situation has radically changed among Israeli Arabs because of their exposure to the dynamic Israeli economy and the relative affluence of Arab-Israeli villages due to work opportunities in urban and industrial parts of Israel. Nevertheless, barriers to mobility still exist: Arabs are not readily accepted in government services that are not strictly confined to the internal affairs of Arab-Israeli communities. It is very difficult for them to buy or rent a house in Jewish neighbourhoods. They are rarely accepted socially or culturally, and mixed Jewish–Arab social events are not frequent. Consequently, the Israeli Arab's economic situation may be better than the fellah's standard of living in neighbouring Arab countries, yet socially

147

and culturally he is still confined to his village or to the semi-urban community in which he lives, particularly to his extended family. Arab society is very much a familial society in which the most important membership group, and more often than not the reference group, is the *hamula* (extended family). For the fellah, the extended family is the most important source of authority, but the urban Arab also imputes legitimacy to the normative control exerted over him by the family, which often takes a decisive part in the choice of mates, profession and domicile. Therefore, social position among Arabs is highly influenced by a familistic ascribed status and by social, cultural and political barriers that curb both their horizontal and vertical social mobility. This limited mobility of the Arab is linked to the inaction and constancy orientations of the participant social character.

Dreams and Visions

The Sisyphean Israeli pioneer is pushed by visions of Utopia. He believes that his frantic activism and violent change of the environment will carry him and his kin on fluctuating waves of dialectics to the Promised Land. The pioneers' Utopianism expressed itself in the total subjugation of their present reality to a remote vision. "To make reality subservient to our vision," wrote one of the Second Aliya ideologists, "was the essence of our labour movement and its prime mover. This frenzied drive towards the Vision did not let us rest and stall. It constantly pushed us for further action and for more conquests."[72] The quest of this "Vision" was in itself considered a means for personal fulfilment. This is the mark of Utopia, which promises complete harmony between Ego and his social and spatial environment. Sisyphus believes that sometime in the future there must be a cosy niche up there on the peak of the mountain for both himself and his stone.

The Jewish pioneers seemed to have sacrificed their personal well-being, health and aspirations for the common cause. Other freedom movements also burned with patriotic zeal, but with the Zionists, the extreme subjugation of social institutions, norms and values in their special brand of Utopian vision was almost unique. Zionism retained the intense and single-minded messianic zeal of Judaism, but lacking a God and an ever-after, it cathected its visionary ecstasy to a national homeland and socialist Utopia for Jews.

The Arab, on the other hand, rejects Utopianism because he does not believe the dialectic conflicts between Ego and the object lead to "progress". He is a believer in Parmenidean constancy. Nothing changes and nothing really moves forward or backward. "What has always been in the past will be in the future", goes an Arab saying, and "one never goes places, but one brings everything with oneself." Movement, change and progress are illusions. The only reality is God; salvation is to be sought through acceptance by Him and partaking in Him. Consequently, religion permeates and governs the Arab's life, and even those who are not overtly observant are predisposed by their social character to seek spiritual ascent. "The name of God," says Patai, "is always on the lips of the people of the East . . . reflecting the psychological omnipresence and ever-presence of God . . ."[73] The Arab is preoccupied with the purity of his soul as a prerequisite for salvation. Because the fellah is mostly poor, he prides himself on having "God in his soul", and one of the most derogatory insults is that so and so has "no God in his heart". Because of the fellah's poverty, and the legendary scarcity of personal possessions of the nomadic Bedouin, the fellah readily renounces, with or without a "sour-grapes" *ressentiment*, the importance of worldly wealth and achievement, and focuses on spiritual salvation. Islam does not prescribe the mediation of an ecclesia as a collective guide to salvation. It lets the individual Arab seek his own private way to God. More often than not he will choose the mystically flavoured Sufi *tariqah* for the partial extinction of the self and partake in the saving grace of Unity (*al-tawhid*).

We have surveyed the polarities of the social characters of the Arabs and Jews as a primary empirical anchor and illustration of the sociocultural dimension of the Tantalus Ratio, the way we used the Besht and the Maggid to illustrate our polar personality types in **chapter 2**. We may conclude this part of our analysis with the rather topical observation that the abysmal depths and intricacies of the Arab–Jewish conflict in the Middle East may be better understood if analyzed within the matrix of our separant–participant social character polarities and not primarily as a function of political power struggles.

In *Valhalla, Calvary and Auschwitz* (1995) we made a similar attempt to decipher the inevitably disastrous encounter between participant European Jewry, with its projected myth of victimized Isaac (to be discussed in **chapter 8**), and Nazi Germany, with its separant Nordic mythological anchors. The last section of this chapter places the social characters on the extreme poles of our continuum, thereby providing an explanation that history alone cannot supply.

The Extreme Poles of the Separant–Participant Continuum

Social Change and Social Character

The ideal-type polar social characters lie at the extreme edges of a continuum along which all cultures may be placed based upon the frequency and intensity of the ten pairs of traits we analyzed in **chapter 3** and illustrated in the present chapter. Cultures and social characters may of course change from one type to another in the course of history, or through the conflict of cultures when one social character leaves its own

149

cultural area and enters another by migration or conquest. In the present work, we are not really concerned with social change, and we shall not indulge in explanations cyclical, dialectical or otherwise of why one social character changes into another. Consequently, we shall assume the movement of social characters along our continuum as a given phenomenon, without asking for explanations. We shall also envisage these to and fro movements as the mechanical swinging of a pendulum without trying to find the shape of the arc or the velocity and acceleration of the swinging movement.

Cultural relativists have studied in detail the changes of social character as a corollary of social change. Arnold Toynbee tells us about a separant Egypt dominated by the activist Ra, the Sun God, whose cult was linked with the stupendous building frenzy of the Great Pyramids that changed into a participant society reigned by the priests of Osiris and their Cult of the Dead.[74] In his classic study on the metamorphosis of Greek religion, Gilbert Murray traces the changes from the separant, activist, politically aggressive Greece of the Heroic age, with its anthropomorphic gods competing with men for worldly goods and the favours of women, to the participant Hellenistic society influenced by the mysticism and the rejection of spatio-temporality of the early Gnostics.[75]

We have already mentioned the Weberian thesis and the studies by McClelland and Sebastian DeGrazia, which analyzed the separant revolution of the Reformation that changed the quietist traditionalism of Western Europe, sanctioned by the Catholic ecclesia, into a seething cauldron of activism kindled by the Protestant Ethic. David Riesman has also focused his analysis, which still holds today, of the changing social character on the transition from a more participant tradition and inner-directed culture to a largely separant other-directed "Lonely Crowd".[76]

These processes of change and transition from one social character to another take place continuously. Modern China, for instance, waged a battle against the deeply rooted participant traits of quietism, traditionalism and resignation that the Maoist cultural engineers attributed to Confucianism. "The struggle between those who want to go forward and those who want to go backward," drone the mass communication channels of China, "still exists . . . To struggle is to advance. Not to struggle is to retrogress, to collapse."[77]

However, after the demise of Maoism, modern China still has some basic vestiges of Marxism, but it has readapted Confucianism to keep its social structure intact. It is ironic that, today, the technologically-advanced West is threatened by terrorism from Fundamentalist Islam in countries it has helped advance from the early Middle Ages to the twentieth century. This could be poetic justice inflicted by a vengeful East on the trespassing West, which dragged the participant oriental societies out of their somnolence and blissful, suspended animation. This issue is the focus of **chapter 5**. These are some instances of social change linked to change of social character over time. Other changes of social character are related to the clash, symbiotic give and take, adoption, subjugation and merger of two or more social characters into one cultural space. We have already dealt extensively with culture conflict as related to social change and deviance[78] and with Levantinism, i.e. the shallow absorption of cultural traits of one social character by another social character or diverging cultural traits.[79] These forms of social character transformations are also outside the scope of our present analysis, because here we are concerned with the study of the social character at a given time and place as related to a given personality type, and not with the changes and transformations of the social character in the course of time and within the dynamics of cultural change.

Finally, it is necessary to point out that the processes of social change may indeed be incidental to a change in social character. Cultures also undergo phases of growth and decline in a manner similar to the maturation curve, which we have described in relation to individuals. It is also possible to study the Tantalus Ratio of entire cultures *vis-à-vis* their phases of growth, maturation and decline. But the present work is a study of individuals who are socialized within a given culture; it is not a study of cultures. Consequently, we shall not concern ourselves with the various changes of the social characters and their movement along our continuum resulting from the varied and numerous forms of social change, but with the consequences of a polar personality type growing up and living in a culture with a concordant or a discordant social character.

151

Personality Type and Social Character

Chapter 1 studied the growth, maturation and decline of the individual as related to the Tantalus Ratio. **Chapter 2** analyzed the fixation and formation of the Sisyphean and Tantalic personality types. **Chapter 3** and the present chapter have dealt with the separant and participant continuum of social characters. Analysis of these three components of the Tantalus Ratio has been presented separately solely for didactic purposes, because in reality they intersect with one another into a dynamic whole. It is now necessary to discuss some forms of the dynamic interrelationship among the three components of the Tantalus Ratio.

Our basic premise is that the Tantalic personality type is ill fitted to perform the roles of the separant social character, so that if a Tantalic-fixated personality grows up in a separant culture, we may expect deviance, conflicts or innovations. The same dynamics apply to the Sisyphean personality type growing up in a participant culture. Indeed, one personality type asked to perform the roles of a divergent social character seems unable to comply, irrespective of the amount of external pressure exerted on him. We may visualize a Martin Luther hurling at his tormentors: "I cannot otherwise" when pressed to change his views, or the grotesque and pitiful performance of the professor in *The Blue Angel* when forced to act as a clown. An individual with a personality type that is placed in a culture of a discordant social character would be predisposed to social deviance. Whether or not this individual eventually becomes a social deviant depends on the flexibility and tolerance of the normative controls of a given society, the availability of institutionalized outlets for deviance, and the readiness of the normative and power structures to label individuals and groups as deviants. This predisposition to deviance as related to the processes of social control and labelling has been dealt with extensively.[80] Our purpose here is to see how a given personality type may play some roles, although marginal and esoteric, in a culture of a discordant social character and not be cast out and rejected as a deviant (see the paradigm in **figure 4.1**, which relates personality type in both its growth and decline phases to social character).

Personality type	Sisyphean Social Character		Tantalic Social Character	
	Growth	*Decline*	*Growth*	*Decline*
Separant	1. *per aspera ad astra*	2. *Ressentiment*	3. Woodstock nation	4. Institutionalized deviancy
Participant	5. "Young Turks"	6. "Guardians of the Holy Spirit"	7. "Pneumatics"	8. Monastic retreat

Figure 4.1 Relationship of personality type, in growth and decline, to social character

1 The Sisyphean personality growing up in a separant culture deems himself a round peg in a round hole. He pursues the roles prescribed for him by an achievement-motivated society, striving hard to find the right placement for himself on the social pyramid. At his "growth" stage he aims to find a proper niche as close as possible to the top. But when he starts declining in the second half of his life, and after he becomes subject to various anomic pressures (that we have described elsewhere[81]), he may find himself in the grip of *ressentiment*.

2 We have already described how the object-fixated Sisyphean character type – who has been pushed, prodded, cajoled and reduced all his life, first by parents, then by the socialization agencies and later on through the constant chatter of modern communications prodding him to acquire as many offices, apple pies and nipples as he can – is embittered by the "system". It turns out that the social structure is not geared to supply the goods as advertised by the achievement norms of socialization and *arriviste* cultural mandates. Separant

society has also wilfully broken down the normative barriers of aspiration, so our Sisyphean *arriviste* sinks into a sour-grapes *ressentiment* towards "the world", i.e. his surrounding object, which cheated him out of his childhood dreams of wine, women, song and power, reinforced by his *arriviste* upbringing. This has been aptly stated by Frederico Fellini, the genius interpreter of *ressentiment*:

People are psychologically polluted. They are losing faith in the future. Our education, unfortunately, moulded us for a life that was always tensed towards a series of achievements – school, military service, a career and, as a grand finale, the encounter with the Heavenly Father. But now that our tomorrows no longer appear in that optimistic perspective, we are left with a feeling of impotence and fear. People who can no longer believe in a "better tomorrow" logically tend to behave with a desperate egotism. They are preoccupied with protecting, brutally if necessary, those little personal gains, one's little body, one's little sensual appetites. To me, this is the most dangerous feature of the seventies.[82]

Fellini does not realize that this *ressentiment*-ridden bitterness is a result of a fixation on the object. When a person looks outside himself for quietist contentment, he looks on a moonless night, in a dark room, for a black cat that isn't there. "He could have looked inside," we can hear Fellini arguing, "to find solace within himself." To this we may sadly answer that he is unable to support his old age with self-directed longing for non-awareness and spiritual Unity, because he was fixated in the opposite direction, i.e. towards the object, at a very early stage of his life.

3   The drug culture, the Jesus freaks and the worshippers of the Guru Maharaji are more likely to attract Tantalic personality types ill at ease in a stifling, smoggy, polluted, violent, impersonal separant America. In a participant society, drugs are institutionalized and contained within a routine that is geared by other cultural attributes to a quietist, traditional self-effacing way of life. A water pipe of hashish for an oriental is nice but not necessary for a quick transition into forgetful meditation and non-awareness, which may last for hours. For the American Woodstock nation, drugs are the sole levers for participation trips because the separant culture does not provide other participatory outlets for temporary "opting out" and attaining the "high" of self-oblivion. Consequently, many "flower people" in the United States became junkies because they concentrated most of the energy in their Tantalus Ratio towards the only outlet in sight, which may satisfy their fixation on early oral non-being, even if it leads them to the pusher, the needle, crime, sickness – and the "greatest high of them all" – death.

The Jesus freaks may also serve as participant outlets for the Tantalic personality in a harassing impersonal havoc of a separant culture. "The Jesus movement", says Robert Ellwood, "epitomizes the evangelicals' 'survival Christianity', in which alienated groups find religious stability amid social turmoil."[83]

It should be noted that Tantalic personality types might effect some innovations that are related to the participant fixations in their separant culture, and especially in its art. The impressionists, for instance, especially the self-destructive Paul Gauguin and Vincent Van Gogh, have broken and dissipated the rigid contours and spatio-temporal concreteness of academic painters like Ingres. In like manner, the jazz virtuosos and the pop music of the Beatles (who were seeking the path to transcendental meditation through a commercialized, fake Indian yogi and introduced Far Eastern themes into their music) softened the formalized pace and structure of baroque music and drove out of business the saccharine, schmaltz and Horatio Alger optimism of the crooners of the forties and fifties.

4   When the citizens of the "Woodstock nation" became older and managed to stay off opiates, they found themselves with steady, lucrative jobs on Wall Street and Madison Avenue. To their amazement, or solace, they discovered that many of their colleagues also had long hair, painted wide ties and gay coloured trousers, widening towards the cuffs. They also found themselves rubbing shoulders with other Mid-Western shoe manufacturers and New England insurance brokers who flocked to hear their old hero in huge concert halls, and enriched multi-millionaire and expert manufacturer of instant nostalgia Bob Dylan even more. In middle and old age, the Woodstock participant rebels may turn into institutionalized peddlers of Tantalic non-conformism. The "squares" like it. After a hard day at the office, they pour out to Greenwich Village or to Soho and buy some non-conformist unwinding from the institutionalized deviants who dress and act exactly like the "camp" image of a non-conformist ordered to specification by the "squares".

5   These days "Young Turks" may be found everywhere in participant Eastern communities. They introduce new tractors and harvesters into the medieval agricultural methods at Mount Hebron. They fight for co-education in the Arab village, where women are hidden and boys killed if they invite a girl on an unchaperoned date. They fight against the authority of the village elders, and introduce Western pop music to the village square coffee house. And yet a discerning eye may detect an oriental muted spasm in the Arab pop singer rendering the latest pop hit. He has all the necessary external appearances of a pop singer: long hair, a drooping moustache and a glittering unisex overall, but his mood is self-effacing and his half-closed eyes long for oblivion.

6   When the "Young Turk" becomes older, his fires of rebellion mellow. However, having been fixated on the object, he cannot really

partake in the quietist self-manipulative participant culture. But even in the participant cultures of non-doers there are many roles to be performed by busybodies, organizers and manipulators. They will be the ones to collect, organize, record and interpret the ways of Buddha. They will sponsor construction of a mosque and commission the best artists to decorate its dome. They will build religious bodies and institutions for Taoism, Hinayana Buddhism and Sufism, although the mere thought of institutionalized religion is abhorrent to a true mystic.

7 The "pneumatics", those who partake of the Sacred Knowledge and have learned the way of spiritual ascent, are the mystic innovators whose personality was fixated at early non-differentiation and who were raised in a participant culture. Still in their young phase of growth, they had the urge to spread the word. They were not yet ready to delve into a solitary search for awakening into the non-self.

Buddha was a young prince when he decided to save not only himself but also the entire world, so he left his pleasure girls and went out to preach the extinction of desire and the renunciation of the self.[84]

Rabbi Isaac Luria, the Holy Ari and the founder of Lurianic Kabbalah, came to Safed as a young man and in a few years initiated the vast Kabbalistic movement that bears his name.

Joachim of Flora was not content to immerse himself in the great inner splendour revealed to him in the well on Mount Tabor, but he collected a circle of disciples around him and formed the mystic order of Flora. However, in the later phases of their life when the fires of proselytizing and sharing their experiences with others had consumed themselves, the disciples were ready for their ultimate calling: the life of a secluded quest for the annihilation of the self.

8 The life of a Buddhist monk in Burma is the epitome of participation since it presumably combines both the Tantalic personality type and the extreme participant social character. Many people in the West were amazed when U Nu, the Burmese political leader, retreated into a monastery after having been deposed from the premiership. What they failed to realize was that for a practicing Buddhist in a participant culture, a peaceful monastery was a welcome change from the intrigues of government and Western-style power politics. Monastic orders are not as prevalent today as in antiquity, yet in participant cultures like India one does not have to enter an institution in order to pursue Nirvana. However, in the more participant European society of the Middle Ages, aspiring mystics could lose themselves in the innumerable monasteries (by the year 1100, there were some 540 monasteries in France alone): they could choose a Carthusian monastery, usually situated in a secluded place, where each monk worked, ate and slept in his own separate cell and practiced almost perpetual silence. They could join

155

a Cistercian monastery, where even literacy was unnecessary. The clochards in our separant societies, which have little tolerance for deviance, would have had it very good in the Middle Ages. All they had to do was join one of the holy orders of mendicants, and drift and tramp not only with impunity but also with the halo of a saint.

We have now analyzed the three components of the Tantalus Ratio and their interrelationships. In **chapter 5** we shall describe the conflict of social characters as extant in the war of fundamentalist Islam on Occidental culture.

The
Twenty-First Century
Kulturkampf

5

Fundamentalist Islam vs. Occidental Culture

I thank God that my sons Oudai and Qussai and my grandson Mustafa have sacrificed themselves for this country.

Saddam Hussein in a recorded message to the Iraqi people

Fundamentalist Islam, like all extremist movements, is fuelled, led and dominated not by middle-range personalities but by extreme activists. In order to be a leader of Al-Qaeda, Hamas, The Front for the Liberation of Palestine and the Martyrs of El Aqsa, one needs to outdo the other militant and fundamentalist organizations in terms of causing loss of life and creating spectacular havoc. Hence the relevance of a personality theory that can explain the formation of the leadership of Fundamentalist Islam in the frame of reference of deviance. We seek to understand the *Kulturkampf* of fundamentalist Islam against Western culture within the context of a culture conflict. It will be useful to examine this culture conflict frame of reference in some detail. Thorsten Sellin states:

Culture conflicts are sometimes regarded as by-products of a cultural growth process – the growth of civilization – sometimes as the result of the migration of conduct norms from one culture complex or area to another. However produced, they are sometimes studied as mental conflicts and sometimes as the clash of cultural codes.

The theoretical premises of a culture conflict may be expanded on both a relatively well cultivated social level and a meagrely explored personal one. The following will guide our analysis:

I   Normative conflict situations take place, presumably, within the arena of the personality of the potential criminal or deviant prior to his first criminal act or his initial "recruiting" into a deviant subculture. These internal conflicts and their subsequent manifestations are crucial in the differentiation process of defining a person to himself and to his relevant others as delinquent and deviant. This is the rather abrupt transfer from the "right" side of the legal and social fence to the "wrong" side.

2 The increasingly deeper integration of an individual within the criminal or deviant group, and his corresponding rejection of the "legitimate" or "square" normative systems, involves rather elaborate conflict processes: the narrowing of socio-economic opportunities, the rupture or jeopardization of marriage and other domestic affiliations, the stigmatizing rejection and counter-rejection of friends, community, voluntary associations and most of the former membership and reference groups. The last step in this process is full-fledged membership in the criminal or deviant group. Resolution of the internal conflicts with the "right" side of the fence at this advanced stage of deviance occurs by severing most relevant normative ties with it. The normative clashes of social control becomes a vestige of external conflict between the deviant's own group and the organs enforcing the laws of the "legitimate" groups.

3 Fluctuations of crime rates in a given community over a given period of time, the genesis and volume of special types of crime and deviance, urbanization, industrialization, internal and external migration, disintegration and secularization of traditional and tribal structures, are the link between most forms of social change and the conflict of conduct norms.

A Frame of Reference

A frame of reference is a common boundary of phenomena that has an empirical common denominator. The common denominator may not necessarily characterize the *whole* phenomenon under consideration; it is sufficient that a part of its factual manifestation fits into the common boundary of the frame of reference. By exclusion, we may note the culture conflict premise is not a theoretical system in the engulfing Parsonian sense, nor is it of similar scope to the conflict theory of society where society (according to the expounders of Georg Simmel's thought) is held together in dynamic equilibrium by diverging normative discord. We hold, moreover that a culture conflict is also not a "middle range theory" by which Robert Merton denoted the relatively limited theories applied to rather narrow and well-defined areas of study. A culture conflict is both wider and deeper and at the same time less systematic than a middle range theory. The latter operates on one level of analysis whereas a culture conflict may include in its premises phenomena that occur on different planes of a space that need not have clear-cut delineations.

Before we launch our own analysis of the clash between fundamentalist Islam and Western civilization it would be beneficial to examine two celebrated attempts to cope with this phenomenon. One is a journalist's effort and the other a wide-ranging essay.

In "The Rage and the Pride"[1] Oriana Fallaci strongly urges the West to realize that an inverse crusade is going on: Fundamentalist Islam is marching against Western civilization. A Charles Martellus[2] – the Frankish king who at Poitiers in the year AD 732 stopped the *Khaliffa*, Abd-ar-Rahman, from conquering Europe – would be of no avail today. The twenty-first century Muslim *Jihad* (holy war) against Western civilization is being waged not by regular armies but by guerrillas, terrorists and the most formidable of weapons: suicide bombers. In 1945, during World War II, 21 US battleships were destroyed by Kamikaze pilots near Okinawa. This was the main reason for President Truman's decision to authorize use of the atom bomb on Hiroshima and Nagasaki. Akijo Alshoka, a Kamikaze pilot, wrote the following before his mission:

I am going to battle with a smile on my face. The moon will be full tonight when I fly to the open sea on the shores of Okinawa . . . I shall target an enemy battleship and I shall show you Caesar that I can die bravely.[3]

Similarly, the suicide bomber who sacrifices himself in a jihad for Allah is not deemed to be a suicide (*intihar*), which is forbidden by Islam, but a sacred Martyr (*shahid*), which is saintly heroism that brings paradise and exposure to God.[4] Indeed, Sheikh Muhammad Sayyid Tantawi of El-Azhar University of Egypt, the highest authority in Islam, decreed in a *fatwa* (religious ruling) in 1996 that suicide bombers are the most privileged sacrificial victims with God since they carry out His *jihad*.[5] Thus, not only are the terrorist exploits of Al-Quaeda, El Islami, Hizbullah, Hamas, the martyrs of El-Aqsa and many other militant Islamic groups vindicated, they also receive religious sanction.

For example, in an Islamic conference held in Stockholm, Sweden in July 2003, Sheikh Yousef Al-Qaradhawi preached for, legitimized and sanctioned terror and suicide bombing. This is of special importance in our present context since Al-Qaradhawi is the leader of the Islamic Committee for Adjudicating the *sharia* (religious law) in Europe. This committee convenes every few months in a different location in Europe; its decisions are binding on all Muslims in Western countries.

Under the guidance of Sheikh Al-Qaradhawi, a decision was adopted at the Stockholm conference stating that suicide bombing is prescribed, stipulated and ordained when a militarily more powerful nation subjugates a morally or spiritually superior one. This was the experience with British, French and American colonialism (against the Indians) and Israeli occupation of Palestine. It was further stipulated that in the case of a terrorist state, the foremost example being Israel, which subjugates and demeans its Palestinian inhabitants, suicide bombing is not only justified but is, in fact, legitimate.

159

Accordingly, the United States is a legitimate target of suicide bombings since it strives to impose its dictatorship around the world. When suicide bombers seek to release prisoners from the Israeli *goals* or to force the trespassing Israeli army to pull out from the occupied territories, suicide is not only legitimate but also moral; it is viewed as the epiphany of Gods' justice on earth.

Of utmost importance is the conference's statement that the blood and property of all the *Dar-el-Harb* (non-Muslims who eventually should be eliminated) are not immune from the wrath of the Muslim warrior. By being antagonistic to Islam the infidels make themselves legitimate prey to Allah's *shuhada* (martyred bombers). It is a measure of the somnolent vulnerability of the West that this kind of macabre decision by the chief Muslim authority in the West did not make glaring headlines in the press. Fallaci is warning that fundamentalist Muslims in Afghanistan, Sudan, Israel, Pakistan, Malaysia, Iran, Egypt, Iraq, Algeria, Senegal, Syria, Kenya, Libya, Chad, Lebanon, Morocco, Indonesia, Yemen, Saudi Arabia, Somalia and other countries with large Muslim populations are out to vanquish and destroy Western civilization.[6] Those in the West who fail to realize this are very similar to the somnolent European countries in the 1930s that witnessed Nazi Germany arm itself to the teeth yet allowed themselves to be cheated by the Munich Pact in the belief that Adolf Hitler actually wanted "peace in our time".

Fallaci warns us that no military victory like the American one in Iraq will ever extinguish the fires of terrorism and jihad. On the contrary, it will kindle more flames of bloodshed and destruction, especially among Shiite Muslims for whom martyrdom is evidence of self worth. Moreover the *Shuhada* are certain to have a place in *Jahana* (paradise) with its 72 black-eyed virgins whose sole role, desire and aim is to entertain Jihad martyrs.[7] Fallaci rejects the notion that the struggle between fundamentalist Islam and Western civilization can be analyzed within the framework of a culture conflict because she holds that Western culture is far superior to Islamic culture; the two cannot therefore be compared fairly.

Unlike Fallaci, Samuel P. Huntington is not a journalist, but a renowned political scientist; as such, he does not avail himself of value judgments. In *The Clash of Civilizations*[8] he analyzes the conflict between fundamentalist Islam and Western civilization within the culture conflict frame of reference. The perennial dichotomy made by Islam is between them and us, the "us" being *Dar-el-Islam,* the Muslim realm, and the "them" being the *Dar-el-Harb*, the realm of war.[9] Still, there was a time in which many Muslim socialists tried to emulate *in toto* Western civilization so as to jumpstart modernism and compete with the West economically and militarily. Huntington calls this emulation *Kemalism* after Kemal Pasha (Kemal Ataturk), the Turkish leader who by force Europeanized Turkey after World War I through such actions as outlawing use of the Arabic alphabet, limiting the practice of Islam, and authorizing police to remove the *tarbush* (traditional red headdress) from people's heads. Similarly, in the 1920s Rezah Shah Pahlevi firmly placed Iran on a diet of Westernization, industrialization and secularization, which continued under his son until the Ayatollah Khomeini ousted him 1979. Concomitant with colonialism in the Middle East and Africa, a self-effacing imitation of the British and French cultures was carried out by the indigenous élites, the results many times being Levantinism.

The extreme manifestation of the Levantine is behaviour based on the external forms and attributes of a culture, while at the same time being ignorant of or disregarding its contents and intrinsic values. It is manifest among members of oriental and Eastern cultures exposed to European culture. The Middle Eastern Levantine adopts Occidental languages, dress and mannerisms. He is not acquainted with, nor has he had the opportunity, to become interested in European literature, art or history, and he has not internalized the values of European culture.

In many instances, Levantinism results from a failure to imitate or rebel. Individuals or groups in a society regard the adoption and absorption of a more advanced and progressive culture as a panacea for all miseries and social ills. Eventually the task proves too formidable or the internal cultural mixture is thought to be impossible, and the innovation or rebellious zeal to integrate with the so-called "enlightened" culture deteriorates into a superficial and shallow imitation of its external manifestations. On the group level, this can take the form of an Ataturk or a Zaglul Pasha burning with the fervour of making Turkey and Egypt modern Occidental nations, but ends in the pitiful image of Levantine bourgeoisie in Alexandria and Constantinople whose original oriental values and culture are still latent below the surface. The group's reaction towards this behaviour is far from derogatory, because usually those who display the external trademarks of an advanced and modern culture belong to the social élite and are idolized by the ignorant multitudes.

European culture followed Oswald Spengler's design. It towered in its technical achievement to space flight and nuclear energy and declined in spirit to the abysmal nausea of Jean-Paul Sartre, the hopeless men of Samuel Becket, the monstrosities of Eugene Ionesco, the agonies of Friedrich Durrenmatt and the obscenities of Jean Genet. This is a tired spirit – desiccated, inanimate. But in the not-too-distant past the spirit of Europe was a carnivore, devouring, swallowing, destroying, incorporating and changing less predatory cultures than itself. On its way it left many victims. European gluttony is Levantinism. The Levantine is essentially a shallow absorber of culture, because Levantinism was mainly associated with Middle Eastern culture, which was exposed to European cultural influence. However, this may happen and must have happened with other predatory cultures like the Islamic, Hindu, Hellenic, Egyptian, Mayan and other carnivores that swept up, clashed with, and devoured herbivores or less aggressive cultures.

Historically, a Levantine, in the sociological connotation of the term, was a European who had "gone native" in the Middle East. Only lately has Levantinism been used (but not studied) in the sense of the present context.

A blending of cultures can produce a new organic entity whereas the Levantine melange is bound to remain a barren admixture. Alfred Kroeber states:

> Cultures can blend to almost any degree and not only thrive but perpetuate themselves. The classic Greek civilization was a mixture of primitive Greek, Minoan, Egyptian and Asiatic elements; Japanese civilization is partly indigenous, partly Chinese, partly Indian and Western in its technology . . . the greater part of the context of every culture is probably of foreign origin, although assimilated into a whole that works more or less coherently and is felt as a unit.[10]

However most clashes of Western culture with other cultures have resulted in various degrees and shades of Levantinism. Arnold Toynbee notes:

> In the struggle for existence the West has driven its contemporaries to the wall and entangled them in the meshes of its economic and political ascendancy but it has not yet disarmed them of their distinctive cultures. Hard-pressed though they are, they can still call their souls their own.[11]

This would be the case if the subjugated cultures managed to preserve the core of their indigenous cultures, which is hardly likely in the modern era of rapid social change. More often their cultural soul, to use Toynbee's simile, has withered away and in its place has adopted a watered-down version of Western culture.

Sociologically, this phenomenon is one aspect of the individual's experience of social culture conflict; as such, it was analyzed by Sellin in his discussion on culture conflict, and by Everett Hughes as a part of the problem of marginality.[12] Sellin was well aware that the disjunction between the new norms and the internalized value structure might be associated with deviant behaviour. Indeed, this was confirmed in a study conducted by the author together with Gideon Rahav and Esther Segal, which suggested that Arab villagers in Israel who adopted some of the European secular norms of Israeli society were more vulnerable to delinquency and crime.[13]

The aetiology of Levantinism can generally be traced to a failure of innovation. The Afro-Asian intellectual, the South American revolutionary and the idealistic communist bring from abroad – or from books – new ideas, techniques and schemes for raising the standard of living, eliminating malaria, trachoma and syphilis, introducing more efficient and less corrupt bureaucracies, and installing a postal service or a telephone system that really works. Reality is rarely cooperative: there are no roads for the heavy trucks to convey equipment; there is no money or trained workers to construct the roads; very few people understand technical matters; the population is so entrenched in its traditional routine that few avail themselves of new services – or are even interested in them. The Western idea of hard work and the concepts of accuracy or even of time itself are foreign, undesirable or meaningless – what is the big hurry? So the great dream deteriorates into rusty, unused, broken equipment, the clerks continue their perennial slumber undisturbed, while the timetables and efficiency charts are slowly covered with dust from the scorched desert plains or with entangled vines from the humid jungle. The innovator is discouraged, deflated and disgusted, and succumbs to his private hibernation retreat surrounded by the external remnants of his dream, a few gadgets, a few beverages, a few clothes and half-baked knowledge sent over to him from the faraway "progressive" culture. This is the main current of individual Levantinism.

With time, emulators of Occidental cultures realized that they were in love with a mirage. There can be no admixture between their indigenous cultures and Western culture, especially when the latter exploits the former through political or economic colonialism. Freedom fighting and wars of independence marked most of the second half of the twentieth century. Furthermore, the conflictual encounter with Occidental culture and the relatively shallow absorption of their patterns of cultures and norms was linked to a disintegration of the familial and traditional normative structures of Muslim societies. Middle Eastern and North African Muslim societies witnessed the disintegration of familial ties and the exposure of their young to drugs, alcohol, pornography, gambling and prostitution, all of which they attributed to the encounter with the West. Hence, fundamentalist Islam howled a rallying cry back to the purist Islamic norms of family asceticism, thrift and sexual mores. The enemy was the Occident, the harbinger of all those ills. Hence, *Jihad* should be waged to the bitter end against Western nations, culture, religion, technology, art and literature.

Huntington argues that Westernization and modernization are two parameters that are only tangentially correlated. Westernization would enhance modernization of indigenous cultures. But then, when economic and technological progress reaches a fair level of political, military and economic might and independence, a sense of dignity and self-esteem sets in stimulating pride in one's roots and traditions and rejection of Occidental values and of Western culture as a whole.[14] On the personal level the clash between Western values and norms and indigenous traditional ones that are liable to give way and disintegrate, temporarily leads to a value vacuum, and to alienation and anomie that may lead to the embrace of fundamentalist Islam. This could create a renewed sense of belonging – "rootedness" and "ego-identity", in the Eriksonian sense.[15] Our stance differs from the culture conflict frame of reference as applied to the clashes between Western and Islamic cultures and their resolutions. Huntington bases himself on research by Ronald Dore,[16] whereby the first generation élite of a newly independent colony are educated in the former colonial power's universities, and thus bring back with them an admiration and adherence to Western norms and culture. However, second generation youth, studying at home in their indigenous languages, are influenced by their own culture and religion and hence are more likely to adhere to fundamentalist Islam. Our claim is that the second generation is still uncertain and confused from parental influence on the one hand, and local culture, on the other. Hence, the second generation is culturally passive; rarely does it actively reject Western culture. Usually, this role is assumed by the third generation, who are sure of their origin, firmly anchored in their indigenous culture and fiercely proud of their heritage, which they consider far superior to any Occidental normative system. They are the natural candidates to fight Western culture and embrace fundamentalist Islam.[17]

The rejection of Western mores and values by Muslim fundamentalists despite their willingness to accept Western technology in industry, science, medicine as well as in the military, is mainly due to the fact that the largely Sisyphean diachronic *arriviste* tool-oriented West does not really agree with the Tantalic, synchronic, passive and meditative East. Unlike regimented, stratified and specialized Christianity, Islam is unified holistically and embraces the whole human life, both individual and group. The Muslim's customs, mores, morals and laws are regulated in the realm of the family, tribe, nation, subject and object, physics and metaphysics, faith and logic. Huntington claims that Islam is well on its way to dominate holistically the Muslim's life, the way Marxism ruled the body, soul and society of its adherents in a totalitarian manner.[18] The Muslim Brotherhood aims and – in many Islamic societies succeeds – in dominating the educational systems, from kindergarten to university, and thus infiltrates in a relatively short period the social and political infrastructures of a large number of Muslim nations.

Muslims, points out Huntington, are more likely to resort to violence to deal with internal and external conflicts. The *New York Times* counted 59 ethnic conflicts in 1993, half of which involved Muslims. In 1993–94, Muslims were involved in 26 out of 50 ethno-political conflicts. Ruth Seaward found that of the twelve wars waged in 1992 with at least 1,000 deaths, nine were between Muslims and non-Muslims. The most frightening statistic is that the mean military strength of Muslim countries on a predetermined scale is 11.8 compared to 7.1 for other countries; the military budget in Muslim countries is an average of 17.7 compared to 12.3 for other countries.[19] Indeed, *Din Muhammad Beseif*, The Law of Muhammad, as decreed by Islam – is by way of the sword.

The Second Law of Thermodynamics

Another parameter, which is rarely related to human behaviour, is the entropy gradient of the second law of thermodynamics. This law was formulated for physics and mechanics by the Frenchman Sadi Carnot in

1827 and by the German Rudolf Clausius in 1868, respectively. The law states that in a closed system, entropy (the dissipation of energy) must ultimately reach a maximum. Entropy then ordains that in closed systems the physical or chemical processes will degrade.[20] The second law of thermodynamics also states that work is dissipated into heat but that heat cannot be completely converted into work. This is the principle of irreversibility in nature.[21] This law of entropy increases, with nature becoming more disordered and thus determining the diachronic "arrow of time". However, the work that is most relevant to our present context was carried out by Ilya Prigogine and his associates. It concerns the second law of thermodynamics as related to open systems with inward and outward flowing energy that is not in equilibrium.[22] The work of Prigogine and his associates shows that non-living systems, such as lasers, and living systems that are dependent for their viability on outside energy, can maintain themselves by using energy from the external source, thus reducing their systems' entropy by maintaining a distance from the equilibrium order yet increasing the entropy of the larger source of energy. The variation on the theme by Joseph Kestin states that systems with temperature, pressure and chemical equilibrium would resist the dissipation of this equilibrium by opposing the applied gradients, which push the system away from its local equilibrium.[23] An example is the need for humans to retain their fixed body temperature: thus in hot weather the body sweats to reduce body temperature. Air-conditioning, heating devices and clothing can also maintain the body's local thermal equilibrium – at the cost of increasing the entropy of the global energy resources.

165

Prigogine and his associates have investigated the self-organization of dissipative structures by means of fluctuations, which lead to irreversible indeterministic choices at the junctions of bifurcations.[24] This also conforms with the dynamics of structuralism set forth by Claude Lévi-Strauss and Jean Piaget, whereby structures and apparently dissipative structures have self-regulative capacities.[25] As for life, Ludwig Boltzman, the pioneering scholar of thermodynamics, aptly describes the evolutionary struggle as a competitive fight for entropy. He says:

> The general struggle for existence of animate beings is therefore not a struggle for raw materials – these, for organisms, are air, water and soil, all abundantly available – nor for energy which exists in plenty in any body in the form of heat (albeit unfortunately not transformable), but a struggle for entropy, which becomes available through the transition of energy from the hot sun to the cold earth. In order to exploit this transition as much as possible, plants spread their immense surface of leaves and unexplored certain chemical syntheses of which no one in our laboratories has so far the least idea. The products of this chemical kitchen constitute the object of struggle of the animal world.[26]

Evolution is carried out through an adaptive choice of the organism *vis-à-vis* an influx of energy and changing conditions from outside. Plants grow by capturing and harnessing solar energy and dissipating external resources. Hence, for plants, growth and survival is a function of their ability to absorb and dissipate energy on a competitive basis. It follows that ecosystems also obey the second law of thermodynamics since

> Such ecosystem development increases energy degradation thus follows the imperative of the second law. This hypothesis can be tested by observing the energetics of ecosystem development during the successional process or by determining their behaviour as they are stressed or as their boundary conditions are changed.
>
> As ecosystems develop or mature, they should increase their total dissipation, and should develop more complex structures with greater diversity and more hierarchical levels to abet energy degradation. Species that survive in ecosystems are those that funnel energy into their own production and reproduction and contribute to autocatalytic processes, which increase the total dissipation of the ecosystem. In short, ecosystems develop in a way which systematically increases their ability to degrade the incoming solar energy.[27]

Prigogine's ideas can be applied to our context by use of the two dynamics of fluctuations and bifurcations, which he describes. According to Prigogine, fluctuations are disorders within the subsystems of systems. When these fluctuations become very violent through resonance or feedback they can shatter the organization of the system. This process, which happens in a system that is far from equilibrium, is the "bifurcation" junction. At this crossroad, it is up to the organism, in our case the human being, to choose indeterministically to react in a manner that is evolutionarily adaptive and thus reach an "order through fluctuations", or chose not to intervene or react in a non-adaptive manner with catastrophic results for the system.[28] Applying these dynamics to human society we claim that the transformations and exchange of energies between social characters obey the rules of thermodynamics and entropy: Muslim societies in the Middle East and North Africa have perennially been Tantalic participant social-characters of low entropy, while Occidental cultures have mostly been close to the Sisyphean pole of social characters with high entropy. When the West invaded Muslim societies by sheer force of colonialism, economic domination, or technological, scientific or managerial superiority, an influx of violent fluctuations occurred leading to a bifurcation junction with nefarious, evolutionary non-adaptive and structurally destructive results for the Muslim societies. First, traditional Muslim values of asceticism, frugality, self-sufficiency, lack of worldly ambition, cohesion of family, tribal mores, sexual virtuousness and belief in God, were assaulted and harassed by the carnivorous, covetous, ambitious Occidental invaders. Second, industry, oil, conspicuous consumption, fast food, hedonism and present orientation, brought an avalanche of high entropy, waste, pollution and the tyranny of diachronic time in low entropy societies that lacked the means and structures to deal with these ecological catastrophes. Kemal Pasha Ataturk, Reza Shah Pahlevı, Zaglul Pasha and many others who tried to emulate the West, destroyed the low entropy infrastructure of their societies but could not possibly build, erect and transform their cultures into high entropy Western type social characters; thus their societies slumped into what Halper calls incoherence. The Levantine's shallow absorption of Western culture, on top of the ruins of traditional norms and values, makes for an incoherence of *weltanschauungen*[29] crippled "ego-boundary" and resultant low self-esteem, powerlessness, meaning-lessness, alienation, anomia and accidia. All this may be the consequent pathological states for societies of low entropy and for the individuals who comprise them and who have been invaded, harassed and subjugated by social characters of high entropy. In order to understand the alienating havoc wrought by Sisyphean high entropy cultures when clashing with Tantalic low entropy cultures, a conceptual clarification is required

We propose a conceptual revival of "accidia" ("acedy" or "accidie") to denote an individual's breakdown of involvement with social norms and values, just as "anomie" ("anomy", or "anomia") has been resurrected from sixteenth century usage to denote normative disintegration in society. The need for a distinct and specific concept of accidia stems primarily from the fact that anomie was conceived by all its exponents, from Emile Durkheim to Merton and beyond, as an attribute of groups, not individuals. For Durkheim, anomie was a collective hangover from a social (mainly economic) shock. One of its manifestations was the break-down of controls over Man's aspirations: "Whatever class has been especially favoured by the disturbances (of affluence) is no longer disposed to its former self-restraint, and, as a repercussion, the sight of its enhanced fortune awakens in the groups below it every manner of covetousness. Thus the appetites of men, unrestrained now by a public opinion, which has become bewildered and disoriented, no longer know where the bounds are before which they ought to come to a halt . . . Because pros-perity has increased desires are inflamed . . . The state of rulelessness or *anomie* is further heightened by the fact that human desires are less disci-plined at the very moment when they would need a stronger discipline."[30]

Durkheim is speaking of a normative rupture of society. The effect of this on individuals is almost taken for granted: the normative enclosure has burst open. Containment by the bumper effects of boundaries and lim-its has suddenly disintegrated. Individuals are exposed to the disrupting effects of limitless desires and boundless aspirations. Merton, Durkheim's contemporary apostle, also stresses the societal nature of anomie. This might come as a surprise to some students of human alienation, because in his now classic exposition of Social Structure and Anomie,[31] Merton expressly deals with *individual* modes of (mal)adaptation. However, the crux of Merton's analysis rests on the group, on the disjuncture between the social structure and the cultural system, between social goals and the normative avenues to achieve them. The individuals in Merton's paradigm are affected by these social disjunctions but *his units of analysis are still societies and not individuals*. He expressly excludes mental processes, which cannot be anchored on the social and cultural levels of analysis from his study. He explicitly states that: "Anomie refers to a property of a social system . . . Anomie, then is a condition of social surroundings, not a condition of particular people . . . to prevent conceptual confusion different terms are required to distinguish between the anomic state of the social system."[32] This conception of anomie is focused, therefore, on a societal state and the individual's confrontation with it is secondary; the individual himself is left in the shade and his subjective state of mind is entirely disregarded. No doubt, Merton realizes that the socially focused conceptualisation of anomie leaves a *lacuna* and calls for a separate personal concept of anomie. He refers us, therefore, to *anomia,* a term coined by Leo Srole to describe the anomic state of the individual. Still, accidia[33] is more of a personal subjective state of mind than anomia. The latter, as measured by the five variables in Srole's scale,[34] is again the confrontation of an individual to some societal states and not a description of individuals as such. Srole thus implies that anomie, as a property of society, may be measured by the distribution of anomia as a property of individuals and vice versa. This assumes, quite unwarrantably, that objective social properties are always accurately reflected in objective individual properties, as if individuals' subjective perceptions and societal experience was irrelevant. For us, this is untenable because any acute state of social anomie must be subjectively perceived as such by individuals, otherwise it would not necessarily be correlated with anomia as an objective property of individuals. This may be likened to the common sociological and Marxist fallacy, which is at best a crude simplification, of regarding an objective state of economic need, measured by a low standard of living, as a predisposing factor to crime and delinquency. Perhaps the ultimate and most objective human deprivation is the threat of starvation. But this would not be regarded by most human beings as sufficient justification for cannibalism. Hindus would not regard it as an incentive to slaughter sacred cows, nor would Orthodox Jews resort to eating pork no matter how available it was. On the other hand, the lack of funds to buy a mink coat for a new mistress might be subjectively defined by some individuals as a need potent enough to induce them to embezzle money from their employers. The relationship (or lack thereof) between anomie and anomia seems rather similar to the problematic correlation, asserted by crude versions of Marxism, between economic need as objectively measured in society and economic need as subjectively conceived by individuals.

Melvin Seeman, in a well-known paper, identifies five types of alienation.[35] The first three – powerlessness, meaninglessness and normlessness (anomie) – are clearly attributes of society. The other two types of alienation, isolation and self-estrangement, are subjective states of mind, but they do not cover the same ground as accidia, for reasons that we shall specify later. We note here that powerlessness was the mode of alienation originally imputed by Karl Marx in his early writings on capitalist society. He conceived powerlessness as a state in society where the worker does not have any means of control and decision over the processes of his work and its outcome.[36] A subsequent conceptualization in the Marxist tradition led to the term Fetishization, which George Lukacs coined to denote the estrangement of Man's creations from himself, his reification into a mere object in a surrounding world populated by an increasing number of thing-objects and people-objects.[37] These have lost their normative or affective meaning and have turned into neuter, dead weights in his cognition. However, Fetishization still relates primarily to Ego's surroundings: it is a condition of his environment and not of his subjective self. Although the comparison would be vehemently disputed and abhorred by Lukacs, in some ways this is similar to Martin Heidegger's *Das Man*, which also refers to the meaningless reification of things and persons. The existentialist counterpart to our conceptualization of accidia as a property of individuals consists of their conceptualization of the situation where a person becomes reified and objectified *to himself*. We may think here of Sartre's estranged consciouslessness of *l'être en soi*[38] when applied to Ego's self-image as perceived by Ego himself. We can say, then, that the objectification of Ego's self as subjectively perceived by him is the core of our conceptualization of accidia as an attribute of individuals and not of social structures.

The dynamism of our conception of accidia rests in its being the final link in a triadic chain. The three elements of the chain are as follows. First there occurs an initial normative gap between previously internalized norms and newly transmitted ones. Second, there is a congruity-motivated involvement by the subject to bridge this gap. And finally, if this involvement-effort fails, there is a value-breakdown, a disengagement; or, to use current slang, the subject mentally "cops-out". Our dynamic conception of accidia is anchored on the congruity principle, which is a basic ego defence mechanism that motivates human beings to resolve their normative conflicts and thus re-establish their otherwise threatened cognitive balance and consonance.

Pious saints like the Talmudic Reish-Lakish and the Catholic Augustine were notorious lechers in their youth; the switch from a "life of sin" to a life of religious fanaticism and apostasy is quite common. The accidiac would tend to agree with Sartre that "it seems that Man is incapable of producing more than an impotent God".[39] Similarly, when the examining magistrate brandishes a crucifix at Meursault, his natural reaction is barely to react at all. The Existentialist outsiders are anaesthetized to *all* value-systems and commitments, particularly religious ones (including *committed* atheism). Similarly, accidiacs, to use Camus' Judge-penitent's simile in "The Fall", would like some of Dante's angels to be neutral in the fight between God and Satan.[40]

Among the types of alienation presented by Seeman, the nearest to our present exposition is "self-estrangement". The latter is quite in line with our conceptualization insofar as it relates to Erich Fromm's description of a mode of experience in which the person experiences himself as an alien and has become estranged from himself.[41] This is similar to the element of self-objectification, which we have identified as one of the components of accidia. However, Seeman considerably relies on an "other-directedness" element in his conceptualisation of self-estrangement. The former, as expounded by Ortega y Gasset and David Riesman, is a very common personality trait among individuals comprising "the mass society" and "the lonely crowd". Other-directedness makes for "joyful obedience" and a Dale Carnegie type contentedness. But for the accidiac, other-directedness is non-existent. Albert Camus' Meursault regards the judge who is trying him for murder, the courtroom and its audience as having hardly anything to do with him. At most his trial appears to him as a game.[42] He assumes the spectator and not the participant role, and at times is interested in the proceedings because it is his first time at a criminal trial. Sometimes he even feels *de trop* – at his own trial.[43] The Judge-penitent in *The Fall* is also "playing at doing things, and not doing, being and not being there".[44] The accidiac regards his environment as an arena where games are staged incessantly, but where he is a watcher and not a player. To him, Man is a *game-player* dabbling in semi-serious games, but the accidiac himself is not one of the players. Accidia is a hangover of the Tantalic low entropy social character that was dissipating in his levelling encounter with a high entropy Sisyphean social character.

The aetiology of so-called Third World societies is linked very significantly to the invasion of high entropy, socio-political and economic patterns of cultures into low entropy societies which cannot contain the resultant destructive fluctuations. These assault and destroy the traditional normative infrastructure with nothing but brute force, violence, corruption, managerial abuse and stifling mindless bureaucracy to take its place. The mineral and other natural resources in which the Third World is rich, work to its detriment in a positive feedback cycle. The low entropy Third World countries do not have the technology to mine and process their natural resources, hence the high entropy Western nations do it for them. They erect petrochemical plants mining industries and wood processing projects which enhance an accelerated urbanization, which takes the form of huge shantytowns. These processes destroy the traditional villages and create a vast population of a poor, homeless, undernourished and diseased population.[45] Since most of the food and consumer goods and gadgets are imported, they are handled either by Western agents and distribution companies aided by the local corrupt hereditary or by the military-backed oligarchy. This is the frightening saga of the aftermath of the violent encounter between the high entropy West and the low entropy Third World. Moreover, since low entropy countries are unable to develop their own industries, invading high entropy aggressive salesmen induce the already impoverished shantytown dwellers to buy more consumer goods that they cannot afford, hence they are sucked into the vicious circle of never-ending debt to "the company store".

Since oil revenues in the Middle East and North Africa go to a small minority of power crazed and money debauched potentates, most Muslim countries seem to have the pomp and ostentatious lavishness reminiscent of a *Thousand and One Nights* – for the exclusive consumption of corrupt and degenerated despots, with few resources allocated to social welfare, socialization, medicine and education for human rights and their awareness. Of course, this results in even greater poverty, more subjugation, less democracy, and less freedom for women. The only refuge left for the downtrodden masses seems to be the sole solaces that cannot disappoint and let down: Allah and the Koran. Since the shallow absorption of Western culture inherent in Levantine dynamics made for a distorted perception of Western social-characters, particularly as reflected by colonial bureaucracies or greedy executives of Western conglomerates, an us/them dichotomy has been created in the self/other perception of the Muslim populace.[46] Consequently, those who fall back onto purist Islam create a vision of themselves as worthy martyrs, mostly crushed, subdued and enslaved by the Western *wiedergeist*, usurper, Satan. Hence, all means are appropriate to combat this demonic trespasser. No moral scruples, legal restraints or pity should curb the fight against the hellish adversary. Since the United States and its ally, the Wise Men of Zion,[47] have never shown any compassion to their Muslim victims, the war against them should be to the bitter end. This is the ideology, war plan and strategy of Al-Qaeda, Hizbullah, Hamas and their ilk. Because the war against the West is a *Jihad*, no human can declare an armistice; only Allah can decide on the conduct of the war against the accused foes through his emissaries: Osama bin Laden, Sheikh Hassan Nassralla and (the late) Sheikh Ahmed Yassin. Their circumstances, and the view presented above, conforms with the work of entropy theorists, such as Ilya Prigogine and Hermann Haken,[48] who point out that when an extreme choice is followed in a bifurcation, all other alternative possibilities undergo a cognitive collapse as if they never existed.

Finally, we are left the question of whether it is possible to avoid, halt or curb this catastrophic collision between Islamic cultures and Western civilization. To approach this question seriously, we must divide it into two: First, do we have a model or experience of changing a low entropy culture into a high entropy culture? Second, could such a model or experience be applied to the clash between Islam and Occidental culture? We have an answer to our first query in the form of two examples, one a micro illustration of the absorption of Jewish immigrants in the hills of Jerusalem; the second, the ongoing experience of East Asia *vis-à-vis* modernization, social management and economic development.

The official ideology and strategy of the Jewish Agency in the 1950s was to force new immigrants, who at the time were mostly from low entropy cultures, to quickly discard the traditions, norms and values of their countries of origin and absorb the normative system of Israel, which at that time was largely a high entropy community. Consequently, at the new immigrant settlement of Beit Shemesh, located near Jerusalem, Jewish

Agency bureaucrats took great pains to create a "true melting pot," mixing all manner of ethnic groups so they would abandon the culture and norms of their countries of origin and become integrated Israelis as quickly as possible. Thus, a Yemenite family was settled near a Moroccan one, and both were placed opposite the asbestos shed of an extended Iranian family. This strategy resulted in strife, tension and social conflict, as well as twice the rate of delinquency in Beit Shemesh as compared to Jerusalem. *Per contra,* when the bureaucrats might have been away, sick or inattentive, a whole tribe of Kurdistani Jews replete with their leaders, Rabbis, *gabbais* (community functionaries) cantors, soothsayers and witchdoctors settled near by. At first, when the nurse came to offer medication to the sick, she was scolded and chased away. Gradually the tribe members learned that antibiotics were as effective as the incantations of the witchdoctor. Hence, every box of medicine had to have the benediction of the witchdoctor before actual use by tribe members. When people finally realized that the medicine was effective even without the blessing of the witchdoctor – they were immediately assigned to irrigate the old orchard, which didn't need irrigation to begin with. Today, with the coming of age of the third generation, delinquency is no longer part of the landscape at Ness-Harim, the tribal village. It is flourishing economically. Many second- and third-generation members are doctors, lawyers, senior army officers, and the rest are successful farmers who grow fruit, grapes and olives, and raise chicken, cattle and goats using the latest science and technology. On the Sabbath and on holidays, the entire tribe comes to the synagogue and kisses the hand of the barely literate tribal octogenarian headman.

Here the low entropy tribe has absorbed the high entropy patterns of the absorbing culture, yet the normative and traditional structures, having remained intact, did not allow the fluctuations caused by the absorption of innovations to disrupt the tribe. Hence, the fluctuations resulted in bifurcations, which adaptively enhanced the evolutionary synthesis and cultural growth of the whole tribe and its individual members. On the other hand, the traditional normative infrastructure of the Beit Shemesh families was disrupted because of the absorption of high entropy patterns of culture-generated fluctuations, which played havoc with the new immigrant families and their members.

On the macro level we have Japan, China and the so-called Four Tigers – Hong-Kong, Taiwan, South Korea and Singapore – initially all low entropy cultures that absorbed high entropy modernization and technology. Because they succeeded in keeping intact their traditional normative structures the fluctuations of modernization did not disrupt their infrastructures but instead bifurcated into evolutionary adaptation and synthesized into economic growth and cultural flourish. Kishore Mahbubani informs us that it took Britain 58 years and the United States 47 years to double GDP. Japan required 33 years; Indonesia, 17; South Korea, 11; and China, 10.[49] This brings to mind Napoleon's warning that we should let China sleep because the world will be sorry if she awakes. Western conglomerates must have difficulty sleeping when they consider that China and the Four Tigers already enjoy annual economic growth of approximately 8 percent. This remarkable feat was possible because modernization, industrialization and scientification were kept in check and balance by traditional Confucian values of asceticism, thriftiness, hard work, family cohesion, and individual responsibility for the welfare of the community.[50] Hence, high entropy patterns of culture generated fluctuations in the low entropy absorbing structures, but the Confucian values served as shock absorbers, and the fluctuations led to a bifurcation of growth and adaptive viability.

In sum, on both the micro and macro level, it is possible to achieve a viable and adaptive synthesis between low entropy and high entropy. Fundamentalist Muslims must realize with Camus that revolutions failed: the French Revolution ended with the Terror; the German Revolution, with Auschwitz; and the Russian Revolution, with the Gulag.[51] Also, the West realizes that the days of colonialism and economic exploitation of low entropy countries are just about over. Eventually, President Bush, the Israeli security forces, and anti-terrorism units around the world will demonstrate to militant fundamentalist Muslims that terrorism will not achieve its disruptive goals. The only way is viable synthesis between low entropy cultures backed by traditional normative infrastructures absorbing in a controlled manner the fluctuation-generating high entropy pattern of cultures resulting in adoptive evolution and growth. In the tenth and eleventh centuries, Jews and Muslims lived in Spain in a mutually fructifying symbiosis; later Christians joined in a *convevencia* with Alfonso (El Sabio) the 10th, which kindled the renaissance in Europe, the expansive discoveries of new worlds, and The Age of Enlightenment. Fundamentalist Muslims, and for that matter their Western adversaries, must realize the profound wisdom of Rabbi Akiva, the second-century sage, who said: "The forces of the world are determined, but Man is endowed with the Freedom of choice."[52] Hence, the stochastic bifurcation is given but a clear choice should be made between suicide, destruction and bereavement, and viability by dialogue and growth through the complementarity of opposites.

Interaction, Objectlessness and the Self-Continuum

Men are blind to the inner significance both of their own nature and everything around them.

Heraclitus, *Concerning Nature*

Now you see that the hope and the desire of returning to the first state of chaos is like the moth to the light, and that the Man who with constant longing awaits with joy each new springtime, each new summer, each new month and new year – deeming that the things he longs for are ever too late in coming – does not perceive that he is longing for his own destruction."

Leonardo da Vinci, *The Literary Works*

These two ways of thinking, the way of time and history, and the way of eternity and timelessness, are both part of man's efforts to comprehend the world in which he lives. Neither is comprehended in the other nor reducible to it . . . each supplementing the other – neither telling the whole story."

Robert Oppenheimer, *Science and the Human Understanding*

Earlier chapters have described the core personality vectors and some basic mechanisms that constitute parts and segments of the personality. The next task is to trace the form and manner in which these vectors, partial mechanisms and processes are structured into the self-continuum.

Empiricists tell us that the concept of self is useful because it may help us predict and understand behavior.[1] The self, the *proprium*, may only partly be warranted by the Cartesian *cogito*, but its overt and covert essence may be inferred from the whole range of human cognitive, conative and intuitive processes, as well from mystic experiences, when everything melts into Unity and nothing is but the omnipresent self.

The self-concept involves consistency and continuity, so that the same self is felt and defined by an individual from the moment his separate awareness has coagulated, until his death. The exceptions to this principle of the continuity and consistency of the self are morbidity and temporary dissolution or weakening of the self in extreme situations of hallucination and mystical experience.

Extreme exponents of symbolic interactionism argue against the consistency of the self. They claim that the self varies with each role that the individual plays in different social groups.[2] We hold the outward presentation of the self à la Erving Goffman, i.e. the social mark of a person changes with the individual's different membership group, but not the core structure of his self, which remains consistent throughout his life. The self, then, is the consistent and continuous inner sameness of the individual *separatum vis-à-vis* his environment. The "inner sameness" element of our definition of the self has, no doubt, an Eriksonian flavour to it.[3] But for Erik Erikson "ego identity" is the meaning of this inner sameness to others, whereas for us, the self is the structured barrier between the separate individual, as conceived by himself, and the flora, fauna, others and inanimate objects that are excluded from within the confines of this barrier. It would be superfluous to compare our definition of the self to other conceptualizations of the *proprium*, because these range from somatic corollaries through conscious processes to the experiential sediments of interaction, depending on the basic orientation of the author.[4]

In order to distinguish our present work from previous expositions, we may point out two methodological premises stand out. First, all conceptions of the self are either anchored on the object or on an inner, "pure", *a priori* self. The symbolic interactionist self is actually initiated and moulded by the surrounding others. Charles Cooley recruits Goethe's Tasso, who states that "only in Man does Man know himself",[5] to construe his "looking-glass self", i.e. the crystallization of the "I" through the reactive mirror-image of the surrounding others. George Mead envisages a self that is built by internalising the roles and expectations of the "generalized other". Only by constantly adopting the attitudes of these others may the self come into being.[6] On the other hand, the phenomenologists, following Edmund Husserl's lead, postulate a "pure-ego", which is the prime core of being reached by the technique of phenomenological reduction of all objects, predicates and attributes of the self.[7] We postulate a self that contains along a continuum both the components of interactive object relationship and the non-objective being, which longs for participant omnipresence; this relates to our separant and participant core personality vectors, the dynamic interplay of which is being structured into corresponding polarities within the self. We propose to denote the participant ontological core of self by the Hebrew word *Ani*. Its etymological meaning is "I", but in Kabbalist doctrine, *Ani* and *Ain* (nothingness) – having the same Hebrew letters but in a different order – are interchangeable and synonymous. Consequently, the *Ani*, the "I" longing for participant nonbeing, is the Tantalic objectless component of the self. We will denote the interactive object-related component of the self by the Hebrew word *Atzmi*, which may be translated into English as "myself". Its root is *etzem*, object in Hebrew, and is therefore most appropriate in denoting our object-related interactive self. To begin, we shall clarify some points of method and concepts; later we shall describe at length the nature of the *Ani-Atzmi* continuum within the dynamic structure of the self.

Another preliminary point is that most personologists describe the self as either an embodied construct or a dynamic system in constant flux. Chad Gordon, for instance, says: "The self is not a thing; it is a complex process of continuing interpretive activity – simultaneously by the person's located subjective stream of consciousness and the resultant accruing structure of self-conception."[8] The *panta rhei*, ever-flowing, dynamically pulsating self is epitomized in Harry Sullivan's conception of the self as a system flowing within and around the dynamisms of social interaction.[9]

An opposite view is that of the body-image psychologists,[10] the exponents of the "personal space[11] and the Gestalt psychologists, who were seemingly influenced by Wilhelm Dilthey's *Strukturzusammanband* of personality,[12] who highlights the boundaries, forms and moulds of the self. We combine both structured boundaries and dynamic systems in our conception of the self. The nature of this combination will be described later.

The self is the ontological essence that defines both its being for itself and for others and manifests its quest of nonbeing. The *Atzmi* is the interactive relational self reaching outward towards the manipulation of the object, whereas the *Ani* transcends spatio-temporality; it waives the object and reaches inwards towards pre-differentiated Unity. The two poles of our self-continuum are illustrated by the two sides of the tenth-century Cross of Lothar. On one side, we may see an imperial cross studded with jewels, while the image of the emperor at its centre is an emblem of power and confidence in one's ability to manipulate and dominate one's environment. On the other side, we have a flat arid dark image of Christ, His head bent as if contemplating His bare navel, His twisted body seemingly oblivious of his surroundings.[13]

It is important to point out that the *Atzmi* – the interactive self – has to have a subject and an object, a perceiver and a perceived. There is a continuous flow of perception to the *Atzmi* from flora, fauna, others and inanimate objects. The *Atzmi* may also perceive the body and the *Ani*, the ontological self, as objects. The *Ani*, on the other hand, does not necessarily have to have an object. The *Ani* has no awareness of itself as being separate from its surroundings in some mystic experiences, forms of madness, drug-induced euphoria, concentrated meditation and, sometimes, in orgasm as well. The boundaries of the self may also melt away and temporary objectless Unity may be achieved.

At this point I need to to confess a change of heart from some of our earlier writings, in which I denied the feasibility of an objectless inner-self.[14] Many of us who were trained in the positivistic tradition – that the science of Man has to follow the same rigour of measurement as in natural sciences – have experienced a scientistic crisis: we felt that the S-R (stimulu-response) matrix and measures of association may indeed be essential to study and understand many aspects of human behavior, but not all of them. The *Atzmi* is by definition a relational entity; therefore its interaction with its surroundings must be studied by measures of stimulus, response, association and correlation. Not so the *Ani*, which in its "pure" form is objectless and non-relational; consequently, measures of logic, deduction and inference do not apply to it. If we wish to study the whole human being and not merely fragments of it, we must rely on intuition, introspection and even meditation in order to grasp the *Ani* component of the self and thereby understand fully the dual nature of our personality.

Our study of the personality is, therefore, holistic and synthetic; it is not analytic. This is contrary to the mainstream of contemporary behavioral sciences,[15] and we are liable to be entangled in many whirlpools while rowing upstream in the established doctrine of personology.

Atzmi and *Ani*: **The Two Faces of Man**

The symbolic interactionist contention that the self is formed only through the mutuality of relationships between the individual and his surroundings, especially his "significant" and "relevant" others, applies only to the *Atzmi*: our interactive self. The *Atzmi* is not only the *persona*, the mask of ego as presented to others, but also the sum total of social roles and experiences internalized by ego. We may envisage the formation of the *Atzmi* as a selective recording and storing by ego of the constant flow of mutual expectations, perception and interaction between himself and his human and non-human environment. The *Atzmi* is both the social self, in the symbolic interactionist sense, and the objective self. It is defined *vis-à-vis* its environment through delimiting and deprivational definitions. We have pointed out elsewhere that the crystallization of the self from the non-self is a process of tearing away region after region of the original omnipresence of the neonate until the separate *Atzmi* is placed within its specific boundaries of spatio-temporality and the confines of a cocoon-like mesh of social norms.[16] The *Atzmi* is the seat of consciousness, the source of action, and a recipient of it. Most of the exponents of the self in traditional personology have been concerned with the *Atzmi*, and we have very little to add to their voluminous expositions. With the *Ani*, however, we are bound to tread on thin ice, because for the established doctrines in personology, the objectless self is either abhorred as anathema or dismissed as metaphysical conjecture. We shall therefore discuss the *Ani* at greater length because there is scant previous treatment of the onto-logical self in the relevant literature.

We shall begin by asserting that the essence of the *Ani* precedes the existence of the *Atzmi*. We therefore differ from the basic maxim of existentialism, that existence precedes essence not on philosophical but on psycho-naturalistic grounds. Earlier chapters have shown that the non-differentiated entity *in utero* and at early orality is an omnipresent, timeless and infinite essence, separated and confined within spatio-temporality by its deprivational interaction with its surroundings. Consequently, this timeless essence, when embedded later within the separate individual, is not a metaphysical phase but rather a natural phase of human development. Our conception of the *Ani* is in line with Husserl's later writings, in which he postulates the phenomenological reduction to the pure ego and says that the knowledge of possibilities (inherent in the pure ego) must precede that of actualities.[17] In like manner, the logically non-verifiable essences of our objectless *Ani*, which has the potential and possibility to interact, must precede the *Atzmi*, which comes into being through interaction. Yet our *Ani* differs from Husserl's pure ego, because it relates to experience and not to *a priori* transcendence. The *Ani* is the structured counterpart of the participation vector of the personality core, which strives to regain the boundlessness of pre-differentiated being. The Zen sage who demands in one of the Koans, "Show me your original face before you were born,"[18] asks to be shown the objectless *Ani* behind the spatio-temporal veils of the *Atzmi*.

At this stage of our exposition we are describing the *Ani* within the framework of the mature self, but its origins, nature and relative predominance within the self must be traced to the pre-natal and early oral fixations, as well as to the dynamics of the participation vector within the personality core. The naturalistic and experiential basis of our conceptualization of the *Ani* makes us reject, within a philosophical matrix, the neo-Kantian notion of an *a priori* space–time construct within the human psyche. Space and time are corollaries of object relationships and, therefore, are attributes of the *Atzmi*, the social self. There can be no space–time conception before the individual has been separated from the pantheistic omnipresence of early orality by its interaction with its surroundings. Moreover, the pre-natal and early oral pantheistic bliss, which is the basis of our exposition of the participation vector of the personality core, as well as the *Ani* component of the self, are also experienced phases of human development and not *a priori* constructs. Consequently, any epistemological hair-splitting about the thing-in-itself or the rift between the phenomenon and noumenon does not apply to the *Ani*. Its longing for Unity stems from its recorded experience of omnipresence at early orality and *in utero*. There the experience is of non-differentiated Unity, and any epistemological query (questioning the feasibility of an objectless subject when no object is yet in existence) is pointless. We agree with Ludwig Wittgenstein that the subject, the "I", is not a part of the world but is a limit of it.[19] We surely know nothing about the world "out there", but the crucial experience of the self is the formation of a boundary, a limit that defines the subject and separates it from the object. This boundary, or the lack of boundary, is the crucial element of the self in both its polar phases: the *Atzmi*, the interactional self, is constantly involved in stressing its own confined existence through the limits, barriers and walls of spatio-temporality; the *Ani*, on the other hand, does not acknowledge limits. It prompts the mystic to search the graces of Unity, the romantic to seek union through love, and the member of the "quiet majority" to look for shelter within the levelling togetherness of the herd. This quest for boundlessness is curbed by the *Atzmi*, which points out the vicissitudes of spatio-temporality to the soaring, boundless *Ani*. The *Ani* is a Don Quixote for whom the boundaries between his inner visions and his surroundings are non-existent or blurred, whereas the *Atzmi* is a pragmatic object-manipulating Sancho Panza.

We searched in vain for expositions that were directly relevant for our conceptualization of the *Ani* in the professional literature. The few we found were made mostly as peripheral *obiter dicta* allegations. It may be a sign of Sigmund Freud's real greatness that he conceded the existence of an "oceanic feeling" in Man, although it stood clearly contrary to his entire theoretical frame of reference. Freud's "oceanic feeling" is the individual's relatedness and Unity with the world. Freud traces this "oceanic feeling" to the pre-differentiated stage of human development. He also agrees that the "oceanic feeling" may be carried on from infancy to adulthood, but he then goes to great lengths to refute the significance of the "oceanic feeling" to the psychoanalytic conception of the personality core.[20] This underlying longing for Unity is the main characteristic of our *Ani*, which is carried over to the structure of the self from the early developmental phase of omnipresence.

Alport also makes an allegation on this aspect of the *Ani*, when he says that the self contains elements that make for inward Unity.[21] Some scattered statements exist in the philosophical literature that may support our conceptualization of the *Ani*. Wittgenstein distinguished between the two statements: "I have a matchbox" and "I have a toothache."[22] The former describes a basic object relationship of the *Atzmi*, whereas the latter does not involve object relationship, or for that matter, any ego at all. This is the nature of the boundlessness of the *Ani*, that it does not have to be related even to a clearly defined subject. The toothache need not be related to a possessor. In like manner, the Cartesian cogito has been paraphrased by Georg Lichtenberg from "I think" to "there is a thought".[23] Consequently, the *Ani* seems to be the master of its realm: it may float as boundless imagery, a daydream, hallucination, meditation towards a mystic union, or it may define itself within a subject. Only when the defined subject interacts with an object does the *Ani* transfer control to the *Atzmi*, which is formed and equipped to interact with spatio-temporality. By imputing to the *Ani* the powers of defining its own realms, we do not postulate any cognitive indeterminism except the ability of the *Ani* to focus diffuse and boundless imagery, thoughts and affects on a specific subject. This is not unlike George Kelly's "personal constructs", by which the random and continuous flow of experience is structured within a specific self.[24] This quality of the *Ani*, i.e. to focus its ontic diffusion and boundlessness on a specific subject, makes it possible for the *Atzmi* to carry out its interaction with the object. Schematically, this dynamism is presented in **figure 6.1**.

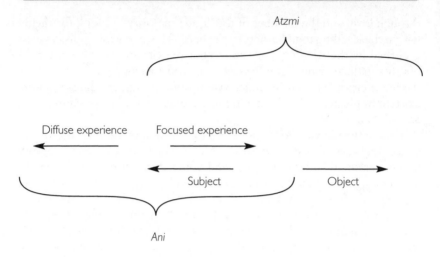

Figure 6.1 *Atzmi* and *Ani*: Polar Components of the Self

To conclude our conceptualization of the *Atzmi* and the *Ani* as the polar components of the self, we must point out again that we are not dealing in ultimates and we are not concerned with prime movers. Our interest in the *Ani's* quest for nonbeing and the melting of the partitions between subject and object in some mystical states is not metaphysical but naturalistic and deterministic. If we state, for instance, that the *Atzmi* manipulates the object mainly by reason, whereas the *Ani* operates mostly by intuition and affect, we base our postulate on the *Ani's* anchor in pre-differentiation, when the lack of plurality and discrete sequences makes reason impossible. Also, the question of why the self strives to crystallize a separate entity out of the pantheistic mass of nonbeing – is metaphysics, yet the relationship between human growth and the participant quest of nonbeing lies within the realm of personology.

Another concept that belongs to the wider context of the self is the "ideal self". Our conception of the "ideal self" differs from the current usage in personology insofar as we base our concept mainly on the sense of choice and uniqueness of the individual *vis-à-vis* others. This conception of the "ideal self", and the comparison between it and the goals that the individual sets to his self-image, which is the current notion of the "ideal self", will be elucidated in **chapter 7**.

Although, our personality model is not yet complete, we have so far provided explanatory sequences for core mechanisms, notably motivation and affect. We were able, for instance, to relate the conflict between growth and self-destruction to the participation vector interfering with the separant–activist vector within the personality core of the object-manipulating Sisyphean personality type. Conversely, the separant factors impeding *Unio Mystica* may well be the same core motives preventing the depressive would-be suicide from pulling the trigger. We linked these varied and wide-ranged spectra of motivations to developmental and psychosocial vectors that may be documented and eventually measured. The contents of the *Ani* and the *Atzmi*, as well as their relative preponderance within a given personality, are related to the participant and separant personality core vectors, the developmental fixations and the given culture in which the individual is socialized. We shall therefore now order the developmental factors within the personality system. Finally, we shall study the *Ity*, which is the Hebrew term for "with me". The *Ity* is the synthesizer of the dialectical conflicts within the self between the Unity-bound *Ani* and the interactive *Atzmi*. The *Ity* is the structured Tantalus Ratio within the self. Its synthesizing function makes it the coordinator of human action, and as such it has more in common with Freud's ego than with the autonomous ego of the ego psychologists.

Another point of method is that ours is more a model of the self than a full-fledged personality theory. Our conception of the self is of a dynamic structuring of basic personality vectors, whereas the whole personality includes traits and peripheral variables and factors. Consequently, we shall confine ourselves to the core personality structure; our concern with peripheral personality variables will be fragmentary and will only be called upon insofar as our focus on the personality requires.

In the course of our presentation of the self we shall refer from time to time to Carlos Castaneda's trilogy on his encounters and discussions with Don Juan, the old Yaqui Indian sorcerer.[25] Our feeling was that there was no Don Juan in the way the author presented him; the account was more of a Socratic dialogue between Castaneda and himself while under the influence of hallucinogens. Even if we are wrong, Castaneda concedes that some of the writings are allegoric. To us they present a striking instance of a dialogue between the student who stands for the spatio-temporal interactive *Atzmi* and the Yaqui Indian, the *Ani*, who is grasping the "other reality" of longing for pantheistic union. These two divergent realities interact conflictually along the continuum between the polarities of the self and reach a dialectic consensus within the *Ity*, the coordinating framework of the self.

The Poles and the Bridge

The relative magnitude and preponderance of the poles of our self-continuum are, no doubt, related to the developmental factors of the personality core. A violent early oral fixation, a quietist participant culture and a Tantalic preoccupation at old age will contribute to the predominance of the *Ani* within the self-continuum. Conversely, a separant fixation on the object at a period of vigorous growth of the individual in an active Sisyphean culture will make for an overpowering *Atzmi*. The strength and weakness of the coordinating *Ity* (described below) will then determine its ability to contain the self within a dynamic system of conflictual balance.

The dual polarity of our continuum stems from the basic fact that the self is subject to two opposing forces. One pushes towards growth and involvement with the object and in the process the painful coagulation of an *Atzmi* takes place. This interactive self is ever grappling with time and space within the matrix of its objective and human surroundings. The other force strives for timelessness and spacelessness when the lack of differentiated objects makes the sequence of time and the discreteness of space impossible, and when there is no-thing and no-being except the omnipresent *Ani*.

Both the poles and the self-continuum are unique in personology; consequently, other conceptualizations relating to the self may not fit on our continuum. Still, many aspects of these concepts, either in form or in content, may be partly linked with or overlap some segments of our continuum. We may scan a few examples, starting with the pioneering exposition of the self by William James. The "I", James's "pure ego", is quite a way from the *Ani* pole of our continuum because James postulates a conscious interaction between his "I" and his "me" – the empirical self. James's "me" is, in like manner, also further away from our *Atzmi* because it contains the "spiritual self . . . The very core and nucleus of our self . . . a direct revelation of the living substance of our soul."[26] To us, these attributes belong more to the objectless *Ani* than to the outward-reaching interactive *Atzmi*. Mead's position is rather extreme. According to him, there can be no self outside the matrix of social interaction. Indeed, the self comes into being, according to Mead, by taking the role of the "generalized other".[27] Consequently, Mead's self will be outside our continuum and further away from our *Atzmi* pole. Mead denies the existence of an *Ani*, an objectless self, whereas for us, the *Atzmi*, the interactive self, is formed by the dynamic relationship of the *Ani* with its objective and human surroundings. Of the eight functions of Gordon Alport's *proprium*, seven will be clustered on our continuum near the *Atzmi* pole because they are mostly concerned with the object and social relationships of the self. His "knower", which is a modified version of Cartesian consciousness,[28] is quite different from our intuitive *Ani*, striving towards non-awareness.

Abraham Maslow's "B-cognition" is quite close to our *Ani* insofar as he envisages a detached passive awareness. However, he conceptualizes this "B-cognition" as an experience or awareness of an object,[29] and in this it differs from our *Ani's* goal of objectless nonbeing.

There are many differentiations in personology of the various attributes of the self, but our continuum seems to transcend these typologies because its poles reach out from object relations to objectlessness and nonbeing. Most taxonomies in personology are based on the dichotomy of the self and its surrounding object, whereas our corresponding dichotomy is of the holistic goal of the nonbeing of the *Ani* and the multitude of pluralities of the *Atzmi*. On one we have Unity and infinity; on the other, a discreteness of number, plurality, sequence and space stemming from the initial division between the individual and his surroundings. The transition is from a partaking in infinity of the *Ani* to the opposition of the *Atzmi* against the finitude of other *separata* and objects.

Far Eastern philosophies and religions, with their preoccupation with quietism and nonbeing, have coined some basic concepts that may be related to our continuum of the self. The Mahayana Buddhist *citta*, which Occidental philosophers have erroneously equated with "mind" as distinct from the body, is actually the undefined, non-differentiated infinity from which the finite, classified thing springs forth. The original (perfect) state of *citta* is nothingness (*sunya*) and nonbeing, and one of its manifestations in the human psyche is the *alya vijnana*, the potential consciousness, which is still in a non-differentiated state. This *alya vijnana*, insofar as it represents in the human psyche the preconscious nothingness, does resemble our *Ani*. *Karma*, on the other hand, with its active object relationship, has many elements of our interactive *Atzmi*.[30] In like manner, in the supra individual, the non-differentiated Upanishadic Atman, we may see some elements of our *Ani*, and in the *jivatman*,[31] the individual separate soul, we may see some similarity to our interactive self.

An apt illustration of our continuum of the self may be found in Castaneda's dialogues with Don Juan, the old Yaqui Indian sorcerer. Ordinary reality as perceived in the dialogues, mostly by the student, is the spatio-temporal object-involved interaction of individuals raised in an activist separant culture, such as the United States. Non-ordinary reality, which was mostly expounded by the Yaqui Indian, has no distinct differentiation between things because Man, in non-ordinary reality, is all by himself and there are no other persons there to make him break down the holistic totality of his perceptions into discrete images.[32] Moreover, the perception of non-ordinary reality can never be attentive or direct, but only vicarious and indirect "like the image created by dust particles in the eyelashes, or the blood vessels in the cornea of the eye, a worm-like shape that can be seen as long as one is not looking at it directly; but the moment one tries to look at it, it shifts out of sight with the movement of the eyeball".[33] Our *Ani* is also ethereal, spaceless, timeless and unique insofar as it does not need an object or partners to populate its pantheistic Unity. It cannot be grasped by direct attention, but only by intuition or contemplative reduction. Castaneda also describes the gradual non-discrete transition between ordinary and non-ordinary reality, which is very much like our continuum, in that it bridges the two poles of the self: the *Ani* and the *Atzmi*.

It is difficult to relate our self-continuum to the psychoanalytic notion of the unconscious. We have already stated that we find the Jungian unconscious, and especially his genetic collective unconscious, hard to accept. We can, nevertheless, relate our self-continuum to the Freudian

183

concepts of consciousness, preconsciousness and the unconscious. The *Ani* would mostly be unconscious because its genesis is anchored in pre-differentiated non-awareness when the space and time of consciousness has not yet developed. Some of the *Ani* would be semi- or preconscious and only a few of its manifestations would be conscious. Even when the *Ani* is conscious, it lurks more on the peripheries of awareness in *déjà vu* – like experiences, or, in the manner described by Castaneda, as resting on the fringes of our field of vision. The *Atzmi*, on the other hand, is largely conscious, partly preconscious, as can be seen in the many semi-automatic functions we perform in daily life, and only rarely unconscious, as in religious ecstasy or drug-induced euphoria when the ego boundary partly dissolves. Schematically, the relationship between our continuum of the self and the states of awareness is presented in **figure 6.2**.

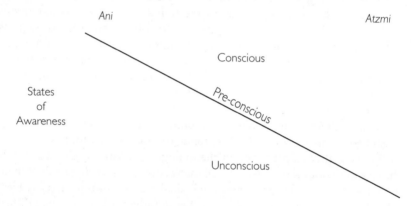

Figure 6.2 Continuum of the Self

Some Dynamics of the Self

Earlier we described the dialectic relationship – the Tantalus Ratio – between the participation and separation vectors of the personality core. We have hypothesized that the energy generated by this dialectic conflict activates the behavior and development of the personality. Below we describe the structured elements of the personality core in the self-continuum, and envisage a dialectic relationship between the polar components of the self, resulting in a structured Tantalus Ratio that coordinates and regulates the functions of the self. This manifestation of the structured Tantalus Ratio has been denoted the *Ity*, the "with me". The essence of dialectics is the creation of a new synthetic state out of two opposing vectors. Consequently, the conflictual relationship between the *Ani* and the *Atzmi* within the Tantalus Ratio of the self provides the structured substance for the development of the personality core, as well as its peripheral traits. This process is not unlike a chemical reaction that produces acids, salts or a new polymer. The Tantalus Ratio of the opposing personality vectors is the source of psychic energy, whereas the Tantalus Ratio of the polar components of the self provides the material for the personality structure. Thus, the Tantalus Ratio is both a regulating and generating mechanism affected by the dialectical process of creating new states through conflictual action.

It is necessary to recall that we are concerned with the interplay between the polar components within the self and not between personalities. In other words, we are concerned with the making of an *Ani*-dominated Abel or an aggressive Cain whose *Atzmi* predominates, but not with the predator–victim dyad of a Cain and an Abel.

The developmental factors, the fixations, as well as the cultural imprints, as described, may converge to make the self more skewed towards the pole of the *Ani* or towards the opposite pole of the *Atzmi*. It is a matter of conjecture whether the types of self are distributed normally on our continuum. We may assume that the selves dominated totally by the ideal-type polarities do not exist as functioning selves. The extreme *Ani*-self might be the Buddhist holy man contemplating his navel while oblivious to the world or an acute schizophrenic immersed in his autism, completely shut off from the outside world. The extreme *Atzmi*-dominated self is the total manipulator of his environment where all men, flora, fauna and objects are pawns in his grand schemes, with himself as the centre. This ideal-type psychopath, who seems to be interchangeable with the "organization man" as described in managerial fiction, hardly exists in real life. These extreme types could not function creatively or even develop their own personality because they do not encounter the dialectic strain of conflicting forces within themselves, which is the ontological basis of existence. It is also the dynamism of the Tantalus Ratio that generates the process of personality development. The Tantalus Ratio within the matrix of the self moves between two goals: the blissful pre-awareness nonbeing of the *Ani* and the total domination of the object by the *Atzmi*. This strain between the impossible and the reality of the middle ranges is the essence of the Camusian absurd, as well as the prime mover and regulator-through-synthesis of the self. The Tantalus Ratio within the matrix of the self provides both the energy as well as the *Ity*: the managerial coordination to keep the self as a system in balance. The energy-producing function of the Tantalus Ratio stems from the continuous clash between the separating forces of growth and deprivational interaction with the object, which is structured within the *Atzmi*, and the participant quietist vectors of the *Ani*. The *Ity* managerial function of the Tantalus Ratio results from the stabilizing fluctuations of the dialectic cycles, which regulate the dynamics of the Tantalus Ratio. We have dealt elsewhere with the dynamics of personality development.[34] In the present context, however, we wish to point out some basic dynamics of the Tantalus Ratio that are instrumental in the development of the self.

The dialectical strain at any given moment within the Tantalus Ratio is related both to the *Ani* and to the *Atzmi*. The separant *Atzmi* aims towards the total domination of the object. This is impossible. Consequently, a compromise is reached in the form of a dialectical synthesis, which may take the form of the internalization of social norms, which in itself is a developmental phase of the *Atzmi* and also enables, in turn, the integration of the individual within a given objective reality or social structure. These mechanisms, which for didactic purposes may be likened to Freudian defences, relegate to the subconscious, to day and night dreams, to visions of imperial dominion, the harnessing of stars or the invention of *perpetua mobilae*. Of course, if conditions permit, these may erupt in the *furor Teutonicus* of a mad dictator and an ever-approaching atomic Armageddon. The more subtle, yet potent participant aims of the *Ani* are equally unrealizable, so the dialectics of the Tantalus Ratio create the participant synthesis of religion, or the "highs" of wine, women and song, while the longing for perfect origins becomes an aim in itself and is relegated to build and reinforce the *Ani* with "oceanic feelings", visions of Unity with the Divine or the vast un-chartered "away and beyond".

The dialectical dynamics of the Tantalus Ratio take place on the continuum of the self. Consequently, at every point of the continuum, even if close to one pole, there are adverse pressures from the other pole. Tired despots, such as General Francisco Franco and unscrupulous power-manipulating tycoons, were known to be attracted by the sea and its boundless infinity, reminiscent of the blissful omnipresence of nonbeing. The *Ani* may inject some participant craving for inaction and failure in the exploits of a successful entrepreneur. His business associates may subsequently remark that there was no apparent reason for failure and the entrepreneur seemed to be motivated by a self-destructive urge. This "Internal Saboteur", which has been described by Ronald Fairbairn in a different context, always lurks as a quietist,[35] "fifth-column" of the *Ani*, to interfere with the enterprises of the *Atzmi*. On a more formidable level, we have Richard Wagner's assertion that *Götterdämmerung* is the occupational hazard of the seekers of absolute dominion and glory. This was proven to the hilt by Wagner's less-sophisticated disciplines in the Third Reich. On the other hand, in many moods of self-negation, one may be jolted back from the precipice by the life-juices suddenly pumped by the *Atzmi* and the Sisyphean assertion that "tomorrow is another day".

The dialectic operation of the Tantalus Ratio within the self makes every synthetic outcome of a cycle a personality element, which in turn interacts with the other personality elements, as well as with the original vectors. The permutations of these composite dialectics are virtually endless and this accounts for the formidable complexity of the personality, as well as for our near impotence in describing, predicting and forecasting human behavior. We may only have an overview of the personality, which is contained by the dialectics of the *Ity*: the regulating Tantalus Ratio, within a force field held in dynamic equilibrium by conflicting forces. Within this structured ego boundary, the Tantalus Ratio operates in a continuous flow of dialectics among the polarities of the self, as well as with the ever newly internalized personality elements.

Our overview of the dynamics of the self does not enable us to delve into a detailed scrutiny of processes within the self, but lends us an insight into some characteristic mechanisms. These are, naturally, related to the developmental factors, fixations of personality type, cultural elements and the manner in which these factors are structured within the polarities of the self. We may envisage, therefore, some typical instances of self-dynamics, which may be linked to a vast array of behavioral modalities. We have already mentioned the Internal Saboteur mechanism in which one polarity of the self interferes with and may hamper the function of the other, which is predominant as far as the structures of the self are concerned. Another typical instance is a self that is skewed towards one pole, say the *Atzmi*, but the opportunities for the activist potentials of the self may be blocked or scarce. Consequently, the individual may find himself a niche in the existing opportunities' structure and let his activist potentials wane or lie dormant, or he may "rock the boat" and effect a change in the opportunity structures. Another typical instance is a relatively quick change of apparent emphasis from one self-skewness to another. This is usually affected by a traumatic experience and may be related to the former instance when a self-skewness, the expression of which may have been blocked by inadequate opportunities, is suddenly revealed and laid bare by the forceful trauma. "The God That Failed" revelations are adequate illustrations of these instances. When the *Ani* engulfs the self with the holistic intensity of a creed, it tends to mar, sift and select the incoming perceptions so that they comply with the dogma or ideology, and it rejects, represses or twists the perceptions that are in dissonance with the creed. These mechanisms, which are studied extensively by the cognitive dissonance theorists, may suddenly lose their grip on the self due to the traumatic jolt, and the disenchanted ex-believer in a theistic or secular creed asks himself in amazement: "How could I ever have believed in this awful nonsense?" What actually happened was that the disillusioning shock pushed the self more to the *Atzmi*, and the *Ani* no longer filters the incoming harsh realities that revealed the pragmatic vicissitudes of the ideology and not only its lofty goals. Another example for a shift of skewness of the self-continuum in the opposite direction than the one experienced by a traumatic hangover from too much ideology is the scientistic crisis of the empiricist. The behavioral scientist totally immersed in matrices of correlations, linear and non-parametric analysis of narrowly defined problems may suddenly experience a sense of futility, bolstered by the holistic *Ani*. He may realize with shock that he has spent his life on significance tests, which suddenly seem trivial, or on the application of Test x to Population y, which appears disconnected from the "real issues". He is therefore prompted by his holistic *Ani* to discard the partial, discrete measurements that seem to him superficial or tautological and launch a *magnum opus*, fuelled by intuition, and affect to search for prime movers and ultimates on a macro-macro level of synthesis. The various techniques of mysticism and meditation are also instrumental in effecting a shift of emphasis of the self from the activist *Atzmi* towards the quietist *Ani*. These techniques lower the exposure of the self to outside stimuli. They dull the sensory system by monotonous routines, they interfere with the dialectic processes of interaction within the self so that the perceptions of time and space are twisted and marred, and the path becomes paved for the temporary surging up of the *Ani* with its holistic strain towards omnipresence and the bliss of Unity and nonbeing. This may be a partial explanation for the "blank-outs" described by research in concentrative meditation and the *Satori* "awakening" of Zen.[36]

It might be useful to recapitulate here that the separant pressures within the *Atzmi* motivate it to overpower the object and introject it within the self. If this is impossible, the *Atzmi* tends to reject, deny or be ambivalent towards the object. We may denote this mechanism as "inclusion", i.e. a reaching-out towards the object, like the submission of the elements to the will of the Besht in Hassidic tales or like the pipe becoming part or an extension of the student's personality in Castaneda's trilogy.[37] The *Ani*, on the other hand, aims at nonbeing, *inter alia*, by melting and fusing with the object into Unity. This we shall denote as "exclusion", which is characteristic of mystical processes and is described by Don Juan, the Yaqui Indian, as the blotting-out of the self in order to achieve a "non-ordinary" transcendental reality. The inclusionary nature of the *Atzmi* is geared towards interaction, whereas exclusion makes for the holistic goal of non-awareness and nonbeing of the *Ani*. These mechanisms may be related to Husserl's phenomenological reduction. Husserl provides us with a method for reaching and identifying the objectless *Ani*. This does not mean, necessarily, that Husserl's end product, the pure ego, is identical with our *Ani*; it is not! The phenomenological epoxy is a method that brackets out or rather peels off the layers of spatio-temporality from the self, so that the *Ani* is laid bare. This method, which in our context means the temporary neutralization of the interactive *Atzmi* in the self-continuum, is rather like the method used by Castaneda's Yaqui Indian to shut off "ordinary reality", but without the help, to be sure, of hallucinogenic drugs. The phenomenological reduction is actually our exclusion in reverse as far as method is concerned, but in content we are worlds apart. Husserl wishes to discover his "pure ego" by suspending the "I" and its attributes and "the man" and his spatio-temporality,[38] which roughly corresponds to our interactive *Atzmi*. Our *Ani*, however, aims to annihilate itself, to melt and thereby become part of the object which, in turn, becomes part of the omnipresence of Unity. Conversely, Husserl's pure ego has no attributes and no vectors. Still, as a method of discovering the *Ani*, the phenomenological reduction may be useful, even if we expect to find at the end of our search a different essence than the one envisaged by Husserl.

In content, the *Ani* might be considered as non-ethical because ethics and morals presuppose relationships among *separata* within a group matrix that are absent in the framework of the *Ani*, which is anchored on Unity and nonbeing. Consequently, we may observe in the *Ani*-skewed self of the mystic a certain indifference or apathy towards morals. In extreme cases of "black religiosity" of a Jean Genet or a Jacob Frank, morals are attacked as an obstacle to the participant goal of salvation by destruction of the ethical structure.[39] The holistic nature of the *Ani* makes for a participant-synthetic *Weltanschauung*, which ignores details. Facts become less and less important for the wider and unified perspectives projected inwards by the *Ani*. Also the *Ani* is responsible for the self's varying concern with ultimates. In the timeless ever-after, one is assured by the *Ani* that one shall have omniscient answers to all one's queries. It is futile, therefore, to be concerned with the trivial problems and riddles of spatio-temporality. "It is better for Man," says the Talmud, "not to have been created at all than to have been born."[40] This, in the literal sense, is sacrilege, which could hardly have been uttered by the pious sages of the Talmud. It seems that their underlying meaning was that ontological nonbeing is preferable to spatio-temporal existence because it brings with it omniscience and the holistic perspective of Unity.

The *Ani* seems to reveal itself more in peak experiences. In the split second just before a road accident one jumps to unprecedented heights of perspective; one's whole life is contrasted with some basic ultimates, coupled with the realization that one's hold on spatio-temporality is both shaky and precarious. One suddenly realizes that the technological triumphs of internal combustion or jet propulsion, which are the *Atzmi*'s successful manipulation of the object, are vulnerable when matters of nonbeing and ultimates are at stake. In peak experience, the *Ani*'s role within the self becomes invariably more prominent. Maslow, who defines peak experiences as moments of the highest happiness and fulfilment (e.g. the creative moment, orgasm or the aesthetic perception)[41] relates them to a holistic or unified perception, a diffusion of space and time and a self-forgetfulness or "egolessness".[42] These are precisely some of the manifestations of our *Ani* when it becomes momentarily more prominent and hence more apparent in the dynamics of the self.

Psychotropic drugs, especially hallucinogens, also seem to impair and sometimes neutralize the *Atzmi*, as well as the coordinating *Ity*, so that the *Ani* gains temporary dominion over the self. How this happens is not really understood, neither by physiologists nor by psychologists. However, there is some evidence that subjects of sensory deprivation experiments experience hallucinations that are similar to those effected by the hallucinogens.[43] The inference might be that both sensory deprivation and hallucinogens block the interactive avenues of the *Atzmi*, with a resultant free rein to the *Ani* and a diffusion of time and space, which characterize visual and audile hallucinations. The drawback of this analogy is that drugs may not only block some forms of interaction but may also twist

189

the rest of the incoming perception. Still, Castaneda's search for the "other reality", which has many common manifestations with our *Ani*, is obviously drug-induced and we shall try to glean insight from his experiences. For now we note that peyote, datura and hallucinogenous mushrooms were the vehicle by which Castaneda and Don Juan, his Yaqui Indian mentor, aimed to reach a different order of reality. This "separate reality" was characterized by a feeling of the melting-down of their bodies, a pantheistic union with their surroundings, and the blurring and sometime total disappearance of the ordinary sequences of time and the basic laws of physics governing the relationship between objects and the concreteness of space. These are, no doubt, the exclusionary aims of nonbeing of the participant *Ani*. Also, each drug seems to be a different, but not alternative, path to reach the "separate reality". "The devil's weed (datura)," says Don Juan, "is only one of a million paths."[44] The "smoke" (hallucinogenous mushrooms) is for those who want to "see".[45] Seeing for Don Juan is looking through the veils of ordinary reality in order to reach the other reality of bliss and Unity. The "smoke" is an "ally"[46] because it is the vehicle – the catalyzer that helps the inner self (rather like our *Ani*) shed its peel of spatio-temporality (very much like our *Atzmi* and coordinating *Ity*) and sees the unifying sameness of Man and object.

The ideal-type *Ani* is timeless and spaceless, and lacks the sequences of logic and inference. These are generated by the interactive *Atzmi* and are structured within the Tantalus Ratio by the coordinating *Ity*. This stems from our basic premise that the *Ani* is anchored on pre-differentiated Unity, whereas the *Atzmi* is a product of post-differentiated object relationship. Consequently, the *Atzmi* is guided by the discrete sequences of reason, but the *Ani* is dominated by a sensile flow of intuition.[47] The *Atzmi* is intentional and attentive to the sequences of experiences and memory, which makes for a distinction of before and after and hence the sequences of time. The *Ani*, on the other hand, is suspended within a *Durée*-like flow of a continuous present.[48]

The *Ani*, having been anchored on pre-differentiated Unity, is also spaceless. It projects into transcendence monistic, universal archetypes like the Upanishadic *Pitrusha*, the Kabbalist Adam Kadmon, or the Gnostic Primordial Man.[49] This holistic view of the universe, characteristic of *Ani*-dominated mystics, regards the discrete, pluralistic image of reality, perceived by the *Atzmi* as inchoate, not unlike the eyesight of an alcoholic whose retina has been damaged by methylated spirits. Still, the perception of space is effected through the relationships and the interaction of the components of the self with its surrounding objects. Like time, space is generated by the interactive dynamics of the Tantalus Ratio and is structured by the regulating dialectics of the *Ity*. The categorizing of experience, and the learning of perspective and spatial dimensions, are linked to the dynamic interplay between *separata*. In like manner, social norms that define, so to speak, the social space of the self *vis-à-vis* others are the internalized deprivational interactions of the individual with his relevant others and social system. The genesis of this social space has been described by us elsewhere[50] and we shall deal with it again later in the context of the relationship of the individual with his surrounding others.

Spatio-temporality, therefore, is a dialectical product of the object relationship of the self. Because these relationships are discrete and linear, they seem to progress in a one-way, irreversible direction, with no possibility for turning round or back. Change in this spatio-temporal sequence can only be effected in the future, and regression back to previous points in the sequences is only found in the time-machines of science-fiction tales – yet even these sophisticated writers cannot straighten out the "cosmic paradoxes" created by the revival of a Caesar because of a messenger from a time-machine. Still, the *Ani*-dominated mystic or Castaneda's Don Juan may effect changes in the "different reality", because in a spaceless–timeless universe, the *Ani* is not only omnipresent but also omnipotent. Within this "separate reality", actions have different meanings and different results. A seemingly harmless act in this world may have lethal consequences in Don Juan's "other reality", or the Kabbalistic manipulation of numbers and names during prayer may bring about a saving grace to a cosmic (or individual) catastrophe. The *Ani*-skewed self, being anchored on pre-differentiated omnipresence, may afford a partial bio-psychological basis for the mystics' and, for that matter, for Castaneda's Don Juan "separate reality". Also the *Ani*-skewed self does not necessarily avail itself of causality, which is linked to the linearity of time and the discreteness of space. It may perceive its own brand of an "other reality" through a Bergsonian *Durée*-like simultaneity or Jungian synchronicity, which is a causal combination or coincidence of events.[51] This is related to the loose hold that spatio-temporality has on the *Ani*, and of causality being a built-in manifestation of the discrete sequences and linearity of spatio-temporality. Thus, non-causal phenomena, like many ESP and spiritualistic manifestations, may be more acceptable to an *Ani*-skewed self than to an *Atzmi*-dominated self.

We close this part of our description of the dynamics of the self by hypothesizing that time, space and the perception of causal association and inference are structured by the regulating dialectics of the *Ity* because they provide the structured form to the dynamics of the Tantalus Ratio within the self. Creativity is the blending of a *Durée*-like intuitive insight and the structured order and discipline of the *Atzmi*, the interactive self. Creativity, therefore, is generated more by the seething dynamics of the Tantalus Ratio itself and is only partially affected by the regulating and delimiting *Ity*.

The Dialectics of the Tantalus Ratio

It is in the nature of our continuum and the dialectics within it that each self-structure, even when skewed towards one pole, is subject to some influence of the opposite polar self-component. If we take creativity as an expression of the self (including the cultural factors internalized by it), we may observe in the muffled, subdued, sad and self-effacing tunes of the East the contrasting, active rhythm of drums and cymbals. Conversely, in the aggressive march of military bands, one often hears in the bombastic beat the sad wails of a bugle or a horn leading the tune through soft and subdued undulations of nostalgia. The fiery Wagner envisaged *Götterdämmerung* as a sequel to his Nibelungen Ring, not only as an inevitable tragic swing of the pendulum by the jealous gods but also as a projection of impending personal disaster following his outbursts of creativity. "It is written in the stars", wrote his wife Cosima, "that nothing in Wagner's life is to be allowed to suffer only a partial shipwreck. Everything must go to pieces precipitately and overwhelmingly."[52] These precipitating eclipses have been described by other artists after an upsurge of creativity. The quietist *Ani* seems to demand its toll whenever the Tantalus Ratio becomes too skewed towards the active pole of the self. Some have been imputed to a whole art movement: viz., the Dada, "non-art" movement of promoting inner goals of inaction and not-being. Creativity was meant to expend itself by Dada into nothingness. "No more painters, no more scribblers, no more musicians, no more sculptors. An end at last to all this stupidity, nothing left, nothing at all, nothing, nothing."[53]

Let us take a closer look at these dialectics within the Tantalus Ratio of the self. Freud envisaged a rather linear flow of "libido quantum", which permeates the organism and then converts into mental energy, not unlike fuel that flows into a power plant and is then converted into energy.[54] We have also assumed existence of an initial flow of energy generated by the developmental processes of growth, and have explained the actual conversion of the growth vectors into mental energy. This conversion, which has been taken for granted or scantily dealt with by other personologists, is effected by the dialectics of the Tantalus Ratio within the self. The vectors of growth and socialization, after having been countered by the vectors of inaction and nonbeing, have been transformed and structured into the polar components of the self. These components contain the potential of the mental energies that are being realized into actual mental processes by the countering clashes and continuous syntheses affected by the dialectical interaction among the divergent polarities of the self. Consequently, the initial "raw material" that flows within the personality core vectors is only a potential, which is totally transformed by the dialectical clashes and subsequent syntheses effected by the Tantalus Ratio. Every mental process, even the most minute, is thus a product of the energy-transforming and -synthesizing Tantalus Ratio, which is then collected, released and coordinated by the *Ity*, the dialectic regulator of the self. Every new stimulus perceived by the organism is processed by the countering forces within the Tantalus Ratio before being integrated into the dynamics of the self as motivation, released as action, and then cathected into the memory reservoirs of experience or deposited as a personality element.

Of late, there has been renewed interest in the different specializations of the two hemispheres of the brain. If indeed the left hemisphere governs logical, analytic, active and object-manipulating action, and the right hemisphere is more holistic, intuitive and contemplative,[55] then the left side would have more of the *Atzmi* components and the right side would be the *Ani*'s favourite site, and many of the dialectical dynamics of the Tantalus Ratio would occur within the interconnecting fibres of the *corpus callosum*. Although this is simplistic and hardly warranted, empirically speaking, the analogy may be of didactic value in illustrating at a low level of abstraction the dynamics of our model. The analogy illustrates a unidimensional mental process, presented schematically in **figure 6.3**.

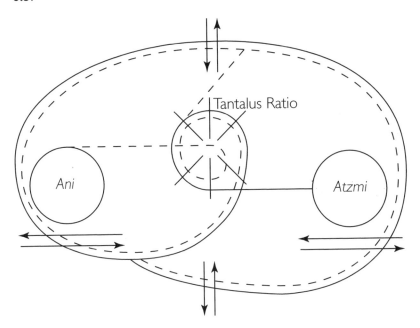

193

Figure 6.3 Dialectic Process Within the Tantalus Ratio

The *Ani* and the *Atzmi* interact dialectically within the Tantalus Ratio of the self to produce and transform mental processes, as well as to sustain the regulating *Ity*, which keeps the self together as a system in balance. It must be stressed that our model envisages that the dialectical processes within the Tantalus Ratio affect every single mental process, regardless of its physiological location. Consequently, the permutations and combinations of the dialectical multi-variations are virtually endless, so our simplistic analogy should only be taken in its didactic context.

All personologists postulate existence of a regulating component, such as the Freudian ego, or its equivalents in the self, that coordinates the structure of the personality and its relationship with "outside reality". Our *Ity* differs from the existing expositions of the ego, because we regard it as the structural product of the dynamic interaction of the components of the self within the Tantalus Ratio. Also, the *Ity* contains the flux of the mental processes within a system in balance, as well as its own structure, by the tensile counter-force of dialectics. The most important aspect of our dialectical conception of the *Ity* is that it explains the homeostatic and other central and stable state tendencies of the ego and its equivalents in personology. We have described elsewhere these homeostatic and central tendencies of the personality and their link to findings in cognitive dissonance and conformity studies; we have elegized the fact that Man, being a *Homo conveniens*, i.e. a conformity-bound animal, and upholder of the Greek *Meden Agan*, i.e. nothing in excess – is disconnected from the wider context of a personality theory.[56] Our present exposition provides the necessary context: the *Ity* being a regulatory, stabilized product, i.e. the synthetic outcome of the conflicting forces within the dialectics of the Tantalus Ratio, is geared and attuned to its very genesis, formation and structure to strive for central, stable and synthetic states. The normative pressures to conform exerted by the group on the individual or some bio-physiological processes within the human organism that enhance homeostasis thus become intervening or contributing factors to the more basic central tendencies and homeostatic-synthetic characteristics of the *Ity*, which are determined by the dialectical dynamics of the self.

The form and strength of the *Ity* is, naturally, related to the structure of the ego boundary, the ego identity and other developmental phases, which we have described elsewhere,[57] and earlier in this work. Consequently, when the personality suffers structural injuries or the ego boundary dissolves, as in some forms of psychosis, the coordinating *Ity* may suffer corresponding damages or become disoriented altogether.

Freud has postulated that all human behavior is "defensive" because the direct expression of the instincts is barred by social norms so that the instinctual energy is transformed by the "defence mechanisms" into socially acceptable behavior. Our dialectical model is rather more elaborate: the social norms are constantly being incorporated within the self by the interactive channels of the *Atzmi*, but even then the goals of the *Atzmi*, i.e. the total domination of the object, are not realizable. In like manner, self-annihilation towards nonbeing, which is the core vector of the *Ani*, is unattainable. Consequently, the impossibility of fulfilment of our polar components of the self is ontological and more basic than the normative barriers to instinctual expression in the Freudian model. Also, it is in the very essence of the dialectical process that the synthetic products differ from the initial components or vectors that entered into the dialectical relationship. We therefore have no need for "defence mechanisms" and their equivalents in personology to explain the dynamics of the self and the structure of the personality. The dialectics of the Tantalus Ratio provide a sufficient explanation for both the processes within the self and its defining contours and boundaries. Therefore, we were able to explain previously[58] the achievement motive and the processes of creativity by the dialectical interplay between our personality core vectors without resorting to the "defence mechanisms" of sublimation, displacement and projection. It should be recalled that we envisage a dual system of dialectics within the Tantalus Ratio: the first is the strain between the goals of our personality core vectors and the ontological impossibility of achieving these goals, and the second is the conflicts among the polar components of the self. The achievement motive, for instance, might be linked to the former, whereas creativity as an ongoing process might be better understood within the context of the latter. These dual dialectical processes in the Tantalus Ratio are presented in **figure 6.4.**

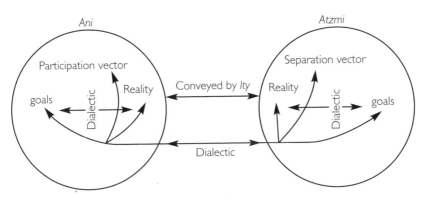

Figure 6.4 Dual Dialectic Process Within the Tantalus Ratio

The strain between the separant wish of the *Atzmi* to overpower and successfully manipulate the object and the impossibility of realizing it as conveyed by the coordinating *Ity* creates the dialectic, which might resolve itself, *inter alia*, by the achievement motive. This, in turn, might lead to the rebellion of the achievement-bound Sisyphus, once he realizes that however hard he tries, the stone will roll down from the peak of the mountain. A Camusian Sisyphus might even become enamoured of his burden and regard his condition as the sole dialectical compromise with the absurd, which in Camusian terms, as in ours, is the gap between our lofty ideals and the painful drudgery of reality.

The dialectic within the *Ani* might lead the Tantalic personality to embrace religion and look for the Upper Jerusalem, the City of God, as a compromise between the impossibility of partaking in Unity and nonbeing, and the vicissitudes of Lower Jerusalem, the City of Man. Creativity and innovation are more likely to be related to the more complex dialectics between the *Ani* and the *Atzmi*. The act of creation is the harnessing of our visions of the bliss of nonbeing into the discipline of form and the aesthetics of harmony. By creative innovation, we impart to spatio-temporality some of our inner "holy sparks" and we effect, thereby, a dialectical synthesis: creativity is the bridge through which we may reach the object, or part of it, and make it our own, or at least dispel its separant petrification by lending it our innermost imprint of uniqueness and quest for the perfection of nonbeing.

Another dynamism of the Tantalus Ratio might explain the seemingly "pointless" failure or the so-called "self-destructive binge" of an otherwise successful career. In medieval Europe and in other theistic societies, these unreasonable and inexplicable self-destructive acts were attributed to the forces of evil and to being temporarily "possessed" by the devil and his disciples. In personology, there have been some vague allusions to these self-inflicted downfalls, notably by Sullivan, in conjunction with the dynamics of his "bad me",[59] and by Fairbairn, as one of the manifestations of his "Internal Saboteur".[60] Sullivan's "bad me" is the person's internalized fear of disapproval guiding his interpersonal relations, whereas Fairbairn's Internal Saboteur is the introjected conglomerate of social norms, not unlike Freud's super ego. Both touch only tangentially the actual process of self-destructive acts. Our self-continuum and the dialectics of the Tantalus Ratio provide a full and direct explanation of these self-destruction processes. We have postulated previously that the dialectic structuring of our self-continuum may have some separant activist elements incorporated in the quietist *Ani* and some self-annihilating elements enmeshed in the object-manipulating *Atzmi*. Also, the dialectical interplay between the *Ani* and the *Atzmi* make each polar component of the self vulnerable to the onslaught of its adversary, especially when its defences are momentarily down. An *Atzmi*-skewed self may have some fantasies or dreams of a blissful, suspended animation of nonbeing, or nightmares of falling and crushing, both of which are the doings of the quietist elements embedded in the *Atzmi*. In contrast, dreams and fantasies of conquest, power and glory are the manifestations of the object-manipulating activist elements incorporated in the *Ani*-skewed quietist personality. As for self-destructive behavior, we may envisage the separant activist *Atzmi*-dominated type being provoked or manoeuvred by the *Ani* into a self-defeating venture or a disastrous decision concerning the promotion of an enterprise so that the quietist goal of inaction may at least momentarily be achieved. The adventurer who seeks dangerous exploits that raise the probability of his death, a Friedrich Nietzsche who preaches, "live dangerously", or a Zorba the Greek who states that "to live means to look for trouble", all court self-destructive involvement, which may bring about their nonbeing. The same holds true for a successful businessman who "makes that stupid move", a celebrated actor who stammers or forgets his lines on opening night, or a Wilbur Mills being ruined at the height of his career by a joint performance with the stripper Fanne Foxe. Conversely, a participant, quietist, contemplative mystic may feel that he has "to be involved", that "life has to be lived" and that "the show", i.e. the daily routines, "must go on". These are the doings of the activist strains embedded in the *Ani*-skewed personality, which prevent it from pursuing its goals of resigned contemplation and the rejection of spatio-temporality.

As a cultural side-glance not entirely in place within the context of a personality theory, we may observe that factors that separate the activist and quietist elements may effect a decline in the dialectical interplay within the Tantalus Ratio, and consequently weaken the culture itself. This may be observed in the independent non-related development of spiritualist contemplative patterns in tribal or quietist cultures, which are totally divorced from newly imported technological innovations and processes. A Levantine mixture, and not a dialectical synthesis, is very often the result. On the other hand, some factors may be introduced to stultify and degenerate the dialectical dynamics of an activist culture. For instance, the introduction of unisex fashion in the West may well effect a further decline in Western culture, which has been perennially bolstered, *inter alia*, by the contrariness and stormy yet stylized dialectics between the sexes.

The *Ani*-Skewed Self

At this stage, we may adopt Husserl's conception of phenomenology as "descriptive psychology"[61] and try to describe the *Ani*-dominated self without being preoccupied with causal analysis. By phenomenological reduction, we may identify the *Ani*-skewed self as striving. We stress striving because, in this context, it is either impossible or irrelevant to reach a state of being without object and without predicates. Therefore, the goal of the *Ani*-dominated self is the holistic rejection of factuality so that true being becomes synonymous with nothingness.[62] The *Ani*-skewed self strives for ontological loneliness, which is at the same time ontological totality, i.e. omnipresence. Its aim of exclusion, i.e. the melting of the self into the totality of Unity, is also the goal of partaking of the Creation and its Creator. The apparent meekness and self-defacing of the *Ani*-skewed self is deceptive because its megalomaniac aim is to partake in Unity and become God. These lofty aims of the *Ani*-dominated self are apparent in the philosophy of Plotinus, who proclaimed that the Unity-bound soul imparted life to the whole of Creation.[63]

Mystics or mystically inclined personalities are bound to have an *Ani*-skewed self, which aims at exclusion, i.e. obliterating separate awareness, so that a direct link with God – even an actual partaking in Him – is affected. The aim of the mystic exclusion may be inferred from the Psalmist's advocation "to taste God and to see that He is good".[64] It is quite remarkable how the various mystical expositions of religions, both Eastern and Western, are very similar in conceiving a mystical union with Divinity, with respect to the exclusionary aims of our *Ani*-skewed self. The Kabbalist Adam-Kadmon, which derives from the Gnostic and early church fathers' Primordial Man, as well as the Upanishadic Atman, are the lonely yet omnipresent archetypes of pre-differentiated perfection. The Upanishads also state that in the beginning Atman was not only alone, but also saw nothing.[65] This is meaningless, unless we interpret seeing in the Psalmist sense of seeing God, and consider the Upanishadic conception of the Atman as a mythical projection of the *Ani* at its perfect stage of non-differentiated nothingness. With slight variations, the various mystic doctrines in the Kabbalah and in Sufism and Hinayana Buddhism also postulate that a Divine Spark is embedded in the temporal self and is linked by a sacred umbilical cord to the Divine Presence or the Universal Spirit. Again, this may be linked to our *Ani*-skewed self, which feels that the "inner" part of its personality is foreign to the vicissitudes of the deprivational interaction with its hostile surroundings. This "inner" self, i.e. the *Ani*, is part of a primordial perfection from which the inter-active self has been separated and expelled into the trials of object relationships and spatio-temporaiity. Consequently, the longing to return to the totality of Divinity, from which the Divine Spark, i.e. the *Ani*, has been separated, is the dominant passion of the *Ani*-skewed self.

We have already pointed out that the goal of nonbeing is unobtainable, although the *Ani*-skewed self may not be aware of this. Consequently, the longing, *per se*, to reach the participant nonbeing becomes a goal in itself and lends meaning to a lifetime of quest for ever-receding goals. The latent meaning in the quest for unattainable goals is the gist of Rudolf Bultman's Kerygma,[66] as well as Martin Heidegger's "meaning of being".[67] Moreover, the quest for nonbeing often becomes a goal in itself, so that the longing for this quest or the longing for the longing may provide the *Ani*-skewed self with a lifetime of meaning. Indeed, in Judaism, the longing for the spiritual and ethereal bliss of *oneg ruhani* (spiritual elation) is a prime preoccupation of the devout. Especially in its mystic strains, this longing for non-temporal being becomes a goal in Judaism, not only a means to an end. Otherwise, one might risk idolatry, because as Paul Tillich claims, the definition of idolatry is the worship of the means towards the fulfilment of the impulse as the fulfilment of the impulse itself.[68] By lowering the stature of longing for nonbeing from an end in itself, one may be tempted to find alternative modes of worship that would be more concrete and less exacting on the devout reservoirs of spirituality or powers of abstraction. One may succumb to worshipping the manifest, a graven image, instead of longing for the unchartered, unmanifest nonbeing. The truly monotheistic Jews are collectively fixated on the non-differentiated Unity of nonbeing, consequently they long and pray for a non-substantive, non-manifest, objectless God who is unreachable, unknowable and unattainable. The monotheistic Jewish God is an arche-typal, metaphysical projection of the *Ani*-skewed self, of its intense longing for nonbeing as an end in itself. Any concretization of this longing on the object; be it in the form of the Son of God or a Golden Calf, is regarded blasphemous idolatry.

In Castaneda's trilogy, this longing for the other "real" reality takes the form of "the will", which makes one see beyond the confines of spatio-temporality. "Will," says Don Juan, "is what sends a sorcerer through a wall; through space; to the moon, if he wants."[69] In our terms, the will to "see the other reality" is the longing of the *Ani*-skewed self to reach the spaceless infinity of nonbeing. This will may be just a longing to see the "other reality", which may not be realized, but one should not lose hope, and wait for it to come. "At least now you know," says Don Juan to his disciple, "you are waiting for your will. You still don't know what it is, or how it could happen to you. So watch carefully everything you do. The very thing that could help you develop your will is amidst all the little things you do."[70] There is a striking resemblance between the apprentice sorcerer waiting for "the will" to take hold of him and carry him away and beyond temporal reality, and the *Ani*-skewed self, forever longing for nonbeing, even if its realization is ever remote and shrouded by uncertainties.

The most conspicuous instances of *Ani*-skewed selves are the mystics. We may, therefore, gain some insight into the dynamics of their selves by examining a random assortment of the teachings of some individual mystics, and not of mystical systems. Dionysus the Areopagite has set forth in his *Mystical Theology* the Doctrine of Divine Darkness. One may reach the "brilliance of darkness" by renouncing the conscious self by a method that has been denoted by us as "exclusion", i.e. by melting into the object. The means to this end are the dulling of the senses, the foregoing of the intellect, the rejection of time sequences, the measurements of space and the notion of causality. This total, sensual deprivation would effect a holistic darkness in which one should plunge in a leap of faith in order to be embraced by the bliss of nonbeing.[71] The mystical doctrines of Dionysus the Areopagite (pseudo-Dionysus), behind his specialized and esoteric terminology, make him fit our description of the *Ani*-skewed self.

Meister Eckhart recounted that when he "came out" from God "into multiplicity" everybody proclaimed, "There is a God".[72] This rather obscure statement may be deciphered by relating it to other writings and sermons of the Meister. God, the origin of everything, and the Meister's own source is formless, modeless, uncaused and is "so elemental that one can say nothing about it except that it is naught".[73] God is the attributeless nothingness, "a Unity alien from all duality".[74] Eckhart's conception of God as a holistic nothingness contrasted with duality is unique. It fits our description of the *Ani*-dominated self, which is fixated on pre-differentiation, as contrasted with the post-differentiated duality of object relationship and activism. Also Eckhart's "root of beatitude" is the total happiness, when Man was not conscious of himself but only of God.[75] This again is the goal of melting into Unity, and returning to the original bliss of pre-separation. Eckhart's statement of coming out of God into multiplicity and being recognized as God may be understood then as the *Ani*-centred self's feeling that part of God is embedded in him. This is the

199

original objectless totality of the *Ani* carried forth by the self from the blissful pantheism of early orality and the self-sufficiency *in utero*. This "God in human nature . . . which is the purest of the soul"[76] is very much like the Kabbalist Divine Sparks, which are the offshoots of the Divine Presence strewn within the profane human bodies. Eckhart's imagery stresses that recognition by others of one's Divine origin is through the outward visibility of this embedded sacredness, which shines like "a lamp of living light".[77] Still, this inner beatitude, which in our context is characteristic of the *Ani*-dominated personalities, is not apparent to everyone because "darkness comprehends not this light".[78] Apparently only other *Ani*-skewed selves that are mystically inclined may recognize these cached Sparks of Divinity, which in our context are the holistic objectlessness of the *Ani*, in one another.

Meister Eckhart is closest to our conception of the *Ani*-skewed self when he described the exclusionary goals of the mystic as follows:

> When I think of the union of the soul with God, He makes the soul to flow out of herself in joyful ecstasy . . . The Divine love-spring surges over the soul, sweeping her out of herself into the unnamed being in her original source, for that is all God is . . . Thus the soul arrives at the height of her perfection.[79]

This is the quest preached by Eckhart for "dying in God", which has most of the aims of our *Ani*-dominated self. It longs for the perfect beginnings of omnipresence at the time when it partook in Unity and hence in God. It wishes to discard its association with space, time and multiplicity and disappear; in effect the aim is to disembody itself from the confines of object relations with its other pole on the self-continuum. It prods the holistic, objectlessness of the *Ani* to take over the entire self, and in the process, to commit an ontological suicide so that the separate self ceases to exist.

Nicholas of Cusa, the mystic mathematician, elaborated his basic notion of the identity of God with Unity and hence the equation of the attributes, or rather the lack of the attributes of God, with the mathematical properties of Unity. Consequently, God for Cusanus is indivisible, all-inclusive, non-sharing, timeless and infinite. God is also not reducible to the discrete manipulation of logic. He has to be approached with "learned ignorance".[80] All the interrelationships of reason, which are the tools of the self interacting with the object, are futile when applied to the holistic Unity of God. Only intuition and belief can apply to the logical absurdity of an uncreated Creator, which makes sense as an article of faith. The *Ani*-centred Cusanus thus describes God in terms of the holistic objectlessness of his *Ani*. His pre-differentiated fixation shows in his imagery of partaking in Absolute Infinity, as being within the Walls of Paradise and the Garden of Delights.[81] There is the bliss and self-sufficiency of egoless participation. Cusanus envisaged a dual reality very much like the two polarities of our self continuum, one invisible, sacred and ultimate in which seeing and being seen, i.e. subject and object, are indistinguishable, very much like our *Ani*, and the visible and derived reality of space, time and multiplicity, which roughly corresponds to our interactive *Atzmi*. Our model of the self envisages a dialectical interplay between the opposing polar components of the self, but the *Ani*-skewed Cusanus makes the holistic objectless *Ani* take over the whole self by affecting a fusion of his opposing realities so that the self-continuum is virtually abolished by the coincidence of opposites. The two opposing realities are not deemed to merge into a third new dialectical state, but spatio-temporal reality is dismissed by the mystical method of Cusanus as a trivial *non-sequitur* when confronted with the enormity of the infinite Unity. In this, the *Ani*-centred Cusanus resembles the Far Eastern Taoists and Hinayana Buddhists, who do not take seriously the outer reality of object relationship and reject it as a chimerical *mayan* veil, to be set aside by meditative techniques.

The most extreme in *Ani*-skewedness of the Christian mystics is probably St. John of the Cross. In a typical passage from his Spiritual Canticle, he describes the fusion of the soul with God in *Unio Mystica* as follows: "The spiritual sleep which the soul has in the bosom of its beloved comprises enjoyment of all the calm and rest and quiet of the peaceful night, and it receives in God together with this a profound and dark divine intelligence and for this reason the Bride says that her Beloved is to her the tranquil night."[82] Darkness for St. John is a symbol of ascent towards union with Divinity by shutting off the temporal world. In like manner, dark Divine intelligence is the wisdom of unknowing and unreason of nonbeing. The description by St. John of mystical union corresponds to our conception of pre-differentiated bliss and the tranquillity and self-sufficiency of suspended animation in the womb. St. John leaves us no doubt as to his fixation on the nonbeing of pre-separation. His inclusionary techniques are also thorough. In his "Ascent on Mount Carmel" he negates methodically, systematically and compulsively every imaginable vestige of sensual perception and every single attribute of spatio-temporality, like extinguishing light after light in a chandelier until dark nothingness reigns supreme. Joy, hope, fear and grief have to be rejected, and detachment, emptiness and poverty bring one nearer to the denial and dissolution of the self into God.

We may mention, finally, that the Christian mystics realized the Tantalic nature of their quest for union. Consequently, the longing for union itself was beautified. "The unground is an eternal nothing," says Jacob Boehme, "but makes an eternal beginning as a craving. For the nothing is a craving after something. But as there is nothing that can give anything, accordingly the craving itself is the giving of it, which yet also is a nothing, or merely a desirous seeking."[83] The *Ani*-skewed self seeks an ever-receding, impossible union with Divinity, but its striving and longing for it may become an end in itself without the need of further reinforcement by actual, mystical experiences.

We have instanced these sporadic glimpses into the inner world of some

Christian mystics as revealed by their writings as initial, empirical illustrations of *Ani*-skewed selves. More substantial empirical support of our model, as well as for our polar types of self, should be sought by the study of a properly chosen sample of practicing mystics as contrasted by a group of achievement-motivated activists representing the *Atzmi*-skewed selves.

Short of being mystics, we must find a method of reaching and identifying the *Ani*-skewed self, and for that matter, the *Ani* itself. With all its shortcomings, this method seems to be the epoxy or Husserl's phenomenological reduction. Husserl's *epoche* is deemed to achieve the same ends and employs basically the same techniques as the mystics. The phenomenological voyage through reduction to the "transcendental pure self" is very like St. John of the Cross's "Ascent on Mount Carmel", extinguishing step by step the attributes and appearances of spatio-temporality until one reaches the ethereal heights of the non-self, which is equivalent to Husserl's "pure self. The Buddhist and Yoga methods also perform phenomenological reductions in their own way, but our Occidental conditioning and background make Husserl's almost compulsive Teutonic orderliness more suitable for our purposes of discovering the *Ani*. Husserl's technique of "bracketing out" spatio-temporality in order to reach the pure self also has another advantage: he does not preclude the "reality" of the "natural world" as perceived by the individual. He just tries to neutralize it in order to reach the core of the pure self. Indeed, the bi-polarity of our self-continuum suits this approach. We claim that the self functions through a dialectical interaction of its components, but in order to reach the *Ani*, we "bracket out" and neutralize the *Atzmi*, the interactive self, and this is exactly what Husserl offers us in his phenomenological reduction. Husserl's technique suits our purposes because he does not exclude the "reality" of the spatio-temporal world – he just devises a technique to unveil its envelopes over the core of "transcendental subjectivity".

We envisage our self to function by a dialectical relationship between the objectless *Ani* and the interactive *Atzmi*. The latter is readily perceived by our senses, whereas the *Ani* is not. Consequently, the phenomenological reduction may be a useful tool to uncover the *Ani*. The phenomenological *epoche* – the "bracketing out" of appearance – is a secular and cerebral counterpart to the Far Eastern religious techniques of mysticism to reach the absolute. Husserl advocates empathy and "turning inwards in pure reflection",[84] the way a Hinayana Buddhist utilizes meditation to extinguish his temporal awareness. Not being Buddhist monks and not having their religious training, the phenomenological reduction is more suited to our Western culture conditioning. The phenomenological reduction starts by positing ourselves at the centre of an ontological drama. Our being is the cause and goal of all perceptions and phenomena, because without us as audience, everything around us loses its existence. Consequently, Husserl's pure self and our *Ani* do not derive their being from perception and spatio-temporality. The *Ani* is the ultimate for which all appearances, sensations and object relationships have been staged. This is more than a Cartesian *cogito* or a Euclidean axiom. It is both an assumption and a hypothesis proved by the irreducible fact of our being. This is the only way to *prove* our being independently of perception and object relationship, and to show the feasibility of an objectless *Ani*. If the objects, flora, fauna and others, as well as our own proprioceptors, are "out there" staging a command performance for the *Ani* as participant observer, there must be an *Ani*. The pure self of Husserl, as well as our *Ani*, is a megalomaniac: "As I am the ego who invests the being of the world," says Husserl, "I now also become aware that my own phenomenologically self-contained essence can be *posited* in an absolute sense."[85] If the whole of awareness, or for that matter, the whole universe, performs for the *Ani*, the curtain may be lowered so that the pure self (and our *Ani*) remains in absolute omnipresent loneliness. This is the gist of the phenomenological *epoche*. Husserl then goes on to describe, with Germanic thoroughness, how all of spatio-temporality may be "bracketed out" and suspended so that only the boundless and limitless pure self remains. Like a St. John of the Cross ascending his spiritual Mount Carmel towards the peak of nothingness, or a Shakespeare killing off his cast one by one, Husserl "disconnects" space, time, causality, science, culture, arts, custom, law, and even God, until the steam of pure consciousness becomes pure nothingness. The phenomenological reduction is also dialectical insofar as it reaches the *Ani* through the reduction, the annihilation of every-thing into no-thing. Only with the removal of the interfering objects-things does the no-thing become "pure", an objectless *Ani*. The phenomenological reduction makes the *Ani* "shine forth and show itself", which is the original meaning of the Greek *phainestai*, which is the root of the word phenomenon.[86] The *Ani* is the Kabbalistic Divine Spark from which the profane covers (*kelippot*) of predicates and objects have been peeled off.

An additional or alternative way to reach the *Ani* is through what Maslow calls "peak experiences". A person may be "turned on" by sex, aesthetic experience, religious ecstasy or chemicals. He then may feel "unified", sense a pantheistic fusion with objects, feel "self-sufficient, cosmic and Godlike".[87] This temporary euphoria may partially anaesthetize or weaken the dialectical controls of the Tantalus Ratio so that the veil of the ego boundary may be lifted and the access to the objectless *Ani* is facilitated.

Alcohol, drugs, and especially the temporary insanity affected by the hallucinogens, have perennially been used by Man to blunt the vicissitudes of social, inter-personal and object relationships. This in turn would weaken the controls of the Tantalus Ratio and let the *Ani* control a wider segment of the self-continuum. It might well be that the main attractions of drugs and alcohol for Man is precisely their weakening of the separating "ego boundary" and their heightening of the sense of Unity and togetherness brought about by a less-restrained *Ani*. Aldous

Huxley takes us on a short comparative survey of drugs, alcohol and religion:

> The swing door opened and shut. God-thirsty from the spiritual deserts of the workshop and the office, men came as to a temple. Bottled and barrelled by Clyde and Liffey, by Thames, Douro and Trent, the mysterious divinity revealed itself to them. For the Brahmins who pressed and drank the Soma, its name was Indra; for the hemp-eating Yaqis, Siva. The Gods of Mexico inhabited the peyotl. The Persian Sufis discovered Allah in the wine of Shiraz, the Shamams of the Samoyedes ate toadstools and were filled with the spirit of Num.[88]

It seems that the drug of choice of separant, activist cultures is alcohol, while the opiates, the hallucinogens and cannabis were originally more prevalent in quietist participant cultures. Why this is so is a matter of conjecture and further research, but the fact is that every culture has its aid for temporary self-oblivion, a means to blur and blunt the interactive *Atzmi* so that the *Ani* gains ascendancy through a flash of ecstasy or the relaxed contentedness of blissful euphoria. Castaneda's Don Juan also preaches that drugs serve only as a tool, an ally to help one "see the other reality". Eventually one may acquire the ability to "see" one's inner self, which roughly corresponds to our *Ani*, without the intermediary of drugs. The goal is the dispersion of perceptual reality so that the "inner reality" shines forth. Drugs are only one means to attain this goal.[89]

Song and dance may serve as additional or even alternative methods to reach one's *Ani*. We have already mentioned the participant role of the monotonous, minoric incantations of the East. Don Juan also assures us that song may help us see "the other reality", provided the songs are sung with "soul" and are not "phony".[90] This test for the authenticity of music might well be based on its ability to lift the veils of routine object relationships and bring one closer to the inner sanctuary of one's *Ani*. Dancing is also a trigger for "men of knowledge" to "see the other reality". "Take Sacateca," says Don Juan, "he's a man of knowledge and his predilection (i.e. something he does in order to know) is dancing. So he dances and knows."[91] This brings to mind the ecstatic whirls of the dervishes and the jerky movements of Jews in prayer, which are meant to dim one's awareness of one's surroundings and facilitate access to Divinity. In our terms, dance may upset the controls of the coordinating Tantalus Ratio so that the quietist *Ani*, subdued and overshadowed by the activist interactive *Atzmi*, may shine forth and take hold momentarily of the whole self. Drugs seem to be for an ever-widening segment of society a prime vehicle of escape into the boundless timelessness of the *Ani*. The author was a victim not very long ago of an accidental overdose of T.H.C. (Ecstasy)[92] in an experimental setting of drug taking. He watched the garden outside the glass window of his living-room and the four seasons passed by in succession: summer turned into autumn; the leaves of the trees turned yellow and fell off; then winter came with rain and winds blowing; spring was marked by the wisteria shrubs bursting into blue bloom; and finally summer came back with its hot winds. When the author looked at his watch, he was amazed to find that the whole cycle of four seasons had lasted only a quarter of an hour. As for spatial perception, the contours of the living room became hazy and a friend who was sitting beside him appeared at the same time to sit also at the far corner of the ceiling. Cheese seemed to reach the mouth without the intermediary of hands and lights turned on and off without the use of switches. The overall effect of the T.H.C. was the congestion and twisting of time, a dispersion of space and the dismantling of causality. These three are the core dimensions of the interactive reality of the *Atzmi*, as well as of the coordinating ego functions of the Tantalus Ratio. It may serve as a primary empirical anchor of our present premise that drugs indeed served to disperse and subdue the spatio-temporal environment and perceptions of the author so that his inner sense of being, i.e. his *Ani*, could spread out through his whole self with a boundless timelessness. Similar experiences have been recorded by Castaneda after taking peyote, and Don Juan assures us that peyote brings about a change in men and teaches them the right way to live by showing them how to "see".[93] "Seeing" in Don Juan's terms is the ability to penetrate into the core of one's being, in contradistinction to just "looking" at the outward sensory perceptions.

Don Juan's method of reaching his objectless *Ani* with the help of hallucinogenic drugs or without them is "controlled folly". In one of the most moving and perceptive passages of the trilogy, Don Juan illustrated what this controlled folly was. He was watching the mangled body of his son, who was crushed by rocks while constructing a highway. Don Juan recounts, while making again the distinction between "looking" and "seeing":

> I stood there too, but I did not look. I shifted my eyes so I would see his personal life disintegrating, expanding uncontrollably beyond its limits, like a fog of crystals, because that is the way life and death mix and expand. That is what I did at the time of my son's death. That's all one could ever do, and that is controlled folly. Had I looked at him, I would have watched him becoming immobile and I would have felt a cry inside of me, because never again would I look at his fine figure pacing the earth. I saw his death instead and there was no sadness, no feeling. His death was equal to everything else.[94]

The controlled folly makes us stop "looking" at the outward plurality of things and start "seeing" their underlying Unity. When one sees oneself and others, even one's dying son, in the context of a pantheistic togetherness, death becomes an illusion. One is reminded here of the Kabbalist doctrine that in the face of eternity, death is a lie. Don Juan is being dominated in his state of controlled folly by his *Ani*. The partitions between his outer and inner realities fade away and everything and nothing, being and death, mingle into Unity.

Controlled folly involves not only a stoic acceptance of disaster but also an overall apathy towards temporal possessions.[95] It is also a Camusian

205

Sisyphus practising the absurd: "We must know first that our acts are useless and we must proceed as if we didn't know it. That's a sorcerer's controlled folly."[96] There is, however, something more: "A man of knowledge", discovering his *Ani*, does not have to be a Sisyphean activist. The Camusian absurd is revealed and grasped through and by one's object relationships within the drudgery of daily routines. Not so our "man of knowledge", who can see himself without the activist setting of object relationship. A man who has reached his innermost being by "controlled folly" does not have to practice the Sisyphean rituals of action or the Protestant sanctification of work. He has a choice: he may go through the motions of object relationships without being dominated by the object, or he may remain altogether impassive. For a man who "sees", who has unveiled his *Ani*, action and inaction are just the same.[97]

Don Juan's techniques of "seeing" and "controlled folly", with or without drugs, were aimed at effecting a fusion of ordinary and non-ordinary reality.[98] In our context, Don Juan's goal would be the fusion of the *Atzmi* with the *Ani* by a partial dissolution or transparency of the ego boundary. Consequently, the dialectics between the polar components of the self would be impaired, with a resultant feeling of harmonious Unity and pantheistic participation instead of conflict and deprivational interaction. The drug-aided voyage of Castaneda to his inner self was characterized by a centripetal suction to the centre of a mandala-like bubble: "soft and dark like a uterus".[99] The anchor here on pre-differentiation is obvious. He then describes his feeling of omnipresence: "I was everywhere; I could see up and down and around, all at the same time."[100] This is the *Ani* in its original phase of timeless, spaceless synchronism in early orality and *in utero*. The end of the voyage was reached when he felt that "everything is filled to the brim and everything is equal".[101] No good and no evil. No victory and no defeat. No life and no death. This is the ultimate of participation in the Unity of the *Ani*.

A man who embarks on a voyage into his inner self, seeking the "other reality" of his *Ani*, finds his "given" reality sterile, futile and trivial.[102] When we are on the verge of discovering our *Ani*, we are gripped by a feeling that our spatio-temporal environment is unreal; that we are moving around in a dream world that is mostly painful, unpleasant or indifferent. We do not attach much importance to it because we feel that we are soon to wake up into the blissful weightlessness of the *Ani*. When we experience a disaster or a personal calamity, we let ourselves be drawn even further and rapidly into the realm of the *Ani*, dismissing the disastrous object relationship as too "unreal" or too absurd to be actually happening to us.

Becoming a "man of knowledge" is an experience, a "happening", like the Gnostic awakening or the *Satori* of Zen. Don Juan specifies the stages of reaching this knowledge, which are not unlike the fourfold way to the Hinayana Buddha. Also, this knowledge is not a permanent state, but a temporary one. Sometimes it lasts for a brief instant only.[103] The revelation of the inner self is a short-lived mystical experience. The veils of the interactive *Atzmi* are lifted for a short time only. One's illuminating contact with the *Ani* is short-lived and the *Atzmi*, as well as the coordinating ego functions of the Tantalus Ratio, soon regain control over the whole self, which is faced again with the trials of object relationships. But the effects of the revealing contact with the *Ani* are everlasting. A man who has experienced "knowledge", even for an instant, can place the vicissitudes of daily routines in their right perspective. The importance, or rather the lack of it, in the Sisyphean drudgeries of temporal interaction is placed within the revelation of the timeless boundlessness of the *Ani*. Don Juan's vision of the "other reality" is an undulating flux: a *panta rhei* of fleeting togetherness and the world of discrete space, melting into ethereal movement.[104] This could be a correlate of the fixation on pre-differentiation, or even on the cushioned soft movements *in utero*. Another aspect of this holistic fixation of the *Ani*-bound "man of knowledge" is that he has no use for logic or the cerebral thinking based on space, time and the discrete sequences of object relationship. When one learns to see, teaches Don Juan, one unifies, but when one just "looks", one thinks too much, and thinking is bad for "seeing", because it divides and compares.[105] This illustrates our premise that the *Ani* cannot be discovered by logic or inference, because the notion of objectlessness itself is illogical. The way of *seeing* the *Ani* is through intuition, holistic Gestalt or an experience of revelation described by the numerous accounts of mystics.

207

Those who search for their inner self, their *Ani*, start with a longing to *see*. They have an inner craving to "find themselves", accompanied by a distaste for their temporal surroundings. Don Juan says that a man who longs to see, "to know his heart", develops a single-mindedness that makes him lose interest in his surroundings, as well as in his fellow men.[106] The Existentialist of the Sartrean brand also develops a distaste for his surroundings and his fellow men, but he stops at that. Negation becomes a goal in itself: Roquentin's nausea becomes his sole *Weltanschauung* and Carcin's "hell is other people" is raised to the stature of a foundation for a philosophy very much like the Cartesian *cogito*. Don Juan and Husserl go further: their rejection of spatio-temporality is a technique, a means to reach the "pure ego", the "other reality", and the core of the *Ani*. We can now better understand Sartre's rejection of Husserl's transcendental self.[107] By denying the *Ani*, Sartre entangled himself in the ontological one-sidedness of object relationship.

Don Juan describes vividly the peripheral vision, which may bring one into the closest contact with the other reality of one's inner self. The Indian "seeing with the third eye" and the "sideways glance" of Zen are also instances of peripheral vision, aimed to grasp the fleeting images of "inner realities" behind the veils of *maya*, but Don Juan's imagery is less abstract and self-explanatory. "One can feel with the eyes," explains Don Juan, "when the eyes are not looking right into things";[108] one can see the other reality when it is on the edge of one's field of vision. Don Juan's student recalls:

> Whenever I tried deliberately to trap the voice, it subsided altogether or became vague and the scene faded. I thought of a simile. The voice was like the image created by dust particles in the eyelashes, or the blood vessels in the cornea of the eye, a worm-like shape that can be seen as long as one is not looking at it directly; but the moment one tries to look at it, it shifts out of sight with the movement of the eyeball.[109]

This more than anything points out the Tantalic trials of the *Ani* seekers. One cannot approach it with the sensory perceptions of ordinary reality. Any deliberate attention makes the vague glimpses of inner reality fade away. The search for the *Ani* is the quest of union and nothingness, and these may be sensed on the fringes of our holistic Gestalt of perception and not in its centre. The moment we try to focus on the visibility of our *Ani* and try to define its contours, we have already lost it. The *Ani* can be experienced but not defined in spatial terms or communicated with the symbolics of language. One may lose one's quest for one's *Ani* by trying to define it, as did Charles Stuart, who lost his monarchy by trying to define it. One cannot also confine the timeless *Ani* into the discrete sequences of communication. The "true self" cannot be communicated because the "Tao that can be expressed is not the eternal Tao".

We may sum up our description of the *Ani* by stating, first of all, that it is a psychobiological entity that may be construed empirically from the non-differentiated core of the self at early orality and *in utero*. Second, the anchor of the *Ani* on pre-differentiation is related to the rejection of discrete sequences and hence of past and future. The *Ani* is ever-present and timeless. The phenomenological counterpart to the timelessness of the *Ani* is the primordial now of Husserl's pure ego.[110] Third, the *Ani* is anchored on Unity, whereas space is derived from the interrelationship of multiplicity, consequently, the *Ani* is spaceless. Indeed, Castaneda describes his "other reality" as accompanied by the melting away of his body and the loss of the concrete tangibility of the things around him.[111] Fourth, the *Ani*, not being relational, is not necessarily governed by rules of causality. A causal simultaneity and synchronicity may be acceptable to the *Ani* as different manifestations of one phenomenon and stemming from one source. Fifth, the *Ani* may be reached by the phenomenological technique of "reduction", rituals of meditation, mystical experiences and catalyzed by ecstatic or drug-induced "peak experiences". Logic is inapplicable as a means of discovering the *Ani*. Intuition and not cognitive attention is the proper medium for the unveiling of the *Ani*, as well as for the grasping of the holistic Gestalt of objectless-ness, which is a patent logical absurdity.

Sixth, the *Ani*-dominated person is detached. True detachment if not a *ressentiment* negation of hedonism by an ascetic or the food-involved fasting of a weight-watcher, is the quietist indifference of the accidiac. Don Juan does not get angry because the acts of other people are not important enough.[112] Social justice, or injustice, leave him cold because human society is hopeless to begin with. For a "man of knowledge", riches and poverty, happiness and squalor, social change or social stagnation are equally meaningless because they do not belong to the "other reality" of the *Ani*.

Finally, the search for the *Ani* is the courting of the nonbeing of death – the annihilation into nothingness of the temporal world. "Upon learning to *see*," says Don Juan, "a man becomes everything by becoming nothing",[113] i.e. he reaches his innermost *Ani*. For a "man of knowledge" who has learned to "see" and has mastered the arduous art of discovering his *Ani*, death is the ultimate touch.[114] Death becomes a central force, a means to discard the appendages of spatio-temporality so that one is fully exposed to the core of one's being.

The Interactive Self

When Goethe's Faust started to translate the New Testament into German, he revealed to us through his semantic deliberations the making of a Faustian activist:

> It is written: "In the Beginning was the word." Here am I balked: who now can help afford? The Word? – impossible so high to rate it; And otherwise must I translate it, if by the Spirit I am truly taught. Then thus: "In the Beginning was the Thought." This first line let me weigh completely, lest my impatient pen proceed too fleetly. Is it the thought which works, creates? "In the Beginning was the Power, "I read. Indeed? Yet, as I write, a warning is suggested, that I the sense may not have fairly tested. The Spirit aids me: now I see the light. "In the Beginning was the Act," I write.[115]

The evolution of a Faust is from the word, the core of a holistic idea; he then progresses to the thought: the derivation of being from the Cartesian *cogito*. The power is the dialectical energy that is generated within the Tantalus Ratio, which finally finds its outlet in the act – in the object manipulation of the *Atzmi*. Indeed, there could be no better description of the flow of energy from the self to the object as this outward-bound progression of the Faustian *Atzmi*.

Our deliberations on the interactive component of the self would have to be less rigorous and not as wide as our exposition of the *Ani*. One of our major innovations in this work, based on the bio-psychological development of the personality, is the introduction into the self of holistic objectlessness. Not so the *Atzmi*, the interactive self, as well as the coordinating *Ity*, which have been dealt with exhaustively by most personologists, although in different conceptual frameworks and not in a dialectic framework. The classic symbolic interactionists award not only primacy but also exclusiveness to the interactive self, whereas we see the *Atzmi* as only one polar component in the self-continuum. Mead expressly says that: "Selves exist only in relation to other selves."[116] We go even further by claiming that whatever the reality of the object "out there", it is revealed by the interactional attributes of space, time and causality inherent in the relational nature of the *Atzmi*. Cooley sees "the looking glass self" [117] as the reciprocal attuning of ego and his relevant others. For him, there is nothing more in the self than this structuring of relationships with others. For us, "the looking-glass self is only part of the *Atzmi*, because the latter is generated by a constant dialectic of object relationship and the holistic *Ani*. Goffman, the contemporary symbolic interactionist, goes so far as to deny any stability of the social self, and his behavioral unit of analysis is a specific role in a given social Gestalt. When the role and social setting change, the whole person changes.[118] This is a far cry from our conception of the *Atzmi*, which is anchored on rather stable developmental phases that determine the vectors, scaffolding and hence the forms (not the contents) of object relationship.

The Freudian psychoanalysts follow their master in regarding the "Pleasure Principle" as underlying the cathartic release of repressed libido *quanta* through object involvement.[119] In contrast, we envisage a dialectical conflict within the Tantalus Ratio of the self, which provides the motivation for the inclusion, i.e. the swallowing of the object, by the outwardly-reaching *Atzmi*. When this proves to be impossible physically, or is proscribed by social norms, the interactive *Atzmi*, with the help of the coordinating *Ity*, devises surrogate modes of exclusion, which manifest themselves as socially accepted or deviant object relationships.

The ego psychologists, notably Heinz Hartmann, David Rapaport, Erik Erikson and their disciples,[120] who are influential in the United States, especially among clinicians, see the ego as an autonomous entity in the personality. This ego, which controls the individual's interactions and object relationships, is believed by the ego psychologists to be partly inherited and partly acquired by experience as a "conflict-free" structure within the personality. Throughout this work, we have tried to avoid undue polemics. Consequently, we shall just state that the notion of inherited structures of behavior is foreign to our basic premises in this work; we had the same reaction to Jung's idea of a genetically transmitted collective subconscious. Also our whole personality model is based on dual conflictual cycles: one within the self between the *Ani* and the *Atzmi* components, which generate the Tantalic psychic energy; the other is the *Ity*, the controlling function of the Tantalus Ratio, which creates through constant dialectic conflicts among the components of the self and its environment a system in balance that holds the personality in a dynamic equilibrium. Consequently, a "conflict-free" autonomous ego is a far cry from our model. The British "oralists" – Melanie Klein, Donald Winnicott, Harry Guntrip, and especially Fairbairn[121] – are close to us in the crucial role they attribute to the oral phase of development and in their description of the "mouth ego", which strives to swallow the object. We place the utmost importance for the formation and structure of the *Atzmi* on the differentiation of the self from the pantheistic mass of early orality. This separation of Unity into plurality, which marks also the division between early and later orality, is virtually ignored by the oralists.

After this brief survey of the relevant literature, we shall now point out the main attributes of our *Atzmi*, the interactive component of the self.

The *Atzmi* is based on the discrete perception of space and the linear perception of time. The perception of the rhythm of time may change from one person to the other and also may be heightened or slowed by drugs or "peak experiences". Nevertheless, the *Atzmi* perceives only the linear sequence of past, present and future as meaningful. The necessity of time and space for the object relations of the *Atzmi* underlie its need for logic, symbolics (language), causality, association and inference, as the *modi operandi* in its interaction with things and other people. Social norms are then incorporated within the self, in a manner that we shall describe later, by the coordinating functions of the *Ity*. The *Atzmi*, in contradistinction with the holistic *Durée*-like flow of intuition, operates by soberly focusing attention on the object and relating to it intentionally. The *Atzmi* is basically a carnivore that aims to "swallow" the object through the numerous modes of surrogate inclusion. The charismatic leader aims to dominate others, irrespective of the different noises he makes on the election platform or at party rallies. A Nietzsche envisions dreams of power and a Valhalla in which a Superman dominates the whole of creation; "his vision and power . . . complete and boundless and who, in his universality, lives in and with Nature",[122] or a Faust aims to achieve the Utopian fusion of subject and object by the saving grace of the act. These are the visions of glory of the *Atzmi*, but the coordinating *Ity* orders the dreamer to "come back to earth" and to face the reality of his stone. The rules of the object-relations game have been spelt out expressly in the Myth of Sisyphus.

Self, Choice and Uniqueness

7

Life may be terrifying, but oblivion is sadder. It's true, I suppose, that oblivion can be a mercy in some cases. But I want to be sure I'm one of those cases before I embrace it.

Tennessee Williams

Behold but One in all things; it is the second that leads you astray.

Kabir

Even from infancy I remember that I marvelled at the sense of my existence. I was already led by instinct to look within myself in order to know how it was possible that I could be alive and be myself.

Marie Maine de Biran

I am the Alpha and the Omega, the beginning and the end.

Paul Tillich, *The Eternal Now*

So far we have described the core vectors, mechanisms and dynamics of the self; the next step is to see how these are structured into a system. Once again it is necessary to point out that we have confined our model to the core of the self and not to its peripheral traits. We have described elsewhere and earlier[1] the developmental phases of the self that serve as background forms or moulds in which the self is, so to speak, cast. These forms are sustained by our two core personality vectors, which serve both as scaffoldings for the self and for its energy sources.

Developmental Forms of the Self

The developmental phases of the self, as structured by the core personality vectors, are presented schematically in **figure 7.1**. The vector of separation embodies the bio-physiological processes of growth, sex and their psychic correlates. The nascent self registers the three developmental phases that we have marked on the schema as catastrophes. The first is the *Geworfenheit* of birth: the violent expulsion from the blissful suspended animation in the womb. This catastrophe may be registered differently by the various neonates, depending on their biological structure; also the various pathologies of the birth process itself may augment or reduce the birth trauma. We do not follow here the Rankean birth trauma hypotheses; rather, we point out the influence of the fact of birth on the relative potency or weakness of the quest for nonbeing, i.e. the reversal of birth, which remains as a life-long participant counterpart to the processes of growth.

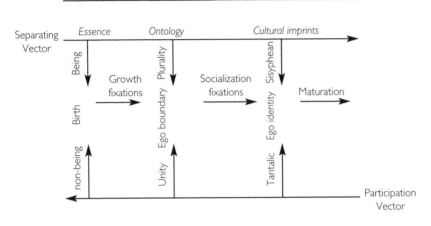

Figure 7.1 Developmental Phases of the Self

The separation of the self from the pantheistic omnipresence of early orality marks two crucial events, which are related to the crystallization of personality types. The first is the fixation on pre-differentiated Unity or on the post-differentiated object that determines the generalized profile of the personality towards Tantalism or Sisypheanism. The second is the process of the coagulation of the separate self through the deprivational interaction with the object, which marks the division between early and later orality and determines the structure of the ego boundary. We have described elsewhere how the interaction with a rejecting, indifferent or absent mother or her surrogate may account for some pathological forms of ego boundaries, which may be linked in turn to predispositions to morbidity or deviance.[2] The formation of the ego boundary, i.e. the basic duality of the "I" and the "not I" (object), is the scar-tissue formed as a shield against the vicissitudes of the deprivational interaction of the early oral omnipresent self with its surrounding objects and the breast–mother, who is not as promptly and fully nourishing as the umbilical cord *in utero*. In other words, if all the needs and wants of the neonate would be immediately and automatically fulfilled, no ego boundary and no separate self would be formed. On the other hand, if the deprivational interaction at early orality is harsher and more severe, we may expect more scar tissue and a stronger, i.e. a more effectively insulating, ego boundary. The cultural imprints through socialization provide the participant-quietist and separant–activist dimensions of ethics, norms, roles and values. As specified earlier, we do not envisage the acquisition of social norms as a function of a specialized personality component, like the super ego or its equivalents in other personality theories. Acculturation in our model is a continuous process, which is more predominant, however, in the third developmental phase of social separation by the various *rites de passage* leading to "ego identity" and to the normative loneliness of responsibility. The dialectical dynamics of the Tantalus Ratio not only take place between the two opposing vectors of the personality core, but also within the various developmental structures. This is presented schematically in **figure 7.2**, which is a cross-section of the dynamic structures of the self. The broken lines represent the participant vector and the continuous lines show the separant core vector. The concentric circles are the developmental phases and the double-headed arrows are the dialectics of the Tantalus Ratio.

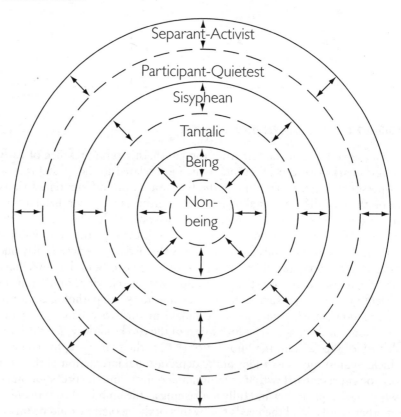

Figure 7.2 Dialectic Dynamics of the Tantalus Ratio

In **chapter 2**, we described how the process of the separation of the self, as well as the fixation on Unity or the object, are related to some core personality characteristics. Here we describe the end product. The structure of the self as related to its polar components, after it has undergone the major phases of development, is presented schematically in **figure 7.3**. The *Ani*-skewed self is represented by a self-continuum that has a predominant *Ani* and a diffuse *Atzmi*, whereas the *Atzmi*-skewed self has in its extreme form a strong ego boundary enclosing the object-related *Atzmi* and a diffuse *Ani*. Any observed structure of the self may then be placed on the continuum of **figure 7.3** according to the diffusion or strength of its polar components. The figure presents not only a continuum of self-structures but also elements of self-contents, because the diffusion or strength of self components is related to the relative predominance of quietist or activist elements within the self system.

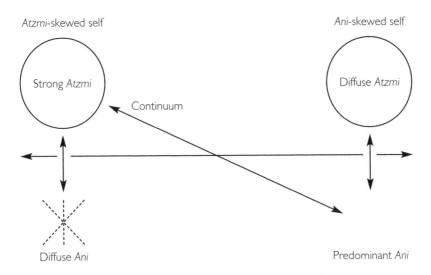

Atzmi-skewed self

Ani-skewed self

Strong Atzmi

Diffuse Atzmi

Continuum

Diffuse Ani

Predominant Ani

Figure 7.3   Structure of the Self

215

Core Dynamics

We envisage the Tantalus Ratio as having a dual function: first is the processing of the psychic energy involved in the clashes between the separating vectors of growth and the countering participation vectors to regress to previous developmental phases and to nonbeing. Second is the regulating *Ity*, which keeps the self as a system in balance through the dialectical conflict between the polar components of the self. The first function of the Tantalus Ratio is related to the channelling of the flow of psychic energy and its cathexis towards the object and the self, whereas the second function actually explains some core attributes of the self that have been regarded as non-explainable basic assumptions by other personologists. Homeostasis, for instance, was regarded as the most important underlying principle in some personality theories,[3] but its "whys" were never explained. Our regulating *Ity*, on the other hand, may explain homeostatic phenomena as the dialectical balance affected by the conflicting components of the self. Another dynamism that is more directly related to the formation of personality structures, as well as to the core fixation of personality types, is the deprivational interaction of the organism with its internal and external environment. This deprivational interaction is a direct corollary of the impact of the processes of separation on the immediate environment of the organism. We have demonstrated earlier how the crucial signposts of developmental separation of birth – the formation of the ego boundary and the *rites de passage* incidental to the acquisition of ego identity – are registered by the individual as catastrophes. In the present context the deprivational interaction is a specialized dynamic in so far as it occurs at the immediate areas of contact between the organism and its environment. Consequently, the perception of the conflicts and clashes of the developing self with its environment are taken in and processed by the Tantalus Ratio as a *Gestalt*, which signifies for the separant vector the obstacles to its aims of growth and to the participation vector the pains and trials that may be avoided by reverting back to a prior developmental phase. Figuratively, the deprivational interaction may be described as the hue and cry of the elements and the surrounding others against the unruly expansion in the physical and the social space of the growing individual. The pain and conflicts inherent in the deprivation interaction of the individual and the environment serve as the naturalistic motivation for the participant vector to refrain from the pain-causing growth. It also generates the scar tissue at the points and areas of contact that is the raw material for the structuring of the self.

The symbolic interactionists claim that the self is created by the mutual role expectations and interrelationship with the relevant others. Our claim is that the self is structured by the deprivational interaction of the organism with the surrounding objects and others as perceived and processed within the Tantalus Ratio. The Freudians envisage the reality principle as a corollary of the inability of the individual to realize fully and satisfy his instinctual drives, but they do not describe and explain how the ego is actually separated from its surroundings. We do this by depicting the clashes of the growing organism with its surroundings after it starts its life as a separate entity and not just as a cushioned appendage of its mother *in utero*. The expelled neonate disturbs, so to speak, a surrounding, which has to adjust to it as a novel system of actions and reaction. Our point of vantage is the perception of the developing self, which is bound to perceive its surroundings as more painful and ever more depriving with each consecutive phase of development. These clashes create traumatized points or areas of experience, which are processed by the dialectical flow of action and inaction within the Tantalus Ratio and deposited as layers of experiential insulation between the growing self and its existentially strange and many times hostile environment. The deprivational interaction of the organism with its immediate environment and relevant others is related both to the formation of the body image and its somatic contours and to the psychic division between the self and the non-self, i.e. the object.

As for the dynamic contents of the self, the energy of growth that constitutes the separant core personality vector, together with the deprivational interaction of the organism with its environment, conflicts with the quietist participant vector of nonbeing. These conflicts within the synaptic junctions of the opposing vectors of the personality core constitute our flow of being, which is processed dialectically and cathected to the quietist *Ani* or the activist *Atzmi* components of the personality, depending on the fixations, socialization, cultural factors and the processes of maturation and ageing. These dialectics of the Tantalus Ratio, which govern motivation, affect and thinking, deposit within the self, layers of peripheral personality traits, not unlike the films of salt crystallized after a chemical reaction. The differences between the Freudian and other personality theories that regard "defensive" processes as the raw material for the structuring of the personality core, as well as its peripheral traits, and our theory, become apparent: defence mechanisms are the sublimated manifestations of repressed instinctual energies, whereas our deposits of personality components are the results of dialectical reactions, which are totally different from the opposing vectors, the course of which was blocked by head-on collisions within the Tantalus Ratio.

In **chapter 2**, we described the formation of fixations that determine a life-long predisposition of the personality towards quietism or activism. These turbulent traumas, which leave their indelible mark, may be anchored on pre-differentiated totality or on the post-differentiated object. The fixations are related to a host of personality traits previously discussed. As dynamism within the self, the fixations relate to a motivational continuum ranging from exclusion (the participant wish for self-annihilation by melting within the object) to inclusion (the separant aim of overpowering and swallowing the object). The relationship here between structure and dynamism is that inclusionary motivational traits would be predominant within the *Atzmi*-skewed self, whereas the exclusionary traits would prevail in the *Ani*-dominated self.

Of special importance are the self-destructive or dysfunctional dynamisms within the self. We do not refer now to pathology or deviance; with these we have dealt with extensively elsewhere,[4] but to the self-destructive mechanisms that are incidental to the core dynamisms of the self. These are considered by some personologists to be so prevalent and so entrenched within the self that they have given it the stature of a structured personality component. Ronald Fairbairn, for instance, made the

217

Internal Saboteur an integral part of his central ego.[5] We maintain that the Internal Saboteur is not a structured component of the self, but the dynamic, momentary, rebellious upsurge of a subdued self component against the dominant polar component of the self. A quietist self-defacing urge may ruin the exploits of an activist object-manipulating *Atzmi*-dominated self, and a sudden burst of activity may destroy the peace of mind and contemplative serenity of a mystical *Ani*-skewed self.

The dynamics of the *Ity*, the regulating dialectical system of balance of the self, is also different in our model from the ego of other personologists. For the ego psychologists, the ego has an autonomous standing that does not stem from the basic drives and core components of the personality. Our *Ity* is different. It is the dialectical force field created by the conflicting pressures within the personality and outside it. Its structure, like the rim of a tornado, is a function of the force and direction of the turbulence and pressures from within and from without it. The dynamic balance held within a stable system may be observed in a wide range of phenomena, such as the fixed courses of stellar bodies. The position, strength and balance of the regulating *Ity* are a function of the potency of the conflicting personality components and a measure of their inability to attain their contradictory goals.

The dynamism of personality change – the maturation curve – is determined biologically and structured psychically; the movement on the maturation curve and the developmental changes of age constitute a prime dynamic within the structure of the personality core.

We are the Chosen

"When Man mints coins," states the Talmud Sanhedrin, "every coin resembles the other, but God made Man in the image of Adam, yet no Man resembles his fellow men. Therefore, each one of us has to say: For me alone has the world been created." [6] In theology and metaphysics, the two customary cardinal questions asked about the whereabouts of Man are: "Where from and where to?" Here the Talmud poses a third cardinal question, which is rarely asked yet is not less important, i.e. "Why me?" This question is the gist of the ontological choice and uniqueness of the self as perceived by the self and has, therefore, a direct bearing on the nature and scope of the individual's self-concept.

Hegel complained of the scandal of the plurality of consciousness, but it seems to us that the real paradoxical "scandal" is the plurality of chosen consciousnesses and the ontological sense of uniqueness of each individual self.

The basic existential fact underlying self-awareness is that the self has been chosen as the channel through which all the flow of existence is perceived to flow. The self knows by inference that other individuals also perceive themselves as chosen in the same way, but the *immediate* awareness of choice is exclusive to the self alone. This awareness of choice *vis-à-vis* others is rife with conflicts because others also assign choice to themselves. On the level of the objectless *Ani*, the awareness of choice becomes unique because the *Ani* relates itself to the core of being and not to the object or others. Consequently, choice, i.e. the selection of the self from others to be the channel of awareness, is an *Atzmi*-based interactive existential, whereas the exclusiveness of uniqueness is an *Ani*-based ontological existential. This is presented schematically in **figure 7.4**.

Existential		Dialetic	
		High	Low
Ani-based		*Ani*-based	
Uniqueness:	Ontological	Autonomy	Hübris
Atzmi-based		*Atzmi*-based	
Choice:	Statistical	Election	Rejection
Burden:	Dynamic	Absurd	*Ressentiment*

Figure 7.4   Dialectics of Choice and Uniqueness

The *Ani*-based ontological uniqueness may range from a high level sense of autonomy, as with the Unity-centred self-sufficiency of a Taoist, a Christian mystic or Castaneda's Yaqui Indian engulfed by his inner reality. The autonomy of uniqueness here relates to the freedom from the object, which we have encountered in the doctrines of Hinayana Buddhism, the quietist Hassidim and the Sufi Muslims. Autonomy from the bonds of spatio-temporality, and hence relationship, is the underlying theme in the celebrated yet esoteric teachings of theologians from many denominations, the common base of which is the longing for and the partaking in the absolute. The Protestant Tillich, for instance, declared his allegiance to the Timeless Now. The Catholic Teilhard de Chardin, shunned for many years by the hierarchy of the ecclesia, recognized the supra-personal goal of Man in his striving for the absolute: the omega point of the collective and universal pantheism.[7] The autonomy of the self, which anchors on the Absolute and frees itself, thereby, from the bonds of object relationships, is the common ground of these otherwise widely divergent thinkers. This sense of autonomy, by partaking in the Absolute, may be lessened if object involvement sets in. Even the most rudimentary object relationships effect a comparison: the *Ani* is no longer viewed as partaking or longing to partake in the Absolute, but as a channel through which the object may be perceived. On the ontological level, this may lead to *hübris*: to a "holier-than-thou" attitude of being above and superior to the object. The Gnostic, or Hassidic *pneumatics*, "the spirited one", is an example of this ontological sense of uniqueness. As we have expounded in *The Bridge to Nothingness* (with regard to Rabbi Nachman of Bratslav), the holy man, the *Tzadik*, is imbued with a sense of sanctity, which makes him high and above the rest of Creation and not subject to its laws. The transition from the ontological sense of uniqueness through partaking in Unity to the *hübris* of seeing oneself as the channel through which sanctity flows into the world is many times a matter of a change in emphasis. The shift is from seeing oneself as an indistinguishable part of the Absolute to regarding oneself as the emissary of the Absolute to the world. The dialectic here is between myself as part of Unity and myself as a particle of Unity *vis-à-vis* and contrasted with the rest of Creation as an object.

The *Atzmi*-based choice is a statistical one. If I am the excellent and the elect, this has to be shown by comparing myself with others. Here the point of reference is not the Absolute, but things and other human beings. Indeed, the achievement motive may well be based in some cultures (as Max Weber claimed) on the quest for a metaphysical proof of worth and a sign of grace, yet the actual manifestation of achievement is the accumulation of wealth and status objects and symbols more than others. There is nothing absolute about achievement: it is all relative to the relevant others within the membership or reference groups. The achiever, whether motivated by the Protestant Ethic or an Ayn Rand elitism, has no other criterion for his worth but to measure himself against others. Choice here may be affected either by raising one's exploits in the relevant parameters above the average of the group or lowering the achievement of others so that one's position on the ladder is relatively raised. This is why social stigma is a prime tool of relative achievement: ego may raise himself by his own bootstraps by explaining away alter's achievement. Consequently, one's role within a group and one's election to, or rejection from, a social position can never be defined by oneself for oneself, but always in conjunction with the judgment of others.

The dynamics of choice are related to the self's deprivational interaction with the object. The *Atzmi's* life-long fate to grapple with the object is manifest in the individual's burden of having to constantly cope with the obstacle course inherent in his interaction with his environment. The dialectic here moves from an optimal pole of the Camusian absurd, in which the strain between Sisyphus and his stone is the most one can hope for in one's temporal life. The interaction between the individual and his stone burden is all there is in object relationship. This, in itself, must be the aim in life, which should be enough to make Sisyphus happy, or at least stoically content. If one looks for aims and meanings beyond mere interaction and beyond the sheer task at hand, one is bound to be disappointed. One is destined to carry one's burden of interaction as an aim in itself. If one looks for meaning beyond the burden of object relations, one is bound to experience *ressentiment*: the bitter disenchantment of those whose expectations can never be fulfilled. Our ontological exposition of the self stems from the point of vantage of the individual. This is why the notions of uniqueness and choice are so crucial for us. We also have no need to delve into the arguments indulged in by semanticists, as to whether the body is or is not included in the concept of self.[8] Our sense of uniqueness and choice takes care of this. We assign a positive sign of worth to all the tissues, bones and juices of our body. The urine and saliva in our body are as acceptable to us as any other part of our body, which is included in our overall sense of uniqueness. Our saliva, for instance, becomes repugnant to us the moment it leaves our bodies, when it is no longer protected by the halo of the self's choice and uniqueness,

Ontological uniqueness is fixated on pre-differentiated holistic Unity. There is no way for the individual to relate this uniqueness to his conscious daily interaction with other human beings. Consequently, the individual can never grasp fully the relational implications of his own uniqueness. He is either constantly baffled or dismayed by his being the channel or even the source of cosmic awareness, or he reveres it as his own cherished sign of Divine grace, which cannot be shared or comprehended by other human beings. This may be the source of the Judaic doctrine that killing one person amounts to the killing of the whole universe. In a similar vein, the Lurianic Kabbalah and the quietist Hassidim believed that human awareness is actually the trapping of Divinity in one's thought. This accounts for Man's sense of Divine uniqueness. The participant aim of the quietist Hassidim was to blot out cognitive awareness so that the trapped particles of Divinity may be released and revert back to their source.[9]

In the last analysis, the sense of ontological uniqueness is the main characteristic of the *Ani*, the holistic component of the self. All other individuals have bodies, roles and positions, but my sense of serving as the channel of awareness and the source of being is uniquely my own. Castaneda's Don Juan also postulated a sense of being chosen (*escogido*) as a corollary of grasping the "other reality".[10] This in our context would be more related to ontological uniqueness, since Castaneda experienced his sense of choice while gaining "knowledge" beyond the confines of spatio-temporality.

On the philosophical level, the exponent of ontological uniqueness is Husserl. His transcendental ego is the subject not the object of being. It exists prior to all cosmic being and is independent of spatio-temporality. The world draws its being and is actually staged as a setting for the transcendental ego.[11] This indeed is the exposition *in extremis* of the ontological uniqueness of the objectless ego. We may proceed now to trace the transformation of ontological uniqueness into the *hübris* of egoism, in the philosophy of Max Stirner. He begins his exposition by describing the emptiness of the self, which is very much like our objectless *Ani* or the mystical *annihilatio*: "I am not nothing in the sense of emptiness, but I am the creative nothing, the nothing out of which I myself as creator create everything . . . I am (therefore) unique . . . equally with God the nothing of all others, who am my all, who am the unique one."[12]

This, in our context, is the uniqueness of the ego, which anchors on the totality of emptiness, i.e. the lack of objects and spatio-temporality and the omnipresence of nothingness and nonbeing. But then Stirner goes on to preach his ownness, which entails ownership "of what I have in my power or what I control . . . if I am only powerful, I am of myself empowered . . . Right is above me, is absolute . . . Power and might exist only in me the powerful and mighty."[13] Stirner's uniqueness becomes a source of power over the objects and all others. From the freedom of objectless uniqueness, Stirner subjugates himself to the Sisyphean task of overpowering the object. This is the *hübris* and snare of the egoist, who does not realize that an ontological sense of uniqueness may be all his own, but power is subject to no monopoly: one may have it for one moment only to lose it in the next.

The individual's sense of choice makes for his ethical partiality to himself. We have dealt elsewhere at great length with the ethical selective perception of the individual and his ethical double standards when related to himself or to others. This ethical egocentricity[14] biases social interaction, and we shall demonstrate in **chapter 8** how it prevents meaningful communication between the individual and other human beings. Indeed, this egocentricity seems to be a basic trait of the personality in its formative years; indeed, Jean Piaget tells us that the logical and ontological egocentricity of the child extends to a more advanced age than is commonly believed, until he learns the hard way that there are other points of view and other interests than his own.[15] Many personologists, including Salvatore Maddi, are not clear why Harry Sullivan sees an inevitable conflict between the individual and society.[16] Sullivan himself takes this conflict as almost axiomatic, which need not be explored for further causality. We claim that our core personality characteristics of uniqueness and choice do explain this inevitable conflict between the individual and the group.

Our ontological conception of uniqueness and choice may or may not be related to the differences among personality profiles and peripheral traits, which make each personality Gestalt or conglomeration of characteristics different from the other. Our uniqueness and choice is viewed phenomenologically from the individual's point of vantage, whereas the differences among personality traits depend on the observer and his measurement tools. Ontology and measurement are on two different conceptual and operational levels.

One important distinction between uniqueness and choice is that the latter needs outside reinforcement, whereas the former does not. The *Ani*-bound participant sense of uniqueness is not related to an object. One does or does not "feel it in one's bones" intuitively. Choice, on the other hand, needs the reinforcement of consensus. One musters "proof" from more

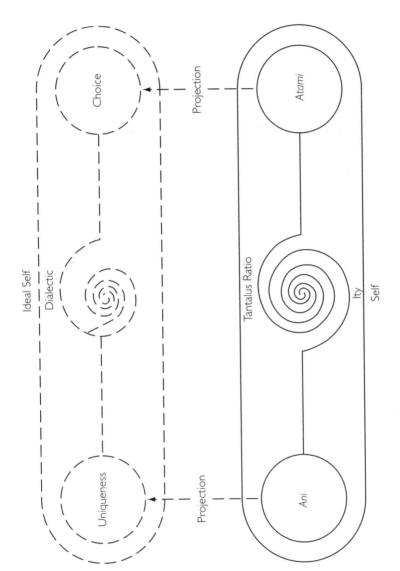

Figure 7.5 Schema of Composition of Ideal Self

223

and more sources that one is better than others. Achievement, as a criterion of choice, needs a constant reinforcement from outside sources; consequently, self-assertion is not enough. Our worth, both in quantity and quality, needs the approval of others. Another aspect of choice is that it may also be expressed negatively. Our statistical excellence is measured by so many standard deviations away from the mode towards the "right", "positive", "great", "more" segment of the normal curve. However, if this is impossible one may be motivated to "excel" in negativity and move towards the other extreme in order not to become a "mediocrity". Some people have a "horror of the fringes". The typical conformist finds comfort in the modes, means and medians of behaviour. Others abhor the middle range, and if they cannot make it on the "right" side of the barricade, they move quickly to the far end of the other side, in order not to remain in the middle. Previously published works by the author have dealt with the differential pressure towards conformity and deviance.[17] As an extreme case, we exampled Jean Genet, who when rejected by the "right" side of the normative barricade, honed to perfection his extreme negativity. He even beautified his own inverse trinity of treachery, theft and homosexuality, contrasting the cherished bourgeois virtues of loyalty, the sanctity of private property and heterosexuality. Genet makes his satanic Archibald in *The Blacks* preach to his followers: "I order you to be black to your very veins. Pump black blood through them. Let Negroes negrify themselves. Let them persist to the point of madness in what they are condemned to be."[18] This is the reinforcement of negative choice. One should pursue excellence in the depth of depravity.

Choice and uniqueness are related to the cherished, desired and longed-for conceptions of the self. Consequently, they would be related to what personologists term as the ideal self. We hold that the ideal self is composed of idealized projections of the core components of the phenomenal (or actual) self (presented schematically in **figure 7.5**).

Uniqueness is the projection of the ideals of pantheistic exclusiveness of the *Ani*, whereas choice is the achievement-bound projection of the interactive *Atzmi*. These two polar aspirations of the components of the self interact dialectically to form the ideal self, which hovers halo-like over the phenomenal self. The ideal self, like the aims of the core personality vectors, is looked up to, striven to and longed for – but never achieved. It may be a measure of our elegiac insight into the structure of our psyche if we realize that our ideal self is composed of hazy projections of the aims of our personality core vectors, which are unattainable by definition.

Man, Others and Things

The Phenomenology of Interaction

Who sees the variety and not the unity wanders from death to death.
Katha Upanishad

I do not want the liberty of men, nor their equality. I want only my power over them, I want to make them my property, material for enjoyment.
Max Stirner, *The Ego and His Own*

Association with the unpleasing is suffering, separation from the pleasing is suffering, not to get what one wants is suffering.
The Pali Canon

So far we have studied the components and dynamics of the self; our unit of analysis was the individual. We shall now be concerned with the interaction of the individual with objects, flora, fauna and other human beings. The difference in relationships between human beings and other life forms and objects lies in the value-laden feedback that only humans can redirect to the acting individual. Consequently, we shall concentrate on the value-laden projections of the individual towards himself and towards his environments and his perception of the feedback of these projections from other individuals. We shall not be unduly preoccupied with group processes and the role and positions of individuals within groups (the customary domain of social psychology and the current publications of symbolic-interactionists and ethnomethodologists). Our ontological exposition of relationship is based on the sense of uniqueness of the individual and its anchor on monistic transcendence, as contrasted with his struggle to reinforce his choice *vis-à-vis* other individuals who compete for the same or similar reinforcement of worth.

The paradigm shown in **figure 8.1** presents our matrix of relationship on three levels. The monadic level deals with the relationship of the self with Unity and transcendence. We have dealt with this mode of relationship at length previously and elsewhere.[1] The second dyadic mode of relationship will be the main focus of interest. With the third multiadic mode of interaction, we shall deal only partially and with topics not customarily dealt with in the main currents of social psychology and sociology.

Mode	Exclusion		Inclusion	
	Goal	*Process*	*Goal*	*Process*
Monadic	Annihilation of self	Projection of the quest for nothingness; inner sanctuary; mystical union with God	Harnessing the object	Objectification of God
Dyadic	Fusion with the other	Diologica: selfless love	Absorbing the other	Subjugating of alter
Multiadic	Utopia	Self-sacrifice	Ideology	Sacrifice of others

226

Figure 7.1   Paradigm of Relationship

The dynamics of inclusion and exclusion are a key process in our paradigm of relationship, because it is the dynamic translation of the polar personality types. The *Ani*-skewed self aims to disappear and melt away or fuse with the object, whereas the *Atzmi*-dominated self aims to include the object by overpowering it, so that the chosen self reigns supreme. To recapitulate: inclusion is fixated on pre-differentiated Unity, whereas exclusion is anchored on the post-separation object. Consequently, the inclusion–exclusion dynamism as a motivating base for human interaction has in our model a bio-psychological foundation, and this has far-reaching implications. When explaining the achievement motive, for instance, we need not resort to the Weberian thesis about the Protestant Ethic. The need to excel and reinforce my sense of choice may be related to my aim to possess the object or prevent others from gaining more dominion over it than myself. No Marxist expositions on the competition for scarce economic resources and no Oedipal explanations of status rivalry may add much on the personality level to the inclusionary aim of overpowering and possessing the object. Inclusion works both ways: the *Atzmi*-skewed self wishes to gain dominion over as much of the object as possible and prevent others from having a share in the object-pie. Inclusion is the means by which the self tries to assert its statistical worth. Exclusion, on the other hand, with its aim of self-defacement and anchor on Unity, may be the underlying motive for mystical experience, transcendental meditation and the dimming of awareness by drugs. Exclusion may be the core motive for these and related phenomena, which have been studied and documented on other levels of analysis.

We have also pointed out earlier that the deprivational interaction of the nascent self with its surroundings actually triggers and affects the process of separation. The painful encounter with hard objects, changing temperatures and the gap between hunger and thirst and their satiation makes for the delimiting of the infant's body contours and the division between the self and the not-self. After the coagulation of the scar tissue of the ego boundary the deprivational interaction of the self continues in both the realm of inclusion and exclusion. The *Ani* component of the self longs for reversal into the non-differentiation of Unity. However, the object-involved *Atzmi* prevents this, because even in the most *Ani*-skewed self there still is an *Atzmi* that pulls towards involvement with the outward objective reality. Consequently, the inclusionary aims of the *Ani* for *Unio Mystica*, for a euphoric "eternal love" fusion with a person, or for Utopia, interact dialectically with the "realistic facing of facts" as presented by the object. A compromise synthesis is then reached, which is registered as a partial disillusion by the self.

The inclusionary aim of affecting a union surrogate by gaining dominion over the object is not realized because the object cannot be fully manipulated and because other people, while competing for the same dominion over the object, will do their utmost to have our self topple down and leave the race. Others, as we shall see later, can never be incorporated subjectively within the self. Consequently, they are prime objects for our domination, and we are objects for their carnivorous greed to assert their own choice. The materialist dialecticians assure us that eventually the clashes between subject and object and Man and his fellow Man shall result in a perfect harmony between Man, object and beast; this remains to be seen. Short of Utopia, the dialectic conflict between the quest to dominate the object and the object's resistance to total subjugation creates here too a synthesis, a compromise, which is experienced as a spiteful *ressentiment* or as a Sisyphean drudgery.

Figure 8.2 presents the deprivational interaction of the self as dialectic of inclusion and exclusion. The *Ani's* quest for participant nonbeing is checked by the separant forces of growth, the *Atzmi*, as the interactive component of the self and finally the whole self as an object. The resultant dialectic is Tantalic in so far as the original participant quest is checked by the sensual concreteness of the self and the longing for participation is relegated to the *Ani* as experiences of hope and faith. The self as object encompasses the *Ani* with a tight sensory barrier and, except for psychosis, hallucinations and non-communicable mystical experiences, participant exclusion in the spatio-temporal world can only be longed for as an unattainable goal. As for the exclusionary aim of dominating the object, the Sisyphean futility starts at the very beginning. Granting the *Atzmi* exclusiveness over the object cannot reinforce the choice of the indi-

227

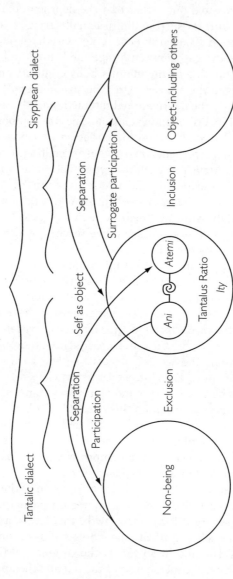

Figure 8.2   Deprivational Interaction of the Self as a Dialectic of Inclusion and Exclusion

vidual. Not only does the object not lend itself easily to subjugation, but the others also compete greedily for the same ever-scarce wealth, status and power. The Sisyphean compromise is the only one available, and with each failure one is bound by one's fate to try again. One is advised by Albert Camus that the Sisyphean cycle of deprivational interaction is all there is to it, and one might as well resign oneself to one's rock and find some stoic contentment and even occasional happiness in one's burden. The alternatives are the pain of *ressentiment* and the horrors of defeat, when one has not yet reached the top of the mountain and the rock is already rolling down the slope towards the abyss.

The relationship between ourselves and the object seems to be a lone tightrope on which we wobble with a dialectical gait from our Tantalic quest for holistic communion and back again to our Sisyphean rock.

Communion

The process of exclusion towards Unity and transcendence seems to be non-communicable. The accounts of mystical experiences and the quests for them sound so verbally meagre and conceptually shallow that one often is not convinced of their authenticity. The reason for this is that each individual has his own perception and interpretation of what a direct immediate experience of transcendence should look or feel like. For one, it is a glowing dewdrop on a rose petal; for the other, it is the moment of silence after gasps of blowing winds on a mountaintop; and for the third, it is the climax of bodies roaring in unison.

The inability to communicate one's quest for exclusion makes the goals of communion, as well as the striving towards it, the most cherished secrets in one's inner sanctuary. These are secrets because the projections of one's quest for nothingness cannot be communicated by the symbols of language or logic. "The Tao (the way) that can be told," says Lao Tzu, "is not the eternal Tao."[2] Also one cannot communicate one's experiences with the quest of the Absolute because these are unique to the specific self-seeker. Indeed, this uniqueness of one's exclusionary experiences, which is related to the uniqueness of the *Ani* component of the self, makes it both impossible and superfluous to communicate them. "It is the height of stupidity," says the Zen master, "to ask what your self is, when it is this self that makes you ask the question."[3] The Zohar, the Kabbalah and other bodies of Jewish mystical knowledge are traditionally denoted as the "secret doctrine". The secrecy here relates basically to the mystery of the infinity of God, which cannot be grasped by reason but only by intuition and direct experience.[4] The projection of Unity in various mystical doctrines has been conceived as a non-transferable personal mystery. Exclusion in the transcendental realm seems to be a strictly personal process. It is a projection of the sense of uniqueness of the self into holistic Unity. It also seems to fade away the moment one focuses attention on it

229

in order to concretize it with spatio-temporal attire or with the symbols of language.

The assertion of uniqueness through exclusion seems so arduous, uncertain and erratic that its practitioners usually doubt whether they are on the right track at all. We have already pointed out that the goal of exclusion, i.e. the total annihilation of awareness, is not attainable. One can only strive for transcendental exclusion, but never achieve it. One cannot also compare notes with other aspiring mystics because exclusionary experiences are non-communicable. One is sometimes gripped by a wild science-fiction suspicion that an infinite Unity has thrown out some of its "Sparks of Divinity" so that they may interact with one another in order to enjoy vicariously the thrills of their tragedies and short-lived triumphs. The way of these *separata* to rejoin timeless Unity is hermetically blocked; otherwise they might not wish to play the games of life "for real". Short of actual death, the show must go on, and their longing to regain the fold of the Absolute must remain a Tantalic article of faith, never to be realized in the here and now. Cardinal Newman once asked himself how to explain the abject, degraded, painful, aimless, hopeless, impotent condition of Man. "I can only answer," he said, "that either there is no Creator, or this living society of men is in a true sense discarded from His presence . . . If there be a God, since there is a God, the human race is implicated in some terrible aboriginal calamity." To this we may add a no less macabre alternative, that we are forced to perform in a weird circus to amuse a God bored by his monotonous, uneventful timeless infinity.

Metaphysical exclusion manifests itself in a desire to lose oneself in a pantheistic union with the inanimate objects, the flora and fauna, in one's environment. Metaphysical inclusion, on the other hand, is the aim of gaining access to the object as a means of transmitting to it the Divine uniqueness embedded in the self and binding, thereby, the object to the self. It may be that flora and fauna, which are the two entirely different life forms on earth, have as a rule a symbiotic relationship, whereas flora and fauna among themselves are mostly in conflict with one another. These relationships do not seem to have accepted naturalistic reasons and they may belong to the basic unknown of a metaphysically charted design.

The process of exclusion involves the dissolution of the ego boundary and, for that matter, of all perception of discrete sequences, so that the existential basis and with it the structure of spatio-temporality is annihilated and a boundless Unity is achieved. Transcendental inclusion, on the other hand, is philosophically more complicated. The process here is envisaged as the reaching out of the Divine Spark in the self to engulf the object. This is the *hübris* of the projected transcendental uniqueness of the self, which must reinforce its holiness by dominating the object. Our process of metaphysical inclusion runs contrary to most doctrines concerning the relationship of Man and Creation to the Divine. The Platonic idea is the epitome of Divine Truth: the perfect thing in itself to which everything else, which is per force inferior, longs for.[5] This is the traditional longing of all Creation for Divinity, which runs contrary to the goals of our inclusion, i.e. the longing of Divinity through the mediation of Man for the object. The Aristotelian *orexis* – the longing of substance for the perfection of form – has also been interpreted by Christian dogma as the aim of the inferior substance to partake in God.[6] *Orexis*, like *Unio Mystica*, is the desire of the less-than-perfect created matter and individual *separata* to deface themselves and melt into perfect Divinity. Consequently, the opposite trend of inclusion is contrary to the accepted dogma in most religions, with respect to the relationship between the whole of creation, including Man and Divinity. In a preceding volume, *Rebellion, Creativity and Revelation*, we substantiated our claim that the *hübris* of inclusion, i.e. the effort of Man as a self-appointed agent of God to dominate the object, is the objectification of God and the essence of idolatry. Indeed, Nietzsche, that great iconoclast, envisaged his Godless Superman "that finally . . . will appear, who feels . . . his power to be complete and boundless, and who in his universality, lives in and with Nature, as the judge and appraiser of all human values."[7] This is the ultimate *hübris* of exclusion, when Man as an agent of God is transformed into the Superman who does not need the grace of God to proclaim himself an overseer of Nature.

In Search of Dialogue

When Anton Chekhov, in his masterful portrayal of the misery of a father who has lost his son, makes the father ask in desperation: "To whom shall I tell my grief?"[8] The answer is obvious: to no one! The father, a sledge-driver, tries to share his sorrow with his drunken fare, with a tired cabman and finally with the mare that drags the sledge – but no one cares or can listen. The bereaved father, who to be sure is in extreme emotional agitation, seems to be on another plane of awareness. Although he uses the same language, there is a barrier of meaning between himself and his environment. He tries to reach out to the people around him in order to share with them some of his grief, which is too heavy for him to bear all by himself. But in a true Tantalic manner, people become more remote the more he tries to approach them.

We claim that the impossibility of dialogue is not confined to people in stress or in extreme situations. We join the Existentialists and the Theatre of the Absurd in holding that a meaningful dialogue between human beings is an ontological impossibility. The aim of dyadic exclusion is to effect a fusion, a meeting of the minds, an inter-subjective link, or at least a meaningful communication, but this aim is never fulfilled. Human beings seem to be on parallel planes as far as inter-subjective communication is concerned. Any meaningful dialogue, therefore, must be based on the non-sensical, illogical or the miraculous meeting of parallel lines or planes. The main reason for this is that the self sees itself in a different way than others see it. This is compounded by the fact that we interact with the image that others transmit to us of themselves, which is different from the image they have of themselves. The same holds true for the image we have of ourselves and of the one we transmit to others. We have dealt elsewhere with the various discrepancies between the perceived and transmitted selves of both ego and alter, and the barriers to communication that these discrepancies create.[9] Here we shall try to examine the gap between the quest for a union of meanings and for an inter-subjective communication, and our ability to achieve it.

The impossibility of dialogue may be traced to our ontological feeling of both uniqueness and choice. Our sense of uniqueness cannot be communicated because it is based on pre-differentiated and hence pre-symbolic partaking in Unity. Also this feeling of uniqueness, being linked to our early oral pantheistic omnipresence, may not be shared or appreciated by others who have a sense of uniqueness of their own. *In extremis*, this may be likened to the *Three Christs of Ypsilanti*, in Milton Rokeach's celebrated study, trying to convince one another that each one of them is the one and only true Christ.[10]

Our subjective perception of ourselves and others imputes first-hand, immediate and therefore authentic experiences only to ourselves; the perceptions of others may only be conveyed to us vicariously and therefore in an inauthentic manner.

This brings us to our sense of choice, which calls for the reinforcement of our worth *vis-à-vis* others. Our positive choice makes all the others either actual or potential competitors. Consequently, we are bound to be biased in varying degrees to the communications relating both to ourselves, to our surrounding objects and to relevant others.

The basic problems of object relationship and interaction with others may be differentiated according to our polar personality types. The *Ani*-skewed type has full confidence in his subjective sense of uniqueness, which is anchored on holistic transcendence. His problems are with objects and others that do not comply with his projections on them of his non-communicable uniqueness. He also expects all others to share his inner link to non-differentiated Unity, which they cannot do. His own ideational Gestalt as to how things "out there" are and how they should be, are clear to him. He "knows them in his bones", but his knowledge is, alas, not communicable. Consequently, the designs and expectations that the *Ani*-skewed self projects onto others are usually not comprehended and not acceptable by others. This, *inter alia*, is the Achilles' heel of Immanuel Kant's categorical imperative and other neo-Kantean non-relative systems of ethics. The *Ani*-skewed type is rigid in his expectations of others and he demands of them a grasp of his subjective meanings. He is bound to learn the hard way that inter-subjective communication does not exist, and unless he trains himself to be satisfied with a rather shallow level of inter-personal communication, he is liable to be constantly frustrated and misunderstood. The *Atzmi*-dominated self, on the other hand, has a weak sense of uniqueness and he has to reinforce his self-esteem, i.e. choice by the consensus or cues from others. This is so because his fixation on the object makes him dependent on space–time and others for the determination of his place in reality and his social position. The interactive *Atzmi*-skewed type is a "realist". Things and others make up his world, and whatever their allocation of space for him or the social judgment they pass on him, he has to accept them or fight to change them in their terms and on their grounds. He literally has to face "objective and concrete reality" because the reality of deprivational interaction with objects and others becomes his sole relevant frame of reference after he has virtually repressed his sense of uniqueness and has relegated it to his unconscious, to be expressed occasionally by spells of intense longing for things unknown. The Sisyphean *Atzmi*-skewed type finds himself obstructed by the non-resilience of the object and by the competitive claims of worth of the relevant others, whereas the Tantalic *Ani*-skewed type finds it difficult to convey to others his projected self-concept based on his sense of uniqueness. These are the basic disjunctures to which we may link all barriers to meaningful communication between the self, objects and others.

The dyadic exclusionary aim of the self is to fuse with and disappear into the other. This aim is manifested in the selfless love of children by their parents. The parents may see their children as their continuation and reincarnation. Their identification with their offspring may be so strong as to effect a vicarious reliving of their own youth. This may lead to a resentment by the children of the parents' over-identification with them, with a subsequent rejection of the *Yiddishe mamma* who "kills herself for her children", or to the cruel egotistical exploitation of the parent *à la pere Goriot* who has trained his daughters from infancy to disregard his needs in order to satisfy their slightest whim. The exclusionary aims of the parents here did not result in a dyadic fusion or dialogue, but in the unilateral exploitation of the parent as an object.

The exclusionary goal of fusion through sexual love, which is momentarily hinted at by orgasm, may take the form of intense emotional dependence of the self on the loved other. It is claimed that in most cases (and some, notably Jean-Paul Sartre,[11] claim that in *all* cases) this emotional dependence cannot be mutual and results in the subjugation of the self as an object to the loved other.

The inclusionary aim in a dyadic relationship is the absorption of the other and his subjugation, either affectively or socially or both. Emotional subjugation is the relationship in marriage or in love where the self who is less emotionally attached dominates the other, who is more emotionally dependent. The social-interaction modes of dominion of the self over the other are presented in **figure 8.3**.

We are not concerned here with the self's relationship to the generalized other, with which we shall deal later in the context of the achievement motive. At this point we are dealing with the self's dyadic relationship with a specific relevant or significant other. The labelling reaction is the self's attempt to overpower the other by either trying to stigmatize him by derogatory tags or to explain away his achievement and powerful (relative to the self) social position.[12] When the other is a failure or suffers a misfortune, pity (especially its public manifestation), is a prime mode of displaying superiority over the other. The ethical mode of ascendancy over the other is either to deny the legitimacy of his power or to justify his failure. The exploitation of the powerful other is by flattering him and showing outward deference towards him in order to gain handouts or favours from him. A special case in this context is women, whose role in most societies in their dyadic relationships is subordinate to the role of the male. Consequently, the woman's sexuality has become a formidable weapon with which she may attain the most varied range of desires and goals from the formally more powerful male.

Other's social position	Labelling	Justification	Exploitation
The powerful other	Explaining away the other's success	The other does not deserve it	Flattery
The powerless other	Pity	The other had it coming to him	Bullying

Figure 7.3 The Self's Modes of Dominion over the Other

The polar, more direct exploitation of the powerless by the powerful is to bully the downtrodden other who has been underprivileged from the outset or has experienced a sudden fall. The latter is the favourite victim of all those who have been dependent on him before his fall.

The Oppressive Dyad

One major impediment to a meaningful dyadic dialogue is what we denoted earlier as the least interest principle.[13] Willard Waller has described this principle in courting relationships where the less emotionally involved party dominates the relationship in the dyad.[14] We claim that the least-interest principle has a universal application. One has better chances of winning the heart of a lady when one is indifferent, and displays a façade of studied indifference towards her. One is offered friendship when one does not need it, and the proverbial "friend in need" finds to his sudden dismay that he has no friends left. Friendship and love seem to obey the laws of financial credit. One has a much better chances of getting a loan from the bank when one does not need money, but one encounters the sour face of the credit manager of the bank whenever one asks for a loan while the account is deep in the red. Deep emotional involvement makes one impatient, greedy and demanding. These make the other party to the dyad uneasy, irritated or fearful, and the chances are that he will initiate a breaking of the relationship altogether. In other more complex dyadic relationships, the self-effacing submissive party is taken for granted: he is "in the purse", whereas the "trouble-maker", the one who "makes problems", has all the attention because he has to be "broken in", wooed or gained over.

The least-interest principle is in line with our model on the exclusionary nature of dyadic relationship. When the self aims to overpower and dominate the other, his interest and effort invested in his relationship with the other is a function of the chances of winning the love, friendship or allegiance of the other. If these chances were high, the efforts invested to win him over would be low, but if these chances were low, effort, charm and wooing would be directed towards the other in full force.

Another related obstacle to meaningful communication is the effort of the more emotionally, socially or economically dependent party of the dyad to be liked, accepted and approved by the other party. The employee in front of the boss, the mental patient in a therapeutic session with his psychiatrist, the interviewee in front of the researcher are all armed with emphatic antennae to detect the desired behaviour or response, and they give it in order to gain approval or avoid sanction. Response sets and "social desirability" biases are examples of the twisting of perceived reality by the need for approval.[15] The messenger who lied to his Mesopotamian king is an extreme example of avoiding negative sanction, because the messenger knew that the harbinger of bad news is more often than not decapitated. Bruner aptly described the middle-range cases: "The protective need of avoiding the sense of being disliked leads perception into all sorts of traps."[16]

Another impediment to a dyadic dialogue stems from our polar personality fixations. The extra-punitive Sisyphean object-fixated type would ever be aware of the depriving others who constantly encroach upon his authenticity. His deprivational interaction with others is the matrix of a "good me" surrounded by a "bad object/others". Consequently, the others are perceived as cutting off slice after slice, by "salami tactics", the subjective sense of choice and worth. This is our psychological counterpart to Sartre's philosophical exposition of the levelling-down by others of the self's *pour soi*, the authentic being-for-itself. For the object/others-fixated Sisyphean, hell is indeed "other people".

The Tantalic intra-punitive type tends to accept the deprivational interaction with his surrounding others as a corollary of his "bad me" "good-object" fixation. Consequently, he would be ambivalent towards his daily trials with others. *In extremis*, he would covertly welcome his daily crucifixions. We have pointed out elsewhere that the Jungian idea of Christ as self-image might well apply to the self-defacing aims of nonbeing of our polar Tantalic type.[17] This need to be martyred has been described by us in relation to the labelling process of the criminal, in which he seems to be a willing victim.[18] In like manner, the predisposition to morbidity may be related to the acceptance by the child of his role as scapegoat, with a resultant process of depersonalization leading to schizophrenia.[19] This willing role of victim has been noted in many dyads, e.g. the schizophrenogenic mother and her autistic child, or the criminal and his complacent victim. One also encounters the type who provokes aggression, who "attracts" violence or who "brings out the worst in people". These are very likely "bad me" "good object" Tantalic types who are drawn to enact a passion with themselves as inevitable victims by their core personality fixation. Consequently, both the power-hungry object-devouring Sisyphean and the Tantalic "accident-prone" willing scapegoat are bound to twist from the outset the dyadic relationship according to the core polarities of their personality, which are rarely related to the ad hoc dynamics of the actual issues in the dyadic interaction or the expectations of the other party to the dyad. These are also biased by the other's core personality fixations, which are not necessarily complementary.

The initial lack of communication between the self and the other as to each other's core dynamics and their mutual expectations makes one unable to help the other effectively in case of ontological distress or the breakdown of some core personality dynamism. This may account for the fact that except for bio-physiological correlates, and the treatment of some peripheral personality problems, we are relatively helpless in treating the severe psychotics. Even in less-acute emotional problems, communication is, to say the least, rather patchy and blurred: one may try to "understand" the other by empathy or identification. The former is usually quite shallow and the latter is coloured by the projection of one's own problems and experience, which very rarely correspond to the problems and experience of the other.

We have examined elsewhere the Existentialist stance as to the impossibility of meaningful communication between the self and others, and the petrifying effect that the others have on the authenticity of the self.[20] This especially has been expounded by Sartre in the chapter on "bad faith" in his philosophical essay on "Being and Nothingness"[21] and dramatized in his play *No Exit*, the closing lines of which are that "Hell is other people." In our context this could mean that love, friendship and sympathy, when directed towards others, cannot be met by the others at the same level, tone and intensity of affect as transmitted by the self. Moreover, the transmission of affect exposes the self to the other in its innermost sensitivity. But the self's exposure cannot be reciprocated by a correspondent emotional exposure by the others because inter-subjective communication is impossible. Consequently, the attempts of the self at reaching affective links with others are marked by awkwardness, shame, guilt and pain.

The lack of meaningful communication between the self and others is also a function of the inadequacy of language to express and describe the subtleties, nuances and intricacies of our feelings and thoughts. This is why language seems to the self a shallow and rigid means of conveying to others his subjective experiences. Also because our sense of uniqueness and choice makes us rather egocentric, we are more interested in conveying our experiences to others than listening to theirs. We are not interested, as a rule, in the experiences of others, unless we can relate to them by identification or projection. However, our interest in what others have to say is instantaneously heightened if it relates to our self-image or to our social position and roles. This holds true even if, otherwise, we have a low view of the judgment and wisdom of these others.

The paradox of an affective dyad is that deeper and more authentic relationships raise mutual expectations for an inter-subjective attunement. As subjective expectations cannot be effectively transmitted, the possibility of conflict is augmented with the widening and deepening of mutual affect. The vicious circle here of hurt sensitivities and lack of communication due to different levels of expectation operates as a negative feedback cycle. The areas of friction and the points of conflict generated by mutual expectations, which were not communicated, non-communicable or cannot be met, serve as repelling agents, which hurt and finally terminate the affective relationship.

As we shall see later, some personality parameters determine the levels of sensitivity that are linked in their turn to our emotional expectations from others. Those who are more sensitive are more vulnerable in the dyadic relationship because they expect more and they can see the meagre emotional contact they may hope to achieve. Because we cannot expect any equalities or even similarities in emotional sensitivity between ourselves and others, we cannot expect an enduring mutually satisfying affective dyad. As if all this is not intricate enough, the covert, subconscious expectations, especially of the "Internal Saboteur" type, complicate dyadic emotional relationships even further. The subdued polar personality component, which may influence covertly or suddenly sprout forth to divert the previous skewness in favour of the other polarity of the self, may effect a sudden change in the self's expectations of which even it may not be aware. The self cannot possibly transmit to the other his covert expectations, so that the fulfilment of these emotional expectations by the other is remote indeed. Consequently, the subconscious expectations of the "Internal Saboteur", which cannot be transmitted to the other and met by him, contribute to the dyadic emotional relationships being a self-defeating venture.

We also hold that the inevitable failure of dyadic affective relationship is a prime source of shame and guilt. Gerhart Piers states: "Whereas guilt is generated whenever a boundary . . . is touched or transgressed, shame occurs when a goal . . . is not being reached. It thus indicates a real 'shortcoming'. Guilt anxiety accompanies transgression; shame; failure."[22] By reacting to the other without having grasped his subjective expectations from us, we have transgressed on his innermost sensitivities, like a bull in a china shop; this may cause subsequent feelings of guilt in us. If we have exposed ourselves to the other, but failed to reach him, and in his reaction he makes clear that he has perceived us as something different than we have intended him to perceive, we feel ashamed. This brings us to the theme of emotional violence in a dyad, which even if not accompanied by physical violence, may nonetheless be devastating. When there is a gap between our self-concept or ideal self and the feedback of our self-image as transmitted to us by the others, the predisposition for emotional violence is generated. The lack of meaningful communication makes us prone to be misunderstood, and our sensitive expectations to be disregarded. This may shame us and make us lose face, which may give way to the violence of anger. On the other hand, our sheer reaching out and reacting to alter, without having fully grasped the nuances of his expectations and the subtleties of his sensitivities, makes us, *ab initio*, violent trespassers and emotional transgressors.

Earlier, we traced the developmental stages of the personality core. We have seen that a vast number of variables associated with bio-psychological growth interact with cultural factors to form a statistically *sui generis* personality core. This, together with the infinite permutations of the peripheral personality traits, determine our self's action and reaction in a specific manner, which is inevitably different from the other's. The other's maturation curve, his fixations and cultural imprints converge to create a core self, peculiar to the other, which is bound to colour and bias his communication with our self. This is another reason for the lack of a common denominator for inter-subjective communication.

Another barrier to inter-subjective communication is that a great deal (some personologists claim all) of behaviour is defensive, i.e. diverted from its original core needs by defence mechanisms. These dynamics, as well as our Tantalus Ratio, process our motivation, affect and cognition, and consequently our reaction, to the other in a manner peculiar to our self and different from the other. A good example of a barrier to inter-subjective communication, or for that matter to any dyadic communication, is provided by a single personality trait as measured by Petrie. The "augmentor" is averse to stimuli because he cannot cope with too many of them. He is more sensitive and consequently more vulnerable. The "reducer", on the other hand, is hungry for stimuli. He is less sensitive, he needs constantly to be aroused and stimulated from the outside and he is less vulnerable in dyadic relationships.[23] The augmenters tend, therefore, to concentrate more on less stimuli. They would furrow deeper and be preoccupied longer with even a single stimulus. Consequently, their subjective perception of stimuli tends to be stronger, their sense of shame more intense and their guilt more damning. Naturally, they would view their inter-personal relationships as more complex and intricate. They would tend to be swept into a vicious circle of sensitivities, which would make their relationship in the dyad unbearable both to themselves and to others. The reducer, on the other hand, needs more stimuli to reach a level of excitation experienced by the augmentor with far less stimuli. Because the reducer anchors on the quantity of stimuli, he can spend less time and effort to examine the subtleties and nuances of each individual stimulus. Perforce, the reducer would be more concerned with the categories and outward contours of the stimuli than with their contents. He would be shallow and less complicated in his dyadic relationships. Being himself less sensitive, he would tend to dismiss the augmentor's over-sensitivities as an exaggeration of trivialities. We can see, therefore, that a meaningful relationship in a dyad, the parties of which possess, for the sake of illustration, only this single augmentor–reducer polarity, has as much chance of success as a dialogue between the deaf and dumb.

Other impediments to an inter-subjective dialogue are the reductions and categories that are used by us to process our incoming stimuli. The choice of categories and reductions are peculiar to each individual and are rarely equally shared by the others in the dyad. Also the perception of incoming stimuli are coloured by an emotional halo effect, which is related to the specific experiences of each individual, which provide the particular emotional halo effect. As Marcel Proust's emotional associations with the taste of the Madeleine cake in *Remembrance of Things Past* cannot possibly be shared by others, so the emotional halo effect on the perception of the self, which cannot be shared by the other, makes for additional disconnectedness in the dyadic communication.

Our own polar personality types also illustrate the vicissitudes and many times the impossibility of dyadic dialogue between polar personality types. The activist separant sees in the successful manipulation of the object a panacea for the problems of society, as well as his personal salvation. The quietist participant, on the other hand, is rather indifferent to most of the outside world. He is attracted only to the objects that are linked directly or symbolically to his inner transcendence. An Apollo space capsule is taken for granted by him, not unlike the lever that flushes his toilet. He is entranced by his inner moods and his search for the "truth" behind appearances. Consequently, the separant Sisyphean and the participant Tantalic have few tangential points of communication.

The little we know about the processes of cognitive perception also supports our thesis on the impossibility of a mutually meaningful dyadic dialogue. The output of the brain seems to be very much – or even totally, as some researchers claim – determined by the bio-psychological attunement of the brain at a given moment so that it actually selects its sensory input (afference). Consequently, the *Gestalt* of awareness of the person at that moment, programs the content of perception. This not only reduces and selects the flow of incoming data but also creates a different perceptual base for each individual cognition. The ingenious experimentation with the tachistoscope and binocular reveals that we see more things that we want to see and that we are attuned to see, and conversely we tend to block our perception to data that is unacceptable or painful to us.[24] In extreme cases, the selective perception is so strong that a whole range of data is not registered. For instance, patients who are dying of terminal illnesses block out information that reveals their hopeless condition, so that they continue to hope for a recovery, despite the overwhelming evidence to the contrary, which is filtered out and not registered in their cognition. This selective perception by both the self and the other of the same or similar stimuli make for another major barrier to meaningful dyadic dialogue.

On an entirely different level of analysis, one may view dyadic relationships as a form of exchange that reinforces or punishes each cycle of interaction.[25] We know, for instance, that the relief of anxiety is a most potent reinforcer of behaviour. Thus, if the other arouses in us directly or symbolically a high level of anxiety, the avoidance of the other relieves anxiety and reinforces our shunning him. The anxiety we feel may very often have nothing to do with the person or behaviour of the other, except that he triggers in us in a symbolic and mostly unconscious manner a process that relates the dynamics of our own self to the creation of a barrier to communication, which is foreign to the actual or potential contents of the dyadic interaction.

In social psychology and the action frame of reference, "definition of the situation" by the individual is considered to be a cognitive condition precedent for further action.[26] But as this definition of the situation is governed by the selective perception of each individual and coloured by his core personality traits and their cultural imprints, it is highly unlikely that there could be a common denominator for a joint definition of a situation by the self and the other within a dyad.

We have pointed out earlier that the postulates of Alfred Schutz and his ethnomethodologist disciples on inter-subjective understanding and communication[27] are theoretically unsound and empirically untenable. Even the more modest claims by Renato Tagiuri as to the "mutually shared" field of interaction between persons[28] do not seem to hold water. Tagiuri points out three elements necessary for inter-personal perception. The first is the "situation". Here we may avail ourselves of the illustration of a grimacing face presented to the viewer. The perception of the grimace was "disgust" if the accompanying caption read that the owner of the face was viewing a hanging, while the perception of the viewer became "determination" if the legend described a runner breaking the tape at the finish-line.[29] The second element relates to the "person" perceived in the situation. Tagiuri claims that if we look at a mourner, we may discern his grief. Some many years ago, the author saw a picture of Niarchos, the Greek shipping magnate, taken at his wife's funeral. It seemed to convey the ultimate in uncontrollable and inconsolable mourning. Yet later, we learned that Niarchos himself killed his wife in premeditated cold blood. As for the third element, the "perceiver", we have shown here at length how selective perception filters and twists the incoming data to fit the ad hoc *Gestalt* of our selves. Consequently, all we may hope for is to receive a biased, vague and twisted glimpse of the other's *Ity*, much less of his interactive *Atzmi*, and never of his innermost subjective *Ani*.

Also we are prone to apply different semantic and value criteria to the *Ani* and *Atzmi* components of our selves, which are liable to differ from the semantic and value criteria employed by others to their own self-components, which again adds to the communication barriers between the self and the other.

We may regard the currently fashionable analysis of Erving Goffman's human interaction [30] as the impressions of an outside observer as to the rituals people use in order to reach working consensus: a *modus vivendi* for the routines of everyday life. The units of analysis are not the persons, but the overt flow of interaction between them. This in a sense is interactional behaviourism, with the inter-actionists being "black boxes" to the observer. But here we are concerned with the subjective interpretations of the intercommunication and interaction by both the parties to the dyadic interrelationship between the self and the other. Nevertheless, some of Goffman's expositions are relevant to our present context: a person's "face work", i.e. the rituals and techniques of face-saving, involve the selective non-perception of the humiliating stimuli.[31] On the other hand, in a society where face-saving is a prime value, one person may present to the other erroneous factual communications in order to save the other's face. For instance, if one asks a pedestrian in some villages in the Middle East if one is walking in Main Street, the pedestrian might agree, even if it were a side alley, because to contradict the stranger is impolite and would reveal his ignorance and cause him to lose face. This is an extreme example, but many of us have retained some gross mistakes in French or Italian pronunciation because our polite hosts invariably praised our less-than-perfect mastery of the language because of their belief that they would hurt us if they corrected our mistakes. The whole process of "face work" is an impediment to dyadic interaction in so far as it involves the transmission or perception of twisted communications of fact.

Another "Goffmaniana" is the presentation of self in social situations.[32] It is of course true that the way one presents oneself to a personnel manager is very often more decisive in getting a job than one's material qualifications. This and other outward façades we present are many times deemed to cache, divert and change our unmasked image or parts of it that we think we display and we deem undesirable in a given set of relationships. If we are successful in presenting a masked image to our partner in a dyadic relationship so that he accepts it, we have deliberately "doctored" the communication cycle. However, many times, especially in intimate emotionally charged situations, we aim to reveal our "true self" to our dyadic partner, only to find ourselves misunderstood, neglected because of the least-interest principle we have described earlier, or we may find that our partner is conditioned by his social norms to regard a display of strong emotions or the revelation of one's "true self" as weakness, bad manners or both. To this, we should add the transcultural presentations of self, which because of the divergencies of social norms may encounter hostility, ridicule or just miscomprehension.

241

In *Society and the Absurd*, we pointed out the delimiting and levelling effects of the expectations of the other from us and our need both external and internal to relate ourselves to these expectations.[33] This is in addition to the Existentialist's exposition of the impersonal "third", the faceless yet petrifying *das Man* – the "man-about-town". Even Sartre's hell was played by a triad – and "three is a crowd". The mere need to relate ourselves to the other musters our attention on some aspects of his physical person and personality, whereas he might want us either covertly or overtly to relate ourselves to other parts of his personality, or ignore him altogether. Once a dyadic relationship has been launched we become enmeshed in it by concentric, overlapping and cross-purpose cycles of attentions, which divert our original course of existence before we encountered our party to the dyad into a delimiting dependency, not unlike the gravity dependencies between two masses, or rather like the dance of spring spiders, who entangle one another in almost invisible yet sturdy webs. This is also true for anthropomorphized objects, flora and fauna, which hold us in their grip, like Carlos Castaneda's Yaqui Indian's hallucinogenic plants or the totemic animals of the Amazonian Indians.

An encounter with a friend was considered a divinity in ancient Greece. The Greeks were stark realists and they sensed that true *dialogica* might be within the realm of Divinity, but not within the grasp of mortals. This is why many people find it difficult or embarrassing to focus attention on other people. The Medusa's stare is implicit in many people's inability to withstand the direct stare of others, or for that matter to focus a direct stare on the eyes of the other. Interlocking stares or the meeting of eyes involve, many times, an intuitive, albeit inchoate stumble on each other's selves. This frightens and makes us uneasy. We are conditioned by our all-important oral phases of development, both earlier and later, to a painful deprivational interaction with our surroundings, including others. When our eyes interlock with the eyes of the other, we are prepared to encounter abysses of duplicity, indifference, rejection or defiance. The author recalls that a person who had broken his trust, but was not aware that the author knew about his betrayal, came to a meeting at night wearing dark glasses, which he had never worn before. He apparently was afraid that his naked eyes would reveal his guilt.

Only in rare fleeting seconds of grace does the stare soften into acceptance or submission, but almost never does it shine with full understanding. An inter-subjective meeting of the selves borders on the miraculous, and miracles can only be believed but not proved to exist.

The Self and Others

The relationship between the self on the one hand and the collectivity of all the others on the other hand is the traditional realm of social psychology. On the philosophical level, the Existentialists have dealt intensively with this relationship and we have devoted to it a volume-length analysis.[34] Consequently, we do not propose to delve in it here at too great a length. However, we must relate ourselves to the interaction of the self with the collectivity of others in so far as this becomes part of the *Atzmi* component of the self. Our interaction with the collectivity of others depends first of all on how we regard this collectivity and how we envisage its structure and dynamics. We subscribe to the structuralist–functionalist view of the human collectivity, i.e. society as a labyrinthine superstructure composed of layers of systems and subsystems. Talcott Parsons tried to reduce the social system within multiples of four squares. Others tried to discover some paradigms of social relationships that are structured into arabesques, Gothic spires or Byzantine domes. If some structural interrelationship is not apparent, it does not mean that it "isn't there"; all we have to do is try again, look further, until we discover the missing structural link. We join the conflict theorists, who regard the social structure and human relations within it as a perpetual obstacle course where the pendulum swings between contradictory and conflicting pressures towards the dialectical progress of the synthesis. For the conflict theorists, tradition and conservation of structures, both for romantic and pragmatic reasons, lead to staleness and decadence. Rejecting Emile Durkheim, they assign a negative mark to adjustment and stability. For them, the synthesis resulting from a clash of conflicting forces is the essence of progress.

Finally, we may agree with the symbolic interactionists and their modern offspring, the ethnomethodologists, who do not see any grand system or design in the social system and human interaction. For them, there is no way of tying one pattern or human interaction to the wider matrix of personality structure of the behaviour of groups. Human, face-to-face interaction is like a minuet; one move may be predicted from the other, but one ball cannot be coordinated with other dances taking place in another space and time.

Whatever our view of the collectivity of others, we tend to impute to it more than just the sum total of the individuals comprising it. We give to it an additional halo effect of an abstraction, which the self anthropomorphizes as having behavioural qualities of its own; sometimes the self may beautify it into an omnipotent image of a deity, e.g. the nation, the dictatorship of the proletariat, or the "people's will". This imputation of reality to a human collectivity, beyond the sum total of the individuals comprising it, may land the self into trouble once he seeks a reward for his adulation, devotion or services rendered to this collectivity. Then he finds out to his chagrin that he imputed reality to a mirage. The ideological constructs superimposed on the collectivity by its power élites serve as the basis and justification for any sacrifice, however great, on the part of the individual. Yet when the individual is being hurt or is in need, many times because of his sacrifice to the ideological constructs of the collectivity, and he cries for help, he may find out to his dismay that these

243

constructs are manipulated like marionettes by the power élites or bureaucracies, who seem amazed at the audacity of the individual who seeks redress from them for the sacrifices he has made to the ideological marionettes. Consequently, we tend to agree more with Søren Kierkegaard, who regards the idealized self-images projected by the groups and their élites as the "all-embracing something which is nothing".[35] We know by now that every cruelty and injustice can be and has been imputed to the welfare or the glory of an almost endless number of group goals and their ideological constructs. Personal enmities within an institution are invariably translated into ideological conflicts pertaining to the progress of the institution. There are, of course, real idealists, but these, like Arthur Koestler's Rubashov, are quite often liquidated by *apparatchiks* like Gletkin, as an "ultimate service to the Party". In like manner, President Richard Nixon justified the Watergate burglaries by the need to safeguard the American way of life, and Indira Gandhi's attempt to prevent further judicial probing into her election frauds by arresting the opposition leaders was done in the name of the Congress Party and for the sake of the people of India.

There is a sinister air to some monumental symbols of group values if one remembers the human lives and the amount of suffering that were offered to them in selfless sacrifices. The outsized statues of Joseph Stalin evoked the macabre spectres of concentration camps, whereas the monstrous white "wedding-cake" monument at the Piazza Venezia in Rome is downright ridiculous. The glory of a Horatio Nelson on top of his column in Trafalgar Square is tarnished daily by the droppings of pigeons, and the author once saw a used contraceptive hung by someone with a keen sense of drama on Napoleon's tomb in the Dôme des Invalides in Paris. Serves him right! He perfected the atrocious art of exchanging young lives for pieces of metal hung on strips of multi-coloured cloth.

When the individual tries to apply phenomenological reductions to the group values, ideologies and systems of norms for which he is prepared to kill and be killed, he may discover that they consist of slogans and abstract symbols that may evoke emotions and visions pertaining to a higher reality that are as real as the unicorn or the Pegasus. Stripped of their mythological connotations, the slogans become mere sounds, which have no meaning for the subjective core of the individual's self. A dialogue between an individual and the abstract construct of the group is impossible because it is a dialogue between an entity and a non-entity. The same holds true for the demands of the normative system from the individual. Norms are supposed to mean the same thing for everybody, but they do not! Kant's categorical imperative was deemed to provide an objective base for ethics. But if I want a certain rule to have a universal application, I impose my own specific view of the rule on others, who might not conceive it in the same or similar way. The relationship between social norms, including laws, and the individual is similar to his relations with other social constructs. The self's conception of a rule of conduct is peculiar to himself and cannot be conveyed to others. Normative dialogues are ontological impossibilities.

The relationship of the self with the others as a group can largely take the form of competitive achievement. This is mostly in the realm of the interactive *Atzmi* and is dependent on the personality polarities and the cultural imprints, whether they lean towards separate activism or participant quietism. However, the achievement motive is relevant in this context because it underlies the individual's relationship with the others within the framework of social institutions. We shall not deal here with the individual's alienation from groups and their goals, since we have dealt with it extensively elsewhere.[36] But we shall try to describe the individual's possible achievement avenues within an institutional setting. Also our conception of achievement is quite different from the Weberian thesis, because we envisage it as a surrogate participation mechanism through the wish to overpower and control the object.

The basic fact in an achievement-oriented group is that all or most of the individuals comprising it compete for the same or similar commodities. Consequently, the individual may be disappointed to find that his peers rarely judge his performance by meritorious standards, because for them his success is not a merit but a demerit. The conflict here is between our own achievement motivation, the group norms that sanction it and the green jealousy of our peers. The latter, in itself, may give us intense satisfaction, but in order not to hinder our further success, we may find it politic to play down our achievements in order not to augment their jealousy. Also we may help them to explain away our own achievement, which they would be inclined to do as a surrogate achievement technique. In *The Mark of Cain* we have pointed out that stigmatizing the other may serve as a surrogate achievement device.[37]

Consequently, social stigma in an achievement-obsessed culture serves as an illusory achievement technique where real achievement has failed or is insufficient (as defined by the stigmatizer). Because achievement is relative, an individual can "achieve" by derogatorily branding (stigmatizing) others. When an achievement-obsessed individual or group craving for success as compensation for insecurity and anxiety does not achieve these goals, they will try to "achieve" status by lowering the status of the stigmatized. This is the actual function of stigma, and is recognizable in the gossiping matron belittling the looks of a rival, as well as in the perennial inclination of the socially insecure lower middle class to hatred of outgroups, anti-Semitism and racial discrimination.

Stigma related to a person's successful innovation or imputed to his achievement can "explain away" his performance so as to narrow the gap of "relative achievement" between the stigmatizer and the stigmatized. "If I cannot be as good as John Smith, I can at least neutralize his success by bringing it down to my level." The Nazi ideology stressed that Germany did not actually lose the war, the war that should have been fought "properly" as among knights of the Nibelungen. "It was not they, the celestial

Teutons, who had lost the war, it was the Jews and the Marxists, who slyly and surreptitiously had administered the fatal stab in the back which made them reel and falter." It was not a fair fight. However, no logical or material link need be apparent between the stigma and the superiority of the stigmatized. Usually the connection is superfluous or non-existent. Cause and effect seem to be irrelevant for "explaining away" success by means of stigma. It follows, therefore, that the more my own achievement, as defined by me, is more satisfactory, the less is my need to belittle the achievement of others by stigma. Conversely, if I define my achievement as unsatisfactory, I would be more inclined to tag my peers by derogatory labels, explain away their achievement or actually interfere, mostly by covert intrigue, in their task, so that they are more likely to fail and be closer to my own level of success or failure as defined by me.

Achievement is a Sisyphean process and we have already illustrated how the achievement motive launches one into a vicious cycle of separation and more greed where the coveted control of the object keeps ever receding. This led Sartre, the master phrasemaker, to sum up that life is a useless passion. In similar vein, Alexander Solzhenitsyn counsels his fellow inmates in the universal prison to "own nothing" because ownership "transforms you from a free though hungry person, into one who is anxious and cowardly".[38]

The
Isaac Syndrome

9

The Third Coming of Civilization: black veils of mourning; after alcohol and syphilis.

From a letter of Paul Gauguin to Manfried

This good man is accursed
By an ancestral dudgeon, stern old grudge,
Inherited from the first
Forefather of his surly race,
Which has imprinted on his brow
The vehement prophet and inveterate judge.
These you will see,
Looking at him, and the wrongous dignity
Of an old, obstinate half-sculptured stone
That will not bow
To the artist's gentle hand and be,
What it should be, a kindly human face,
The dudgeon, which is ours, we must forgive.
But why should he hand on
The wrong so ostentatiously,
And if to bear that burden were to live,
And there were nothing to say
But that we must, and yet can never repay?
Lord, fling into his face
The gift, it seems, that never can be
His choice, Your grace."

Edwin Muir, *A Righteous Man*

The People of Israel; the Israeli Defence Forces and the Armoured Divisions will not be ensnared by deceit. They will continue to forge the force to encounter every enemy. On the families of the fallen depends the Victory. Not only a victory on the battlefield but also a victory which will extricate us from the burden of exile.

David Giladi, the father of Amnon and Gideon who fell in the Wars of Israel

"When Isaac again saw Abraham's face it was changed, his glance was wild, his form was horror. He seized Isaac by the throat, threw him to the ground and said, 'Stupid boy dost thou then suppose that I am thy father? I am an idolater. Dost thou suppose that this is God's bidding? No it is my desire.'"

Søren Kierkegaard, *Fear and Trembling*

Education is a stupendous fraud perpetrated by the liberal mind on a bemused public and calculated, not just not to reduce juvenile delinquency, but positively to increase it, being itself a source of this very thing.

Malcolm Muggeridge, *Things Past*

"And Satan came to Abraham and asked, 'how is it that you lost your heart? A son was born to you when you were a hundred years old and now you go and slaughter him.'"

Genesis Raba

Infinity, according to Lurianic Kabbalah, is characterized by a constant predisposition to transmit grace.[1] However, with the *Tzimtzum* (the contraction) signifying the first phase of emanation, which in our model stands for pregnancy, one is incarcerated and contained within a womb, like a depth diver who must use a high-pressure chamber before he may surface. After the catastrophic expulsion of birth – the breaking of the vessels, which signifies the exile into demiurgal temporality – one is again exposed to the Edenic grace of pantheistic early orality. However, this soon gives way to the deprivational interaction with the breast–mother and with objects, and the resulting incarceration in the scar tissue of the ego boundary. In the third social phase of development, the child basks in the graceful forgivingness within the family, only to be inducted into the normative system of society by the harsh, sacrificial rites of passage. This rape of the normative innocence of the young into the coercive rules and morals of the groups by their elders forms the subject of the current chapter. We claim that this sacrificial normative placement of the young is countered by a complementary normative aggression of the young against their elders. This rebellion, manifested in the "generation gap", is Oedipal only in the normative sense, since the proscription of incest is not paternal, as Sigmund Freud thought, but rather maternal; it is ingrained into the oral infant by the mother or her surrogate. We do not claim any diachronic sequences between paternal aggression and filial reaction, but rather envisage a synchronic complementarity between paternal sacrificial normativeness and the corresponding reaction of the young. The mytho-empirical manifestation of the normative sacrifice of the young is the sacrifice of Isaac, denoted as the Isaac Syndrome. Its female counterpart is the sacrifice of Iphigenia by her father Agamemnon. Yet the sacrificial cycle returns to the parents, because the life of an Abraham or an Agamemnon becomes unbearable due to their guilt and pain following the act of sacrifice, even if Isaac, Iphigenia, or Jesus were willing victims.

On the socio-psychological level, the Isaac Syndrome may be related to the process of norm sending and norm reception. The socio-psychological theoretical systematization of the processes leading to conformity to social norms analyzes the transmission and enforcement of norms by the group (norm sending) and the degree to which the norms have been received and internalized by the individual.[2] The norm sending process first requires a statement by the group as to the desired behaviour and the consequences to the individual if he does not comply. The group should then maintain surveillance over the person in order to determine the extent (if any) of his compliance to the norm; and, lastly, the group should apply sanctions to non-complying individuals.

The degrees of conformity to the norm by the individual are graded from mere compliance, where the individual is induced to conform by constant surveillance and by threat of sanction (negative – i.e. depriving); to identification, where conforming behaviour is induced by sanction (positive – i.e. rewarding) and conformity becomes, thus, autonomously rewarding; to the most complete conformity, which is the internalization of the norm by the individual. In the last case, surveillance and sanction are not necessary because the internalized norm, when incorporated by the individual as a personality element, becomes "just," "right," and "true". The last phase of the internalization of the norms would, presumably be experienced by the "willing victims". The more or less effective transmission of norms within the family and by the other socializing agencies depends on the maintenance of a system-in-balance between the Isaac Syndrome and Oedipal pressures. When this system-in-balance is disrupted there is a tendency to anomie, deviance and crime, both on the individual and group levels.

Oedipal pressures of children against their parents for bringing them into the world are subconscious, ontological and existentialist, as well as psychosexual (as Freud claimed). More consciously, they rebel against their socialization by harsh rites of passage. Thus, in tandem with the guilt and grief of the parents for having normatively sacrificed their offspring, children bear guilt at not having done everything to prevent the suffering of their parents in old age and sickness and for not being able to prevent their deaths. Man is thus ever vacillating and torn between his guilt as a parent and his guilt as a child. The Oedipal rejection of the parents also stems from a child's wish to experience life; the child disregards the parents' counsel not to engage in certain ventures or to perform in a given manner. The rebellion of youth and the "generation gap" are Oedipal, and suppression of that rebellion by parents relies on the primacy of moral "righteous indignation". "Law and order," and the assumed sovereignty of the "rule of law", stem from the Isaac Syndrome.

The primal need of the parents to reproduce makes the offspring infinitely more important to the parents than the parents to the offspring. The parents' need to care for their young is far more intense than the child's wish to be cared for. As the saying goes, "The cow craves to feed the calf more than the calf wishes to be fed." Consequently, the parents' expectation of thanks and appreciation from their children, and a reciprocation of care when they reach old age, are mostly bitterly frustrated. These disillusioned parents should have been more observant; they should have realized that our programming intended parents to care for their children, but not vice versa. They should also have heeded the saying that "when parents give to children both are happy but when children give to parents both are miserable". Our programming makes it quite clear that the offspring – the children, the coming generations – are all-important and the parents, once they have fulfilled their procreative functions, are all but superfluous.

However, parents who are not otherwise creative regard their children as their sole creation. This might lead to a Sisyphean clinging to children as objects, which in extreme cases manifests itself in a Medusan petrification of children by their subjugating parents. Moreover, when parents possessively regard their children as objectified chattel they cannot bear the child's efforts to liberate from the stifling parental yoke by trying to establish an inter-subjective liaison with a lover or a mate. Worse still, parents may try to resuscitate their own amatory longings and fantasies by involving themselves vicariously in the love affairs of their children, often with disastrous results for both young and old. Parents often emotionally blackmail their children for love and attention with the proverbial crudeness of a *Yiddishe mamma*, yet on a more sophisticated level they may prod their children to achieve some creative goal that the parents could not or did not have the opportunity to accomplish. "I want to give my children the education I could never have," may translate itself into a fierce achievement orientation on the part of the children. Indeed, the maternal Sisyphean socialization of children at orality is very much linked to their achievement orientation, whereas the later paternal normative indoctrination should mould the young into the accepted socio-transcendental cast, as conceived by the mediating authority of the father.

J. H. Brenner, one of the early, morbidly existentialist Israeli authors, called one of his books *Bereavement and Failure*. For many years this combination seemed rather incomprehensible, until it dawned that the loss of an offspring represents the ultimate failure for the parent. Parents are programmed metaphysically and biologically, conditioned psychologically, and indoctrinated culturally to reproduce and rear offspring, so that their loss is tantamount to the destruction of their ontological *raison d'être*. The loss of a parent for an adult child is many times painful, but it is ultimately accepted as the natural course of life. The parents, on the other hand, inevitably experience the loss of a young child as a catastrophic blow, usually resulting in a permanent emotional handicap and, in many cases, in mental incapacitation. The death of a child causes for most parents a traumatic change of their *Weltanschauung*, and in some cases a radical change in their order of priorities, meanings, and even the course of their lives. "There is no armistice for bereaved mothers" and daughters, and the patriotic glee of victories in wars is rarely shared by bereaved parents whose sons were killed in these wars. They feel cheated and experience rage at themselves for having either actively or tacitly participated in the sacrifice of their ontological sequel and embodiment to the mirage of patriotism – to abstract notions of glories, ideologies and creeds reinforced by the waving of coloured rags, the shouting of slogans by bemedaled marionettes, and the self-important verbosity of hypocritical politicians. Worse still, their pain can never be communicated to anybody who has not experienced the same loss; even communication with their partners in bereavement cannot dull the pain.

The Maternal Proscription of Incest

The proscription of incest is not part of the paternal Oedipal process; it is inculcated by the mother at the oral stage of the child's development. The proscription of incest at the oral stage by the mother has the widespread cultural implications that the Oedipal prohibitions had for the Freudian system of thought. The cardinal difference is that for Freud the originator of the cultural sublimation of incest is the father; in the Kleinian oralist frame of reference the origin of the proscription of incest, and hence of its cultural sublimation, is the mother. The Kleinian system of thought has the primacy in contending that the Oedipal processes actually take place at the oral phase of human development, yet neither Melanie Klein nor her leading disciples have traced rigorously the cultural implications of their contentions. Moreover, Klein's contention that because the breast does not continue to nourish the child, the child turns "Oedipally" to the father's penis is both disconnected and far fetched. First, the breast is concretely present in front of the infant's face, whereas the father's penis is not, and Klein does not credibly explain how the child may be exposed to and be aware of it even symbolically at early orality. Second, Klein bases her theory on the nourishing function of the breast and the purely sexual function of the penis. The breast produces food, whereas the penis does not. Klein claims that the mouth–ego feels Oedipal guilt at its weaning because it imputes the drying of the breast–mother to its sucking of it. This seems a spurious association between cause and effect, in that it unduly imputes to the mouth–ego sophisticated inference techniques it cannot possess. Oedipal pressures, we believe, are felt as a sexual arousal by both child and mother while nursing at the breast. This incestuous desire is incidental but different from the food intake and extraneous to it. It is also harshly suppressed by the mother. The child is inculcated with guilt for feeling a forbidden sexual desire for his mother by a direct tactile transmission from her as well as by empathy and nonverbal cues. The Oedipal guilt is thus transmitted directly and forcefully by the mother or her surrogate, so that both the proscription of incest and the guilt for having felt desire for it are ingrained into the child at early orality. Even shallow introspection may reveal that we are aware of a powerful injunction against incest at a much earlier age than Freud claimed – that it was in fact there as early as we can remember. The crucial point is that the direct proscription of incest and the transmission of guilt by the mother to the child launches the sublimatory processes of culturally accepted avenues at the outset of early orality. Emphasized here is the sexual desire of the child and its suppression at early orality rather than on food intake as a sublimatory basis for guilt, marital bond formations and cultural creativity, because the sexual drive is so much more pliable than our need for food. Food intake is a binary continuum with one pole of satiety and the other of starvation and death. With sex, the variety, combinations, permutations and nuances are endless. This is why our programming utilizes sex and not food or air to spur our separant processes of growth, to bait us by short-lived instances of participant bliss into multiplying and procreating, and, by a controlled deprivation of sex, to create culture. A direct suppression of the incestuous desires of children at early orality by their mothers may also be related to the development of gender differentiations. This is so because the phallic images are transmitted to the child by the mother in conjunction with her incestuous feelings and their suppression. Sexual images of breast and snake are interchangeable because they are sexually anchored, whereas the food based Kleinian image of the breast and the phallus are not so readily interchangeable. Finally, the continuous sexual desire of the human animal, unlike other life forms, may also be related to the suppression of sexuality at early orality. By suppressing the natural outlet and manifestations of sex at early orality, we become sexually traumatized and hence sexually sensitized for life.

Another difference between the Kleinian stance and ours lies in her stress upon the anal–erotic reinforcement of toilet training. We agree with Ronald Fairbairn that while the breast and the genitals are biologically based sexual objects, faeces are not.[3] Moreover, Bronislaw Malinowsky has already shown that the Trobrianders, who did not make an issue of toilet training, were not concerned at all with the decency or indecency of bowel movements.[4] Consequently, some symptoms are found among neurotic, European bourgeois patients due to severe toilet training, while they are not found in some other cultures that are less strenuous in the toilet training of their young; therefore, there is no evidence of a universal anal–erotic phase of human development.

Philip Slater makes the ingenious observation that in the Oedipus myth the father, Laius, was a secondary figure. He was a homosexual who refused his wife Jocasta's bed. She had to seduce him when he was drunk in order to conceive Oedipus.[5] The main dramatis personae of the myth are Jocasta and Oedipus, mother and son, whose forbidden desire for each other is the essence of tragedy. The sexual dialectics of desire and its proscription between mother and child are so crucial for the child's development because they first happen at the plastic formative phase of early orality, during which the neonate's surroundings impinge on its nascent self with brute force. Moreover, the desire proscription dialectic creates an approach–avoidance conflict and a double bind; these in themselves are severe traumatizers.[6] But when the subject of the conflict is sex, which is both the prime mover of procreation and the anchor of our participant quest for love, its effects become cardinal for both personality formation and cultural sublimations.

The link between mother and child is based on a direct, non-verbal flow of communication, because of the close tactile proximity between them and because during the first year of his life symbolic communication with the child is nearly impossible. However, the child is not a passive receptacle of the mother's attitudes and behaviour. He can and does direct her behaviour towards him by selectively manipulating the mother or her surrogate by his crying, restlessness, or signs of contentedness.[7] The mother–child dyad at early orality is, therefore, truly symbiotic, and the differential attachment behaviour of mother and child as shown by John Bowlby and his associates[8] may be the expression of the differential flow of emotions within the mother and child. Of special importance is the study of breast-feeding carried out by Winter. She concludes, *inter alia*, that while suckling her child the mother feels very close or "fused" with it and senses a "weakening of the sense of separateness between mother and infant".[9] Also, this attachment and proximity may be for both mother and child a manifestation of their participant quest for union. Stated inversely, the reciprocal participant quest of proximity, attachment, and union of mother and child may be regarded as part of our inbuilt programming to induce the mother to feed her child and for the child to attach himself to the mother. This quest for union might also provide the deeper core reasons for the attachment behaviour of infants observed by Bowlby and his associates. The second "baiting" mechanism that attracts the mother and child to each other for the feeding and the protection of the latter is the sexual pleasure felt by both mother and child while nursing at the breast. This is the separant function of early oral mutual sexual arousal of mother and child, to enhance the nurture and survival of the young of the species. The separant function of sex is baited even at early orality by the participant quest for union inherent in sexual desire and attraction. It is precisely this primacy of the early oral sexual attraction of mother to child and vice versa that makes its suppression so devastatingly traumatic – so much so that it was projected empirically as the Original Sin and was mainly responsible for the sublimatory creation of culture.

Before continuing, two points of method must be made. First, the theoretical framework is based on breast-feeding, but what about bottle-feeding mothers and bottle-fed babies? The studies relating to this topic are contradictory and inconclusive. One representative study states: "Women who do not whole-heartedly desire to breast feed are less likely to be motherly individuals. They are apt to feel that childbirth is hard . . . more apt to feel men have a more satisfying time in life, and are more likely to reject children." [10] Another well-designed and controlled study arrives at the diametrically opposite conclusion – that mothers who bottle-feed their children were not any more rejecting or cold towards them than mothers who breast-feed their children.[11]

Three possible attitudes to this point of method are as follows. (1) It is a bio-psychocultural evolutionary relationship between mother and child that was based on breast-feeding for millions of years, so the relatively recent period in which bottle-feeding has been practiced is insignificant; (2) the mother holding the child in her lap to bottle-feed has the same feelings towards the child as breast-feeding mothers; (3) bottle-feeding mothers and bottle-fed children feel differently towards each other than breast-feeding mothers and breast-fed children. Our theory holds true only for the last case. There is no way of ascertaining which one of these three possibilities is more feasible, and until clear-cut empirical evidence is provided, each one of the three possibilities is as viable or non-viable as the other.

The second point of method relates to a surrogate mother, e.g. nurse, wet nurse, stepmother, adoptive mother, etc. The possibilities here again are either that the surrogate mothers feel and behave towards the child in a similar manner to the natural mother, or that our conclusions do not apply to surrogate mothers.

Both the mouth and breast are primary erogenous zones. When the mother suckles her child she is sexually excited by it. Indeed, nursing women describe the nursing experience itself as sexually stimulating.[12] As for the mouth–ego, the sucking of the breast involves sexual excitement because the breast is not only a source of food for it but also, or mainly, a sexual object. The sexual essence of oral sucking has been stressed by Fairbairn[13] and was heavily relied upon by Karl Abraham who pointed out that the act of sucking in itself has an erotic significance independence of the food intake.[14] This supports the contention that sex is used at the oral phase of development too as a participant bait for the separant business of survival. The sucking of food is reinforced by sexual pleasure incidental to the nourishment. We are, naturally, not able to glean information from the mouth–ego as to the nature of his sexual feelings, but Abraham infers the independent, erotic significance of sucking from the prolonged thumb and hand sucking of children who seem to derive erotic pleasure from it not necessarily in conjunction with food.[15] As already mentioned, as for mothers, the participant nature of their erotic pleasure incidental to nursing may be inferred from their statements that nursing their children gave them a feeling of the weakening of the sense of separateness between them and their infants.[16] It should be stressed that the mutual sexual excitation of mother and child operates by a positive feedback cycle, so that the arousal of the mother by the infant's sucking is transmitted back by the mother to her nursing infant, thus augmenting his sexual arousal, and so on. This positive feedback cycle of incestuous arousal is cut off by the mother – with far-reaching psychological and cultural effects.

Although the mouth–ego's sexual arousal is incidental to feeding, it may be linked to it by conditioning and by association, so that the feeding itself gains a sexual meaning. This has been noted by Abraham, who tried to explain some cases of compulsive eating and obesity as an expression of oral sexuality.[17] The oral–sexual significance of eating was masterfully portrayed in the feast scene in the film *Tom Jones*. It was evident in the Roman orgies and can be seen in the function of dinners as oral preliminaries to love-making, and in dates and other rituals of seduction.

Indeed, Abraham had the pioneering insight to note the overwhelming importance of oral sexuality.[18] This is even more noteworthy if one bears in mind that Abraham was a member of the inner circle of psychoanalysis presided over by an autocratic master who relatively neglected the theoretical potential of oral sexuality. The overwhelming importance of oral sexuality is evident from the fact that the kiss in many cultures is the prime overt display of eroticism. This should be linked to some infantile fantasies that women become pregnant by being kissed, analyzed by Abraham.[19]

The proscription of incest inculcated by the mother into her children at their oral phase of development manifests itself in the boy as a fear of castration and in the girl as fear of penetration. The enormity of this proscription, which is depicted empirically in the Original Sin, is also manifest in the fact of its contrariness to the primary biological functions of the male and female genitalia. The participant quest of the male penis is to penetrate and be absorbed, and the female's vagina is structured to be penetrated and separantly absorb. The primary identification of daughter with mother makes for a more effective internalization of the fear of penetration. This, together with the biological barrier of the hymen, made virginity in many cultures the most prized asset of a girl, to be bartered at puberty for the biological fulfilment of raising children, the social status of marriage, the security of a family, and the protection of a husband. The boy's fear of castration is more complicated, because it is ingrained not by identification with the mother but through the vicarious and more elaborate complementarity with her. This fear is strong enough to curb incestuous desires throughout man's life and to generate lifelong feelings of guilt and shame for having had them. Moreover, this proscription of incest has sexualized the life of *Homo sapiens*. Unlike all other fauna and flora, the human being is sexually sensitized and impassioned throughout life.

In summary, the present premise points to the socio-normative importance of the suppression of incest within the oral mother–child dyad, not only for the regulation of familial relationship, but also for the creation of a basis for socialization and acculturation. The implications of this conclusion are so vast and relate to so many frames of references, focal interests, and areas of knowledge that they transcend the limits of the present work. However, we shall point out some attributes of these implications, which have an overall relevance to the present context.

The Freudian conception of the formation of the human family and, for that matter, the sustenance of human culture – as masterfully expounded in *Totem and Taboo* and Sigmund Freud's other writings – is related to the suppression of the incestuous attraction towards the mother and the normative resolution of the Oedipal conflict with the father. This primal renunciation by the son of his instinctual drives, and their sublimation into normatively accepted channels, is directed and carried out under the terms set by the father and his abstraction – i.e. the law and the normative system. One can make some wild and, at this stage, rather vague conjectures as to how this male chauvinist Freudian system would be affected by our model which posits the mother and not the father as the main suppressor of incest at the oral stage of human development, and thereby views the mother as the prime initiator of human culture. It would be presumptuous to develop this theme more extensively in the present context. However, in *The Bridge to Nothingness* (chapter 6), we did examine possible origins for the matriarchal origins of culture including, of course, the myth of the Original Sin itself.

Noted earlier was women's tendency to be more later orally fixated and hence more separant. This again is developmentally appropriate: in the first year of his life the main problems of the infant relate to the need to learn to adjust to his objective environment and to reach a *modus vivendi* with it. Consequently, the earlier separant directives of the mother and her instructions for acculturation are geared to the infant's needs. Later on, at the social phase of normative placement, the father adds his more abstract and more normatively participant acculturation mandates. The mother, as the joke goes, deals with the small matters of culture (the way the children should be fed, dressed, and sheltered), whereas the grand issues of culture she leaves to her husband (the nature of God, the essence of morality, and whether Man possesses free will or is spurred by strict determinism).

The Isaac Syndrome

Ego's normative relationship with its environment is viewed as the third social phase of separation. Indeed, most of the transitions from childhood to adulthood involve the introjection of the burdens of responsibility by means of painful rites of passage.[20] The socialization into the mesh of social norms involves deprivational and conflictual relationships with the normative authority within the family, i.e. the father or his surrogate. The Freudian Oedipal pressures have been perennially associated with the acquisition of morality and social indoctrination by (male) children. We claim that the actual process of normative separation is initiated by the father or his surrogate through a dynamic which is diametrically opposite to the Oedipal pressures. This dynamic involves deprivational pressures from the father towards the son and is meant to effect the normative separation of the adolescent from the family fold into the loneliness of social responsibility. These pressures may aptly be called the Isaac Syndrome, after the biblical myth of the offering of Isaac by his father. As has been pointed out in *Salvation Through the Gutters*, myths are personal realities insofar as they constitute, many times, a projection of personal developmental history.[21] The myth of the offering of Isaac may therefore be taken in its psychological context as a basic family dynamic that counteracts the Oedipal pressures postulated by Freud. We have chosen to denote the normative pressures directed from father to son as the Isaac Syndrome rather than the Laius complex, because the *Akedah* (the myth of the offering of Isaac as denoted in the Bible in the original Hebrew) is more explicit, dramatic, and forceful than the persecution of Oedipus by his father Laius.[22] We shall expound below the mechanisms of the Isaac Syndrome: how it generates the normative separating pressures within the family and its role as the separating dynamic that links the socialization within the family with the expulsion into normative loneliness outside it.

But first, it is necessary to take a closer look at the *Akedah* myth itself. When Abraham built the altar, bound his son, and took the knife to slay him, an angel of the Lord ordered him not to lay his hand upon the lad and showed him a ram caught in a thicket by his horns. The scriptures then relate that: "Abraham went and took the ram, and offered him up for a burnt offering in the stead of his son." [23] The original Hebrew version states that Abraham offered the ram as a burnt offering *tahat* his son. *Tahat* can mean not only 'instead', but also 'after' (e.g. Zechariah reigned *tahat*, or after, Jeroboam).[24] Consequently, some interpreters claim that Abraham offered Isaac and afterwards slaughtered the ram.[25] They cite traditional sources, according to which Abraham did slay Isaac and a quarter of a log (a large liquid measure) of his blood was poured onto the altar.[26] Also, Isaac's ashes were believed to have been strewn and scattered on the altar,[27] and Isaac's soul was raised to paradise as a reward for his noble sacrifice.[28] These interpreters base their theories on the nineteenth verse of Genesis 22, which states expressly that after the *Akedah*, "Abraham returned unto his young men." Abraham returned by himself; there is no mention of Isaac, who must have indeed been offered as a burnt sacrifice on the altar on top of Mount Moriah. This interpretation of the *Akedah* myth has been expounded by a wide range of scholars, both Jewish and Christian.[29] But the interpretation raises a number of problems and queries, most of which relate to the contradictory facts stated by Genesis 22 and the question as to the identity of the actual patriarch of Israel, if Isaac was indeed offered on Mount Moriah. One rather confusing answer is that the story of Isaac presents more than one myth, or more than one Isaac. However, our concern is not with the historical accuracy of the biblical myth, but with the interpretations of the myth dating from as early as the third or fourth centuries AD, according to which Isaac was slaughtered and burned as an offering. If myths are a projection of personal history, then the *Akedah* myth is of prime importance as psychological source material, irrespective of its historical truth. Consequently, the *Akedah* myth may serve as an archetype of covert father–son relationships both in its version as a temptation of Abraham or its interpretation as a consummated burnt offering of Isaac. In short, our interpretation is that Isaac was actually slaughtered on the altar, and not just bound on it. Biblical exegesis on issues of Isaac's "binding", Abraham's "test" and his unwavering compliance, make for fascinating reading and prolonged discussion, but whether the event is viewed as fulfilled command or deliberate etymological confusion in action, the impact on the father–son relationship is the same.

The interpretation that Isaac was slaughtered as a burnt offering is in line with the custom in the Middle East in biblical times, to offer children, especially the first-born, to the gods.[30] The Bible recounts the sacrifice of the crown prince by the Moabite king, when the battle went badly for him; by sacrificing his son, he hoped to regain his martial fortunes. The Jews imitated the Canaanites and Phoenicians by offering their children to the Ba'al, or by throwing them into the red-hot bosom of a metal Moloch. These offerings were practiced, *inter alia*, in the valley of Hinnom, which became synonymous in Hebrew with hell.[31]

Later, the gods were cheated and had to make do with domestic animals instead of a human first-born. The offerings of the animals were conducted as if they were human. The calves offered to Dionysus, for instance, were attired with children's clothes and babies' shoes so that the deity would think that he was receiving real children and not animal substitutes.[32] In times of great stress, parents reverted to the sacrifice of their children; but gradually, substitutes of human sacrifice received full religious sanction and became symbolic of the archetypal sacrifice of the *Akedah* myth. Circumcision thus became a ritualized substitute for the sacrifice of the newborn son, and the sounding of the ram's horn on the Jewish New Year and Day of Atonement is symbolic of the sacrifice in the myth of the Akedah.[33]

Father against Son

In Grimm's *Fairy Tales*, and in numerous equivalents in other cultures, the step-parents plot cannibalistic and infanticidal schemes against children,[34] suggesting that overt aggression of parents against their children is inconceivable. But the *Akedah* myth – with its universal analogies ranging from the Indian myth of the offering of Cunacepha to the god Varuna, to the slaughter of Icelandic princes at the shrine of Odin in the *Ynglinga Saga*,[35] – shows that a deprivational attitude of father towards son is an archetypal dynamic of the human family. Many demographic, economic and emotional reasons have been offered for the overt and covert aggression of the father against his male offspring. First and foremost is the ageing father's fear of being overthrown.[36] Sexual rivalry is another covert basis for paternal aggression, and as such is closest to its instinctual counterpart of the son's incestuous attraction to his mother. An ontological basis for paternal hostility is provided by the father's feeling that he is being reincarnated in his son, as evidenced by physical and behavioural similarities. Some Hindus, for instance, believe that the father literally dies when the son is born.[37] On a more symbolic level, the father may have an unconscious feeling that the son has inherited him existentially and that he, the father, has become ontologically superfluous; this, no doubt, may serve as a potent incentive for paternal aggression. The most common economic motivation for the Isaac Syndrome and, *prima facie*, the least convincing, is that another child is "another mouth to feed".[38]

The strength of the Isaac Syndrome is related to the anxiety felt by the father due to his waning strength. This is epitomized by Abraham, a hundred-year-old patriarch, whose son Isaac was quite likely conceived not by him but by Pharaoh, who had taken Sarah into his harem,[39] or by one of the angels who came to announce the birth of Isaac,[40] or by Abimelech, King of Gerar, who took Sarah for a few days into his tents.[41] The relative incidence of fact or fiction in the biblical stories is not important for this context. It is interesting to note that the archetypal sacrifice of the first-born should be preceded by three stories that cast doubt on the paternity of Abraham. This may point to a dynamic of sexual anxiety on the part of the father that is related to the Isaac Syndrome and perforce to the Oedipal pressures on the son. As an over-generalized abstraction, one may state that there is a positive linear relationship between the Isaac Syndrome and the Oedipal mechanisms. The Isaac Syndrome will be stronger as the Oedipal dynamics of the son raise, directly or symbolically, the father's sexual and status anxieties. All this lends a macabre hue to the advice of the scriptures: "Honour thy father and thy mother that thy days may be long upon the land." [42] Because the shortening of the sons' days may be a figurative warning that the Oedipal urges must be suppressed, otherwise the scourge of the Isaac Syndrome is liable to be unleashed.

The Isaac Syndrome is, to be sure, only one of the developmental conflicts within the family matrix. The "Medea complex", for instance, could serve as the maternal counterpart of the Isaac Syndrome insofar as it expresses the infanticidal urges of the mother.[43] However, of concern here is the separant normative aspect of the parent–child relationship; and as such, the Isaac Syndrome, as a counterpart to the Oedipus complex, is of unique relevance.

Salvation Through the Gutters dealt with the separant significance of rites of passage,[44] but with new insight into the Isaac Syndrome, one may regard these rites of passage as surrogate sacrifices. The dynamics in these cases may be regarded as a symbolic resolution of both the Oedipus complex and the Isaac Syndrome. The growing son is reminded by a painful rite of passage many times involving a token mutilation of the body (or circumcision) that the Oedipal pressures should be suppressed and repressed; otherwise, the archetypal memory of the original sacrifice will be invoked. The adolescent at puberty assumes full responsibility and undertakes the burden of loneliness outside the protective cocoon of the family fold. In the ceremony of the bar mitzvah, for instance, the father declares ceremoniously that he relinquishes all responsibility for the son's deeds or misdeeds. A preconscious pact of non-aggression takes place here: the son introjects the normative system of society as represented by the authority image of the father. He undertakes to leave the family fold, figuratively in some societies, symbolically in others, so that he is not exposed to the hazards of Oedipal pressures. And the father undertakes to waive his Isaac Syndrome and make do with a symbolic representation of the real sacrifice. This has a dual purpose: it obviates the necessity for an actual sacrifice and serves as a symbolic reminder to both parties of the preconscious pact to abide by the terms of the deal. Normative indoctrination involves, therefore, a covert process of sacrifice and renunciation of sanction and reinforcement, directed equally towards the lawgiver and towards the socialized law receiver and norm absorber. If this reciprocity is disrupted, the process of normative indoctrination becomes less effective and faulty. Examples of this are numerous: there are parents who demand from their children adherence to rules that they themselves do not obey; teachers who pay lip service to values and norms; social institutions that promulgate rules that the power élites have no intention of following and that the people readily violate, if they can get away with it.

The Isaac Syndrome conceives of the father as a stern authoritarian. The *Midrash* interpretation of the *Akedah* myth explains that God ordered Abraham to go to the land of Moriah (three days of travel) so that he sacrifice his son not out of hurried obedience to God's command but rather after three days of thinking and in a sober and determined state of mind.[45] There is an empirical significance to the fact that the *Midrash* describes a geographical proximity between Mount Sinai and Mount Moriah, hence the link between the sacrifice of Isaac and the acquisition of law and morality by the people of Israel on Mount Sinai.

The other dramatis personae in the *Akedah* myth supplement the image of the archetypal dynamics of separant socialization in the family. The angel who orders Abraham not to slay Isaac is invariably depicted in the iconography of the *Akedah* as female.[46] It would therefore not be farfetched to regard the female angel as representing the mother – Sarah – asking for grace, representing the participant protection of the family fold. This is also apparent in many primitive rites of passage that are presided over by the elders, where the mothers wail for their suffering sons.[47]

Wellisch was the first to compare the *Akedah* and the Oedipus myths. He accepted the Freudian theory of superego formation as a resolution of the Oedipus complex, whereas the psychological significance of the *Akedah* for him lay in an entirely different mechanism leading to altruistic object love.[48] We, however, regard the Oedipal pressures and the Isaac Syndrome as the two vectors inherent in the dialectic of socialization and normative indoctrination. The Isaac Syndrome is basically a separant dynamic. The father is covertly motivated to harness his son into the separating social norms, with the ultimate aim of "making a responsible adult out of him", and in the process he is ejected from the family fold. The son counters these pressures by Oedipal rejection of the authority of the father and attraction to the grace of the mother and the forgiveness of the family fold. The Oedipal pressures are in essence participant: the generation gap, youth revolt, the hippie movement and familial communes. These illegitimate offspring not only reject the authority of social norms, which stem from the archetypal father, but also long for the togetherness of the family fold or its surrogates. The love-ins, the group drug rites, the Woodstock nation, the flower children, and the diffuse, multi-mothered commune family are all in league with participant Oedipal pressures. The separant Isaac Syndrome, as well as the participant Oedipal pressures, are not "resolved" into another dynamic, as Freud and Erich Wellisch believed. They are, rather, kept in a dialectical balance by their constantly opposing and contradictory pressures. One may be pushed or attracted to one of these dynamics, but a precarious balance has to be maintained. When this balance is severely disrupted, a predisposition to crime, deviance, or madness might ensue. Consequently, it is superfluous to argue, as Wellisch and Bakan do,[49] as to whether the Isaac Syndrome (they call it the Laius complex) precedes or follows the Oedipus complex. These two are not consecutive developmental phases, but rather opposing yet simultaneous vectors that constitute the third state of normative separation and contain dialectically the introduction of the adolescent male to the harness of social norms and the loneliness of responsibility.

Frequently the son (or a group symbolizing the son) willingly accepts the burdens of the social norms like the "Bnei Israel", which in Hebrew means "the Children of Israel". Thus Isaac himself is believed to have welcomed his own sacrifice, in compliance with divine, i.e. paternal, command as did Jesus Christ, the archetypal victim. Whereas the Isaac Syndrome and Oedipal pressures oppose each other dialectically, the Isaac Syndrome and the willing victim complement each other.

The dialectics of normative indoctrination can sometimes constitute a special case of labelling and stigmatization within the family, with a resultant predisposition of the son towards crime and deviance. This may happen when the covert aggression of the father and his preconscious pressures of violence are projected onto the son. The latter accepts these projections, just as Isaac accepted his role of victim. The son may then act out the violent and deviant behaviour covertly projected onto him. Consciously, the father is not likely to accept the deviant behaviour of the son, which he himself has projected. Here, the Oedipal pressures may be strong enough for the son to reject his stigmatizing father; or the son may carry on his deviant behaviour in compliance with the covert expectations of the father. In this manner, the dynamics of the Isaac Syndrome may be linked to the stigma theory of crime and deviance, which has been discussed elsewhere.[50]

The following paradigm (**figure 9.1**) presents the dialectics of the Isaac Syndrome and the Oedipal pressures as related to the core personality vectors of participation and separation. This paradigm views the father-son relationship from the son's point of view. We have already discussed the separant nature of the Isaac Syndrome and the function of the rites of passage and their surrogates in Western societies in enmeshing the adolescent into the pigeonholes of social norms and the Sisyphean drudgeries of socio-economic duties. The Oedipal pressures, per contra, constitute a rebellion against the estranging socialization inherent in the authority of the father coupled by a participant attraction for the grace of the ever-forgiving mother and the irresponsibility within the family fold.

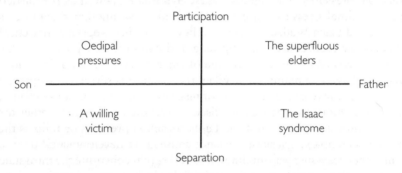

Figure 9.1   Dialectics of Isaac Syndrome and Oedipal Pressures

The victim is the son who accepts willingly, and often enthusiastically, the burdens of the separating social norms. This is characterized by Isaac himself, who is believed to have welcomed his own sacrifice in compliance with divine, i.e. paternal, command; it is also characterized by Jesus Christ, the archetypal victim. Whereas the Isaac Syndrome and the Oedipal pressures oppose each other dialectically, the Isaac Syndrome and the willing victim complement each other. The same is true of the Oedipal pressures and the "superfluous elders" who are the victims of their rebellious sons. Anthropologists have recorded many cases of "superfluous elders", e.g. among the Crannas of South Africa, the son of a chief, after attaining puberty, is supposed to knock his father down with a stick before being proclaimed chief of the Kraal.[51] In Tahiti, the king abdicated in favour of his newly born son and ruled as his son's regent.[52] The euthanasia of elderly Eskimo parents is also well documented. On a wider social scale, there is a considerable segment of the older generation, especially in Western cultures, accepting the derogatory judgments of the younger generation. Some even go to the pathetic length of growing long, white hair around their bald crowns and joining the drug parties of their teenage children and their friends.

One may hypothesize that the complementary relation between the Isaac Syndrome and its willing victims may be stronger among Sisyphean personalities in separant cultures. A prime example is the harsh authoritarian upbringing of children in Protestant Germanic cultures with a resultant "*Ordnung muss sein*" legitimization of almost every social norm. One may also hypothesize that a Tantalic personality type may be more inclined to regard himself as superfluous in old age, in keeping with his quietist, self-effacing disposition.[53] But we cannot offer any corresponding hypothesis concerning the link between Oedipal pressures and a participant culture.

The socio-normative consequences of the Isaac Syndrome are many, and diverse, starting with the basic rules of conduct preached by the father or his surrogate and carried on by teachers and other socialization agencies. These rules involve being truthful and loyal, obedient to the law, helpful to others, etc. The child learns the hard way that these norms actually impede his progress towards the achievement of his goals. The overt goal of normative socialization is to "make an honest man and a responsible citizen out of you"; but the covert outcome of the Isaac Syndrome is that the young fail because they are sent to the front with faulty ammunition.

On the level of ideology, the need to sacrifice oneself for the fatherland (a striking, tell-tale expression), for the party, or for the cause – the Isaac Syndrome – reigns supreme: sons are socialized to devote themselves to ideals and group goals, to serve the welfare of society selflessly, to defend their country, and to be brave in battle. Precisely these very same norms, if internalized successfully by the sons, often may be the direct cause of their death and destruction. Every soldier knows that "the good and the brave go first and are killed first", and physical injuries and mental suffering are very often the wages of selfless devotion to a cause. The vicious paradox inherent in the Isaac Syndrome is that those youths who are a success story from the point of view of ideological indoctrination are most likely to be destroyed and injured, as an actual, not symbolic, sacrifice, to the normative system that they have internalized. The paradox is even more accentuated in modern times, when cultures are more and more child-centred. Children are the centre of attention, not only of their parents but also of educators, health authorities and welfare systems. Yet these very idols and *raison d'être* of cultures are being more effectively exterminated and maimed by the ever-developing lethal weapons and more sophisticated physical and mental violence of wars, conflicting ideologies and internal political strife. The paradox inherent in the Isaac Syndrome highlights more than anything else the basic incompatibility between the individual and the normative system of the group. The death of a son in war, for instance, which is the worst blow to the cognitive system of a parent, is mourned officially by the group with parades and monuments; the dominant atmosphere is of romantic glory accepted by the group as a rite of noble sacrifice. This raises in the bereaved father a hot fury that may subside into a stale emptiness. When his son is dead, the preconscious dynamics of the Isaac Syndrome are consumed by his grief, which is too painful to bear; and the glorified idealization of his sacrifice by the group as well as its values and ideologies become worthless verbiage in the face of his crushing personal disaster. The ultimate rationalization of the grieving father might then be that his son, the dying god, has been projected unto eternity with the halo of perfect beauty and permanent youth. Yet, this rationalization may not save the father from his abysmal guilt, which may plague him for the rest of his days, at having partaken in the enactment of the ever-recurring *Akedah* episode.

The Isaac Syndrome also fulfils the covert participant components of the father's psyche: the youth hero dies and is projected onto eternity as the image of permanent youth and perfection. A striking support for this premise may be found in the *Akedah* myth itself. The *Midrash* asked why Abraham built the altar himself and did not let Isaac help him in the sacred task. The reason given by Rabbi Levi was that Abraham let Isaac stay away from the site of the construction of the altar lest a stone or splinter injure him, thereby rendering him unfit for the sacrifice. A burnt offering has to be whole and perfect.[54] A macabre yet apt analogy is that only the best, the fittest both physically and mentally, are chosen for the crack units of armies, which also suffer the highest mortality rates in battle. This is the theme of the sacrifice of the young god, so prevalent in ancient mythology and contemporary anthropological studies. The father identifies with his dead son – the embodiment and reincarnation of his younger image. The son becomes a god and the father, through the son, partakes vicariously in divine perfection. The Isaac Syndrome may be seen, therefore, as a rare successful combination, a psychic dynamism in its own right as well as a defence mechanism. It is instrumental in the socialization of the young into the separant mesh of social norms and, at the same time, vicariously fulfils the covert participant wishes of the father. This may be one of the reasons for the potency of the Isaac Syndrome: it allows the father to eat his mental cake and have it as well.

In summary, we offer a conjecture that is made hesitantly because of its enormous implications: we suggest cautiously that the Isaac Syndrome may be linked to society's need for holy martyrs, for mythic heroes to boost its ideologies and group goals. The Isaac Syndrome may therefore underlie and covertly legitimize the mass destruction, slaughter and pain inherent in wars and political strife.

Another equally far-fetched yet possible corollary of the Isaac Syndrome might be the increasing prevalence of mediocrities in the power structure of social institutions and among the pacesetters of culture, art and science. The ideology of the revolution, to cite Vladimir Lenin, sees men as "insects to be virtually crushed for the good of the cause".[55] The select, idealistic, revolutionary avant-garde are consumed like insects by the fires of the revolution, like the front rows of a horde of locusts that hurl themselves into the man-made defensive water channels so that their comrades in the rear can pass the obstacle over their dead bodies. Then come the *apparatchiks*, who sweep the revolutionary terrain with a levelling fury. They work by the book and they cater to the needs of the totalitarian bureaucratic machines that are operated by no-nonsense, middle-range comrades. A similar mechanism may have occurred in the wars of the twentieth century. In previous centuries, wars were mostly fought by professional soldiers and mercenaries, while the social institutions were still manned by the traditional élites who operated by a rather elaborate yet stable division of labour. Not so in the two world wars: their total mobilization exposed millions of budding scholars, scientists and artists to the slaughter in the European trenches of the First World War and the mechanized destruction by the lethal weapons of the Second. On a smaller scale, one may observe a similar process in Israel. The constant wars for the first thirty-five years since becoming independent have virtually erased entire age groups. The mortality rate was naturally higher among the physically fit and more intelligent in the army and among the volunteer units, which carried out the more daring, dangerous tasks. Consequently, the prevalence of mean fitness, modal intelligence, and median creativity is more apparent among politicians, leading scientists, and the *arbiteri elegantiari* of contemporary culture and art. The ultimate paradox may well be that the Isaac Syndrome is instrumental in sacrificing the best, the fittest, the brightest, and the most excellent of the youth, not to the perfection of God but to the Molloch of mediocrity.

The Rationalization of Sacrifice

The potent rationalization inherent in the Isaac Syndrome is that the sacrifice is made at God's command and is therefore sacred and cannot be questioned. In the Bible, in Middle Eastern traditions contemporary with biblical sources,[56] and in some anthropological studies, the first-born of man and beast belongs to God and should be sacrificed unto him, in order to guard against the wrath of God being hurled on the whole flock[57] or tribe. A direct corollary of this rationalization is that the sacrifice of the first-born expiates the sins of the tribe and the community. This is symbolized by the sacrifice of the Passover lamb, which is linked to the Messianic redemption through "the blood (sic) of the binding of Isaac".[58] The Midrash elaborates this theme and states that the sacrifice of Isaac is the basis of the yearly forgiveness of the sins of all the Jews at the New Year and the Day of Atonement.[59] This adds another dimension to the unique dynamics of the Isaac Syndrome: not only is it instrumental in the normative indoctrination of the young and fulfils the covert participant quest of the father to partake in eternal glory through his identification with the

ever-young, "dying gods", their sacrifice also expiates the father's sins –
i.e., guilt, for having been motivated by preconscious infanticidal urges.
The Isaac Syndrome is, therefore, one of the most effective psychic defence
mechanisms as well as a self-cleansing device for a guilty conscience. A
common rationalization of the Isaac Syndrome, which is linked to the one
of divine command, is an economic one: God will be pleased with the
sacrifice or his wrath will be appeased by it, and he will bestow on Man
wealth and bountiful crops. The Irish Celts, for instance, sacrificed children in order to ensure more milk and corn, and the Mexicans sacrificed
children to the rain god Tlaloc. "If the children wept it was regarded as a
happy omen for a rainy season." [60] Another sinister rationalization, which
is not readily voiced by its exponents, is that wars save humanity from a
Malthusian catastrophe; thus the Isaac Syndrome saves humanity from
overcrowding and starvation.

On a different level of rationalization, there are the legends, sagas, and
glorification of dead heroes and their bravery in battle. These, together
with ceremonies in which posthumous decorations are awarded, are
meant to boost the morale of nations at war. In this category may be
included the accounts of parents who stoically receive the decorations of
their dead sons, without the howl of anguish they felt like exhibiting. Also
included here is the glorification in the Israeli media of parents who have
lost one son in the war but have nevertheless allowed their other sons to
serve in fighting units, although they are entitled by law to be transferred
to non-combatant services.

The normative religio-metaphysical rationalization of the Isaac
Syndrome, as distinct from the one invoking God's will, makes the sacrifice an absolute duty towards God. This is Kierkegaard's leap of absolute
faith, the suspension of all ethical considerations, which leaves blind
submission to God as the sole *raison d'être*.[61] This absolute duty to God
may well be the normative projection of an absolute duty to the father; as
such, it constitutes a further legitimization of the father's separant role as
a rule setter and norm giver, by divine agency. Indeed, the Midrash
imputes to the *Akedah* myth the pure manifestation of an absolute,
unequivocal and unconditional faith, which sets the standards of an
imperative that cannot and should not be questioned. This is why
Abraham is portrayed as wishing to carry out the sacrifice, although the
angel commanded him to stop. Abraham then asked the angel if he might
strangle Isaac, or at least shed some of his blood.[62] This is the image of
the pious doctrinaire turned into a compulsive ritualist. The rule begets a
life of its own and the command becomes sacred in itself. As already
mentioned, the most humane figure in the *Akedah* episode proved to be
none other than the Devil. The Midrash recounts that when Abraham was
about to slaughter his son, the Devil came and reprimanded him: "What
happened to you old-timer, you seem to have lost your heart. A son was
given to you when you were 100 years old and now you are about to
slaughter him."[63] When the Devil saw that Abraham was adamant, he

came to Isaac and said: "Lo you poor son of your poor mother. How much pain and suffering did she undergo until she beget you and now this old father of yours went out of his mind in his old age and is about to slaughter you."[64] The fact that the Devil is the one to invoke ethics, pity and grace is important in this context: if absolute and abject submission to the command of the Lord (as the projection of the archetypal father) is the epitome of pious righteousness, then any attenuating emotional considerations must come from the Devil. This is even truer if the Devil speaks with the voice of the preconscious dynamism that identifies the absolute command of God as the covert infanticidal wish of the father.

Isaac and Christ

The most conspicuous characteristic of Isaac's role in the *Akedah* myth as described by the Midrash is that of a willing victim.[65] The fragmentary *Targum* describes Isaac's active role in the sacrifice as follows: "Abraham stretched out his hand and took the knife to kill Isaac his son. Isaac answered and said to Abraham his father: 'Bind my hands properly that I may not struggle in the time of my pain and disturb you and render your offering unfit'."[66] Josephus recounts that when Isaac heard that he was going to be sacrificed, he ran to the altar with joy.[67] This symbolizes the son's legitimization of the divine, i.e., paternal, authority. Some interpreters go even further and claim that Isaac bound himself upon the altar.[68] This is literally the self-enclosing and enmeshing within the boundaries of the delimiting and separating social norms promulgated by the archetypal father.

On the socio-ideological level, there is also the willing victim who complies with the stereotyped image of the patriot, hero and revolutionary. The martyred hero is an absolute necessity for a nation at war or a revolutionary movement, and if one does not exist, one is manufactured synthetically.

Willing victims may sometimes overdo their compliance. One gruesome example is provided by the groups of German Jews who partook in Nazi demonstrations, carrying signs that proclaimed: "*Raus Mie Uns!*" – (Out with us!). As shown in *Valhalla, Calvary and Auschwitz*, the Isaac Syndrome as a Jewish myth served as a catalyst for the disaster following the encounter with Nazi carnivorous myths. Precisely this complete submission to sacrifice, total acceptance of the role of victim, is the common denominator of both Isaac and Jesus. Isaac (the "tame dove") and Jesus (the *Agnus Dei*), both sacrificed themselves to archetypal perfection. There are other salient parallels: both Isaac and Jesus were sanctified by their sacrifice; both were believed to have been slain and then revived by a divine miracle; Jesus carried his own cross, and Isaac carried the wood for his sacrifice on his shoulders, forming a cross with his body;[69] the sacrifice of Isaac redeems and expiates the sins of all Israel, and the crucifixion of Jesus saves and forgives the sins of all mankind. As with the *Akedah* episode, there is also a dialogue about Calvary between an Apostle of God and a disciple of the Devil. "If God is for us," says St. Paul "who shall be against us? He who did not spare His own Son, but surrendered Him for us all, will He not grant us every favour with Him?" [70] By Aristotelian logic, this does not make sense. Why should we get more favours if Christ granted us the ultimate favour of having sacrificed himself for us? It does, however, make sense according to the dynamism of the Isaac Syndrome. If our inner guilt at having wished the sacrifice of our archetypal son has been expiated by his own willingness to be our scapegoat, then we may carry on asking divine providence to fulfil our wishes. To this Friedrich Nietzsche retorts in the voice of the Antichrist, "God sacrificed his son to expiate the sins of all humanity in the most nauseating and barbaric manner. The sacrifice of the innocent for the sins of the sinners." [71] This is the outraged sense of fair play of a moralist and the protest of a humanist against violence performed in the name of righteousness. Who, but the Antichrist – the Devil – could have sensed the sinister vicissitudes of the Isaac Syndrome?

We may note finally that the Talmud states that those who bury their sons absolve their sins.[72] What sins and what sort of guilt are related to the loss of sons if not the sacrificial guilt of the Isaac Syndrome?

Whereas the first victimization of the child at orality is maternal and blocks the free expression of its incestuous desires, the second is the paternal coercion of the child into the normative system of society of which he, the father, is deemed to be the agent within the family. Usually this coercive and normative victimization is backed by the absolute authority of God, the fatherland, or the secular deity of materialist dialectics. As in the empirical model of the offering of Isaac, there is usually a symbiotic relationship between the stern, doctrinaire father and a metaphysical source of absolute authority. This continuing victimization of the child by his parents from early orality onwards is an integral part of the separant processes of development and socialization. The maternal victimization leads to the Sisyphean sublimation towards cultural creativity, and the paternal victimization leads to the separant insertion of the pubescent individual within a normative pigeonhole sanctioned by society. At this stage the mother is the symbol of grace. She stands for the child's participant longing for the forgiveness and irresponsibility within the family fold, prior to taking on the normative burdens of society. In some tribes the rites of passage from childhood to puberty are presided over by the elders, while the mothers join in the wailing of the circumcised, aching and suffering sons.[73]

The Isaac Syndrome constitutes paternal normative aggression against children, countering the Oedipal urges of children against their father. The main thrust of the empirical offering of Isaac consists of the sacrificial enmeshing of the young into the disciplinarian boundaries of the normative system of society. All normative initiation involves varying measures of sacrificial curbing of the well-being and freedom of the pubescent young in favour of the right and the just rule, and the welfare of the group. These sacrificial indoctrinations are performed by the father as intermediary between the young and the social rules that are sustained through his authority by secular or divine transcendence.

Literature abounds with examples of the sacrifice of children to the carnivorous exigencies of the normative system. Franz Kafka's letters to his father, for instance, exude the agonies of a son being abused by his father in the name of bourgeois morality. Kafka's relationship with his father was, no doubt, related to his description in *Metamorphosis* of Mr. Samsa – the petty bourgeois father, who degrades and crushes his misfit son out of shame and fear of social norms.

Mothers often warn their children when they are naughty: "You wait till Daddy comes home and I tell him about your behaviour today." She implies that she herself does not wield the normative rod; rather it is the role of the authoritarian figure in the family i.e., the father, to apply sanctions to whomever they are due. The doctrinaire role of the father is directed equally towards the son and the daughter. The contents of the social norms imposed by paternal authority vary with gender: the son is coerced to undertake the burdens of social responsibility, whereas the daughter is harnessed into her feminine roles of marriage, household duties and child bearing.

The most striking feminine parallel to the Isaac Syndrome, with the gory sacrificial details and the enormity of its socio-normative implications, is the sacrifice of Iphigenia to the exigencies of the socio-religious commands through the authoritarian agency of her father Agamemnon. Iphigenia was sacrificed for the glory of the group and to patriotic honour, which constituted the extension of the glory and honour of Agamemnon himself, just as the normative power of divinity is the extension of the authority of Abraham. Unlike Abraham, who never doubted the commands of God, Agamemnon wavered and raged against the need to sacrifice his daughter for the glory of the army and the honour of the mob. This stems from the difference in the Judaic and Greek conceptions of divine authority. For Abraham, God's commands were the epitome of justice and could not be doubted and should not be questioned, whereas the anthropomorphic Greek gods make no pretence of being just. Yet they are the pronouncers of *ananke* (necessity) and *moira* (fate), which are the prime movers of Greek religion and the normative system.[74] The outcome was the same: both Isaac and Iphigenia were sacrificed to the divine projections of socio-normative mandates. Iphigenia was not as willing a victim as Isaac. She pleads with Agamemnon, in one of the most shattering monologues in world drama:

> Had I the voice of Orpheus, O my father,
> If I could sing so that the rocks would move,
> If I had words to win the hearts of all,
> I would have used them. I have only tears.

See, I have brought them. They are all my power.
I clasp your knees, I am your suppliant now,
I, your own child; my mother bore me to you.
O, kill me not untimely! The sun is sweet!
Why will you send me into the dark grave?
I was the first to sit upon your knee,
The first to call you father.[75]

At the end she accepts her fate and goes to the altar with the patriotic announcement of "bid my father come and torch the altar. I will bring this day victory and salvation unto Greece."[76] And like Sarah in the offering of Isaac, Clytemnestra, Iphigenia's mother, is the figure of grace condemning paternal cruelty, as expressed in the divine mandate to sacrifice her daughter for the glory of Greece.

Figure 9.2 summarizes the present premise; it is based on **figure 9.1**, with some new components added.

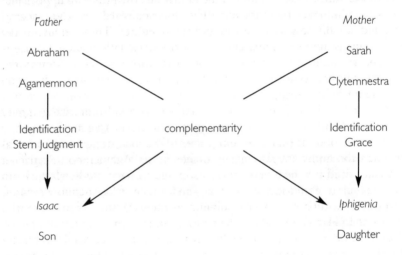

Figure 9.2 Models of Sacrifice in the Mythic Family

The implications of this model for the theoretical system of the present work are that whereas the oral maternal inducement to creativity is mainly in the realm of a separant organization of one's environment and its instrumental manipulation, the paternal socialization is directed towards socio-normativeness and its transcendental and ideological bases.

The vicissitudes of social separation, the cruel rites of passage from childhood to puberty, the harsh coercion into the delimiting social norms, and the sacrificial horrors of the Isaac and Iphigenia syndromes, all presided over by the father, induce both male and female children to long for the forgiveness and lenient protection of the mother. For the homosexual Marcel Proust, this longing became so intense that he closed himself in a padded, womb-like room and wrote volume after volume, idolizing his beloved mother. For the fiercely heterosexual Albert Camus, his great love for his mother may have manifested itself in a generalized longing for the grace of womanhood, rather than for a specific woman. Hence, Camus had "a lifelong quest for the tender friendship of women".[77]

Morals are promulgated primarily through the family. We have already mentioned that for the family to serve as an effective medium of norm transmission, it has to effect a system-in-balance between the Oedipal pressures and the Isaac Syndrome. The complete pardon of the prepubescent child – i.e., "let him be, he is just a kid" – the absence of criminal responsibility of children, and the reduced responsibility of young adults gives way to the rites of passage, the expulsion into the stern normativeness, the harsh social placement, and competitive achievement outside the family. Here too is a continuum between the Sisyphean and Tantalic cultures. In achievement anchored activist Sisyphean cultures, the rites of passage are harsher, and the young are pushed out of the family sooner, to seek out their fortune and prove their worth by success in the achievement motivated society. In participant societies, on the other hand, the young are more thoroughly indoctrinated in the traditional normative mesh, which is more authoritarian, but they are not quickly or harshly pushed out of the family fold. On the contrary, many times the extended family creates a larger cocoon of protectiveness around the young adults, although the norms existing within it are authoritarian and strict.

The normative role differentiation within the nuclear family in most cultures ranges again along a continuum. The participant pole is occupied by the paternal authority, who sets curbing limits on action, devises systems of doctrines, and links these to divine authority. The maternal pole, on the other hand, supervises Sisyphean object relations: order, "cleanliness next to godliness," achievement and success. These roles are archetypal and may be blurred or even are interchangeable in some families. Yet in essence, this normative role differentiation is related to the identification and complementarity of son and daughter with the paternal and maternal roles, as discussed earlier.

The identification of the son and the complementarity of the daughter with the norm-promulgating father are reinforced by the desire to gain his normative approval. The internalization of the father within leads to a complete moral orientation towards paternal norms and the feeling of automatic gratification from the very compliance with them, without any further reward or sanction. The morally oriented, "willing victim", gains a self-image of righteousness by obeying the norms of the internalized father. After introjecting Abraham within his inner self, Isaac could not but obey. The father thereby becomes, as Kierkegaard has stated, an immediate normative absolute. In introjecting the father, the son performs a Baron Münchausen feat: he can thenceforth lift himself by his own normative bootstraps. Even the mother, who provides the separant motivation for proficiency and pragmatic achievement – reinforced by maternal love, grace, and acceptance – needs the father for normative authority. However, the distortion of participant paternal norms are not checked and balanced by separant maternal norms, and vice versa; or when norms become monstrous in their extremity, compulsiveness, misery and horror may ensue. In an over-achieving, authoritarian family a non-conformist such as Gregor Samsa saw himself as an oversized cockroach, as reflected in the eyes of his Kafkaesque, bullying father.

Rebellion and Yearning

10

Forget your personal tragedy. We are all bitched from the start . . . but when you get the damned hurt use it – don't cheat with it.

Ernest Hemingway, in a letter to F. Scott Fitzgerald, 1934

So far we have traced the petrifying effects of the generalized other, the painful and coercive subjugation to normative structures and the breakdown of communication between Man and his surroundings, and especially with his fellow men. We have also described the conditions that give rise to barriers against dyadic communication and to the disruption of human encounter (**chapter 7**). Not that all human encounters end in failure, but a great many do and our concern is whether this is inevitable. Is there a way out of the multi-phasic petrification of Jean-Paul Sartre's *No Exit*? If not, why not? And if yes, how?

Our answers have been triggered partly by some of the ideas of Martin Heidegger but mostly by the teaching of Albert Camus. The author has been curious for a long time about the meaning of authenticity in conjunction with his formulation of notions of existential choice and ontological uniqueness. When he had hesitantly and tentatively clarified to himself some of the attributes of authenticity, he reread Heidegger's *Sein Und Zeit*, which on a previous occasion he despaired of deciphering. Eventually I realized that Heidegger's conception of authenticity was similar to his own. This brought to mind Ralph Waldo Emerson's experience that: "In every work of genius we recognize our own rejected thoughts; they come back to us with a certain alienated majesty."[1] The source of light for the silver lining of the cloud of Man's petrification is Albert Camus' rebellion. Like Camus, the author has a Mediterranean outlook on life, coupled with an exposure to Teutonic metaphysics. It is the subterranean affinity of one *pied noir* to another who has been baffled by Occidental thought.

For the author, Camusian rebellion is a *Weltanschauung* and a way of life. This chapter is a tribute to Camus' rebellion which, short of the engulfing bosom of religion, in all its theistic and secular forms, is the only ray of light at the end of the dark tunnel of life in which we blunder, stumble on each other and stifle one another with our petrifying presence.

This chapter will sum up the main attributes of both Sisyphean and Tantalic rebellion. We do not include here a lengthier study of all the figures that represent this rebellion; two such great figures are Søren Kierkegaard and Rabbi Nachman of Bratzlav, to whom we dedicated a chapter in *The Bridge to Nothingness*.

Defiance

Our concern in the present context is not with revolutions, political rebels or with anarchists aiming to disrupt societies and destroy social institutions. Our focus is on individual ontological rebellion as a means of asserting one's authenticity and of escaping the Gorgonian petrification by the generalized other. Ontological rebellion inevitably involves varying measures of metaphysical defiance against a silent Transcendence. The unknown Away and Beyond was at least an accomplice for throwing us into this world for a relatively short journey rife with misery and pain, and short spells of joy culminating in an inescapable death. This Transcendence was an accomplice before shanghaiing us into this world without asking us whether we feel like being taken for that specific ride and an accomplice after conspiring to hide from us the reasons for our enforced journey unto death.

We differ from Camus' conception of the metaphysical rebel who declares "We are alone",[2] by envisaging our ontological rebel as defying a silent God who treats us very much like a rather dumb-witted, silent partner who should not be told what or whose business it is all about.

Ontological rebellion makes the rebel assert at least a part of himself as an authentic being.[3] Consequently, rebellion may replace the Cartesian *Cogito* by stating: "I rebel, therefore, I exist authentically." Heidegger"s assertion of authentic *Dasein*, Camus' ontological rebellion and Kierkegaard's preaching of the gospel of personal truth to the generalized other may help extricate Ego from the clutches of petrification and hence make him ready for the quest of dialogue if he chooses to pursue it, even if the achievement of dialogue on the terms of ego seems to be impossible.

A common quest and longing for dialogue, even if not realizable, following both ego and alter's rebellious extrication from their ontological petrification, may be, at least, a partial refuge from the impossibility of inter-personal communication. Finally, we conclude our preliminary remarks by pointing out that rebellion may be separant or participant, assertive or negative, as illustrated in **figure 10.1**.

At the centre of the paradigm we posit Sartre's dead-end petrification with no way out of the stultifying clutches of Man over his fellow men. The horizontal axis signifies the continuum of the separant's inclusionary efforts to achieve rapport with the object by overpowering and controlling it, whereas the participant aims to close the rift between himself and the object by fusing with it or immersing in it. The vertical axis presents a continuum of assertive rebellion and a negative destructive one. The rebellion of the Camusian Sisyphus is in trying to find a *modus vivendi* with his object-stone by imbuing meaning to his daily routines and finding thereby a limited yet viable ontological assertion to his "throwness-unto-death". Samuel Beckett's stranded and desolate tramps are waiting in vain for salvation by Godot; yet the strain, the hunger and the longing for Grace are by themselves enough to fill the tramps with glimmers of hope, which are continuous and self-sustaining. Sade incarcerated in the Bastille is foaming at the mouth and spewing all around him visions of Armageddon against everyone and everything, fuelled by his *ressentiment*, deprivation and craving for vengeance. Jean Genet strives to achieve the ultimate fusion of murderer and victim by the *coup de grâce* of mutual annihilation performed by the solemn rituals of a black passion.

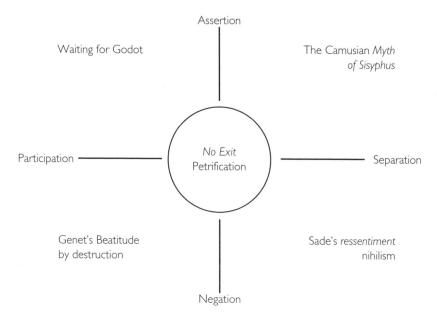

Figure 10.1 Separant, Participant, Assertive and Negative Rebellion

These are only extreme illustrative instances to highlight the contours of our following description of the various manifestations of ontological rebellion. The Camusian Sisyphus rejects first of all the metaphysical programming, which posits Man's life on an inevitable scaffolding of pain and suffering. Camus' Rieux in *The Plague* resents the pointless deprivation, injury and hurt inherent in human interaction and especially the obvious injustice of the torturing of innocent children.

"Why was there that anger in your voice just now? What we'd been seeing was as unbearable to me as it was to you."

Rieux turned toward Paneloux "I know. I'm sorry. But weariness is a kind of madness. And there are times when the only feeling I have is one of mad revolt."

"I understand", Paneloux said in a low voice. "That sort of thing is revolting because it passes our human understanding. But perhaps we should love what we cannot understand."

Rieux straightened up slowly. He gazed at Paneloux, summoning to his gaze all the strength and fervour he could muster against his weariness. Then he shook his head.

"No, Father. I've a very different idea of love. And until my dying day I shall refuse to love a scheme of things in which children are put to torture."

A shade of disquietude crossed the priest's face. "Ah, doctor", he said sadly, "I've just realized what is meant by 'grace'." [4]

Sisyphus does not have the hesitation of Ivan Karamazov. For him, Original Sin and the children born guilty are lies. He is not interested in the redemption of the ever after. He wants to find the answer to his plight in the here and now. We might add that our model of human growth and development envisages pain and suffering from the very moment of the neonate's expulsion from the womb, his fall from the pantheistic unity of early orality and the rites of passages from the forgiving grace of the family fold. Man's deprivational interaction with the hostile object and other people is ordained throughout his "thrownness-unto-death" without the additional trials of plagues and the Nazi Holocaust. The defiance of Sisyphus consists first of all in his acceptance of the limits of his manoeuvrability. Like a good soldier he has to "read and forecast the battle". He must concede the immense powers of his adversary and the total lack of information in the intelligence files on anything before his *Geworfenheit* and after the end of his journey in the here and now. Yet fight he must in order to assert his ontological worth against a silent, yet immensely powerful manipulator. Also, no judgments can be postponed to the ever after. All accounts must be settled in the here and now. There are also no places for illusions or make-believe fantasies: Sisyphus has to plan his rebellion realistically because both the rock burden and the mountain up which he has to push it are real indeed.

Sisyphean rebellion is usually a sequel to petrification. There are hardly any shortcuts to it. One has to experience the stagnation of the separant daily routines before discovering the authenticity of rebellion. Many people end their lives in the petrifying first stage of Camus' judge penitent in *The Fall*, having become entangled in the cycles of the rat race, illusory achievements and servitude to the generalized other without ever embarking on the arduous "fall" towards authenticity. After the transition of the child from one developmental phase to the other, which is registered[5] by the organism as catastrophes, the child is usually indoctrinated with one or other brand of the achievement ethic. After some years,

276

decades, half a lifetime, a lifetime and with most people not at all – a potential Sisyphus may realize that he was chasing a mirage – that achievements and triumphs are briefly cherished for a fleeting moment, for a Heideggerean *Augenblick* to be quickly catalogued, filed and jotted down in the curriculum vitae of the frantically galloping separant who is sweating his way to the next coveted goal which, when achieved, will be discarded and forgotten *da capo*. This realization is the first step on ego's road to rebellion. It is the beginning of the Heideggerean *Verstehen* (understanding) and the discovering of the significance (*bedeutsamheit*) of his being-in-the-world.[6] It is also the judge penitent's realization of the shallowness of his daily encounter with his friends and colleagues, and the ritualistic emptiness of his discourse with his fellow men. At his moment of truth the judge penitent says:

> Living among men without sharing their interests, I could not manage to believe in the commitments I made. I was courteous and indolent enough to live up to what was expected of me in my profession, my family, or my civic life, but each time with a sort of indifference that spoiled everything. I lived my whole life under a double code, and my most serious acts were often the ones in which I was the least involved. Wasn't that after all the reason that, added to my blunders, I could not forgive myself, that made me revolt most violently against the judgment I felt forming, in me and around me, and that forced me to seek an escape.[7]

The second stage of the making of a Camusian Sisyphus is his realization that there is a limit to his potentialities decreed by the "before and after" blackout of his "thrownness-unto-death". Moreover, there must be limits to Sisyphus' potentialities. To paraphrase a variation on one of Friedrich Nietzsche's themes, "If everything is possible nothing is true." If so, then Sisyphus' search for authenticity becomes pointless. Freedom can only be conceived as a leeway, as a range of choices within normative limits. This is why the Camusian rebel rejects the "everything is permitted" of Ivan Karamozov, which leads to murder. Sisyphus seeks a meaningful way to live in the here and now; he does not wish to die or cause others to die. Dying is the end of the journey and one need not concern oneself with what kind of authentic existence one may lead, if at all, in the away and beyond. The metaphysical programming is dead silent on this matter. Suicide is also outside the terms of reference of the Camusian Sisyphus. It is an escape, that obviates both rebellion and the search for authenticity in the here and now, which is the only *raison d'être* of Man's existence. Death is sure to come anyhow and there is no point in hurrying our "thrownness" – it is already galloping towards death.

Sisyphus has to discover ways of authentically and meaningfully living within the confines of being-in-the-world. This, as it happens, is a choice of rebellion against the metaphysical programming which binds us to our burden-rock of life's drudgery between the limits of an involuntary birth and unknown death engulfed by a silent mystery and totally ignorant as to life's beginnings and ends. Finding meaning in the processes of life and not in their culturally sanctioned and achievement obsessed ends can be achieved by beautifying every minute routine and experiencing in full every episode in life, be it joyful or sad; by imbuing with strains of creativity our object relationships and by yearning for dialogue with our fellow men, even though we know that the achievement of an inter-subjective dialogue is impossible. In this way we attack our metaphysical programming in its own backyard. Its original intentions, as apparent from the Sisyphean lot of Man, seem to be vitiated and confounded. The defiance of Sisyphus in managing to discover a viable and creative mode of existence in the here and now, against enormous odds, makes him a junior partner to the metaphysical programming. The latter has all the advantages, the best strategic positions and the control of the beginnings and ends, as well as an intelligence report on the future moves of its grotesquely vain opponent. Yet the omnipotent metaphysical programming has to reckon with the cock-like dignity of a rebel who refuses to succumb to his burden and hence deprives God of a small crumb, however minute, of His omnipotence.

The Camusian rebel casts some side-glances to Greek mythology. By accepting the confines of his being-in-the-world and striving to achieve authenticity and creativity within limits our rebel accepts the Greek doctrine of "nothing in excess" and rejects the excesses of *hübris*. *Hübris* is the attempt to rebel against insurmountable limitations of our being-in-the-world, like death, ageing, blindness, deafness, being in prison, having a Mongoloid child and other irreversible handicaps. To rebel against these limitations is not only futile but also detrimental to the search for authenticity and creativity within the given limits of our handicaps because we divert our psychic energies to overcome our limitations and handicaps over which we cannot have any control. An authentic rebellion, on the other hand, concentrates its efforts on the viable areas within the insurmountable limits. A paralyzed war veteran in a wheelchair may find creative avenues for self-expression and authentic being even if he cannot regain the use of his legs; and parents of a Mongoloid child may find ways of treating their handicapped child which could be deeply rewarding for both parents and child. However, one may indeed rebel against that part of Man's fate in life, his *Fortuna* or *Sors*, which was aptly defined by Gilbert Murray as the denial of the value of human endeavour.[8] Against the illusory decrees of luck, chance, fate and its other synonyms, Man should rebel viciously and fight hard. The success of his rebellion will depend precisely on his ability to imbue authenticity and meaning to his endeavours. It happened to the author many times that he found himself in the same or similar quandary that he was many times before; the least resisting way out was to attribute it to an inevitable tough luck. The Sisyphean rebel does not accept this chance or luck even if it repeats itself as many times as his rock rolls down the slope of the mountain. He tries to attack the converging factors which constitute his quandary in such a way that they fit into his creative strain with his surroundings and thus reveal themselves to him in a Heideggerian *Befinlichkeit*. His quandary then becomes authentic in its uniqueness and not just another senseless event in a row of drudgeries.

The Sisyphean rebel resists the urge to "go under" and "let himself go" even in the face of extreme hardship and pain. The least resistant avenue of going to pieces is unacceptable to the defiant rebel. Giving in to inevitable disaster, personal injury, the death of a beloved person and other handicaps, are as giving in to the plague against which Dr. Rieux, a Camusian Sisyphus, fights with all his might even if he knows that ultimately the plague is bound to win. The saving of even one life, the alleviation of even the minutest amount of pain, is a proper reinforcement for the Camusian Sisyphus in his rebellion against the metaphysically programmed plague. It is worthwhile pointing out in this context that succumbing to pressures of de-personalization and madness may also be a form of giving in to the pressures of the Sisyphean burdens of life, which the patient "couldn't take any more". Hannah Green has described how her personal onslaught of psychosis was preceded by the feeling that the crutches of sanity did not support her any longer and that by becoming mad she felt a cathartic sense of ease, of not having to sustain any longer the outward façade of sanity.[9] Indeed, two recent theories of psychosis regard schizophrenia as succumbing to a vulnerability crisis which is not contained homeostatically and depression as giving in to "learned helplessness".[10] Rebellion denies, therefore, capitulation to the vicissitudes of life, however hard or painful they may be. In similar vein the Sisyphean rebel rejects the lure of the achievement based rat race, and the *ressentiment* and envy which are its inevitable camp followers. The strain of creativity provides a sense of purpose to the rebel's relationship with objects and other people provided he anchors on the process of his creativity and not on its culturally sanctioned remunerations.

An apt illustration of our present premise is the case of the astronaut Edwin (Buzz) Aldrin. He was trained to be the superman of the most achievement-motivated (separant) society on earth. American technology and human excellence in the person of Air Force Colonel, West Point graduate, Doctor of Science, Edwin Aldrin, launched the most ambitious programme to the stars and succeeded. Aldrin stepped on to the moon on 21 July 1969, with the entire world watching. "All my life," said Aldrin "was conducted to achieve one aim, to step on the moon, and I never thought of anything beyond it. When the operation was over I did not know what to do with myself."[11] This is the typical aftermath and anticlimax of a separant arriviste hero who achieved a competitive triumph, which was soon catalogued, filed and forgotten. The trouble was that he had no other peaks to conquer. Neither his surroundings nor he himself could provide alternative avenues for his devastating competitive drives. As for his fellow men, said Aldrin: "Astronauts are terribly competitive, they don't even meet to exchange memories, they are still afraid of one another."[12] Then came the fall: Aldrin started to drift, left his family, sunk into depression and became a drunk. But he proved to be a Camusian Sisyphus. He went on to sell cars in Beverly Hills, California. Aldrin found himself. Sisyphus achieved a *modus vivendi* with his rock.

The Sisyphean rebel does not need the grandiose and self-defeating separant competitive aims, goals and ends. Only the processes, the continuous dynamics of creativity, can be imbued with an *agape*-like elation, which beautifies Man's daily routines and tasks. Creativity provides the struggling Sisyphus with a sense of meaning and dignity. The "small things in life" and one's daily tasks thus become a vocation, a *raison d'être* and "the great things" which lend a sense of purpose to Sisyphus' being-in-the-world. This beautification of Man's daily tasks is voiced by the priest in William Golding's novel *The Spire*, who tells the Master builder: "My son. The building is a diagram of prayer: and our spire will be a diagram of the highest prayer of all. God revealed it to me in a vision, his unprofitable servant. He chose me. He chooses you, to fill the diagram with glass and iron and stone, since the children of men require a thing to look at. D'you think you can escape? You're not in my net – It's His. We can neither of us avoid this work. And there's another thing. I've begun to see how we can't understand it either, since each new foot reveals a new effect, a new purpose."[13] The creative involvement of Sisyphus with his stone thus also provides reinforcement to his existential sense of choice.

Bertolt Brecht's dictum that it is never too late to begin again one's failed endeavours, even with one's last breath, or the Kiplingesque hero starting to rebuild from scratch his ruined life work with "worn out tools", have a romantic aura in their poetic contexts. But for us they are Sisyphean rebels who are acting in the only authentic manner possible within the confines of their "thrownness-in-the-world". Sisyphean rebellion means trying again and again to perform a given task; this constitutes the rebel's creativity, even if he fails repeatedly and even if he knows that the chances of achieving his goal are meagre. In the same vein the Sisyphean rebel strives to achieve dialogue with his fellow men even if he fails in his endeavours many times.

The creative processes and the quest of dialogue are in themselves the *raison d'être* of the Sisyphean rebel. Rebellion and quest are the two entwined redeeming anchors of the thrown Sisyphus who is bound to his rock by an absurd metaphysical programming and is ever petrified by his deprivational interaction with the generalized other.

The Two Faces of Rebellion

The Sisyphean rebel seeks authenticity within the Heraclitean strife between himself and the object, whereas the Tantalic rebel seeks the Parmenidean all-engulfing reality behind the appearances of spatio-temporality. This other reality ever eludes him behind the metaphysically programmed Mayan veils of sensory perception. The Tantalic rebel searches for dialogue in the Greek etymological sense of "going through" spatio-temporality and "reaching out to" the eternal constancies. The separant Sisyphean rebel is concerned with the vicissitudes of his object-relationships and the means to achieve a meaningful *modus vivendi* with objects and other people; whereas the Tantalic rebel seeks the ideational links between himself and his surroundings and the manner in which his inner self relates to some unknown ultimates. The Sisyphean rebel puts great store by his ability to distinguish between events he can control and those he cannot; whereas the Tantalic rebel is not interested in controlling his environment but in understanding and wrenching from the silent metaphysical programming the ways in which he fits into the wider scheme of things. The separant Sisyphean rebel is baffled by the competition over his sense of existential choice with other people and objects; whereas the Tantalic participant rebel is filled by a desire to know and to understand how his feeling of ontological uniqueness is related to the all-embracing Unity. Camus just hinted at the possibility of Tantalic rebellion but he did not develop this theme the way he described and documented Sisyphean rebellion. We shall stray, therefore, from his giant strides and try to describe more fully the Tantalic rebellion in line with the main theses of the present volume.

We are not dealing here with a dichotomy but with a continuum having at its extremes the two "ideal type" modes of rebellion. Also, one type of rebel may perform a summersault from one pole to the other. Two illustrative cases are those of Paul Firehabend and John A. Wheeler. Firehabend, one of the leading contemporary philosophers of science, launched a campaign against the tyranny of science. He claims that science is just another ideology, which curbs Man's freedom of choice; that scientific methodology is a myth and that the intuition of "outsiders" may sometimes enhance our knowledge much more than the logic and measurements of scientists. Wheeler, a world-renowned physicist, who also participated in the Manhattan Project, claims in his article "Genesis by Observership" that according to quantum mechanics the observer of reality is a full partner in the definition of this reality. There is no world "out there" independent of the observer. Consequently the existence of the observer is as necessary for the existence of the world as the existence of space and time is necessary for the genesis of Man.[14] This brings to the fore the Buberian conception of dialogue between Man and the world, and various mystical teachings according to which Man actively participates in the creation of the world. These conceptions are obviously light years away from mainstream theories of contemporary physics.

The Sisyphean rebel tries to solve the recurring pain, nausea and despair involved in his separant preoccupation with objects and other people: his urge to amass money and property as an extension of his inflated self; his

281

compulsive attachment to objects, the loss of which hurls him into a morbid anxiety; his need to build structures, raise students and "leave his imprint on the future" which does not leave him time or energy to live in the present; his feeling that every day he is running for re-election by the generalized other and woe to him if he fails; his need to be approved by his audience in whatever he does and his morbid fear of loneliness; and, finally, the petrifying need to conform to the wishes, mandates and decrees in the choice of his occupation and profession. The Sisyphean rebel has to shed layer after layer of these petrifying effects of the objects and other people. Only then is he ready for a creative involvement with objects and an authentic relationship with other people. Above all he should beware of pseudo-rebellion motivated by a sour grapes *ressentiment* rejection of the object and by his desire to revenge himself on some real or imaginary injustice or injury inflicted on him by some relevant others. A pseudo-rebellion is liable to lead to an even more complete petrification by the object-burden and to an abject slavery to the shifting whims of the generalized other.

The Tantalic rebel, on the other hand, seeks revelation, the Heideggerean *Befindlichkeit* and especially self-revelation. He longs to understand (*Verstehen*) and to feel the relationship between himself and the unifying whole. The Tantalic rebel is not so much concerned with life as with reasons for living.[15] He knows that he is part of an event, of an experiment conducted by a non-communicative metaphysical programming, the nature of which is totally incomprehensible to him. Yet he is fired by his craving to know and understand his relationship with this secretive unifying whole of which he felt an integral part in his pantheistic early orality (at which time he was fixated as a personality type). This, incidentally, is the possible link between the manifestations of Tantalic rebellion and our developmental personality model. The Tantalic rebel has a Nietzschean core in him in so far as he aims to immerse himself into the cosmos in order to rediscover the link between himself and Eternal Divinity.[16] He rejects the Nietzschean *Amor Fati* because unlike the Sisyphean rebel, he does not seek involvement with his surroundings. He accepts them as an inevitable nuisance, which he has to neutralize or "see through" in order to unveil the wider relationships between himself and the unifying whole away, beyond and "behind" spatio-temporality. The Tantalic rebel keeps seeking these ultimates even if they constantly recede from him.

The search for ultimates itself becomes then the *raison d'être* of the Tantalic rebel even if he knows from all his experience up to a given point in his life that it is well nigh impossible to wrench any secrets from the chronically silent metaphysical programming. The inferential pieces of information gleaned by the science and logic of the separant Sisyphean rebel leaves the Tantalic rebel cold. He longs for a direct link with the Absolute; for an immediate sense of partaking in Unity; for a return to the way he felt *in utero* and in the blissful omnipresence of early orality.

Power does not infatuate the Tantalic rebel. He is bored like Diogenes with the brute omnipotence of an Alexander. The Tantalic rebel is prompted by an insatiable curiosity and a thirst for knowledge not of unrelated facts and processes, but for aetiological models and meta-theories leading to prime movers, grand designs and ultimate causes. The Tantalic rebel seeks a Johnsonian "integrated sense of himself . . . a liberation through creative uses, of qualities of mind, of readiness of a range of interest, and imaginative perception that he had discovered he might really have".[17] Armed with this insight of his potentialities the Tantalic rebel embarks on his quest to discover and decipher the meaning of his being-in-an-absurd-world, and his relationship with a silent metaphysical programming.

The Tantalic rebel seeks information like the prisoner in the British television series of the early 1960s by that name. Each new instalment opened with a person (the prisoner) being abducted from a flat in London, drugged and brought to a prison camp, which is run like a village where all the inmates go about their routine business as if they lead a normal life. This is a variation on a Kafkaesque theme, except for the opening scene in which the prisoner is brought before the headman of the village who is always Number Two. Number One, the prime mover is not known and remains clandestine throughout the series. The prisoner then tries to escape and find out why he has been shanghaied to the village. His escapades and surrealistic adventures revolve around his strenuous efforts to unravel the reasons for his abduction as well as the identity of Number One and the system by which he controls the village prison. He invariably fails in his efforts and at the end of each instalment he is brought back to the village and to Number Two only to begin again his Tantalic search for freedom and for the ultimate reasons and answers to his plight. This portrays the Tantalic rebel who is not so much bothered by his "thrownness" into this world as by the silence of the metaphysical programming, which has posited him there. His quest for information about his being-in-the-world and his relationship to things and people is the Tantalic rebel's main concern in life which he keeps pursuing even if he fails time and again to wrench some glimmerings of knowledge from the tight-lipped universe.

Tantalic rebellion – as conceived by us here – is quite apparent in Camus' writings. After Tarrou, Dr. Rieux's friend, died in the plague, the doctor contemplated "what had he (Rieux) won? No more than the experience of having known plague and remembering it, of having known friendship and remembering it, of knowing affection and being destined one day to remember it. So all a man could win in the conflict between plague and life was knowledge and memories. But Tarrou, perhaps, would have called that winning the match."[18] This is the triumph of the Tantalic rebel who knew both friendship and sorrow – and experienced them to the hilt. Knowledge was revealed to him and the memories of grace became part of him so that even the death of his friend could not diminish his triumph, which took place on a totally different plane of his inner reality.

Camus' *Adulterous Woman* is a classic instance of Tantalic rebellion, which is especially apparent in the following passage:

> Over yonder, still further south, at that point where sky and earth met in a pure line – over yonder it suddenly seemed there was awaiting her something of which, though it had always been lacking, she had never been aware until now. In the advancing afternoon the light relaxed and softened; it was passing from the crystalline to the liquid. Simultaneously, in the heart of a woman brought there by pure chance, a knot tightened by the years, habit, and boredom was slowly loosening . . . After so many years of mad, aimless fleeing from fear, she had come to a stop at last. At the same time, she seemed to recover her roots and the sap again rose in her body, which had ceased trembling. Her whole belly pressed against the parapet as she strained towards the moving sky; she was merely waiting for her fluttering heart to calm down and establish silence within her. The last stars of the constellations dropped their clusters a little lower on the desert horizon and became still. Then with unbearable gentleness, the water of night began to fill Janine, drowned the cold, rose gradually from the hidden core of her being and overflowed in wave after wave, rising up even to her mouth full of moans. The next moment, the whole sky stretched out over her, fallen on her back on the cold earth.[19]

This is the upsurge of a subdued inner-self from the misery of everyday life and the squalor of a lacklustre domestic slumber into a defiant roar against a silent universe, which seems to give in to her tempestuous and irresistible longing to partake in it. The woman's adulterous submission to the world is an offering of rebellious affirmation, which may make her daily trials less unbearable.

Another Tantalic rebel is Beckett's Molloy. Like many other of Beckett's characters, Molloy is in the gutters and sinking into a progressive inaction. Molloy, like Beckett himself, seems to have had an urge to go back to the womb,[20] and one way to simulate it and regain the blissful pantheistic union *in utero* is to ignore the separation from his surroundings and from his mother by calling her and himself by the same name and identifying with her as well as with Teddy, the dog. Molloy's Tantalic rebellion manifests itself first of all in trying to prod into his inner self and then trying to relate it to his surroundings even if this relationship continues to be incomprehensible and not subject to elucidation. "Not to want to say, not to know what to say, not to be able to say what you think you want to say, and never to stop saying, or hardly ever, that is the thing to keep in mind."[21]

To keep trying to expound his relationship with his surroundings, even if it seems utterly impossible or absurd, is the essence of Molloy's Tantalic rebellion. He also tries to gain insight into his inner self by some weird techniques of meditation so as to annihilate his spatio-temporality and reach out towards his surroundings and other people, until his soul is strained like a tight cord. Molloy vows to carry on his Tantalic

284

search for meaning even if his chances of success are ever decreasing. He voices a defiant Tantalic credo by declaring that he will continue to advance on his *Via Dolorosa* even if he cannot hope for a redeeming crucifixation.

Like most of Beckett's heroes, Molloy is not too fussy about his living conditions and his animal comfort. He believes that outside reality has very little to do with his inner reality. Outside reality "should not be taken too seriously". What is important is to keep looking for links between one's inner self and the non-intelligible messages behind the grotesque, absurd and dilapidated façade of temporal appearances, even if the chances of success are as high as Godot suddenly materializing on our doorstep.

The Search for Authenticity

The rebel embarking on his search for authenticity must first of all see his "thrownness" in the world as it is, with no illusions, no "romantic" make-up and no metaphysical attenuating circumstances. Furthermore, there must be no comforts of false chemical happiness imbibed through the gut or pumped into the veins. "I personally," says the young hero of Ajar's novel *La Vie Devant Soi*, "spit on heroin. The children who shoot dope get used to this happiness and it takes revenge on them. Because happiness is mainly known for its absence. Only those who really look for happiness use the needle and one has to be a king size dunce to invent such ideas. I personally never used horse but smoked occasionally some hash out of courtesy to the boys. When you are ten years old the grown-ups want to teach you many things but I don't want to be happy, I prefer to live."[22]

One should not, of course, distort one's view of life artificially. But what is the "right" and "true" view? A possible answer is that Man's existential choice and ontological uniqueness makes him feel that the world is revealed to him in a unique manner not shared by others. Consequently, if he was chosen as the sole avenue for the awareness of the world this must also be the authentic way for him to perceive it. The first corollary of this basic premise is that authentic being-in-the-world necessitates liberation from the yoke of the generalized other. The gang, our best friends, our bullying bosses and our *Yiddishe mammas* might be hurt if we disentangle ourselves from their hold. But authenticity starts from the revelation that one's being-in-the-world is first of all for oneself and then for others.

If one lives as if one has to regain every day the approval of the generalized other, that one has to be "nice" to everybody and smile to them even if one does not want to, if one is constantly worried about what "they" say about one, there is no chance of revealing the authentic being-for-oneself. One is an empty shell filled with fear and anxiety because of

285

the expectations of the generalized and relevant others. As for the stigmatizing control by "what people are going to say about me" the authentic attitude coincides with one of the mottos of St. Andrew's College in Edinburgh, Scotland:

"They say."
"What say they?"
"Let them say."

Indeed, the revealing of the authentic being-in-the-world involves, according to Heidegger, the liberation of the self from the hold of the interchangeable "one like many" and becoming the unique *Dasein* of being-for-itself.[23] To achieve this first step towards authenticity one may experience a sudden revelation and "drop out to do one's own thing" or undergo a gradual metamorphosis *à la* Camus judge penitent in *The Fall*. The judge penitent's "fall" into authenticity is like a Husserlean phenomenological reduction. He sheds layer after layer of his bourgeois hypocrisy; his socialite small talk; his manipulation of others through phoney morals and false modesty; his helping others only when there is an audience; his declaration of eternal love for a single fling in bed; and his letting people die when helping them would not gain him anything. All these layers were veils in which he was entangled by the generalized others. When this striptease towards authenticity was complete the judge penitent reached the zero level of being in a bare room, facing himself austerely by himself without the impeding expectations or the false comforts of generalized others. Once the zero level has been reached the ascent, or descent depending on the point of vantage, towards authenticity begins by reassessing one's relationship with spatio-temporality.

Time can also be authentic and inauthentic. There is a difference between Sisyphean and Tantalic authentic and inauthentic time. It seems that Heidegger deals with what we have conceived as Sisyphean involvement with time. He distinguishes between the inauthentic *Vorhandenheit* of time in which ego is indifferent to the passing of time from the future to the past through the fleeting moments (*Augenblick*) of the present (where time is objectified and lingers "out there" without ego being involved or partaking in it), and authentic time where there is a creative involvement (*Zuhanden*) so that the passing of time from the future to the past becomes the horizon of being-in-the-world.[24] In the latter case, time is not neutral for ego but becomes the framework for the revelation, discovery and elation of his creative involvement with the object. In this manner ego may project onto time his subjective moods so as to extend to it his personal subjective imprint. The authentic involvement with time necessitates a setting of an order of priorities for ego in line with the quests of his inner being and his creativity, and not as decreed by the petrifying generalized other. Because Man's being-in-the-world is a "thrownness-unto-death" for a limited time span it has to be utilized in a manner which is relevant to ego's creative interests and not to be sidetracked into irrelevant *ressentiment*, sour grape regrets or into power skirmishes over *non sequitur* points scored in the rat race.

Some years ago the author realized the meaning of this reordering of priorities within the context of authentic time, when he did some stock-taking as to what he wished to do with himself in the foreseeable future. He counted roughly the expected active years still left to him and assessed the amount and kind of work he wanted to do. He realized that if he did not give up administrative duties, involvement in academic power politics and the excessive conference hopping of the international flying academia, he would not be able to accomplish even a small fraction of what he really wished to do with his time. The resetting of priorities necessitates, therefore, a severe cutting back of activities into which one drifts almost inadvertently until they take up a large part and sometimes most of one's time. In order to live the "horizons of one's being" in authentic time one has to be the master of time and not its reified slave. Also, one has to strip one's activities to the bare essentials for achieving creative involvement with one's surroundings. Austerity is therefore one of the attributes of the Sisyphean rebel engaged in creative involvement with his rock burden within authentic time.[25]

For the Sisyphean, rebellion is never too late to start creative involvement with the object because the horizons of being are always developing up to the moment of death. For the Tantalic rebel the discrete sequence of time can never be authentic and it is very often too late. At the end of Camus' *The Fall*, the judge penitent expresses the wish that he be given another chance to rescue the girl whom he knowingly refrained from rescuing many years ago:

> You yourself utter the words that for years have never ceased echoing through my nights and that I shall at last say through the mouth: "O young woman, throw yourself into the water again so that I may a second time have the chance of saving both of us!" A second time, eh, what a risky suggestion! Just suppose cher maitre that we should be taken literally? We'd have to go through with it. Brr . . . ! The Water's cold! But let's not worry! It's too late now. It will always be too late. Fortunately?[26]

To achieve his aim of partaking in Unity the Tantalic rebel aims to emerge out of the separating discrete sequences of time. For example, Marcel Proust's attempts to escape from his stifling present and revert back through the longing for grace to the forgiveness of childhood and the bliss of his mother's lap. The Bergsonian *Durée* is another Tantalic attempt of ecstasy from the sequences of past–present–future into the authentic flow of duration and streamlined continuity. Tantalic quests of authentic time are apparent in the various techniques of mystical union, that try to escape spatio-temporality by annihilating time, which is its more volatile component and hence most vulnerable. Here authentic time is literally no-time. In similar vein, Kierkegaard postulated the bursting of eternity into Time, and Paul Tillich preached the eternal now, which again is a Tantalic collapsing of the sequences of time into a *Durée*-like present. A simple and clear description of the Tantalic rebel's authentic time is described by Emerson as follows:

> These roses under my window make no reference to former roses or to better ones; they are for what they are; they exist with God today. There is no time to them. There is simply the rose; it is perfect in every moment of its existence. Before a leaf-bud has burst, its whole life acts; in the full-blown flower there is no more; in the leafless root there is no less. Its nature is satisfied and it satisfies nature in all moments alike. But Man postpones or remembers; he does not live in the present, but with reverted eye laments the past, or, heedless of the riches that surround him, stands on tiptoe to foresee the future. He cannot be happy and strong until he too lives with nature in the present, above time.[27]

The "fall" into authenticity also involves the ceasing of judging others according to our standards. The judge penitent in the second part of Camus' *The Fall* does not judge any more because his motivations for judging others have been revealed to him and his dismayed disgust from these motives made him incapable of judging. The judge in Genet's play *The Balcony* experienced a similar revelation when he realized that his being a judge depended on his ability to declare the thief a thief. Hence the function of the judge emanates from the thief, but not vice versa.[28] Ego in an authentic existential mood does not judge others because he can never be in their subjective shoes. This is not only because of the simplistic "here but for the grace of God stand I" but also because one cannot and should not judge others as failures, "losers" or sad – one cannot know the extent of the factors and nature of moods which make these others happy or unhappy. The author once realized how foolish and inauthentic he was to judge as "a miserable imbecile" a young student of his in his early twenties, very able and good looking, who married his teacher, a woman in her early fifties. Whatever their covert and overt motivations, they seemed so happy together that the author decided that for whatever period it would last no one has the right to impose on them the petrifying judgment of the generalized other. "They say" and "everyone knows" that a marriage between a boy of twenty-two and a woman of fifty-two is not good, unhealthy and sad, but the actual couple apparently do not know it.

Being with Fear and Anxiety

Our being-in-the-world and our interaction with our surroundings and with other people is deprivational and conflictual. It is characterized by fear and anxiety. This is the Heideggerean dread (*Angst*) and anxiety (*Sorge*).[29] How can one live authentically in a world the interaction with which is constantly marked by fear and anxiety. This is especially the case in Western cultures, which do not as a rule train its young how to experience and confront failure, pain, anxiety and fear.

The authentic rebellion here is to experience fully both happiness and pain as the inevitable attributes of being-in-the-world. Fear and anxiety as manifestations of existence have to be lived through and experienced through all their nuances and intensities of feelings and perceptions. For the Tantalic rebel longing for a meaningful relationship with ultimate meanings, suffering and pain may also be interpreted by him as a condition precedent to the longed for partaking in Unity.[30] The rebellion expressed here is by maintaining a keen interest in the experiences of being-in-the-world even if they include stunning blows. Failure should not blunt one's sensitivities but be lived through as an existential phase of being-in-the-world. Memories should not be evaded because of fear that remembering the happy experiences will bring up the painful ones too. For the existentialist rebel, both the Sisyphean and Tantalic pleasure and pain, success and failure, are just two different poles of experiential continua, which should be lived through authentically. The existentialist rebel is, therefore, the antithesis of the *arriveste* go-getter spurred by the Protestant ethic or mamma's image of a "good Jewish boy" whose sense of worth can be reinforced only by success as measured by money, power and status. Kierkegaard with his "Absolute Affirmation" even goes to the extreme of welcoming pain, fear and suffering as an integral part of Man's lot in the here-and-now as decreed by Divinity. He maintained that all experience should be willingly accepted and experienced ecstatically and in a mood of elation.

289

The logic behind this mode of authenticity and rebellion is that being "thrown" into the world to a constant deprivational interaction with one's surroundings masked by fear and anxiety, the existentialist rebel may express his defiance of the silent metaphysical programming by experiencing fully and deeply every event and gaining the insights from having lived them intensively. This has many examples and applications to Man's everyday life. A son or daughter telling their parents that they do not want to take their parents' word for it that a certain course of action is good or bad just because the parents have experienced it as such, expresses the wish to go through the relevant experiences themselves and glean from them the insights which are relevant to their own life. The insights they gain might not be as meaningful to their parents or, for that matter, to anybody else who cannot share their sense of ontological uniqueness. Pain, blows and traumatic experiences may also raise one to experiential peaks, as Abraham Maslow has noted, so that one may see one's "thrownness" in the world with unprecedented authenticity and clarity. Ezra Pound, for instance, recounts how his rough treatment by some Piazza toughs generated and triggered the creative insight for some of his more celebrated cantos. Even death may be regarded existentially as a peak experience – as the last phase of one's *Geworfenheit zum Todt*. Everyone, including those we very much love or hate, have either experienced this final exit or are sure to go through it in the foreseeable future. One's death may be conceived as a stunning precipitation into nothingness, as a prelude to some religiously backed ever after, or death may be thought of as the final peak experience of the existential rebel's ontological uniqueness, the limit which has yet to be experienced fully by his horizon of being.

The final phase of the rebel's search for authenticity is his pursuance of a dual freedom: the first is the disentanglement from the petrifying yoke of the generalized other so that the rebel may experience his being-in-the-world through his sense of ontological uniqueness; the second is the rebel's quest to fully experience all the events and phases of his "thrownness-unto-death", including death. The meaningful living, through these events, both pleasurable and painful, allows the existentialist rebel to find authenticity within the confines of his being-in-the-world as programmed metaphysically. In this way he gains a measure of freedom and independence from his metaphysical programming and a silent God.

Creative Rebellion

Creativity, says, Camus, abrogates the abject relationship between master and slave.[31] Indeed, the creative involvement of Man with his surrounding objects and people allows him, as we have pointed out previously, to find a measure of authenticity in his metaphysically programmed "thrownness" amidst these objects and other people and hence be, partially at least, liberated from this silent programming. The Sisyphean rebel's creative involvement with his object–burden substitutes the jerky, achievement-motivated jumps from one interim goal to another which become stale the moment they are achieved by a strain process of cathecting psychic energy towards objects and moulding, carving and structuring them according to the relevant mental images of the creator. Sisyphean creativity tries to achieve a Buberean dialogue between the self and object. Inauthentic creativity is the petrified manufacturing of books, paintings and music to satisfy the tastes of the generalized other, so as to make it to the best-seller list or to top the hit parade.

Authentic creativity, on the other hand, is the extreme absorption of the creator in his task to the almost total extinction of the rest of his surroundings, other people inclusive. Stefan Zweig describes the total immersion of August Rodin in moulding a sculpture, that he completely forgot that people were waiting for him outside his atelier.[32] Authentic creativity seems to release the pent-up psychic energy of the creator so that it bursts out and is structured into the work of art. The creator projects on his creation his sense of ontological uniqueness as well as his existential moods so that the authentic work of art bears the unmistakable imprint of the creator's unique personality configuration. The viewers of Vincent van Gogh's paintings, for instance, must be aware of the explosive uniqueness of the artist's expressiveness and his almost desperate involvement with his creation, which is apparent in every stroke of the artist's brush.

The creative Sisyphean rebel grapples with reality in a Nietzschean live wire tension and tries to mould it in his own image, rebelling against God by the most radical defiance possible of imitating His own acts of creation.

The creative innovator is very often a rebel almost by definition. His seeing things differently and depicting them in his novel creation place him almost automatically in opposition to the mainstream cliques in art and literature. Many of the greatest outbursts of creativity have been fuelled by rebellion and protest. The self-exiled Americans and Irish expatriates in the "lost generation" literary salon of Gertrude Stein in Paris generated the most spectacular upsurge in literature and art between the two world wars. Arthur Koestler, Ignacio Silone (*Fontamara*, 1933) and the "God That Failed" group were spurred into new heights of creativity by the Spanish civil war. The protest against the Vietnam War gave some US artists their finest hours, whereas the civil rights movement in the USSR generated forceful new currents in Soviet literature and art. This trend is characterized by an expressive authenticity, which has been absent for almost half a century in the official literature and the stagnant art of the servile legions of party and state-sponsored Soviet artists.

Tantalic creativity rejects spatio-temporality and searches for the surreal, for the worlds of dreams of an Yves Tanguy or a René Magritte, and for the escape of science fiction from this unbearable reality to a world of coherence and of meaning in the away and beyond of a C. S. Lewis trilogy. The Tantalic creative rebel structures in his art his longing for Unity and his quest for understanding his relationship with ultimates. The artist's surroundings and other people are almost superfluous to Tantalic creativity. Of crucial importance is the inner self and its expression into an art with the creator as audience or even sole spectator. The instance of Franz Kafka is too well known to need further elaboration. Camus mentions the case of "The Silent Piano": "Ernst Dwinger in his Siberian Diary mentions a German lieutenant – for years a prisoner in a camp where cold and hunger were almost unbearable – who constructed himself a silent piano with wooden keys. In the most abject misery, perpetually surrounded by a ragged mob, he composed a strange music, which was audible to him alone."[33] For the Tantalic rebel "artistic creation is a demand for Unity and a rejection of the world".[34] The Tantalic artist has a Proust-like distaste for the here and now. Like Proust he anchors on the lost worlds of early childhood and the pantheistic omnipresence of early orality. The Tantalic artist rebels with his art against the silent metaphysical programming and expresses through it his longing for comprehension and for a partaking in the unifying meaningfulness of the Universe.

The creative rebel needs first to be attuned to his inner self and only then to his surroundings. The artist has to rid himself of the petrifying demands of the generalized other if he does not wish to produce entertainment for the mediocre intelligence of the masses. The creative artist is not an egotist but his extreme concentration and absorption in his art makes him oblivious to his surroundings; hence he may be justly seen as egocentric. Here again, we are confronted with the basic paradox appearing throughout the present work: the more one is creatively involved with one's surroundings the more one appears to be detached from it and immersed in oneself.

The Quest

Creativity may be the way out from our petrified "thrownness-unto-death" but not everyone has the talent or the ability to be creative. Also, creativity may fail and become sour. The author many times felt while writing a new book that he finally created his magnum opus and that with each new page he unravelled profound and eternal truths only to slump into near despair when rereading the manuscript and discovering that most of what he really wanted to say remained unsaid. Many people postpone for later the many things they wished to do but this "later" never comes. Many potential Gauguins end their lives as stockbrokers – all that is left is their urge and longing to create. This longing to be creatively involved with the object, the quest for a meaningful dialogue with other people, and the Tantalic yearning to partake in Unity even if the fulfilment of these quests have failed many times and their realization seems as remote as ever, may be also a way out towards authenticity from Man's petrified "thrownness". The Sisyphean quest of involvement with the object, although one can never control the object, is posited by Camus as a universal *raison d'être* and as a basis for ethics. Dr. Rieux in *The Plague* knows that he has no way of subduing the plague or controlling it, and yet his constant search for means to control it and his trying to ease the pain of even one Man was itself enough reason for his carrying on living in a plague infested town and constituted in itself the gist of his moral *Weltanschauung*.

Many people also have a free-floating longing that something interesting or gratifying will happen to them. Even if their actual life has been a succession of miseries and the chances of their extricating themselves from their squalor are almost non-existent, it is this free-floating longing for creativity, dialogue and grace that keeps them going with a light-hearted optimism which is not reinforced by their objective circumstances.

Indeed such grandiose outbursts of poetic creativity – like those of Walt Whitman and Henry Thoreau, or the philosophies of Emerson and Jean-Jacques Rousseau – may be partially, at least, traced to their free-floating longing to be integrated harmoniously into their natural surroundings and partake in cosmic Unity. In similar vein Sigmund Freud confessed that his "oceanic feeling", his rather amorphic wish to partake in a greater whole, was the closest thing to a religious feeling he ever had. For Kierkegaard his ardent wish to cling to the grace of Unity *qua* Unity without knowing its attributes or the means to achieve it was the basis of his existentialist

"Leap of Faith".[35] Beckett's Molloy is also motivated by a quest for dialogue and for grace but he purposely and rather slyly makes his quest diffuse and his longing non-descript because he feels that if his striving is too ardent and too intense he will "frighten" away his goals and his longing itself will perish. This is the reverse of Carlos Castaneda's Yaqui Indian who taught his disciple not to search directly the "other reality" which lurks at the corner of the eye, but that he should be content to feel its presence intuitively somewhere on the peripheries of his field of vision. This also brings to the fore again the Taoist maxim that "The Tao that can be defined is not the eternal Tao."

Kierkegaard went one step further – by relinquishing the hope of implementing his quest he made it "pure", independent and eternal. By giving up his fiancée, Regina Olsen, he made his longing for her continuous and absolute in its fierce intensity. This permits us to make an analogy with Fyodor Dostoevsky's Grand Inquisitor whose main argument seems to be that the actual coming of the Saviour would be a blemish on our longing for Him. Beckett's Godot is not supposed to come because the longing for him in itself and by itself should be enough to imbue with authenticity our Tantalic being-in-the-world.

The impossibility of dialogue and Man's petrification by the generalized other makes for his ontological loneliness. However, Man's constant search for dialogue even after repeated failures is the main buffer, which prevents this ontological loneliness from becoming utter despair. Beckett's Molloy is ever ready for a dialogue and is prepared to fulfil any condition which may be required of him to make this dialogue possible. Bruno Schulz's Broza prays for dialogue: "I need a friend," he pleads, "I long for the nearness of a close person. I search for companionship to my inner world. To bare my inner world all by myself is the strife and burden of an Atlas. I wish I could transfer for a moment my burden to some friendly arms." This transfer is impossible, yet Man is ever going to long for a dialogue. This may have a saving grace in another important way.

Although inter-subjective communication and dialogue are impossible, Ego and Alter may yet have a common longing for communication and dialogue. This common quest for dialogue may give them a common structured framework for a relationship that could be rewarding in itself. A boy and girl may hold hands on the seashore looking at each other and the stars; they cannot reach an inter-subjective dialogue and a two-way direct flow of emotions, yet their common craving for communication and dialogue may serve as a common incentive, catalyzer and framework for their emotions to soar together even when the feelings of each individual cannot be directly communicated and felt by the other. In like manner, two people can be engaged in a discussion, which may send both of them to soaring heights of intellectual euphoria, although no direct communication between them has been effected by their encounter. Consequently, what may be communicated is the common quest and search for dialogue. This may be nothing more (although nothing less) than an encounter between longings for dialogue, the expectations from which are bound to be different with the parties to the encounter. However, it is the most that Man can expect from his being "thrown" in the world, but enough to sustain both Sisyphus and Tantalus in their incessant, absurd, yet dignified and rewarding rebellion against a silent universe.

Notes

Preface

1 Mircea Eliade, *Myth and Reality* (New York: Harper Torchbooks, 1963), pp. 34–48.
2 Uriel Tal, "Political Faith of Nazism Prior to the Holocaust." Jacob M. and Shoshanna Schreiber Annual Lecture (Tel Aviv: Tel Aviv University Press, June 14, 1978), pp. 29–30.
3 Martin Heidegger, *Being and Time* (Oxford: Basil Blackwell, 1962), pp. 17–19.
4 Eliade, *Myth and Reality*, pp. 34–48.
5 Roger Penrose, *The Emperor's New Mind* (New York: Penguin, 1991), p. 414.
6 Thomas Thompson, *The Ancient History of Israel*.
7 Leon Festinger, *When Prophecy Fails: A Social and Psychological Study of a Modern Group that Predicted the Destruction of the World* (New York: Harper and Row, 1964).

Introduction   The Away and Beyond is Right Here and Now

1 Shlomo G. Shoham, *Salvation Through the Gutters*, pt. 2 (Washington, DC: Hemisphere Publishing, 1978), p. 21.
2 Shoham, *Crime and Social Deviation* (Chicago: Regnery, 1966); *The Mark of Cain* (New York: Israel Universities Press/Oceana Publications, 1970); and *Society and the Absurd* (Oxford: Basil Blackwell, 1974).
3 David Bakan, *The Duality of Human Existence* (Chicago: Rand McNally, 1966), p. 5.

I   The Fist and the Open Hand

1 Gordon W. Allport, *Personality: A Psychological Interpretation* (New York: Holt, 1934), p. 48.
2 Silvano Arieti, *American Handbook of Psychiatry*, vol. 1 (New York: Basic Books, 1966), p. 101.
3 Shlomo G. Shoham, *Salvation Through the Gutters* (Washington, DC: Hemisphere Publishing, 1978), p. 21.
4 Ernest Schachtel, *Metamorphosis* (London: Routledge & Kegan Paul, 1963), p. 32.
5 Phyllis Greenacre, *Trauma, Growth and Personality* (New York: Norton, 1952), introduction.

6   Edwin Erickson, "The Problem of Identity", *Journal of the American Psychiatric Association* 4 (1956): pp. 56–121.

7   W. Ronald Fairbairn, *Psychoanalytic Studies of the Personality* (London: Tavistock, 1966), pp. 103–8.

8   Gershom G. Scholem, *Major Trends in Jewish Mysticism* (New York: Schocken Books, 1961), p. 233.

9   Sigmund Freud, *Beyond the Pleasure Principle* (London: International Psycho-Analytical Press, 1922).

10 Otto Rank, *The Trauma of Birth*, 2nd edn (New York: Robert Bruner, 1952).

11 Andras Angyal, "A Theoretical Model for Personality Studies", *Journal of Personality* 20 (1951): pp. 131–42.

12 Angyal, *Neurosis and Treatment: A Holistic Theory* (New York: Wiley, 1965), p. 29.

13 Harry Sullivan, *The Fusion of Psychiatry and Social Science* (New York: W. W. Norton & Co., 1964), p. 235.

14 Lucien Lévy-Bruhl, *Mentalite Primitive* (Paris: Press Universitaire de France, 1960).

15 Mircea Eliade, *Myth and Reality* (New York: Harper & Row, 1968), p. 78.

16 *Ibid.*, pp. 78, 89, 125.

17 Eliade, *The Myth of the Eternal Return* (Princeton, NJ: Princeton University Press, 1954), Foreword.

18 Schachtel, *Metamorphosis*.

19 Sullivan, *Conceptions of Modern Psychiatry* (Washington, DC: William Allanson White Psychiatric Foundation, 1947), pp. 10–21.

20 Shoham, *Salvation Through the Gutters*, p. 21.

21 *Ibid.*, pt. 1.

22 *Ibid.*, ch. 10.

23 Salvatore Maddi, *Personality Theories: A Comparative Analysis*, rev. edn (Homeland: Dorsey Press, 1972), p. 51.

24 Albert Camus, *The Myth of Sisyphus* (New York: Vintage Books, 1961), p. 3.

25 Shoham, *Salvation Through the Gutters*, chs. 4, 8, 13.

26 Robert Graves, *The Greek Myths*, 2nd vol. (Harmondsworth: Penguin, 1955), p. 26.

27 Ecclesiastes Raba, 5:14.

28 Freud, *Beyond the Pleasure Principle*, p. 71.

29 Carl G. Jung, "The Soul and Death", in *The Meaning of Death*, ed. H. Feifel (New York: McGraw-Hill, 1965), p. 6.

30 Jung, "Synchronicity: A Causal Connecting Principle", in Jung, *The Structure and Dynamics of the Psyche* (London: Routledge & Kegan Paul, 1969), Collected Works, vol. 9, p. 446.

31 Talmud Berachot p. 17a.

32 Talmud Avot 4:16.

33 Talmud Kiddushim, p. 39b.

34 Talmud Baba-Batra, p. 10a.

35 Genesis 1:31.

36 Genesis Raba 9:5.

37 Zohar, Midrash Ha-Ne'elam, Genesis, p. 98a.

38 This seems to be in line for the reasons given in Genesis Raba 9:5 for the death of the righteous.

39 Jung, *Psychological Types* (London: Kegan Paul, Trench, Trubner, 1944), pp. 24–5.

40 Talmud Berachot, p. 17a.

41 Talmud Shabbat, p. 152b.

42 Talmud Nidda, p. 31a.

43 Paul Tillich, "The Eternal Now", in *Meaning of Death*, ed. Feifel, p. 38.

44 Jung, "Soul and Death", in *ibid*. p. 15.

45 Shoham, *Salvation Through the Gutters*, Pt. 1.

46 Freud, *The Interpretation of Dreams* (London: Hogarth Press, 1953), p. 511.

47 Jung, *On Psychic Energy*, Collected Works, vol. 8 (Princeton, NJ: Princeton University Press, 1960).

48 Jung, *The Archetypes and the Collective Unconscious*, Collected Works, vol. 9 (London: Routledge & Kegan Paul, 1959), p. 400.

49 Ruth Munroe, *Schools of Psychoanalytic Thought* (New York: Holt, 1955), p. 360.

50 Martin Heidegger, *Sein und Zeit: Erste Haifte* (Halle: Max Niemeyer, 1927), p. 187.

51 Ecclesiastes 3:10–11.

52 Shoham, *Salvation Through the Gutters*, pt. 1.

53 Schachtel, *Metamorphosis*, p. 60.

54 John Bowlby, *Attachment* (Harmondsworth: Penguin, 1972), ch. 11.

55 This is the stand adhered to, *inter alia*, by Sullivan. See Munroe, *Schools of Psychoanalytic Thought*, p. 360.

56 Shoham, *Salvation Through the Gutters*, pt. 2; and Fairbairn, *Psychoanalytic Studies of the Personality*, ch. 11.

57 Jean Piaget and Barbel Inhelder, *The Psychology of the Child* (New York: Basic Books, 1969), p. 25.

58 Fairbairn, *Psychoanalytic Studies of the Personality*, pt. 1.

59 Russell R. Dynes *et al.*, "Level of Aspiration: Some Aspects of Family Experience as a Variable", *American Sociological Review* 21 (April 1956): pp. 212–15.

60 Sebastian DeGrazia, *The Political Community* (Chicago: University of Chicago Press, 1948), p. 59.

61 Raymond W. Mack *et al.*, "The Protestant Ethic, Level of Aspiration and Social Mobility: An Empirical Test", *American Sociological Review* 21 (June 1956): pp. 255–300.

62 Louis Guttman, "The Non-Metric Breakthrough for the Behavioural Sciences", *Proceedings of the Second National Conference on Data Processing*, Rehovoth, Israel, 5–6 January 1966).

63 Richard A. Cloward and Lloyd E. Ohlin, *Delinquency and Opportunity* (New York: Free Press, 1961), p. 95.

64 Shoham, *Society and the Absurd* (Oxford: Basil Blackwell, 1974), chapter 3.

65 *Ibid.*, ch. 1.

66 Camus, *The Fall* (New York: Vintage Books, 1956), p. 133.

67 Camus, *The Myth of Sisyphus*, p. 91.

2   The Sisyphean and the Tantalic – An Ontological Personality Typology

1 This has mainly been presented by Sigmund Freud in his *Three Contributions to the Theory of Sex: The Basic Writings of Sigmund Freud* (New York: Modern Library, 1938), p. 553; Instincts and Their Vicissitudes, Collected

Works, vol. 5; Character and Anal Eroticism, vol. 2; The Infantile Genital Organization of the Libido, vol. 2 (London: Hogarth Press, 1925).

2   Salvatore R. Maddi, *Personality Theories: A Comparative Analysis*, rev. edn (Homewood, Ill.: Dorsey Press, 1972), p. 271.

3   Joseph Nuttin, Psychoanalysis and Personality (New York: Mentor-Omega Books, 1962), p. 35.

4   Freud, *Psychopathology of Everyday Life: The Basic Writings of Sigmund Freud* (New York: Modern Library, 1938), pp. 174–75.

5   Shlomo G. Shoham, *Salvation Through the Gutters* (Washington, DC: Hemisphere Publishing, 1978); and also Chapter 1 of this book.

6   Shoham, Salvation Through the Gutters, pt. 1.

7   Chapter 1 of this book, p. 000.

8   Ludwig Binswanger, *Being in the World: Selected Papers of Ludwig Binswanger* (New York: Basic Books, 1963); and Medard Boss, *Psychoanalysis and Daseinsanalysis* (New York: Basic Books, 1963).

9   Henry A. Murray, ed., *Explorations in Personality: A Clinical and Experimental Study of Fifty Men of College Age* (New York: Oxford University Press, 1938).

10 Hans J. Eysenck, *The Biological Basis of Personality* (Springfield, Ill.: Charles C. Thomas, 1967), p. 37.

11 Shoham, *Salvation Through the Gutters*, ch. 6.

12 Paul Federn, *Ego Psychology and the Psychoses* (London: Imago, 1953).

13 Saul Rosenzweig, "Types of Reaction to Frustration", in *Explorations in Personality: A Clinical and Experimental Study of Fifty Men of College Age*, ed. Murray, pp. 585–99.

14 Shoham, *Salvation Through the Gutters*, ch. 5.

15 Shoham, *Sex as Bait: Eve, Casanova and Don Juan* (St Lucia: University of Queensland Press, 1983), Ch. 6.

16 Karl Abraham, *Selected Papers* (London: Hogarth Press, 1928), pp. 396, 404.

17 Melanie Klein, *Contributions to Psychoanalysis* (London: Hogarth Press, 1948), p. 269.

18 W. Ronald Fairbairn, *Psychoanalytic Studies of the Personality* (London: Tavistock, 1966), p. 144.

19 Klein, *Contributions to Psychoanalysis*, pp. 312–13.

20 Fairbairn, *Psychoanalytic Studies of the Personality*, 23ff.

21 Erich Neumann, *The Great Mother* (Princeton, NJ: Princeton University Press, 1955), p. 10.

22 Genesis 2:25.

23 *Ibid.*, 3:10.

24 Klein, *Contributions to Psychoanalysis*, 267ff.

25 Arthur Koestler, *The Yogi and the Commissar* (London: Jonathan Cape, 1945), pp. 9–10.

26 Carl G. Jung, *Psychological Types* (London: Kegan Paul, Trench, Trubner, 1944), p. 567.

27 Friedrich Nietzsche, *The Birth of Tragedy* (Edinburgh: 1909), 22, 26, cited by Jung in *ibid.*, pp. 172–3.

28 Jung, *Psychological Types*, p. 173.

29 *Ibid.*, p. 418.

30 Erich Heller, *The Disinherited Mind* (Harmondsworth: Penguin, 1961), p. 171.

31 *Ibid.*, p. 450.
32 *Ibid.*, p. 412.
33 Fairbairn, *Psychoanalytic Studies of the Personality*, p. 31.
34 Shoham, *Salvation Through the Gutters*, pt. 3.
35 Murray, *Explorations in Personality*.
36 Eysenck, *The Biological Basis of Personality*, pp. 36–7.
37 *Ibid.*, p. 76.
38 *Ibid.*, p. 77.
39 *Ibid.*, p. 110.
40 *Ibid.*, p. 108.
41 *Ibid.*
42 G. F. Reed and G. Sedman, "Personality and Depersonalization Under Sensory Deprivation Conditions", *Perceptual and Motor Skills* 18 (1964): pp. 659–60.
43 A. Petrie, W. Collins, and P. Solomon, "The Tolerance for Pain and for Sensory Deprivations", *American Journal of Psychology* 123 (1960): p. 114; and A. Petrie, *Individuality in Pain and Suffering: The Reducer and Augmenter* (Chicago: University of Chicago Press, 1967), pp. 138, 140.
44 W. P. Colquhoun and Derek W. J. Corcoran, "The Effects of Time of Day and Social Isolation on the Relationship between Temperament and Performance", *British Journal of Social and Clinical Psychology* 3 (1964): pp. 226–31.
45 Eysenck, *The Biological Basis of Personality*, p. 183.
46 *Ibid.*, p. 163.
47 H. A. Witkin *et al.*, *Psychological Differentiation* (New York: Wiley, 1962), p. 27.
48 S. Cohen and A. J. Silverman, *Body and Field Perceptual Dimensions and Altered Sensory Environment* (Durham, NC: Duke University Press, 1963), p. 27.
49 Shoham, *Promethean Therapy* (Haifa: Ach Press, 1998, in Hebrew), ch. 2; also, forthcoming in English, *The Insatiable Gorge* (Aldershot, Hampshire: Ashgate, 2003, in press).
50 John W. Thibaut and Harold H. Kelley, *The Social Psychology of Groups* (New York: Wiley, 1959), p. 239.
51 Julian. B. Rotter, Melvin Seeman, and S. Liverant, "Internal versus External Control of Reinforcements: A Major Variable in Behaviour Theory", *Decisions, Values, and Groups*, ed. M. F. Washburne, 2 (1962), pp. 473–559.
52 Thibaut and Kelly, *The Social Psychology of Groups*, p. 149
53 David Riesman, *The Lonely Crowd* (New Haven, Conn.: Yale University Press, 1950).
54 Douglas P. Crowne and David A. Marlowe, "New Scale of Social Desirability Independent of Psychopathology", *Journal of Consulting and Clinical Psychology* 24 (1960): pp. 349–54.
55 Jung, *Psychological Types*, p. 416.
56 Shimon Dubnow, *The History of Hassidism* (Tel Aviv: Dvir, 1930), pp. 35–6.
57 Martin Buber, *Befardes Ha'Hassidut* (Tel Aviv: Mossad Bialik, 1945), p. 58.
58 Dubnow, *History of Hassidism*, p. 36.
59 Buber, *Befardes Ha'Hassidut*, p. 71.

299

60 *Ibid.*, p. 73.
61 *Ibid.*
62 *Ibid.*, p. 57.
63 Jung, *Psychological Types*, 15ff.
64 Buber, *Befardes Ha'Hassidut*, p. 54.
65 Eliezer Steinman, "The Legacy of The Besht", *Be'er Ha'Hassidut, Sefer-Habesht* (Tel Aviv: Knesset, in Hebrew), p. 101.
66 Gershom G. Scholem, *Major Trends in Jewish Mysticism* (New York: Schocken Books, 1961), pp. 349–50.
67 Rivka Schatz-Uffenheimer, *Quietist Elements in Hassidic Thought* (Jerusalem: Magness Press, 1968), p. 16.
68 *Ibid*, p. 16.
69 *Ibid.*, p. 97.
70 *Ibid.*, p. 95.
71 Rabbi Benjamin, *Torei-Zahav*, in Steinman, *Sefer Habesht*, Tel Aviv: Knesset (in Hebrew), p. 157.
72 Albertus Magnus, "De Mirabilibus Mundi", in *Synchronicity: An Acausal Connecting Principle, the Interpretation of Nature and the Psyche*, vol. 9 (London: Routledge and Kegan Paul, 1955), p. 448.
73 Or-Ha-Emmet, 14, side 2, cited by Schatz-Uffenheimer, *Quietist Elements*, in *Hassidism,* The Magnes Press, Jerusalem, p. 130.
74 Rabbi Benjamin, *Torei-Zahav*, p. 57
75 Encyclopedia Judaica, "Dov Baer of Mezhirech".
76 *Ibid.*
77 *Ibid.*
78 *Maggid Devarav Le Yaakov* (Jerusalem: 1962), p. 16.
79 Scholem, *Major Trends in Jewish Mysticism*, p. 335.
80 Schatz-Uffenheimer, *Quietist Elements in Hassidic Thought*, p. 93.
81 Shem-Tov, Keter, vol. 1, 11, 19, 23, in *History of Hassidism*, p. 55.
82 Samuel A. Horodezki, *Sefer Shivchei Habesht* (Tel Aviv: Dvir, 1947), p. 7.
83 *Ibid.*, p. 107.
84 Shoham, *Salvation Through the Gutters*, pt. 1.
85 Buber, *Befardes Ha'Hassidut*, p. 56.
86 The Maggid of Mezherich (Rabbi Dov Baer), Maggid Devarav Leya'akov, p. 13.
87 Scholem, *Major Trends in Jewish Mysticism*, pp. 260–5.
88 Steinman, *Be'er Ha'Hassidut*, p. 101.
89 Shoham, "The Swing and The Pendulum: A Note on Method", in *Salvation Through the Gutters*, Introduction.
90 Steinman, *Be'er Ha'Hassidut*, p. 101.
91 Shoham, *Salvation Through the Gutters*, pt. 2.
92 Mezherich, *Maggid Devarev Leya'akov*, p. 13.
93 Schatz-Uffenheimer, *Hassidism as Mysticism*, p. 125.
94 Dubnow, *History of Hassidism*, p. 57.
95 Steinman, *Sefer Habesht*, p. 123.
96 Schatz-Uffenheimer, *Hassidism as Mysticism*, p. 40.
97 Schatz-Uffenheimer, *Hassidism as Mysticism*, p. 48.
98 Buber, *Befardes Ha'Hassidut*, p. 55.
99 Mezherich, *Maggid Devarav Le'Ya'akov*, p. 33.
100 Schatz-Uffenheimer, *Quietist Elements*, in Hassidism, p. 40 and n. 30.

101 Horodezki, *Sefer Shivchei Habesht*, p. 41.
102 *Ibid.*, p. 44; Dubnow, *History of Hassidism*, p. 30.
103 Buber, *Tales of the Hassidism* (New York: Schocken Books, 1961), p. 71.
104 Horodezki, *Sefer Shivchei Habesht*, p. 105.
105 Scholem, *Major trends in Jewish Mysticism*, pp. 348–9.
106 Alan Watts, *Behold the Spirit* (New York: Vintage Books, 1971), p. 72.
107 Buber, *Befardes Ha'Hassidut*, p. 66.
108 Buber, *Tales of the Hassidim*, p. 57.
109 Buber, *Befardes Ha'Hassidut*, p. 66.
110 Buber, *Tales of the Hassidim*, pp. 58–9.
111 *Ibid.*, p. 85.
112 Schatz-Uffenheimer, *Quietist Elements*, p. 101.
113 Dubnow, *History of Hassidism*, p. 53.
114 Buber, *Tales of the Hassidim*, p. 70.
115 *Ibid.*
116 *Ibid.*, p. 66.
117 *Ibid.*, p. 74.
118 Schatz-Uffenheimer, *Quietist Elements*, p. 14.
119 Buber, *Tales of the Hassidim*, p. 73.
120 Buber, *Befardes Ha'Hassidut*, p. 6.
121 Schatz-Uffenheimer, *Quietist Elements*, p. 17.
122 Dubnow, *History of Hassidism*, p. 80.
123 Buber, *Tales of the Hassidim*, p. 84.
124 Horodezki, *Sefer Shivchei Habesht*, p. 110.
125 Buber, *Befardes Ha'Hassidut*, p. 70.
126 Buber, *Tales of the Hassidim*, p. 45.
127 *Ibid.*, p. 43.
128 *Ibid.*, p. 76.
129 *Ibid.*, p. 71.
130 Buber, *Befardes Ha'Hassidut*, p. 119.
131 *Ibid.*, p. 98.
132 Buber, *Tales of the Hassidim*, p. 13.
133 *Ibid.*, p. 54.
134 Scholem, *Major Trends in Jewish Mysticism*, p. 344.
135 Buber, *Tales of the Hassidim*, p. 68.
136 *Ibid.*, p. 48.
137 *Ibid.*, p. 55.
138 *Ibid.*, p. 66.
139 *Ibid.*
140 Schatz-Uffenheimer, *Hassidism as Mysticism*, p. 114.
141 *Ibid.*
142 *Ibid.*, p. 38.
143 *Ibid.*, p. 22.
144 Schatz-Uffenheimer, *Hassidism as Mysticism*, p. 24.
145 Dubnow, *The History of Hassidism*, p. 91.
146 Encyclopedia Judaica, 1st edn, "Dov Ber of Mezhirech."
147 Lammens, H., *Al-Hallag, un mystique musulman au IIIe siècle de l'Hégire*, Rech. sci. rel., 5 (1914), pp. 123–35.
148 Buber, *Befardes Ha'Hassidut*, p. 99.
149 Schatz-Uffenheimer, *Hassidism as Mysticism*, p. 108.
150 *Ibid.*, p. 108–9.

151 Buber, *Tales of the Hassidism*, p. 104.
152 Dubnow, *History of Hassidism*, p. 91.
153 Schatz-Uffenheimer, *Hassidism as Mysticism*, p. 103.
154 The Maggid of Mezhirech (Dov Baer), *Maggid Devarav Leya'akov*, p. 12.
155 Encyclopedia Judaica, 1st edn, "Dov Baer of Mezhirech."
156 Dubnow, *The History of Hassidism*, p. 86.
157 Encyclopedia Judaica, 1st edn, s. v. "Dov Baer of Mezhirech."
158 *Ibid.*
159 Buber, *Tales of the Hassidim*, p. 99.
160 *Ibid.*, p. 103.
161 Shoham, *Salvation Through the Gutters*, pt. 2.
162 Schatz-Uffenheimer, *Hassidism as Mysticism*, p. 43.
163 *Ibid.*, p. 56.
164 *Ibid.*, p. 190.
165 Haim Hazan, *The Limbo People* (London: Routledge and Kegan Paul, 1980).
166 Jacques Brel, *Oeuvre Integrale* (Paris: Robert Laffort, 1982), pp. 236–73.
167 Talmud Shabbat, p. 152.

3 Separant and Participant Cultures – The Social Component of the Tantalus Ratio

1 Oswald Spengler, *The Decline of the West*, vol. 1 (London: Allen & Unwin, 1954), p. 107.
2 Alfred L. Kroeber, *The Nature of Culture* (Chicago: University of Chicago Press, 1952), pp. 23–30.
3 Ruth Benedict, in *Culture and Behaviour* (New York: Free Press, 1962), p. 26.
4 Leslie White, in *ibid.*, p. 52.
5 Kroeber, *Anthropology: Culture Patterns and Processes* (New York: Harcourt, Brace & World, 1963), p. 101.
6 White, *The Science of Culture* (New York: Farrar, Strauss & Cudahy 1949), p. 25.
7 Spengler, *The Decline of the West*, vol. 1, p. 101.
8 Claude Lévi-Strauss, *The Savage Mind* (Chicago: University of Chicago Press, 1966), Introduction.
9 Benedict, *Patterns of Culture* (New York: Mentor Books, 1934), p. 54.
10 *Ibid.*, p. 220.
11 Kroeber, *Anthropology: Culture Patterns and Processes*, pp. 125–30.
12 Lévi-Strauss, *The Savage Mind*, p. 9.
13 Francis L. K. Hsu, *The Study of Literate Civilizations* (New York: Holt Rinehart & Winston, 1969), p. 86.
14 David Riesman, Nathan Glazer and Reuel Denney, *The Lonely Crowd* (New York: Doubleday/Anchor Books, 1953).
15 Erich Fromm, *Escape from Freedom* (New York: Farrar & Rinehart, 1942), p. 277.
16 Riesman *et al.*, *The Lonely Crowd*, p. 19.
17 Lucien Lévy-Bruhl, *How Natives Think* (New York: Washington Square Press, 1966), pp. 3–5.
18 Carl G. Jung, *Psychological Types* (London: Kegan Paul, Trench, Trubner, 1944), p. 616.
19 Lev Shestov, *Athens and Jerusalem* (New York: Simon & Schuster, 1968), p. 61.

20 Spengler, *The Decline of the West*, vol. 1, p. 10.
21 *Encyclopaedia Judaica* (Jerusalem: Keter, 1971), vol. 13, p. 1390.
22 David C. McClelland, *The Achieving Society* (Princeton, NJ: Van Nostrand, 1961), p. 50.
23 Gilbert Murray, *Five Stages of Greek Religion* (New York: Doubleday, 1955), pp. 4–5.
24 Bertrand Russell, *History of Western Philosophy* (London: Allen & Unwin, 1947), p. 383.
25 McClelland, *The Achieving Society*, p. 51.
26 Christmas Humphreys, *Buddhism* (Harmondsworth: Penguin, 1952), p. 81.
27 *Ibid.*, pp. 88–89.
28 Mircea Eliade, *Yoga: Immortality and Freedom* (Princeton, NJ: Princeton University Press, 1969), p. 9.
29 *Ibid.*, p. 8.
30 Humphreys, *Buddhism*, p. 87.
31 *Ibid.*, p. 49.
32 McClelland, *The Achieving Society*, p. 369.
33 Alan W. Watts, *The Way of Zen* (New York: Mentor Books, 1960), p. 108.
34 Spengler, *The Decline of the West*, vol. 1, p. 106.
35 Lévy-Bruhl, *How Natives Think*, pp. 3–4.
36 Lao Tzu, "Tao Te Ching", in Watts, *The Way of Zen*, p. 30.
37 *Ibid.*
38 Lao Tzu, *Tao Te Ching* (Harmondsworth: Penguin, 1963), p. 82.
39 Watts, *The Way of Zen*, p. 28.
40 *Ibid.*, p. 32.
41 *Ibid.*, p. 35.
42 Humphreys, *Buddhism*, p. 78.
43 *Ibid.*, p. 127.
44 *Ibid.*, p. 128.
45 Eliade, *Yoga: Immortality and Freedom*, p. 16.
46 *Ibid.*, p. 16.
47 Watts, *The Way of Zen*, p. 49.
48 *Ibid.*, p. 48.
49 Shlomo G. Shoham, *Salvation Through the Gutters* (Washington, DC: Hemisphere Publishing, 1978), p. 175
50 Humphreys, *Buddhism*, pp. 150–1.
51 *Ibid.*, p. 148.
52 Murray, *Five Stages of Greek Religion*, p. 144.
53 *Ibid.*, pp. 144–5.
54 McClelland, *The Achieving Society*, p. 368.
55 Despite the author's strenuous efforts to locate the source of these terms, the correct reference could not be traced, so the eventual critic is free to make the accusation of plagiarism; but then let him or her kindly reveal the work where these terms were originally used. Thank you.
56 McClelland, *The Achieving Society*, pp. 67, 107.
57 J. Ortega y Gasset, *Man and People* (New York: Norton, 1963), pp. 29–30.
58 Murray, *Five Stages of Greek Religion*, p. 44.
59 *Ibid,*, p. 59.
60 *Ibid.*, p. 125.
61 Humphreys, *Buddhism*, p. 50.

62 Eliade, *Yoga: Immortality and Freedom*, p. 27.

63 These figures were correct forty years ago, but even if the proportions are different today, the figures uphold our thesis. See McClelland, *The Achieving Society*, p. 2.

64 Murray, *Five Stages of Greek Religion*, p. 4.

65 Carl G. Jung, "Concerning Mandala Symbolism" in *Collected Works*, vol. 9, pt. 1 (London: Routledge & Kegan Paul, 1959), p. 356.

66 *Ibid.*, p. 357.

67 Humphreys, *Buddhism*, p. 89.

68 *Ibid.*, p. 81.

69 McClelland, *Achieving Society*, p. 455.

70 *Ibid.*, p. 178.

71 Kroeber, *Anthropology*, p. 109.

72 Shoham, *Society and the Absurd* (Oxford: Basil Blackwell, 1974), chapter 1.

73 Kroeber, *Anthropology*, p. 106.

74 See Arthur Koestler, *The Lotus and the Robot* (London: New English Library, 1964), p. 183.

75 Max Weber, *The Protestant Ethic and the Spirit of Capitalism*, trans. Talcott Parsons (New York: Scribner, 1958), p. 15.

76 Murray, *Five Stages of Greek Religion*, p. 119.

77 Lévy-Bruhl, *How Natives Think*, p. 51.

78 *Ibid.*, p. 24.

79 Lao Tzu, *Tao Te Ching*, vol. 1, p. 57.

80 Henry Bergson, *The Two Sources of Morality and Religion* (New York: Doubleday/Anchor, 1954), p. 99.

81 Lévy-Bruhl, *How Natives Think*, p. 61.

82 McClelland, *The Achieving Society*, pp. 169–70.

83 Koestler, *The Lotus and the Robot*, pp. 172–3.

84 Giuseppe di Lampedusa, *The Leopard* (New York: Pantheon, 1960), p. 146.

85 *Ibid.*

86 *Ibid.*

87 *Ibid.*, p. 151.

88 Eliade, *Yoga: Immortality and Freedom*, p. 373.

89 Ainslee Embree, ed., *Sources of Indian Tradition* (New York: Columbia University Press, 1958), p. 303.

90 Eliade, *Yoga: Immortality and Freedom*, pp. 228–9.

91 *Ibid.*, p. 192.

92 Humphreys, *Buddhism*, p. 149.

93 *Ibid.*, p. 151.

94 *Ibid.*, p. 144.

95 *Ibid.*, p. 155.

96 *Ibid.*, p. 87.

97 *Ibid.*, p. 86.

98 Watts, *Way of Zen*, p. 85.

99 *Ibid.*, p. 94.

100 Guy Ferchault, "Hector Berlioz: Grande Messe des Morts", introductory text to Berlioz's "Requiem", performed by the Bayerischen Rundfunks, conducted by Charles Munch and recorded by the Deutsche Grammophon Gesellschaft, p. 4.

101 Watts, *The Way of Zen*, p. 59.

102 Embree, *Sources of Indian Tradition*, p. 278.
103 Lao Tzu, *Tao Te Ching*, p. 58.
104 *Ibid.*, p. 59.
105 Humphreys, *Buddhism*, p. 121.
106 Lao Tzu, *Tao Te Ching*, p. 57.
107 *Ibid.*
108 Suttanipata (London: Pali Text Society), no. 1076; in H. W. Schumann, *Buddhism* (London: Rider, 1973), p. 83.
109 Spengler, *The Decline of the West*. vol. 1, p. 308.
110 Watts, *Way of Zen*, p. 63.
111 Seyyed Hossein Nasr, *Sufi Essays* (London: Allen & Unwin, 1972), p. 37.
112 Weber, *The Protestant Ethic and the Spirit of Capitalism*, p. 48.
113 R. H. Knapp and H. Green, "Time Judgement, Aesthetic Preference and Need Achievement", *Journal of Abnormal and Social Psychology* 58 (1960): pp. 140–2.
114 McClelland, *The Achieving Society*, p. 302.
115 *Ibid.*
116 Svend Ranulf, *Moral Indignation and Middle-class Psychology: A Sociological Study* (Copenhagen: Levin & Munksgaard, 1938).
117 Talcott Parsons *et al.*, *Theories of Society* (New York: Free Press, 1961), pp. 1262–3.
118 Max Weber, "On Protestantism and Capitalism", in *Protestant Ethic*, pp. 13–31.
119 Robert. K. Merton, *Social Theory and Social Structure* (New York: Free Press, 1964), p. 190.
120 *Ibid.*
121 McClelland, *Achieving Society*, p. 320
122 *Ibid., p.* 361.
123 *Ibid.*, p. 46.
124 R. H. Tawney in foreword to Weber, *The Protestant Ethic and the Spirit of Capitalism*, p. 23.
125 McClelland, *Achieving Society*, pp. 51, 100, 151.
126 *Ibid.*, p. 304.
127 *Ibid.*, p. 316.
128 *Ibid.*, pp. 317–18.
129 Merton, *Social Theory and Social Structure*, pp. 192–93.
130 Willard Waller, *The Family* (New York: Holt, Rinehart & Winston, 1938), pp. 190–1.
131 *Ibid.*, p. 191.
132 Chu Ch'an; in Watts, *The Way of Zen*, p. 103.
133 Shoham, *Society and the Absurd* (New York: Basil Blackwell Ltd., Oxford and Springers, 1974)
134 Joachim Israel, *Alienation* (Boston: Allyn & Bacon, 1971), p. 28.
135 Karl Marx, "Economic and Philosophical Manuscripts"; in *ibid.*, p. 38.
136 *Ibid.*, p. 51.
137 Emile Durkheim, *Suicide* (Glencoe, Ill.: Free Press, 1951), pp. 247–57.
138 Israel, *Alienation*.
139 Richard Schacht, *Alienation* (New York: Doubleday/Anchor, 1970).
140 F.L. Woodward, *Some Sayings of the Buddha* (London: Oxford University Press, 1973).

141 Watts, *The Way of Zen*, pp. 57–8.
142 Cited in Humphreys, *Buddhism*, p. 91.
143 Lao Tzu, *Tao Te Ching*, ch. 38.
144 *Ibid.*
145 Erich Fromm, *Man for Himself* (New York: Holt, Rinehart & Winston, 1947), pp. 83–97.
146 *Ibid.*, p. 97.
147 Sebastian DeGrazia, *The Political Community* (Chicago: University of Chicago Press, 1963), p. 64.
148 *Ibid.*, p. 60.
149 Martin Luther, "An Open Letter to the Christian Nobility", in *ibid.*, p. 60.
150 *Ibid.*, p. 63.
151 *Ibid.*, p. 61.
152 Weber, *The Protestant Ethic and the Spirit of Capitalism*, p. 172.
153 *Ibid.*, p. 182.
154 Humphreys, *Buddhism*, p. 184.
155 *Ibid.*, p. 100.
156 Watts, *The Way of Zen*, p. 29.
157 di Lampedusa, *The Leopard*, p. 151.
158 Seymour M. Lipset and Hans L. Zetterberg, "A Theory of Social Mobility", in *Class, Status and Power* (London: Routledge & Kegan Paul, 1953), p. 569.
159 Ferdinand Tönies, *Community and Society: Gemeinschaft und Gesellschaft* (East Lansing: Michigan University Press, 1957).
160 Weber, *The Theory of Social and Economic Organization* (New York: Free Press, 1964), pp. 115–17.
161 Henri Pirenne, "Stages in the Social History of Capitalism", in *Class, Status and Power*.
162 Douglas P. Crowne and David A. Marlowe, *The Approval Motive* (New York: Wiley, 1964), p. 189
163 McClelland, *The Achieving Society*, p. 160.
164 Riesman *et al.*, *The Lonely Crowd*, p. 32.
165 Weber, *The Theory of Social and Economic Organization*, p. 131.
166 Lévy-Bruhl, *How Natives Think*, p. 74
167 Karl Mannheim, *Ideology and Utopia* (New York: Harcourt, Brace, 1936), pp. 192–3.
168 *Ibid.*, p. 196.
169 *Ibid.*, p. 205.
170 Meister Eckhart, "Schriften und Predigten", in *Ideology and Utopia*, p. 215.
171 Murray, *Five Stages of Greek Religion*, p. 145.
172 Humphreys, *Buddhism*, p. 16.
173 Watts, *The Way of Zen*, p. 59.

4 Jews and Arabs – Relationship between Personality Types and Social Characters

1 Raphael Patai, *Israel between East and West* (Philadelphia: Jewish Publication Society of America, 1953), p. 20.
2 Moshe Beilinson, in *The Rebels Against Reality: The Book of the Second Aliya* (Tel Aviv: Am-Oved, 1947), p. 47.
3 *Ibid.*, p. 19.
4 Itzhak Tabenkin, "The Sources", in *ibid.*, p. 25.
5 Berl Katznelson, "The Miracle of the Second Aliya", in *ibid.*, p. 14

6 Patai, *Israel between East and West*, p. 16.
7 I. Shimoni, *The Arabs in Palestine* (Tel-Aviv: Am-Oved, 1947), p. 25.
8 *Ibid.*, p. 25.
9 Seyyed Hossein Nasr, *Sufi Essays* (London: Allen & Unwin, 1972), p. 30.
10 *Ibid.*, p. 43.
11 "Islam in Medieval India" in *Sources of Indian Tradition*, Ainslee Embree, ed. (New York: Columbia University Press, 1958), pp. 415–16; and Nasr, *Sufi Essays*, pp. 11–13, 18, 32.
12 Nasr, *Sufi Essays*, p. 17.
13 *Ibid.*, p. 36.
14 *Ibid.*, p. 33.
15 Shaykh Al-Arabi al-Darqawi, *Letters of a Sufi Martyr*, trans. Titus Burkhardt; in *ibid.*, p. 29.
16 Nasr, *Sufi Essays*, p. 43.
17 Shlomo G. Shoham, *Society and the Absurd* (Oxford: Basil Blackwell, 1974).
18 Shimoni, *The Arabs in Palestine*, p. 20.
19 *Ibid.*, p. 22.
20 Michael Assaf, *The Relationship between Arabs and Jews in Palestine* (Tel Aviv: Mifaley Tarbut Vechinuch, 1970), p. 80
21 J. Waschitz, *The Arabs in Palestine* (Merhavia: Sifriat Poalim), p. 195.
22 *Ibid.*
23 Joseph Vitkin, "A Manifesto to the Youth of Israel whose Heart is With Their Nation and With Zion", *Hapoel-Hatzair* 1 (1935): p. 33.
24 Joseph Hayyim Brenner, in *Rebels Against Reality*, pp. 22–3.
25 From the charter of the corporation, "The Land and the Labour", incorporated at the beginning of this century by a group of pioneers of the First Aliya.
26 Jonah Horowitz, "From the Conquest of Labour to Settlement", in *Rebels Against Reality*, p. 215.
27 Oswald Spengler, *The Decline of the West*, vol. 1 (London: Allen & Unwin, 1954), p. 171; vol. 2, pp. 314–15.
28 Taufiq-El-Haquim, *The Diary of an Egyptian Rural Prosecutor* (Tel Aviv: Am-Oved, 1945).
29 Nasr, *Sufi Essays*, p. 16.
30 *Ibid.*, pp. 36–37.
31 *Ibid.*, p. 69.
32 J. Waschitz, *The Arabs in Palestine*, p. 193.
33 Assaf, *The Relationship between Arabs and Jews in Palestine*, pp. 66, 68, 74.
34 See Chapter 2 of this book.
35 Netta Harpaz, "The Trials of Conquest" in *Rebels Against Reality*, p. 225.
36 Shmuel N. Eisenstadt *et al.*, *Israel: A Society in the Making* (Jerusalem: Magnes Press, 1972), pp. 66–67.
37 *Encyclopaedia Judaica*, vol. 9 (Jerusalem: Keter, 1971), p. 848.
38 Berl Katznelson and J. Kaufman, eds., *The Collected Works of Nahman Sirkin*, vol. 1 (Tel Aviv: Davar, 1939) pp. 73–4.
39 Nasr, *Sufi Essays*, p. 78.
40 *Ibid.*, p. 79.
41 *Ibid.*
42 "Be Strong", poem by the Hebrew poet David Shimoni.
43 "Strongholds of Jewish freedom fighters", poem in Ze'ev Jabotinsky, "Defiance", the anthem of Betar, the Revisionist Zionist Youth Movement.

44 Yael Dayan, *Envy the Frightened* (London: Weidenfeld & Nicolson, 1961), p. 10.
45 M. Amiad, in *Rebels Against Reality*, p. 437.
46 Joseph Trumpeldor, "The Pioneer: His Nature and Goals", in *The Book of Pioneers*, ed. M. Bassouk (Jerusalem: Jewish Agency, 1940), pp. 24–5.
47 S. Tsemach, in *Rebels Against Reality*, p. 31.
48 Spengler, *The Decline of the West*, vol. 2, p. 362.
49 Haj is a revered title for those who made the pilgrimage to Mecca.
50 Waschitz, *Arabs in Palestine*, p. 135.
51 El-Haquim, *The Diary of an Egyptian Rural Prosecutor*, pp. 49–50, 58, 100.
52 Menahem Cohen, in *Rebels Against Reality*, p. 259.
53 See Chapter 2 of this book.
54 Ben-Zion Israeli, in *Rebels Against Reality*, p. 421.
55 Nathan Shifris, in *Ibid.*, p. 195.
56 See Chapter 2 of this book.
57 *Rebels Against Reality*, p. 232.
58 *Ibid.*, p. 13.
59 David C. McClelland, *The Achieving Society* (Princeton, NJ: Van Nostrand 1961), p. 167.
60 Itzhak Rosenblat, "Wandering", in *Rebels Against Reality*, p. 251.
61 *Ibid.*, p. 225.
62 Eliyahu Even Tov, in *ibid.*, p. 183.
63 Moshe Salomon, *Scrolls of Fire, The Diaries of Soldiers* (Tel-Aviv: Ma'arochet, 1950), p. 390.
64 Uri Fried, *ibid.*, p. 689.
65 *Rebels Against Reality*, p. 191.
66 *Ibid.*, p. 219.
67 *Ibid.*, pp. 251, 426.
68 *Ibid.*, p. 42.
69 *Ibid.*, p. 39.
70 Patai, *Israel between East and West*, pp. 47–8.
71 Nasr, *Sufi Essays*, p. 87.
72 S. Tsemach, "In the Beginning", in *Rebels Against Reality*, p. 34.
73 Patai, *Israel between East and West*, p. 40.
74 Arnold J. Toynbee, *A Study of History* vol. 1 (New York: Dell, 1965), p. 51.
75 Gilbert Murray, *Five Stages of Greek Religion*, chs. 1 and 4.
76 David Riesman, Nathan Glazer and Reuel Denney, *The Lonely Crowd* (New York: Doubleday/Anchor Books, 1953), p. 23.
77 *Time Magazine*. Date not located.
78 Shoham, ed., *Israel Studies in Criminology* (Tel Aviv: Gomeh, 1970), vol. 1; and *Israel Studies in Criminology* (Jerusalem: Jerusalem Academic Press, 1972–3), vol. 2.
79 Shoham, *Society and the Absurd*.
80 Shoham, *The Mark of Cain* (New York: Israel Universities Press/Oceana Publications, 1970).
81 Shoham, *Society and the Absurd*, ch. 1.
82 Frederico Fellini, in an interview given to *Time Magazine*, 4 February 1974.
83 Robert S. Ellwood, *One Way* (Los Angeles: University of Southern California Press, 1973).
84 Christmas Humphreys, *Buddhism* (Harmondsworth: Penguin, 1952), p. 31.

5 *The Twenty-First Century Kulturkampf – Fundamentalist Isalm against Occidental Culture*

1 Oriana Fallaci, *The Rage and the Pride* (Tel Aviv: Dvir, 2003).
2 *Ibid.*, p. 22.
3 Anat Berko, "The Moral Infrastructure of Chief Perpetrators of Suicide Terrorism", Unpublished Ph.D. Thesis.
4 *Ibid.*, p. 9.
5 *Ibid.*, p. 10.
6 Oriana Fallaci, *The Rage and the Pride*, p. 23.
7 *Ibid.*, p. 50.
8 Samuel P. Huntington, *The Clash of Civilizations* (Jerusalem: Mercas Shalem, 2003, in Hebrew).
9 *Ibid.*, p. 20.
10 Alfred L. Kroeber, *Anthropology*, rev. edn (New York, Harcourt Brace, 1948).
11 Arnold J. Toynbee, *A Study of History* (New York: Dell, 1965).
12 Thorsten Sellin, "Culture Conflict and Crime", in *Social Science Research Journal*, p. 41.
13 Shlomo G. Shoham, Esther Segal and Giora Rahav, "Secularisation, Deviance and Delinquency among Israeli Arab Villagers", *Human Relations* and *Megamot* (1975, Hebrew).
14 *Ibid.*, p. 86.
15 *Ibid.*, p. 87.
16 Ronald Dore, "Unity and Diversity in Contemporary World Culture" in *The Expansion of International Cultures*, pp. 421–8.
17 Giora Shoham, Nahum Shoham and Adnan Abd-El-Razek, *British Criminology*, October (1966): pp. 391–409.
18 Huntington, *The Clash of Civilizations*, p. 137.
19 *Ibid.*, pp. 347–9.
20 Eric D. Schneider and James J. Kay, "Life as a Manifestation of the Second Law of Thermodynamics," *Mathematical and Computer Modelling* 19, 6–8 (1994): pp. 25–48.
21 *Ibid.*, p. 27.
22 Ilya Prigogine, *Thermodynamics of Irreversible Processes* (New York: John Wiley, 1955).
23 Joseph Kestin, *A Course in Thermodynamics* (Waltham, MA: Blaisdell Publishing Co, 1966).
24 Prigogine and Isabelle Stengers, *Order Out of Chaos* (New York: Bantam, 1984), pp. 160–7.
25 Jean Piaget, *Structuralism*. (London: Routledge and Kegan Paul, 1971), p. 5.
26 Ludwig Boltzman, "The Second Law of Thermodynamics", in *Theoretical Physics and Philosophical Problems* (1974).
27 Schneider and Kay, "Life as a Manifestation of the Second Law of Thermodynamics, pp. 37–8.
28 Prigogine and Stengers, *Order Out of Chaos*, p. 206.
29 Manfred Halpern, "Four Contrasting Repertories of Human Relations in Islam", in *Psychological Dimension of Near Eastern Studies* (Princeton, New Jersey: The Darwin Press, 1977), pp. 60–102.
30 Emile Durkheim, *Suicide* (Glencoe, Ill.: Free Press, 1951), pp. 131–60.

309

31 Robert K. Merton, "Anomie, Anomia and Social Interaction, Contexts of Deviant Behaviour", *Anomie and Deviant Behavior* (Glenoce, Ill.: Free Press, 1964).

32 *Ibid.*, p. 213.

33 We have used the form of 'accidia' and not 'accidie' to resemble the personalized 'anomia' and not group-based 'amonie'.

34 Leo Srole, "Social Integration and Certain Corollaries. An Exploratory Study", *Am. Soc. Rev.* 21 (1956): pp. 709–16.

35 Melvin Seeman, "On the Meaning of Alienation", *American Sociological Review* 24 (1959), pp. 83–91.

36 Menachem Rosner, *Hitnakrut: Alienation — A Comprehensive Analysis of the Marxist Exposition of Alienation* (Hadera: Givat Haviva, 1967)

37 Georgy Lukacs, *Existentialism and Marxism* (Tel Aviv: Hakibutz-Hameuchad, 1950).

38 Jean-Paul Sartre, *Being and Nothingness,* part 3 (New York: Citadel Press, 1965).

39 Walter Kaufmann, *Critique of Religion and Philosophy* (New York: Harper & Brothers, 1958), p. 259.

40 Albert Camus, *The Fall* (New York: Vintage Books, 1956), p. 84.

41 Seeman, "On the Meaning of Alienation", p. 534.

42 Albert Camus, *The Stranger* (New York: Vintage Books, 1954), p. 103.

43 *Ibid.*, p. 105.

44 Camus, *The Fall*, p. 87.

45 Jeremy Rifkin, *Entropy: A New World View* (New York: Viking Press, 1980), pp. 188–93.

46 Levon H. Melikean, "The Modal Personality of Saudi College Students: A Study in National Characters", in L. Carl Brown and Norman Itzkowitz, *Psychological Dimensions of Near East Studies* (Princeton, NJ: Darwin Press, 1977), pp. 166–209.

47 This Tzarist forgery is a runaway bestseller in the Muslim Middle East and North Africa.

48 Juval Portugali, *Self-Organization and the City* (Heidelberg: Springer-Verlag, 2000), Foreword.

49 Huntington, *The Clash of Civilizations*, p. 127.

50 *Ibid.*, p. 133.

51 Albert Camus, *The Rebel* (London: Hamish Hamilton, 1953), p. 83.

52 Mishna Avot.

6 Interaction, Objectilessness and the Self-Continuum

1 Chad Gordon and Kenneth. J. Gergen, eds, *The Self in Social Interaction* (New York: Wiley, 1968), p. 3.

2 Pitirim A. Sorokin, *Society, Culture and Personality: Their Structure and Dynamics* (New York: Harper, 1947), p. 349.

3 Erik H. Erikson, *Childhood and Society* (Harmondsworth: Penguin, 1969), p. 253.

4 Theodore. E. Sarbin, "A Preface to a Psychological Analysis of the Self", *Self in Social Interaction*, p. 179.

5 Charles. H. Cooley, "On the Meaning of the Social Self", in *ibid.*, p. 89.

6 George. H. Mead, "The Genesis of the Self", in *ibid.*, p. 57.

7 Edmund Husserl, *Ideas* (London: Allen & Unwin, 1958), p. 233; Clark E. Moustakas, "True Experience and The Self", in *The Self in Growth, Teaching and Learning* (Englewood Cliffs, NJ: Prentice-Hall, 1965), p. 41.

8 Gordon, "Self-Conceptions: Configurations of Content", in *The Self in Social Interaction*, p. 116.

9 Harry S. Sullivan, "Beginnings of the Self-System", in *Ibid.*, p. 174.

10 Seymour Fisher and S. E. Cleveland, *Body Image and Personality* (Princeton, NJ: Van Nostrand, 1958).

11 Robert Ardrey, *The Social Contract* (London: Collins/Fontana Library, 1972), p. 226.

12 Robert. R. Holt, "Individuality and Generalization in the Psychology of Personality", in *Personality* (Harmondsworth: Penguin, 1967), p. 42.

13 Kenneth Clarke, *Civilization* (London: BBC, 1970), p. 26.

14 Shlomo G. Shoham, *Society and the Absurd* (Oxford: Basil Blackwell, 1974), p. 168.

15 Holt, "Individuality and Generalization in the Psychology of Personality", in *Personality*, p. 38.

16 Shoham, *Salvation Through the Gutters* (Washington, DC: Hemisphere Publishing, 1978), chapter 1.

17 Husserl, *Ideas*, p. 232.

18 Eugen Herrigel, *The Method of Zen* (New York: Vintage Books, 1960), p. 39.

19 P. F. Strawson, "Persons", in *Essays in Philosophical Psychology* (New York: Doubleday/Anchor, 1964), p. 377.

20 Sigmund Freud, *Civilization and its Discontents* (London: Imago, 1950).

21 Gordon W. Allport, "Is the Concept of Self Necessary?" in *Self in Social Interaction*, p. 27.

22 Strawson "Persons", 381.

23 *Ibid.*

24 Salvatore R. Maddi, *Personality Theories: A Comparative Analysis* rev. edn (Homewood, Ill.: Dorsey Press, 1972), p. 150.

25 Carlos Castaneda, *The Teachings of Don Juan; A Separate Reality; Journey to Ixtlan*, 3 vols. (Harmondsworth: Penguin, 1974).

26 William James, "The Self", in *Self in Social Interaction*, p. 47.

27 Mead, *Mind, Self and Society* (Chicago: University of Chicago Press, 1962), pp. 140, 223.

28 Gordon and Gergen, *The Self in Social Interaction*, pp. 31–2.

29 Abraham H. Maslow, "Cognition of Being in the Peak Experiences", in *Self in Growth, Teaching and Learning*, pp. 172, 182.

30 Alan W. Watts, *The Way of Zen* (New York: Mentor Books, 1960), pp. 81–2.

31 *Ibid.*, p. 56.

32 *Ibid.*

33 *Ibid.*, p. 155.

34 Shoham, *Salvation Through the Gutters*, pt. 2.

35 W. Ronald Fairbairn, *Psychoanalytic Studies of the Personality* (London: Tavistock, 1966), pp. 103, 108.

36 Robert. E. Ornstein, *The Psychology of Consciousness* (San Francisco: Freeman, 1972), pp. 126–28.

37 Castaneda, *The Teachings of Don Juan*, p. 71.

38 Husserl, *Ideas*, p. 233.

39 Shoham, *Salvation Through the Gutters*, pt. 1.
40 Talmud Berachot.
41 Maslow, "Cognition of Being in the Peak Experiences", p. 173.
42 *Ibid.*, pp. 173, 177–8.
43 Woodburn Heron, "The Pathology of Boredom", in *Altered States of Awareness: Readings from Scientific American* (San Francisco: Freeman, 1972), pp. 60–4.
44 Castaneda, *Teachings of Don Juan*, p. 106.
45 *Ibid.*, p. 70.
46 *Ibid.*
47 Husserl, *Ideas*, pp. 246–47.
48 In *Introduction to Metaphysics*, Henri Bergson says: "pure duration excludes all idea of juxtaposition, reciprocal exteriority, and extension" in *Readings in 20th Century Philosophy* (New York: Free Press, 1963), p. 49.
49 Carl G. Jung, *The Structure and Dynamics of the Psyche* (London: Routledge & Kegan Paul, 1969), p. 199.
50 Shoham, *Salvation Through the Gutters*, pt. 3.
51 Jung, "Synchronicity: An Acausal-Connecting Principle", in *Structure and Dynamics of the Psyche*, p. 446.
52 Elizabeth Förster-Nietzche, ed., *The Nietzsche-Wagner Correspondence* (London: Duckworth, 1922), p. 22.
53 Jacques Riviere, "Dada Manifesto" in *The Collected Works of Antonin Artaud* (London: Calder & Boyars, 1968), p. 10.
54 The Jungian conception of libidinal energy is more extended and different in many ways than the Freudian libido. Jung also envisages the transformation of libidinal energy by the clashes of psychic forces. Jung, however, defines these forces, i.e. progression and regression, in a quite different manner than we envisage the dynamics of our components of the self. Also his conflicting forces do not interact dialectically and his conflicting entities, unlike our polarities, seem to be the conscious and the unconscious. See Jung, *Structure and the Dynamics of the Psyche*, pp. 3, 33, 36–37, 39, 71, 406.
55 Ornstein, *The Psychology of Consciousness*, p. 50.
56 Shoham, *Society and the Absurd*, pp. 27 et. seq.
57 Shoham, *Salvation Through the Gutters*, pt. 1.
58 *Ibid.*, pt. 3.
59 Sullivan, *The Interpersonal Theory of Psychiatry* (New York: Norton, 1953), p. 164.
60 Fairbairn, *Psychoanalytic Studies of the Personality*, p. 105.
61 Alston and Nakhnikian, eds, *Readings in 20th Century Philosophy*, p. 624.
62 In order to avoid polemics we shall not delve into comparisons among our *Ani*, Martin Heidegger's *das sein* and Jean-Paul Sartre's *pour soi*. The differences, however, between our *Ani* and the existentialist's "authentic self" are apparent both conceptually and materially. For the basic Existentialist conceptualizations of self, see Heidegger, *Being and Time* (Oxford: Blackwell, 1962); and Sartre, *Being and Nothingness* (New York: Citadel Press, 1956).
63 *The Philosophy of Plotinus: A Representative Book from the Enneads* (New York: Appleton Century-Crofts, 1950), p.97.
64 Gershom G. Scholem, *Major Trends in Jewish Mysticism* (New York: Schocken Books, 1961), p. 4.

65 Alan Watts, *The Way of Zen*, p. 44.
66 Rudolf Bultman, *Kerygma and Myth* (London: Billing, 1960), p. 1.
67 Heidegger, *Sein und Zeit* (Halle: Max Niemeyer, 1927), p. 7.
68 David Bakan, *The Duality of Human Existence* (Chicago: Rand McNally, 1966).
69 Castaneda, *Separate Reality*, p. 147.
70 *Ibid.*, p. 149.
71 "Dionysius the Areopagite: The Mystical Theology", in *Mysticism* (Harmondsworth: Penguin, 1963), p. 190.
72 "Meister Eckhart: Godhead, God and the Soul", in *ibid.*, p. 238.
73 Friedrich Schulze-Maizier, *Meister Eckhart's Deutsche Predigten und Tractate* (Leipzig, 1938), Tractatus XI.
74 Josef Quint, "Meister Eckhart's Predigten Herausgegeben", in *Meister Eckhart: Die Deutschen und Lateinischen Werke* (Stuttgart-Berlin, 1936), Sermon XCIX.
75 Raymond B. Blakney, *Meister Eckhart: A Modern Translation* (New York: Harper Torchbooks, 1957), p. 80.
76 Quint, "Meister Eckhart's Predigten Herausgegeben", Sermon 1.
77 Schulze-Maizier, *Meister Eckhart's Deutsche Predigten und Tractate*, Tractatus XI.
78 *Ibid.*, Tractatus XI.
79 *Ibid.*, Tractatus II.
80 Nicholas of Cusa, *Of Learned Ignorance* (London: Routledge & Kegan Paul, 1914), ch. 13.
81 *Ibid.*, ch. 12.
82 Stanza XIV in Happold, *Mysticism*, p. 334.
83 Jacob Boehme, *Six Theosophic Points and Other Writings* (Ann Arbor: University of Michigan Press, 1958).
84 Husserl, *Ideas*, p. 13.
85 *Ibid.*, p. 17.
86 Medard Boss, "What Makes us Behave at all Socially?", *Review of Existential Psychology and Psychiatry* 4, 1 (1964): pp. 53–68.
87 Maslow, "Peak Experiences as Acute Experiences", *American Journal of Psychoanalysis* 21 (1961): pp. 254–60.
88 Aldous Huxley, *Point Counter Point* (New York: Modern Library, 1928), p. 266.
89 Castaneda, *Teachings of Don Juan*, p. 137.
90 *Ibid.*, pp. 148–9.
91 Castaneda, *Separate Reality*, p. 11.
92 Tetra-hydro-cannabinol, the active narcotic agent in cannabis.
93 Castaneda, *Separate Reality*, pp. 63, 66.
94 *Ibid.*, pp. 90–91.
95 *Ibid.*, p. 93.
96 *Ibid.*, p. 77.
97 *Ibid.*, p. 85.
98 Castaneda, *Teachings of Don Juan*, p. 241.
99 *Ibid.*, pp. 170–71.
100 *Ibid.*, p. 144.
101 Castaneda, *Separate Reality*, p. 88.
102 *Ibid.*, p. 168.
103 Castaneda, *Teachings of Don Juan*, p. 83.

104 Castaneda, *Separate Reality*, p. 112.
105 *Ibid.*, pp. 11, 37, 86.
106 *Ibid.*, p. 153.
107 Sartre, *The Transcendence of the Ego* (New York: Noonday Press, 1957).
108 Castaneda, *Teachings of Don Juan*, p. 33.
109 *Ibid.*, p. 155.
110 Husserl, *Ideas*, p. 239.
111 Castaneda, *Teachings of Don Juan*, pp. 134, 138–139.
112 *Ibid.*, p. 73.
113 Castaneda, *Separate Reality*, p. 153.
114 *Ibid.*, p. 150.
115 Johann W. von Goethe, *Faust* (New York: Modern Library, 1950), p. 43.
116 Mead, *Mind, Self and Society*, p. 140.
117 Gordon and Gergen, eds, *Self in Social Interaction*, p. 37.
118 Erving Goffman, *The Presentation of Self in Everyday Life* (Edinburgh: University of Edinburgh Social Science Research Center, 1958), p. 11.
119 Freud, *Beyond the Pleasure Principle* (London: International Psycho-Analytical Press, 1922), p. 1.
120 Maddi, *Personality Theories*, pp. 43–45.
121 Fairbairn, *Psychoanalytic Studies of the Personality*.
122 Elizabeth Förster-Nietzsche, ed., *Nietzsche-Wagner Correspondence*, p. 217.

7 Self, Choice and Uniqueness

1 Shlomo G. Shoham, *Salvation Through the Gutters* (Washington, DC: Hemisphere Publishing, 1978); and also Chapters 1–3 of this book.
2 Shoham, *Salvation Through the Gutters*, ch. 8.
3 Ross Stagner, *Psychology of Personality* (New York: McGraw-Hill, 1961).
4 Shoham, *Salvation Through the Gutters*, Introduction.
5 W. Ronald Fairbairn, *Psychoanalytic Studies of the Personality* (London: Tavistock, 1966), p. 105.
6 Talmud Sanhedrin, ch. 4.
7 Teilhard de Chardin, *The Phenomenon of Man* (New York: Harper Torchbooks, 1965), pp. 258–59.
8 P. F. Strawson, "Persons", in *Essays in Philosophical Psychology* (New York: Doubleday/Anchor, 1964), p. 377.
9 Rivka Schatz-Uffenheimer, *Quietistic Elements in Hassidic Thought* (Jerusalem: Magnes Press, 1968), p. 124.
10 Carlos Castaneda, *The Teachings of Don Juan* (Harmondsworth: Penguin, 1974), p. 50.
11 Edmund Husserl, *Ideas* (London: Allen & Unwin, 1958), p. 14.
12 Max Stirner, *The Ego and His Own* (London: Jonathan Cape, 1971), p. 41.
13 *Ibid.*, p. 139.
14 Shoham, *Society and the Absurd* (Oxford: Basil Backwell, 1974), p. 53.
15 Jean Piaget, *The Child's Conception of the World* (Frogmore, St. Albans: Paladin, 1973), pp. 188–89.
16 Salvatore Maddi, *Personality Theories: A Comparative Analysis*, rev. edn (Homewood, Ill.: Dorsey Press, 1972), p. 51.
17 Shoham, *The Mark of Cain* (New York: Israel Universities Press/Oceana Publications, 1970), Introduction.
18 *Ibid.*, p. 218.

8 Man, Others and Things – The Phenomenology of Interaction

1 Shlomo G. Shoham, *The Bridge to Nothingness: Gnosis, Kabbalah, Existentialism and the Transcendental Predicament of Man* (Cranbury, NJ: Associated University Press, 1994).

2 Lao Tzu, *Tao Te Ching* (Harmondsworth: Penguin, 1963), p. 57.

3 Daisetz T. Suzuki, *What Is Zen?* (New York: Harper & Row, 1972), p. 1.

4 Fischel Lachover and Isaiah Tishby, *The Wisdom of the Zohar* (Jerusalem: Bialik Institute, 1971), pp. 100–101.

5 Philebus, *The Dialogues of Plato*, vol. 2 (New York: Random House, 1937), p. 389.

6 J. Landau, *The Desire of Matter Towards Form in Aristotle's Philosophy* (Tel-Aviv: Tel-Aviv University Press, 1972).

7 Elizabeth Förster-Nietzche, ed., *The Nietzsche-Wagner Correspondence* (London-Duckworth, 1922), p. 217.

8 "Misery", in *Great Stories by Anton Chekhov* (New York: Dell 1970), p. 11.

9 Shoham, *Society and the Absurd* (Oxford: Basil Blackwell, 1974), chs. 2, 3.

10 Milton Rokeach, *The Three Christs of Ypsilanty* (New York: Random House, 1964), p. 201.

11 Jean-Paul Sartre, *Being and Nothingness* (New York: Citadel Press, 1965), Pt.3.

12 Shoham, *The Mark of Cain* (New York: Israel Universities Press/Oceana Publications, 1970), chs. 3, 4.

13 *Ibid.*, ch. 3, p. 45.

14 Willard W. Waller and R. Hill, *The Family: A Dynamic Interpretation* (New York: Dryden Press, 1951), p. 113.

15 Douglas P. Crowne and David A. Marlowe, *The Approval Motive* (New York: Wiley, 1964), p. 76.

16 Jerome S. Bruner, "Perceptual Processes and the Self", in *The Self in Growth, Teaching and Learning* (Englewood Cliffs, NJ: Prentice-Hall, 1965), p. 125.

17 Shoham, *Salvation Through the Gutters* (Washington, DC: Hemisphere Publishing, 1978), pt. 2.

18 Shoham, *Mark of Cain*, chs. 4–7.

19 Shoham, *Society and the Absurd*, ch. 4.

20 *Ibid.*, chs. 2–3.

21 Sartre, *Being and Nothingness*, chapter 4.

22 Helen M. Lynd, *On Shame and the Search for Identity* (New York: Science Editions, 1961), p. 22.

23 A. Petrie *et al.*, "The Tolerance for Pain and for Sensory Deprivation", *American Journal of Psychology* 123, 1 (1960): pp. 80–90.

24 Bruner, "Perceptual Processes and the Self", p. 127.

25 George C. Homans, *Social Behaviour* (London: Routledge & Kegan Paul, 3973), p. 40.

26 Bruner, "Perceptual Processes and the Self", p. 122.

27 Alfred Schutz, *The Phenomenology of the Social World* (London: Heinemann Educational Books, 1972), p. 97.

28 See Renato Tagiuri and Luigi Petrullo, *Person, Perception and Interpersonal Behaviour* (Stanford: Stanford University Press, 1965), p. xi.

29 *Ibid.*, p. xiii.

30 Erving Goffman, *The Presentation of Self in Everyday Life* (New York:

Anchor Books, 1959); and Goffman, *Interaction Ritual* (New York: Doubleday/Anchor Books, 1967), p. 32.
31 Goffman, *Interaction Ritual*, pp. 15–23.
32 Goffman, *The Presentation of Self in Everyday Life*, p. 42.
33 Shoham, *Society and the Asburd*, ch. 2.
34 *Ibid.*, ch. 2.
35 Søren Kierkegaard, *The Present Age* (London: Oxford University Press, 1940), p. 38.
36 Shoham, *Society and the Absurd*; and Shoham, *Salvation Through the Gutters*, Pt. 1.
37 Shoham, *Mark of Cain*, chapter 2.
38 Aleksandr Solzhenitsyn, *The Gulag Archipelago*, vol. 1 (New York: Harper & Row, 1974), p. 15.

9 The Isaac Syndrome

1 Haim Vital, *Etz Haim* (Jerusalem: Research Center of Kaballah, 1978), p. 27.
2 John W. Thibaut and Harold M. Kelley, *The Social Psychology of Groups* (New York: Wiley, 1959), p. 19.
3 W. Ronald Fairbairn, *Psychoanalytic Studies of the Personality* (London: Tavistock, 1966), p. 31.
4 See Gordon Bermant and Julian M. Davidson, *Biological Bases of Sexual Behaviour* (New York: Harper and Row, 1974), p. 261.
5 Philip Slater, *The Glory of Hera* (Boston: Beacon Press, 1968), pp. 135–6.
6 Paul Watzlawick, "A Review of the Double Bind Theory", *Family Process* 2 (1963): pp. 132–53.
7 D. Lévy, *Behavioural Analysis* (Springfield, Mass.: C. C. Thomas, 1958), p. 25.
8 John Bowlby, *Attachment* (New York: Pelican Books, 1972), p. 76.
9 K. S. Winter, "Characteristics of Fantasy While Nursing," *Journal of Personality* 37 (1969): pp. 58–71.
10 Niles Newton, *Maternal Emotions* (New York: Paul B. Hoeber, 1955), p. 103.
11 Robert R. Sears, Eleanor E. Maccoby, and Harry Levin, *Patterns of Child Rearing* (Evanston, Ill.: Row, Peterson, 1957), p. 96.
12 Seymour Fisher, *The Female Orgasm* (New York: Basic Books, 1973), p. 153.
13 Fairbairn, *Psychoanalytic Studies of the Personality*, p. 144.
14 Karl Abraham, *Selected Papers*, p. 395.
15 *Ibid.*, p. 265.
16 Fisher, *The Female Orgasm*, p. 153.
17 Abraham, *Selected Papers*, pp. 254–65.
18 *Ibid.*, p. 265.
19 *Ibid.*, p. 334.
20 Shlomo G. Shoham, *Salvation Through the Gutters* (Washington, DC: Hemisphere Publishing, 1978), pt. 3.
21 *Ibid.*, introduction.
22 Erich Wellisch, *Isaac and Oedipus* (London: Routledge & Kegan Paul, 1954), p. 27; and David Bakan, *The Duality of Human Existence* (Chicago: 1966), 201ff.
23 Genesis 22:13.

24 Kings 14:29.
25 Genesis Raba 22:13; and Shalom Spiegel, "Meagadot Ha'akedah," in *Festschrift* (New York: The Jewish Theological Seminary, 1940), p. 497.
26 Spiegel, *Festschrift*, p. 491.
27 *Ibid.*, p. 487; and Talmud Zevachim, 62, side 1.
28 Spiegel, *Festschrift*, p. 473.
29 Martin McNamara, *The New Testament and the Palestinian Targum to the Pentateuch* (Rome: Pontifical Biblical Institute, 1966), 164ff; G. Vermes, *Scripture and Tradition in Judaism* (Leiden; E. J. Brill, 1961), pp. 205–7.
30 Wellisch, *Isaac and Oedipus*, p. 66.
31 *Ibid.*, pp. 13–14, 63.
32 Aelianus, *De Natura Animalium*, XII, 34.
33 Wellisch, *Isaac and Oedipus*, p. 58.
34 For a survey of infanticidal impulses in fairy-tales see Bakan, *Slaughter of the Innocents* (San Francisco: Jossey-Bass, 1971), 57ff.
35 Wellisch, *Isaac and Oedipus*, pp. 8, 63.
36 *Ibid.*, p. 19.
37 *Ibid.*, p. 20.
38 Bakan, *Slaughter of the Innocents*, 78ff
39 Genesis 12:15.
40 Bakan, *The Duality of Human Existence* (Chicago: Rand MacNally, 1966), pp. 212–14.
41 Genesis 20:1–2.
42 Exodus 20:12.
43 Edward S. Stern, "The Mother's Homicidal Wishes to Her Child," *The Journal of Mental Science* 94 (British Journal of Psychology, 1948): pp. 324–5.
44 Shoham, *Salvation Through the Gutters*, pt. 2.
45 Genesis Raba 22:1.
46 Wellisch, *Isaac and Oedipus*, 95ff.
47 Y. A. Cohen, *The Transition from Childhood to Adolescence* (Chicago: Aldine Publishing Co., 1964), p. 105.
48 Wellisch, *Isaac and Oedipus*, pp. 89, 114.
49 Wellisch, *Isaac and Oedipus*, p. 10; and Bakan, *The Duality of Human Existence*, p. 230.
50 Shoham, *The Mark of Cain* (New York: Oceana Publications, 1970), chapter 3.
51 John Campbell, "Travels in South Africa, Second Journey", in *Isaac and Oedipus*, p. 29.
52 *Ibid.*
53 Shoham, *The Tantalus Ratio*, pp. 119–44.
54 Genesis Raba 22:9.
55 *Time Magazine*, 15 July, 1975.
56 Bakan, *The Duality of Human Existence*, p. 211.
57 Spiegel, *The Myth of the Akedah*, p. 24.
58 Mekhilta of Rabbi Ishmael, pp. 57, 88.
59 Leviticus Raba 29:9, and other sources, in G. Vermes, *Scripture and Tradition*, p. 213.
60 Wellisch, *Isaac and Oedipus*, pp. 11–12, 15.
61 Søren Kierkegaard, *Fear and Trembling* (New York: Doubleday Anchor, 1954), p. 78.

62 Genesis Raba 22:12.
63 Genesis Raba 22:7–8.
64 *Ibid.*
65 Spiegel, *The Myth of the Akedah*, pp. 21– 3.
66 Geza Vermes, *Scripture and Tradition in Judaism*, p. 194.
67 *Ibid.*, p. 198.
68 Sifre Deuteronomy 32, cited in Vermes, *Scripture and Tradition*, p. 197.
69 Genesis Raba 22:3.
70 Romans 7:31–32.
71 Friedrich Nietzsche, *The Antichrist* (New York: Arno Press, 1972), p. 293.
72 Berochot 11B.
73 Cohen. *Transition from Childhood*, p. 105.
74 Graves, *The Greek Myths*, vol. 1, p. 91.
75 Euripides, *Iphigenia in Aulis*, *The Complete Greek Drama*, vol. 2 (New York: Random House, 1938), p. 323.
76 *Ibid.*, p. 334.
77 Herbert R. Lottman, *Albert Camus* (New York: Doubleday, 1979).

10 *Rebellion and Yearning*

1 Ralph W. Emerson, *Selections* (Boston: Houghton Mifflin Co., 1960), p. 147.
2 Albert Camus, *The Rebel* (Harmondsworth: Penguin, 1962), p. 19.
3 *Ibid,*, p. 22.
4 Camus, *The Plague* (New York: Vintage Books, 1972), p. 1967.
5 See Chapters 1 and 2 of this book.
6 Martin Heidegger, *Existence and Being*, p. 35.
7 Camus, *The Fall* (New York: Vintage Books, 1956), pp. 88–9.
8 Gilbert Murray, *Five Stages of Greek Religion*, p. 129.
9 Hannah Green, *I Never Promised You a Rose Garden* (London: Pan Books, 1964).
10 Joseph Zubin and Bonnie Spring "Vulnerability – A New View of Schizophrenia", *Journal of Abnormal Psychology* 2 (1977), vol. 86: pp. 103–26; "Learned Helplessness as a Model of Depression", Special issue, *Journal of Abnormal Psychology*, vol. 87, number 1.
11 From an interview reported in *Yediot Ahronot* (Israeli Daily Newspaper) of August 9, 1977.
12 *Ibid.*
13 Samuel C. Florman, *The Existential Pleasures of Engineering* (New York: St. Martin's Press, 1976), p. 125.
14 Paul Feyerobend, "Science – The Myth and its Role in Society", cited in *Machshavot*, Tel Aviv, Vol. 44, August 1976.
15 Camus, *The Rebel*, p. 73.
16 *Ibid.*, p. 66.
17 W. Jackson Bate, *Samuel Johnson* (London: Chatto & Windus, 1978), p. 11.
18 Camus, *The Plague*, p. 262.
19 Camus, "The Adulterous Woman", in *Exile and the Kingdom* (Harmondsworth: Penguin, 1964), pp. 22–3, 28–9.
20 Martin Esslin, *The Theatre of the Absurd* (New York: Doubleday, 1961), p. 6.
21 Samuel Beckett, *Molloy* (London: John Calder, 1958), p. 28.
22 Emile Ajar, *La Vie Devant Soi* (Paris: Mercure de France, 1975), p. 90.

23 Heidegger, *Existence and Being*, p. 66.
24 *Ibid.*, p. 92.
25 Camus, *The Rebel*, p. 65.
26 Camus, *The Fall*, p. 147.
27 Emerson, *Selections*, p. 157.
28 Jean Genet, *The Balcony* (London: Faber and Faber, 1957), p. 20.
29 Heidegger, *Existence and Being*, p. 34.
30 Shoham, *Salvation Through the Gutters* (Washington, DC: Hemisphere Publishing, 1978), chaps. 1–4.
31 Camus, *The Rebel*, p. 239.
32 Stefan Zweig, Die Welt van Gestern, Erinnerungen eines Europaers (Berlin: S. Fischer Verlag, 1962), p. 116.
33 Camus, *The Rebel*, p. 241.
34 *Ibid.*, p. 219.
35 Søren Kierkegaard, *Purity of Heart* (New York: Harper, 1948), p. 61.

322